Business Modeling with UML
Business Patterns at Work

Hans-Erik Eriksson
Magnus Penker

Wiley Computer Publishing

John Wiley & Sons, Inc.

NEW YORK • CHICHESTER • WEINHEIM • BRISBANE • SINGAPORE • TORONTO

Publisher: Robert Ipsen

Editor: Theresa Hudson

Associate Developmental Editor: Kathryn A. Malm

Managing Editor: Micheline Frederick

Text Design & Composition: Thomark Design

Library of Congress Cataloging-in-Publication Data:

Eriksson, Hans-Erik, 1961–
    Business modeling with UML: business patterns at work / Hans-Erik Eriksson, Magnus Penker.
        p. cm
    Includes bibliographical references and index.
    ISBN 0-471-29551-5 (cloth : alk. paper)
    1. Application software--Development. 2. UML (Computer science). 3. Business--Data processing. I. Penker, Magnus, 1968– II. Title.

QA76.76.A65 E794 2000
650'.0285'5117--dc21   99-058911

Printed in the United States of America.

10 9 8 7 6 5 4 3 2

Advance Praise for Business Modeling with UML

"Attempts to model businesses have been around for a long time. Unfortunately, the confusion surrounding object methodologies and notations that existed before 1997 slowed the progress in this field while arguments ensued over notation and structure of business representation. With the worldwide acceptance of OMG's UML standard, business modellers can now focus on the business mechanics and semantics of interactions rather than the graphical form. Eriksson and Penker leverage this newfound focus with an excellent hands-on book for practitioners eager to document the internal structure and everyday workings of business processes. This clear and practical book belongs on the shelf of everyone dedicated to mapping, maintaining, and streamlining business processes."

Richard Mark Soley
Chairman and CEO, OMG

"Eriksson and Penker have not just written another patterns book; this is a significant contribution to the key field of business-IT alignment. While capturing profound academic insights, what makes the book so refreshing from a practitioner's viewpoint is the richness of accessible, down-to-earth examples and its pragmatic, unpretentious style."

Paul Allen
Principal of CBD Strategies and
Architectures, Sterling Software

"UML may have been designed by and for software engineers, but Eriksson and Penker have defined a practical extension to UML for describing business processes. They put this extended UML immediately to use with a gallery of common business patterns that should jump start any BPR effort."

Philippe Kruchten
Director of Process Development,
Rational Software

"This book is a marriage between proven business modeling concepts and the techniques of the UML. It provides real-world strategies for developing large-scale, mission-critical business systems in a manner accessible to both software and business professionals."

Scott W. Ambler
Author of *Process Patterns*

About the Authors

Hans-Erik Eriksson is a consultant, specializing in object-oriented technology. He has been doing system development for more than 15 years. With a background in program and system design, in the last years, Mr. Eriksson has focused on software architectures and the integration of business processes with technology.

Mr. Eriksson has authored numerous articles and five books on object technology, among them the best-selling *UML Toolkit* (with Magnus Penker), which was one of the first UML books available. He has worked as a trainer in object-oriented technologies for more than 10 years and has taught over 100 courses within this field.

Mr. Eriksson is the Chairman and Chief Technical Officer of Open Training, a company that specializes in advanced online learning solutions and the integration of e-Business and e-Training.

He can be contacted at hanserik.eriksson@opentraining.com.

Magnus Penker has more than 10 years of experience in the field of object-orientation and business process engineering. His previous positions include project manager, senior management consultant, and VP of training (at the European e-Business company Adera+). Mr. Penker has published several books, including the best-selling *UML Toolkit* (with Hans-Erik Eriksson). He is a frequent speaker at conferences and also the author of a number of articles and papers on business and software engineering.

Mr. Penker is the Chief Executive Officer of Open Training, a company specializing in advanced online learning solutions and the integration of e-Business and e-Training.

He can be contacted at magnus.penker@opentraining.com.

OMG Press Advisory Board

OMG Press Books in Print

Building Business Objects by Peter Eeles and Oliver Sims, ISBN: 0471-191760.

Business Component Factory: A Comprehensive Overview of Component-Based Development for the Enterprise by Peter Herzum and Oliver Sims, ISBN: 0471-327603.

Business Modeling with UML: Business Patterns at Work by Hans-Erik Eriksson and Magnus Penker, ISBN: 0471-295515.

CORBA 3 Fundamentals and Programming, 2nd Edition by Jon Siegel, ISBN: 0471-295183.

CORBA Design Patterns by Thomas J. Mowbray and Raphael C. Malveau, ISBN: 0471-158828.

Developing C++ Applications with UML by Michael Sandberg, ISBN: 0471-38304X.

Enterprise Application Integration with CORBA: Component and Web-Based Solutions by Ron Zahavi, ISBN: 0471-327204.

The Essential CORBA: Systems Integration Using Distributed Objects by Thomas J. Mowbray and Ron Zahavi, ISBN: 0471-106119.

Instant CORBA by Robert Orfali, Dan Harkey and Jeri Edwards, ISBN: 0471-183334.

Integrating CORBA and COM Applications by Michael Rosen and David Curtis, ISBN: 0471-198277.

Java Programming with CORBA, 2nd Edition by Andreas Vogel and Keith Duddy, ISBN: 0471-247650.

Mastering XMI: Java Programming with the XMI Toolkit, XML and UML by Stephen Brodsky and Tim Grose, ISBN: 0471-384291.

The Object Technology Casebook: Lessons from Award-Winning Business Applications by Paul Harmon and William Morrisey, ISBN: 0471-147176.

The Object Technology Revolution by Michael Guttman and Jason Matthews, ISBN: 0471-606790.

Programming with Enterprise JavaBeans, JTS and OTS: Building Distributed Transactions with Java and C++ by Andreas Vogel and Madhavan Rangarao, ISBN: 0471-319724.

Programming with Java IDL by Geoffrey Lewis, Steven Barber, and Ellen Siegel, ISBN: 0471-247979.

UML Toolkit by Hans-Erik Eriksson and Magnus Penker, ISBN: 0471-191612.

About the OMG

The Object Management Group (OMG) was chartered to create and foster a component-based software marketplace through the standardization and promotion of object-oriented software. To achieve this goal, the OMG specifies open standards for every aspect of distributed object computing from analysis and design, through infrastructure, to application objects and components.

The well-established CORBA (Common Object Request Broker Architecture) standardizes a platform- and programming-language-independent distributed object computing environment. It is based on OMG/ISO Interface Definition Language (OMG IDL) and the Internet Inter-ORB Protocol (IIOP). Now recognized as a mature technology, CORBA is represented on the marketplace by well over 70 ORBs (Object Request Brokers) plus hundreds of other products. Although most of these ORBs are tuned for general use, others are specialized for real-time or embedded applications, or built into transaction processing systems where they provide scalability, high throughput, and reliability. Of the thousands of live, mission-critical CORBA applications in use today around the world, over 300 are documented on the OMG's success-story Web pages at www.corba.org.

CORBA 3, the OMG's latest release, adds a Component Model, quality-of-service control, a messaging invocation model, and tightened integration with the Internet, Enterprise JavaBeans, and the Java programming language. Widely anticipated by the industry, CORBA 3 keeps this established architecture in the forefront of distributed computing, as will a new OMG specification integrating CORBA with XML. Well-known for its ability to integrate legacy systems into your network, along with the wide variety of heterogeneous hardware and software on the market today, CORBA enters the new millennium prepared to integrate the technologies on the horizon.

Augmenting this core infrastructure are the CORBAservices which standardize naming and directory services, event handling, transaction processing, security, and other functions. Building on this firm foundation, OMG Domain Facilities standardize common objects throughout the supply and service chains in industries such as Telecommunications, Healthcare, Manufacturing, Transportation, Finance/Insurance, Electronic Commerce, Life Science, and Utilities.

The OMG standards extend beyond programming. OMG Specifications for analysis and design include the Unified Modeling Language (UML), the repository standard Meta-Object Facility (MOF), and XML-based Metadata Interchange (XMI). The UML is a result of fusing the concepts of the world's most prominent methodologists. Adopted as an OMG specification in 1997, it

represents a collection of best engineering practices that have proven successful in the modeling of large and complex systems and is a well-defined,
widely-accepted response to these business needs. The MOF is OMG's standard for metamodeling and metadata repositories. Fully integrated with
UML, it uses the UML notation to describe repository metamodels. Extending this work, the XMI standard enables the exchange of objects defined
using UML and the MOF. XMI can generate XML Data Type Definitions for
any service specification that includes a normative, MOF-based metamodel.

In summary, the OMG provides the computing industry with an open,
vendor-neutral, proven process for establishing and promoting standards.
OMG makes all of its specifications available without charge from its Web
site, www.omg.org. With over a decade of standard-making and consensus-
building experience, OMG now counts about 800 companies as members.
Delegates from these companies convene at week-long meetings held five
times each year at varying sites around the world, to advance OMG technologies. The OMG welcomes guests to their meetings; for an invitation, send
your email request to info@omg.org.

Membership in the OMG is open to end users, government organizations,
academia, and technology vendors. For more information on the OMG, contact OMG headquarters by phone at +1-508-820 4300, by fax at +1-508-820
4303, by email at info@omg.org, or on the Web at www.omg.org.

Contents

Acknowledgments

We would like to acknowledge the work of the people who helped us to write this book, and whose efforts have been vital to its completion.

Some very insightful and important comments were made by our team of reviewers, most notably:

- Philippe Kruchten at Rational Software
- Paul Allen at Sterling Software
- Jos Warmer at IBM

Several reviewers were anonymous to us and therefore can't be named, but a sincere thanks goes to them for their constructive and helpful comments.

A tremendous job was done from the Wiley team to get this book ready: Kathryn Malm, Terri Hudson, Gerrie Cho, Micheline Frederick, and others. Producing this kind of book is always an endeavour, and when the authors and reviewers are spread across the world it becomes quite an achievement.

Special thanks goes to the consultants at Astrakan, who have vast experience in business modeling and have provided many of the theories and ideas presented in this book. Many have been individually credited in the pattern chapters, but a thanks also goes to the group as a whole.

Any remaining mistakes or errors in the text are the responsibility of the authors. Readers who would like to contact us to pose a question or to discuss the contents of the book may feel free to do so at the addresses listed below.

The book's Web page is located at www.opentraining.com/bm. Readers are invited to visit for further information, updates, and links to topics related to the book.

Stockholm, December 1999

Hans-Erik Eriksson
hanserik.eriksson@opentraining.com

Magnus Penker
magnus.penker@opentraining.com

Introduction

Since it's standardization by the OMG (Object Management Group) in November 1997, the Unified Modeling Language (UML) has had a tremendous impact on how software systems are developed. The role of modeling in specifying and documenting complex software systems is being accepted, and an industrial approach to software engineering is on its way to becoming reality. With the acceptance of UML, a new generation of tools and processes that use UML have also emerged, and important concepts and techniques such as the role of architecture, requirements engineering, and tool integration also have been emphasized.

However, a common problem is that software systems do not properly support the businesses of which they are an integrated part. There are several reasons for this: a correct requirement specification is not available, the software team does not have a proper understanding of the business, or the business changes so frequently that the software can't keep up. With the emergence of e-commerce, the solutions of tomorrow need to be a combination of technology and business—to provide real excellence you need an understanding of both. Business modeling helps you understand by modeling the actual business and its goals, processes (activities), resources (such as people, machines, and material) and rules.

To identify the proper requirements on the software systems is not the only reason to do business modeling. Business modeling creates an abstraction of a complex business and establishes a common understanding that can be communicated to the business's stakeholders (e.g., owners, management, employees, and customers). A better understanding of how the business functions facilitates improvements to the business, and helps to identify new business opportunities (i.e., business improvement or innovation).

Although UML in its first years has been used mainly for modeling software systems, it is also a very suitable language for business modeling. It has the ability to describe both the structural aspects of a business (such as the organization, goal hierarchies, or the structures of the resources), the behavioral aspects of a business (such as the processes), and the business rules that affect both structure and behavior. Many developers are already familiar with UML since they have used it to model software. Using the same modeling language for both business and software modeling ensures that the documentation is consistent and facilitates communication between business modelers and software modelers. In addition, a large amount of tools become available for use in business modeling when you use UML.

This book shows how to use UML for business modeling, and how to use the business models to identify the correct requirements for the software that supports the business. We use standard extension mechanisms, such as stereotypes, to define new model elements suited for business modeling. This book also presents guidelines for how to produce a business model and what it should contain. It introduces you to how to define business rules using the Object Constraint Language (OCL).

To help you get started with business modeling using UML, 26 business patterns are provided. These patterns are working, reusable, and illustrative examples of how different aspects of a business can be modeled. In addition, you'll learn how the information and knowledge in a business model can be used to identify the proper requirements on software systems that support the business, as well as how the information can be reused in the software models.

Finally, you'll find an example business model. The model applies the concepts, steps, and patterns described through out the book to an example mail order firm that has to migrate into the new world of e-business and network economy. This example is based on our experience modeling these types of projects. The company is fictitious, but the business structure is based on existing businesses.

What the Book Is and Is Not

This book provides valuable information that will help you to effectively use UML to model your business. You'll learn:

- A combination of techniques that melts knowledge and experience in the business modeling field together with object-oriented modeling.

- An approach that shows how to use the well-established UML language for business modeling. UML has so far been used mostly for modeling software systems.

- A set of business extensions, the Eriksson-Penker Business Extensions to UML, that extend UML with adapted model elements for business modeling. The extensions are defined using the standard extension mechanisms in UML.

■ New techniques, such as the Assembly-Line diagram, that integrate the business processes in a business model with the use-cases to define functional requirements on a software system.

■ Common business modeling experience and knowledge packaged in the form of reusable patterns (Resource and Rule Patterns, Goal Patterns, and Process Patterns).

■ An approach to designing support systems that are in harmony with the business they are supposed to support.

■ Many powerful examples of business models and illustrations of nontrivial features of the UML language, such as powertypes and stereotypes.

■ A practical and pragmatic approach to doing business modeling with UML, an approach that can be used together with other techniques or methods.

This book is **not**:

■ A new "method" for either business modeling or software modeling. Most of the ideas presented are acknowledged techniques for modeling, but have not been used with UML before.

■ A book describing the UML language in detail. There are other books for this, such as our previous book *UML Toolkit* [Eriksson 1998].

■ A programming book. The models in this book do not model programs and should not be translated into code. The models, however, can be the basis for other UML models that model the software in an information system.

■ A book about object-oriented technology. Knowledge of the basic concepts of object-oriented technology are required for reading this book.

■ A substitute for doing bad analysis. A very important factor for succeeding with business modeling is staffing the project with knowledgeable, experienced, and dedicated people. There is no "silver bullet" in business modeling either.

■ A book showing statistical proof of the success rate of these techniques. The techniques presented are based on well-established theories and have been used in practice for many years (though not necessarily using UML as the modeling language). There is a vast world of literature related to business modeling that provides further "proof" of the success of these techniques.

Who Should Read This Book

This book is for you if:

- You want to understand the concept of business modeling for creating abstractions of your business that in turn can be used to communicate, improve, or innovate the business.

- You want insight into how UML can be used to describe the complexities of a business instead of just software systems.

- You are a software manager or developer who is looking for an answer to questions such as "But what should I do before I start producing the software system?" and "How do I know if I have identified the proper requirements (e.g., use cases)?"

- You are an analyst or a modeler who is looking for working and reusable patterns that demonstrate how the processes, resources, rules, and goals of a business can be modeled.

- You are an experienced business modeler who wants to understand how UML can be used in a business context, and how business modeling can be integrated with software development.

- You are a CASE Tool vendor who would like to integrate business modeling features with software engineering features in your tool.

You should have a basic knowledge of object-oriented concepts and of UML.

How this Book Is Organized

Chapter 1, "Business Modeling," presents the concept of business modeling and the purposes for modeling a business. It also provides arguments for why UML is suitable for business modeling and what elements are required in UML to do business modeling.

Chapter 2, "UML Primer," is an overview of the UML language. If you are proficient in UML, feel free to skip this chapter. There are, however, some important sections on activity diagrams, powertypes, and UML extensions that highlight some areas of UML that are relevant to business modeling and the rest of the book.

Chapter 3, "Modeling the Business Architecture," defines the major concepts used in business modeling: processes, goals, resources, and rules. It also introduces the Eriksson-Penker Business Extensions that are defined using the standard extension mechanisms in UML to facilitate business modeling.

Chapter 4, "Business Views," describes the different views of a business model. It defines the techniques and diagrams used to capture a specific aspect of a business, and provides examples to illustrate their use.

Chapter 5, "Business Rules," describes how to define business rules using the Object Constraint Language (OCL), part of standard UML. Examples show you how to use different categories of rules in all of the views in order to regulate how to run and structure the business. We also introduce Fuzzy Business Rules, a technique for defining rules without ordinary binary logic.

Chapter 6, "Business Patterns," introduces the 26 business patterns, common solutions to business modeling problems, that are covered in chapters 7 through 9. The chapter defines a pattern, it's structure and characteristics, and how patterns are represented in the UML language.

Chapter 7, "Resource and Rule Patterns," describe patterns that can be used to resolve typical problem situations that can arise when modeling the structures and relationships (including rules) between resources.

Chapter 8, "Goal Patterns," describes patterns for defining the goals of a business. Goals are what the business and their corresponding models strive for, and form the basis for designing the processes, finding the right resources, and tuning the business rules.

Chapter 9, "Process Patterns," defines high quality, well-proven, and easy-to-use patterns that are used to model business processes. The chapter defines the different categories of process patterns, and covers important areas such as layering, decomposition, interaction, process type and instance, and workflow.

Chapter 10, "From a Business Architecture to a Software Architecture," discusses how the business model is used to produce the business's supporting information system. The business model identifies the requirements on the information systems (the use cases of the system), and can also be used to define the architecture of the information system. Using the same business model for several information systems also helps to create systems that are more easily integrated with the business they support.

Chapter 11, "A Business Model Example," demonstrates how the techniques and notation defined through out the book can be used to model a practical example of an e-business. The business views, business extensions, business rules, and business patterns are demonstrated in this case study.

We've also included additional resources, a visual glossary of the Eriksson-Penker Business Extensions, a table summary of the Business Patterns, and a glossary.

Also visit the Web site at www.opentraining.com/bm/ for further articles, information, and links on subjects related to the book, as well as our recommendations for tools that support business modeling. You can also contact us through our email addresses hanserik.eriksson@opentraining.com and magnus.penker@opentraining.com.

CHAPTER 1

Business Modeling

Running a business today is more competitive than ever. The globalization of world markets, brought about by technology in general and the Internet in particular requires businesspeople to acquire and adapt to new business logic. Anyone who doesn't continuously strive to improve the operation, products, and services of their business will find it difficult to succeed in this challenging environment.

To keep up and remain competitive, companies and enterprises must assess the quality of their products and the efficiency of their services. In doing so, they must consider the world around them: their competitors, their subcontractors, their suppliers, the ever-changing laws and regulations, and, above all, their customers. They must also objectively examine their products or services, asking such questions as: Is my internal operation working smoothly? Can I improve my product or service in any way? Is production running as efficiently as possible? Can I expand my product or service portfolios to reach new markets and customers?

Today's businesspeople must also evaluate their information systems: Do they effectively support their way of working? Do the systems adapt easily to change? Is information used as an important strategic resource in the business? Is the information adequate and correct? All businesses will benefit by

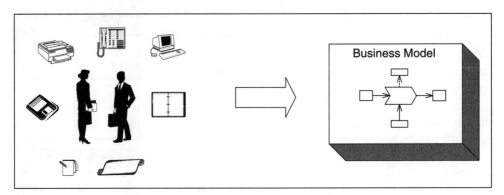

Figure 1.1   A business model is a simplified view of a business.

gaining a deeper understanding of how their business interacts with its environment, which comes from honestly answering these questions.

In today's marketplaces, information systems no longer merely support businesses. Increasingly, they are an integral part of them. All businesses make some use of information technology, and it is important that their systems be designed to support them. The business is, after all, what defines the requirements of the information systems.

To answer these questions, it is essential to make a *model* of the business, a simplified view of a complex reality (Figure 1.1). It is a means of creating abstraction; it enables you to eliminate irrelevant details and focus on one or more important aspects at a time. Effective models also facilitate discussions among different stakeholders in the business, helping them to reach agreement on the key fundamentals and to work toward common goals. Finally, a business model can be the basis for other models, for different information systems that support the business, for example. Modeling is an accepted and established means of analyzing and designing software. To create appropriate software, the businesses in which the software systems operate must also be modeled, understood, and improved as required.

A *business model* is an abstraction of how a business functions. Its details differ according to the perspective of the person creating the model, each of whom will naturally have a slightly different viewpoint of the goals and visions of the business, including its efficiency and the various elements that are acting in concert within the business. This is normal, and the business model will not completely resolve these differences. What the business model will do is provide a simplified view of the business structure that will act as the basis for communication, improvements, or innovations, and define the information systems requirements that are necessary to support the business. It isn't necessary for a business model to capture an absolute picture of the business or to describe every business detail.

The business model is the focal point around which business is conducted or around which business operations are improved. The evolving models also help the developers structure and focus their thinking. Working with the models increases their understanding of the business and, hopefully, their awareness of new opportunities for improving business.

The word business in this context is used as a broad term. The businesses that can be modeled with the techniques presented in this book do not have to be profit making (e.g., a relief organization for the homeless or for war victims is also a business that needs to be organized as effectively as possible). Any type of ongoing operation that has or uses resources and has one or more goals can be referred to as a business. The *owner* of the business sets the goals and allocates resources to make the business run. The *business modeler* then creates the structure, designs the processes, and allocates the resources in order to achieve the goals. The *system developer* then adapts, designs, or develops appropriate information systems that support the running of the business.

This chapter explores the role of models in general, and how businesses can benefit from using them, and, more specifically, where the Unified Modeling Language (UML) fits in.

The Role of Models

Anyone who has played chess knows that you need a strategy or plan, and that even a bad plan is better than no plans at all. During the game, not everything happens as planned, but the plan nevertheless points in a direction, making the decision-making easier and faster. A more skilled player will change the plan, in part or in whole, during the game and think ahead about alternative moves he or she will take as a result of possible moves by the opponent.

The business model functions as the plan for conducting a business. It acts as the basis for decision-making and affects decisions about prioritizing goals, obtaining the right resources, or negotiating with subcontractors. It also serves as an up-to-date description of how the business is performed, and allows for changes and improvements in the process, such as cutting costs, improving quality, or shortening time-to-market. The model can anticipate and forecast changes that are necessary to maintain an edge on the competition. The model can't provide all the answers, but as for the chess player, it is a basic strategy or plan to follow. An advantage of modeling in a language such as UML is that it visually depicts functions and relationships that are usually difficult to visualize clearly.

Ideally, a business model would consist of a single diagram that included all the important aspects of a business. That is, however, never possible, since a business is so complex and has so many aspects that a single diagram can't capture all that information. Instead, a business model is composed of the following:

Views. A business model is illustrated with a number of different views, each of which captures information about one or more specific aspects of the business. A view is an abstraction from a specific viewpoint, omitting details that are irrelevant to that viewpoint. Multiple views are necessary to separate purposes and perspectives in a controlled way, without losing important information about the business.

Diagrams. Each view consists of a number of diagrams, each of which shows a specific part of the business structure or a specific business situation. Several diagrams are necessary to visualize a single view of the business model, since each type of diagram has a different purpose and expresses one important aspect or mechanism within the business model view. A diagram can show a structure (e.g., the organization of the business) or some dynamic collaboration (a number of objects and their interaction to demonstrate a specific process). The diagrams contain and express the objects, processes, rules, goals, and visions defined in the business situation.

Objects and Processes. Concepts are related in the diagrams through the use of different objects and processes. The objects are the "things" in the business; they may be physical, such as people, machines, products, and material, or more abstract, such as debts, instructions, and services. Objects can also represent other objects by containing information about other things in the business. Processes are the functions in the business that consume, refine, or use objects to affect or produce other objects.

A model is motivated by objectives. For example, the purpose of modeling a building might be to construct it or, later, to sell apartments in it. The purpose of modeling a business might be to understand or to improve its functionality. It is important to distinguish models used as an exploration tool from models used as a specification tool (modeling can be used for both). To build a supporting information system, such as a sales system, the surrounding business is modeled in order to understand it, and from that understanding the appropriate information system can be designed. Models facilitate understanding and communicating about systems, but only when the objective of the model is kept in mind. If the objective is to understand a business well enough to specify a supporting system, it is not necessary to model the entire business in detail; producing such a detailed model is simply too time-consuming and too expensive for that purpose. However, if the goal of a serious business process innovation project is to redefine how the entire business is run and to find new and improved ways of conducting business, a more elaborate effort might be necessary. In any case, it is important not to overwork the models; if you keep the objective of the model in mind at all times, you will profit from business modeling.

UML

Since its introduction in November 1997, the Unified Modeling Language has quickly become the standard modeling language for software development. Many users of other methods (Booch, OMT, Fusion, etc.) have adopted UML; a number of books have been written about UML; and most modeling tools have implemented support for the language. All predictions for the future of UML indicate that it will become even more dominant and important, and that the tool support for producing and exchanging UML models will become more advanced.

The UML consists of nine different diagram types, and each diagram shows a specific static or dynamic aspect of a system. The basics of UML are easy to learn, and very powerful constructs, such as stereotypes or powertypes, are available for the more advanced modeler. Chapter 2, "UML Primer," includes an overview of UML and some of the advanced concepts used later in this book.

The UML standardizes notation for describing a process, but it doesn't standardize a process for producing those descriptions (a well-defined order of activities, a set of artifacts produced, and ways to monitor or control the work). UML, in fact, can be used by many different developmental processes, more or less formally specified. This is not an oversight by the developers of UML; a development process for a project involving three persons is very different from a project involving a thousand people who work in different countries. The process is also affected by other factors, such as the type of system or the experience of the developers. Attempts at defining de facto standards for development processes, such as the Rational Unified Process [Kruchten 1998] or Select Perspective [Allen-Frost 1998], are often configurable, meaning that they can be adapted or modified to suit the project at hand. It is important to understand that UML doesn't prescribe a specific way of how it should be used in a project; there is no *one* specific or correct way of using it.

Several development processes that use UML advocate that the system development should start with *use-case modeling* to define the functional requirements on the system. A *use case* describes a specific usage of the system by one or more *actors*. An actor is a role that a user or another system plays. The objective of use-case modeling is to identify and describe all the use cases that the actors require from the system. The use-case descriptions then are used to analyze and design a robust system architecture that realizes the use cases (this is what is referred to as "use-case driven" development).

But how do you know that all of the use cases, or even the correct use cases that best support the business in which the system operates, are identified? To answer such questions, you need to model and understand the system's surroundings.

Modeling business surroundings involves answering questions such as:

- How do the different actors interact?
- What activities are part of their work?
- What are the ultimate goals of their work?
- What other people, systems, or resources are involved that do not show up as actors to this specific system?
- What rules govern their activities and structures?
- Are there ways actors could perform more efficiently?

The answers to these questions come from tackling the entire business and looking beyond the functions of the information system currently being built (and using techniques other than use-case modeling). The ultimate objective of all software systems is to give correct and extensive support to the business of which it is a part. However, when modeling the surroundings of the information system, you are no longer modeling software. Enter the world of *business process modeling*.

Business Process Modeling

A business is a complex system, consisting of a hierarchical organization of departments and their functions. Some of these functions, however, are not restricted to one department; they cross horizontally across several departments. The traditional method for documenting a business is to draw an organization chart, which divides the business into a number of departments or sections (e.g., research and development, marketing, sales, manufacturing, etc.), represented vertically. This documentation method is limited to how the business is built and organized. It does not document the business processes that flow through horizontally and affect all the vertical departments (e.g., the development of a new product will affect all divisions).

Other structures in the business, such as business processes, resources that participate in or are used in the process, rules that govern the execution of the business, the goals, and problems that hinder the achievement of those goals, cannot be captured in the traditional organizational view. A good business model contains all of this information. Capturing and documenting this information in itself can be the basis for making better decisions that result in a business that runs more smoothly, and better documentation for specifying the requirements of the information system.

In the process modeling field, many different theories strive to explain and improve how to structure and run a business. Very few standards, or even methods, exist in this area, and most of the literature concentrates on how to describe a business rather than on the well-defined techniques for actually running a business. The central concept used for process modeling is the business process, which describes activities within the business and how they relate to and interact with the resources in the business to achieve a goal for the process.

A business model can never be totally accurate or complete, simply because no two observers of a business will have an identical perception of the business or agree on an accurate model. As noted earlier, the business model cannot and should not contain all the details of the business. A model that attempts to do so risks becoming just as complex and as hard to comprehend as the business. Not every detail can be captured due to restrictions in the modeling language or the concepts used to build the model. Thus, the model should focus on the core business tasks and its key mechanisms. Pinpointing the core business tasks and determining what to depict in the model is the responsibility of the modeler.

Likewise, a business model of a future view of the business cannot be expected to ever be completely realized as planned. Changes in the real world can affect the basis on which the model was created, rendering the model as no longer completely valid. In addition, during implementation, the model may meet with active or passive resistance by either the business management or the employees.

Even with these limitations, however, the following arguments for producing business models are still very strong:

To better understand the key mechanisms of an existing business. By providing a clear picture of their roles and tasks in the overall organization, the models can be used to train people. (They may be used in both a hierarchical or a process-oriented organization.)

To act as the basis for creating suitable information systems that support the business. Descriptions of the business are used to identify necessary information systems support. The models are also used as a basis for specifying the key requirements of those systems. Ideally, large sections of the business model can be mapped directly onto software objects. As more infrastructure software systems are added, potentially the systems being developed may become more business-driven, and the developers can concentrate more on functionality that supports the business rather than on solving technical incompatibilities or problems.

To act as the basis for improving the current business structure and operation. The models identify changes in the current business that are necessary to implement the improved business model.

To show the structure of an innovated business. The model becomes the basis for the action plan. Innovation suggests that radical change, rather than incremental changes, have been made to the business processes.

To experiment with a new business concept or to copy or study a concept used by a competitive company (e.g., benchmarking on the model level). The developed model becomes a sketch of a possible development for the business. The model can be a new idea, inspired by modeling other businesses, or can take advantage of new technologies, such as the Internet.

To identify outsourcing opportunities. Elements of the business not considered the part of the "core" are delegated to outside suppliers. The models are used as the specification for the suppliers.

Let's take a detailed look at each of these motives for business modeling and see how they differ.

Understanding the Business

One of the primary motives for developing any model is to increase the understanding of the business and facilitate communication about the business. A visual model is easier to comprehend and discuss than a textual description or no description at all (which is often the case). The model is a current snapshot of how modelers currently view the business. The model will change and evolve either as modelers better understand the business or as the business changes. Once the models are fairly stable, because they give a clear picture of the roles and tasks in the overall organization, they can be used to train people.

Information System Support

Today, most businesses use some type of information system. In fact, it may be said that information technology is an integral part of the daily operation of many, if not most, companies. This trend continues to gain momentum with the recognition that the effective use of computer systems will enhance almost any business. In some domains, computer systems are obligatory to handle the massive amounts of information and to respond to the need for fast and reliable communication with other companies and customers. With the Internet as a technical infrastructure for communication and financial transactions, a wealth of new business opportunities is emerging. Existing business models need to be adapted with the new possibilities that the Internet provides.

As widespread as this trend is, however, many companies are dissatisfied with the quality of their information systems, citing they offer insufficient or ineffective business support, they are awkward to use, are not reliable, and are not integrated with other systems. In many cases, this is due to the fact that the systems haven't been developed with a correct understanding of the business it supports. Developing the actual software for computer systems is still a job for qualified computer experts who are familiar with all the intricate details of programming languages, operating systems, and databases. Because of this, software systems development is often technology-driven, rather than business-driven.

The common approach to solving this problem is to have representatives of the business write a requirement specification for the systems that are to be developed. Frequently, though, this requirement specification is often inadequate and incomplete because it is usually written specifically with the information system in mind, but concentrates on describing the appearance of the user interface rather than on the relationships and interactions between the objects used in the business. Often, the authors of the specifications are also technicians who make design decisions. Without a full understanding of the business and its needs, they prematurely make important decisions about how the information should be constructed. Sometimes these choices are in direct conflict with the functions and characteristics the business really requires from the system.

The solution is to create a model of the overall business that can be used to decide which information systems are required, how those information systems should be developed, and what functionality the systems should contain (see Figure 1.2). If the requirement specification is based on a good business model, there is a much greater chance that the information system will support the business adequately. There are several advantages to basing all the information systems on the same basic business model:

- The information systems become an integrated part of the overall business, supporting the business and enhancing the work and the results.

- The systems integrate easily with each other and can share or exchange information.

- The systems are easier to update and modify as dictated by changes in the business model, which result from changes in the surrounding environment, goals of the business, or improvements or innovations to the business model. This in turn reduces the cost of maintaining the information systems and of continuously updating the business processes.

- Business logic can be reused in several systems.

Ideally, the objects presented in the business models translate or map to objects in the information system. Normally, this is not a one-to-one mapping.

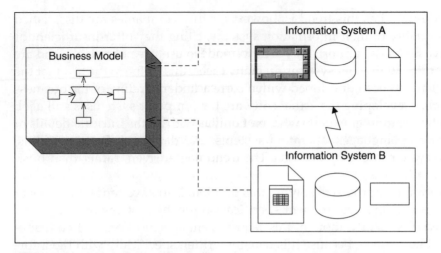

Figure 1.2   A business model can be used as the basis for defining the requirements on information systems.

One object or process in the business model cannot always be translated into one object in the information system, since there are objects in the information system that are not present at all in the business model, and vice versa. This makes a direct mapping between the "real world" as described by the business model and the software system impossible. Nevertheless, even if a one-to-one mapping between the business model and the analysis model of the information system is not possible, the way the business operates and the functionality and design of the information system used to support it are more tightly integrated. Why? Because an information system that is built to support the requirements of a process will offer the appropriate services. Using object-oriented techniques, the modeling concepts and the structures used in the business model can be the same as those used in the analysis models for the information systems. Furthermore, the information system can be implemented using the very same concepts. This book shows you how.

Using business models as a basis for the information systems also presents the opportunity for software reuse. If there are several information systems that support the same business, they often will have an overlapping set of objects. For example, several information systems that act within the same process can use the same objects from the business model. These objects have to be implemented only once and can be reused in other information systems. Often, the objects in a business model participate in several processes, and the information systems supporting different processes then can reuse reoccurring objects. It is difficult to succeed with this kind of reuse if the system has been developed with only one software system in mind. The objects become too "attached" technically to a particular system; they have not been generically modeled after the requirements of the business.

The advantage of reuse also applies to models. If the same business model can act as the basis for several information systems, it can be reused as the basic input for defining the requirements of each system. Without a common business model, each system development team creates its own analysis model to understand the real world. Not only is this redundant work, but this heightens the risk that the different teams will interpret reality differently and thus develop incompatible systems. The trend for reuse within system development is leaning more toward high-level reuse through architectural frameworks or patterns, instead of simple reuse of code (which hasn't lived up to its promise). Reusing business models is another step in that direction.

In addition to new information systems, most businesses already have a number of information systems known as *legacy systems* that are expensive and hard to replace. These systems are functional parts of the business; they actually become a part of the current business model. In many cases, the legacy systems are the parts of the business that are most likely to be the target of an improvement or innovation plan (e.g., to substitute or remove some of these old systems).

There are two ways to depict a legacy system in the business model: it may be modeled as a single entity, such as a person acting in the business, or it may be *reverse-engineered.* Reverse engineering means that a model is created by analyzing the current information system; that is, modeling an already completed system (which is opposite from what normally is advocated). Reverse engineering breaks down the current system in order to discover the set of information objects present in the system. These information objects then become part of the business model. These two techniques are discussed in more detail in Chapter 10, "From a Business Architecture to a Software Architecture."

Improvement

A business model can be used to improve the current business. This technique, sometimes called *business process improvement* (BPI), is used to identify possible ways to make the business more efficient. The current business is modeled and then analyzed for opportunities for enhancement or improvement. The improvement part of BPI suggests that the business is changed incrementally (i.e., step-by-step improvements; see Figure 1.3) rather than through immediate and radical means. When an opportunity for improvement is identified, a new business model is produced to demonstrate how the business should look after those changes are implemented.

A number of activities must be completed in order to change the business and implement the new business model:

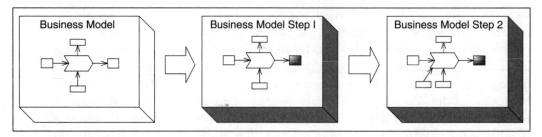

Figure 1.3 Business improvement means that changes are done incrementally.

- Describe new routines and create administrative support for these routines.
- Train the people affected by the changes; teach them the new processes and motivate them to become a part of the changes.
- Change the information systems that participate in the business to better support and enhance the operation of the business.
- Negotiate with subcontractors and other partners who will need to adapt to the changes.

Depending on the extent of the changes, improving the business can be simple or complex work. Changes occur in small steps, but they can be implemented continuously, acting upon changes in the business environment, such as changed customer needs (i.e., whenever a customer need is changed, an incremental step is performed to meet and handle that change in the business).

Innovation

Business innovation involves analyzing the current business and searching the model for new ways of doing things. The business model and its processes are changed significantly to create different and improved processes (see Figure 1.4). Often, routines in a business exist because of historical reasons (it always has been done that way) or because the infrastructure demands them to be done a certain way (the documents or the information systems don't allow them to be made in any other way).

Innovation places even higher demands on correct implementation than business improvement. Motivating and instructing the people involved and ensuring that the new processes are integrated in the existing business are essential for success. To be sure, innovation is a much bigger risk than improvement, but if innovation succeeds, the resulting business can achieve much larger gains in efficiency. Innovation is therefore typically used in companies that require radical change prompted by poor performance, missed budgets, and inefficient productivity.

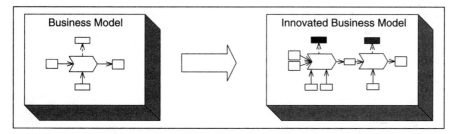

Figure 1.4   Innovation implies making radical changes to the processes.

An extreme form of business innovation is *business process reengineering* (BPR). BPR advocates radical changes to the business processes; this means that everything about the current way of running the business is questioned and, subsequently, often substantially changed. BPR strives to achieve dramatic improvements in efficiency in the order of several hundred percentage points, in comparison with process improvement or traditional rationalization where changes of 5 to 10 percent are deemed satisfactory.

Succeeding with such innovation is much more difficult and bears a higher risk of failure. Consequently, there has been strong resistance to BPR. Many BPR projects have failed because those involved in the business or the environment objected to the radical changes and therefore did not actively or wholeheartedly participate in implementing the new business models. Failures are also caused by incorrect design of the business process; they simply don't work when implemented.

Information systems are the key enablers to achieving process innovation or BPR. The introduction of new information systems is not, however, a guarantee for innovation. More commonly, new information systems are designed according to a current, inefficient business model, which effectively cements the current way of doing things, and makes innovation impossible to achieve. True innovation takes place first in the minds of the modelers, before it can be described and achieved in a business model. Only then can new information systems be built, either as a central and required part of that new business model or simply as a support for it.

Debate continues in the management world over whether improvement or innovation should be used when making changes to the business processes. We will not choose sides in this debate; instead, we point out that the business modeling techniques described in this book can be used for either purpose.

Design New Processes

Business modeling can be used to create new models, not previously part of the business, in order to experiment with how new business concepts fit into the current model. Models are used to determine if the current organization, resources, and information systems can be easily used in or adapted to the new process. Business models also are used to benchmark a business, that is, to copy or study business processes used by competitors in order to measure one's own business against the competition.

Often, new processes are designed based on a vision of new opportunities. Modeling this vision or idea creates a "first try" that tests the feasibility of the process. Obviously, other activities have to be performed before implementing the process, including profit calculations, cost analysis, and market studies. These activities can use the new process model as a specification of the projected goals for the new process and of the necessary resources, and to determine how the new process is implemented within the current business.

New opportunities stem from finding new combinations of or additions to objects that are already present in the organization. For example, a business can identify new ways to use customer information that it already possesses, or new services to add to the products that the business sells. By visualizing the processes in models, it is easier to see the strengths and weaknesses of the business and how to use the strengths and eliminate the weaknesses in order to turn opportunities into successes.

Outsourcing

A common practice among business leaders today is to focus on the core business, fundamental processes at which the company excels and that give them the competitive edge. Processes that are not part of the core business are good candidates for *outsourcing*. The companies hire subcontractors to handle support functions or even entire departments, rather than managing them themselves. Information systems are not the only candidates for outsourcing; other parts of the business that aren't considered vital, such as marketing or maintenance, may be sent out as well.

Business modeling can be used not only to identify and define the core processes, but also to define the processes that are candidates for outsourcing. The model then acts as a resource for the supplier and becomes a valid specification for how these processes should be performed and integrated with the core processes. The business model acts as a map that integrates the processes with each other, indicating where the processes are run by different companies and subcontractors.

Business Modeling with UML

Why use object-oriented modeling techniques to describe a business? Isn't object-oriented modeling and programming restricted to analyzing and designing computer programs? The answer is there are several advantages to using object-oriented concepts and techniques to model a business:

Similar concepts. A business can be described in terms of processes that achieve goals by collaborating with different types of resource objects. Rules define conditions and constraints as to how the processes and resources may relate to each other and how they may behave. All of this can be mapped onto objects, relationships between objects, and interaction between objects; for example, through creating static and dynamic object-oriented models.

Well-proven established techniques. Object-oriented modeling and programming has been used for several years now and has proven that it can handle large and complex systems. New techniques, such as patterns, have been introduced in the field of object-oriented modeling, and a number of patterns are available for modeling businesses.

Standard notation. Business modeling methods and techniques are in need of a standard notation: every method uses its own notation and its own tool, if notation is used at all. Object-oriented modeling finally has a standard notation: UML. That means the tools are already there, and that the same tools that are used to model the information systems can be adapted and used to describe the business models. It also opens up the possibility of enabling continuous traceability of business requirements all the way to the implementation code. The absence of this capability is a major weakness in most tools today.

Short learning curve. It is a major advantage when the same basic concepts (objects, classes, etc.) used to describe the information systems that support the business can also be used to describe the business as a whole. Just as object-oriented models have decreased the semantic gap between those who analyze and design systems and those who program them; using object-oriented techniques and notation will decrease the gap between the business modelers and information systems modelers and architects (assuming both have prior knowledge of object orientation).

New and easier ways to view an organization or a business. The traditional way of describing and viewing an organization doesn't show much of how the business is performed. The functional division of a business into organizational charts can't be used to describe modern business processes that are horizontal to the organization and affect many functions within the business. Object-oriented techniques can easily show these processes, as well as the traditional organizational structure.

There are, of course, a number of other ways to create business models, including using other notations such as IDEF0; it is also possible to simply use textual descriptions of the processes. But UML is a well-defined standard, supported by many tools. It is the dominant modeling language used to model object-oriented information systems.

Summary

The purpose of business modeling is to generate descriptions (abstractions) of a complex reality that capture the core functions of the business. The models show agreed-upon fundamentals, and can serve as a point of discussion. There are many motives for business modeling: to better understand the key mechanisms of a business, to act as the basis for supporting information systems, to improve the business, to radically change the business, to identify new business opportunities, and to identify outsourcing opportunities.

UML has quickly been adopted as the standard modeling language for modeling software systems. This book illustrates how it also can be used for business modeling, based on object-oriented concepts and thus demonstrates that the same modeling language can be used for business and for software models.

This book shows a business model from a number of views. Each view is expressed in one or more diagrams. The diagrams can be of different types, dependent upon the specific structure or situation in the business that it is depicting. The diagrams capture the processes, rules, goals, and objects in the business, and their relationships and interactions with each other.

Naturally, business models alone can't guarantee the success of a business. Good leadership and management are still needed, both in terms of having a long-term strategy and in running and coaching the daily operations. Nor are business models a substitution for finding the right people to work in the business, or for motivating and rewarding these people. All of these issues are very important, but beyond the scope of this book.

Chapter 2 offers a short introduction to the basics of UML and describes some important concepts such as powertypes and stereotypes. Beginning in Chapter 3, "Modeling the Business Architecture," we'll use UML to do business modeling.

CHAPTER

2

UML Primer

The Unified Modeling Language (UML) was created by Grady Booch, James Rumbaugh, and Ivar Jacobson, and later standardized by the Object Management Group (OMG) in 1997. Since then many people and companies have contributed to making UML the language for modeling software systems that it is today.

UML has become one of the most important topics of discussion in modern software engineering circles; and it is becoming of interest to management consulting firms, business analysts, system analysts, software developers and programmers, and people working with requirement specifications. In short, UML has had and continues to have a tremendous impact. Many companies have decided that all their software should be modeled with UML, and thousands of people have taken training courses in the language. Many books have been written about UML, and many software tools support it. All this progress and UML's importance as a generic modeling language is still only in its infancy; its use is expected to grow substantially in the years to come.

UML Basics

A modeling language has a *notation*—the symbols used in the models—and a set of rules that govern the language. The rules are *syntactic*, *semantic*, and *prag-*

matic. The syntactic rules dictate how the symbols should look and how they may be combined. The syntax can be compared to words in a natural language; as in a natural language, it is important to know how to spell them and how to combine them to form sentences. The semantic rules tell us what each symbol means and how it should be interpreted by itself or in the context of other symbols. These rules can be compared to the definitions of words in natural languages (what each word represents). Pragmatic rules explain how to use the language. They may be compared to writing guidelines in natural language. They define the intentions of the symbols, through which the purpose of the model is achieved and becomes understandable to others.

In UML the symbols are geometrical, such as rectangles, circles, and lines. It has a well-defined set of syntactic and semantic rules that define what the symbols mean and how they can be combined. But UML does not have pragmatic rules, that is, specific guidelines for how to use it. Therein lies one of the purposes of this book: to show pragmatic ways of using UML in business modeling.

This chapter gives an overview of the basic UML symbols, syntax, and semantics. The pragmatics of UML in the context of modeling businesses are explored in the remainder of this book. This chapter focuses on introducing UML fundamentals; it presumes a basic knowledge in object-oriented methodology. Those readers with a good knowledge of UML and object orientation can regard this chapter as a refresher and feel free to skim it. The chapter also addresses some special areas, such as powertypes and UML extensions, which will be of interest to readers already proficient in basic UML.

Unified Modeling Language

UML has nine predefined diagrams:

Class diagram. Describes the structure of a system. The structures are built from classes and relationships. The classes can represent and structure information, products, documents, or organizations.

Object diagram. Expresses possible object combinations of a specific class diagram. It is typically used to exemplify a class diagram.

Statechart diagram. Expresses possible states of a class (or a system).

Activity diagram. Describes activities and actions taking place in a system.

Sequence diagram. Shows one or several sequences of messages sent among a set of objects.

Collaboration diagram. Describes a complete collaboration among a set of objects.

Use-case diagram. Illustrates the relationships between use cases. Each use case, typically defined in plain text, describes a part of the total system functionality.

Component diagram. A special case of class diagram used to describe components within a software system.

Deployment diagram. A special case of class diagram used to describe hardware within a software system.

These diagrams capture the three important aspects of systems: structure, behavior, and functionality. Because of UML's unique capability to adapt and extend, it is possible to add new diagrams and elements to UML, making it is a very flexible language that can be used in many situations. Extending UML is discussed in more detail later in this chapter.

Class Diagram

Systems are built from *objects*, which can be physical, such as computers, people, and raw materials, or abstract, such as information or knowledge. Objects are described by their internal properties and their relationships to other objects. For example, Bill's bank account (an object) has attributes common to all bank accounts, such as balance, account number, and credit on current account. In addition, Bill's bank account has relationships to other objects, in this case to a specific bank (a bank object) and to Bill himself (a person object). Attributes are described with a name and a type (integer, Boolean, string, date, etc.). For example, the account number attribute is an integer (a type); and in UML it is shown as 'Account Number : Integer'. Objects also have behavior; for example, one can ask a bank account for its balance. Behavior is described with operations attached to the objects. A bank account could, for example, have "cash withdrawal" and "get balance" operations.

A *class* is a set of objects with the same characteristics. Typical classes are Person, Invoice, Company, Supplier, Order, Product, and Goal. Classifying and grouping objects into classes reduces the complexity and number of elements when modeling and facilitates describing more complicated systems.

Classes are modeled and related to each other in a *class diagram*. The classes are described with names, attributes, and operations. The relationships between the classes are described with a name, roles, and multiplicity. For example, many companies (employers) can employ many persons (employees). This relationship can be described in terms of classes: the class Company has an employ relationship with the class Person. The company plays the role of employer and the person the role of employee. This relationship also has multiplicity, because companies employ many persons, and a person can be employed by many companies.

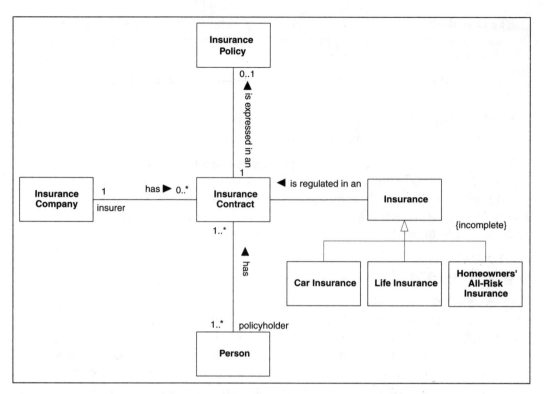

Figure 2.1   A class diagram describing a small system for insurance companies.

Class diagrams are used to describe the objects and relationships of a system. Class diagrams capture and describe information within an information system (physical items in mechanical systems, parties in organizations) or they can be used to describe objects in biological systems, such as the ecosystem. Figure 2.1 is a class diagram for a small system for insurance companies. The model specifies that:

- A person can be a policyholder, and a policyholder has one or many insurance contracts.

- One insurance contract has one or many policyholders, which are persons.

- One insurance company plays the role of an insurer who has zero, one, or many insurance contracts with policyholders. The insurance contracts represent one insurance, which can be a car insurance, life insurance, or homeowner's all-risk insurance. The insurance is regulated by the insurance contract, which specifies policyholder, term of insurance, and policy value. The contract includes all of this information (as attributes) in an insurance policy document.

- An insurance contract is expressed in one (or zero, when it has not been printed yet) insurance policy.

Classes and Objects

Another way to introduce the basic concepts of object technology is to quote from *The Universal Dictionary of the English Language* (Wordsworth Editions Ltd, 1989). All the basic concepts are defined there:

Class. Order, group, category of organisms, etc., which have some essential character or feature in common.

Object. (1) That which is presented to, or observed by, the senses; a material thing, anything visible or tangible. (2) That which is presented to, and grasped by, the mind; that which can be apprehended or known.

Attribute. A quality ascribed to, and considered as inherent in and essential to, any person or thing.

Operation. Act performed, transaction, in the way of business: operation on the stock exchange.

Association. (1) State of being associated, companionship, intimacy. (2) Connexion, bond.

Generalization. (1) Mental process of generalizing. (2) A notion, rule, law, etc. resulting from such a process; derived, evolved, formulated by observation of specific instances.

Multiplicity. Quality, state, of being very numerous or various.

Role. Part played by actor.

In UML, classes are defined as a set of objects with a name, attributes, and operations. The classes can be associated to each other via associations; and the associations have names, roles, and multiplicity. The only concept quoted from *The Universal Dictionary of the English Language* that was not explicitly discussed in the introduction is generalization. The insurance class in the model shown in Figure 2.1 is a generalization of car insurance, life insurance, and homeowner's all-risk insurance. The class Insurance then includes the car insurance, life insurance, and householder's all-risk insurance. In a mathematical sense, a class is a set of objects, and a generalization is just a set of sets. The Insurance class is a superset containing the subsets of car insurance, life insurance, and householder's all-risk insurance.

A class is drawn in UML with a rectangle that is divided horizontally into three compartments. The top compartment contains the name of the class; the middle compartment contains the attributes of the class; and the bottom compartment contains the operations of the class. A compartment can be suppressed in a diagram. Attributes with a plus sign (+) in front of them are public, meaning that other classes can access them. Attributes preceded by the minus sign (-) are private, indicating that only the class itself and its objects can access the attribute. Protected attributes, marked with the number sign (#), can

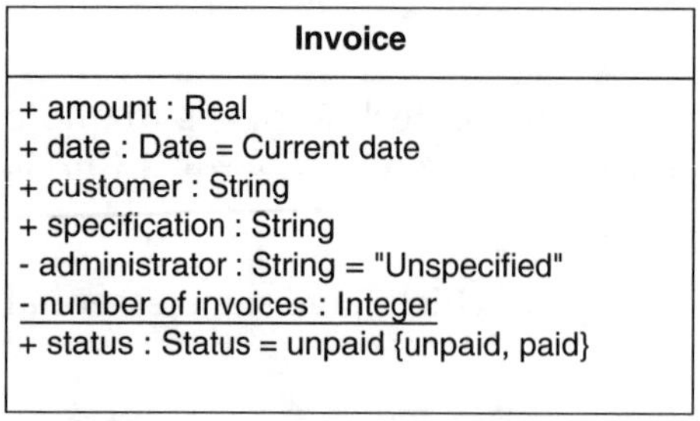

Invoice
+ amount : Real + date : Date = Current date + customer : String + specification : String - administrator : String = "Unspecified" <u>- number of invoices : Integer</u> + status : Status = unpaid {unpaid, paid}

Figure 2.2 A class with attributes.

be used by the class and any descendant (specialization) of the class. Attributes can also be marked as *class scope global* by underlining the attribute. This designates that the attribute has only one value in common with all objects. An example of a class scope global attribute is a counter, such as number of invoices, that is common to all instances of the class. An attribute's possible values can be enumerated, in which case they are shown in the form {a,b,c...}.

Figure 2.2 shows class Invoice with the name and attribute compartments (the operations compartment is suppressed). Invoice has the attributes amount, date, customer, specification, administrator, number of invoices, and status. The amount attribute is of type Real (real number), date is of type Date with the initial value Current date, which means that when a new object of the class Invoice is created the attribute date of that object will be assigned the current date.

Classes also have *operations*, services that the class provides. Operations are similar to functions in programming languages; but the operations in a class have unique access to all the attributes in that class. An operation has a name, visibility, a list of parameters, and a return type. An operation performs some service that the class provides; it sometimes requires parameter values as input; and it returns a result of the return type. Figure 2.3 shows a Bank Account class with the operations cash deposit, case withdrawal, and bank statement.

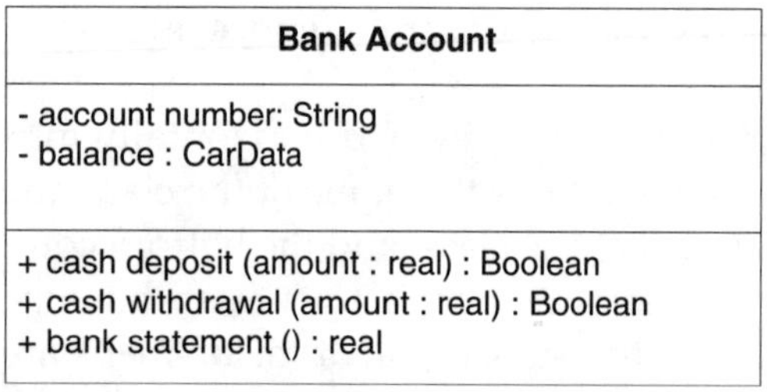

Bank Account
- account number: String - balance : CarData
+ cash deposit (amount : real) : Boolean + cash withdrawal (amount : real) : Boolean + bank statement () : real

Figure 2.3 Examples of operations.

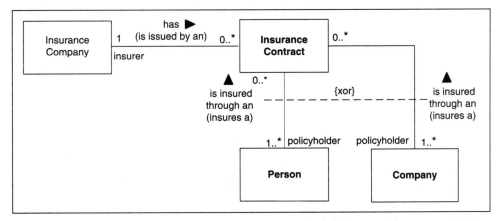

Figure 2.4   A class diagram with classes, associations, association names, roles, multiplicity, and a constraint (xor). The reversed name of the association is indicated in parentheses.

Operations can also be class scope global. Two examples of operations that always are global (for a class) are create and destroy (sometimes referred to as the constructor and the destructor of the class). A create operation is used to create new objects. It is global to the class because it is not possible to ask an object to create itself (because it needs to exist to ask it that). The destroy operation is used to model the destruction of objects.

Associations are given names (usually verbs) and are represented in UML with lines. The association name appears near the association line, and multiplicity and role names appear on each end, as shown in Figure 2.4. Multiplicity is presented as a range, such as 1..5 or 0..* or as a specific number, such as 4. The asterisk (*) indicates many (an open interval). The multiplicity 0..* indicates zero or more. For example, Figure 2.4 shows that the class Insurance Company is associated to zero or more insurance contracts (specified at the end of the association line, near the Insurance contract class). Multiplicity is indicated at the ends of the association, also called the roles of the association. Specifying a name for each role is optional.

Associations can also be given a name direction, specifying how the name of the association should be read. (For example, the Insurance Company has Insurance contracts, not vice versa.) The name direction is drawn near the association name and marked with a small, solid black triangle. If needed, the reversed name (the name in opposite direction) of an association can be indicated in parentheses. The constraint {xor}, drawn between the "is insured through" associations, indicates that only one of these associations can be valid at a time.

The class diagram in Figure 2.4 indicates that the Person class (a noun and a subject) is associated to the Insurance contract class (a noun and a object) with

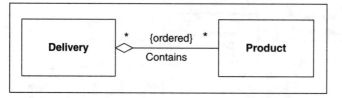

Figure 2.5   A delivery aggregates a number of products.

the association of "has" (a verb) and the multiplicity of 0..* at the end of Insurance contract. The Person is insured through one or more Insurance contracts.

More about Relationships

The *aggregate relationship* is a specialization of association used in situations where a whole is connected with its parts, as shown in Figure 2.5. The hollow diamond on the association in this figure denotes that a delivery aggregates many products (the parts). A delivery consists of a number of products. The constraint {ordered} indicates that a specific order exists between the different products.

   Object composition, shown with a filled diamond, is a stronger form of aggregation. This relationship indicates that the parts can only be in one entity at time. Figure 2.6 shows object composition.

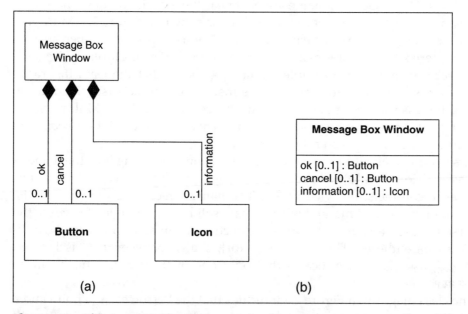

Figure 2.6   Object composition. Buttons and an icon compose a message box. The right side (b) is another way to show object composition.

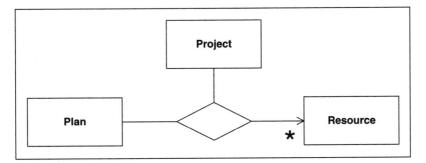

Figure 2.7   A ternary association is shown with a large open diamond.

Where three classes are connected, a *ternary association* is used, as shown in Figure 2.7. Associations are normally bidirectional but there may be unidirectional associations in which the association is only valid in one direction. The association in Figure 2.7 is unidirectional. In this figure, a Plan and a Project are connected to several Resources. Ternaries can be used with both unidirectional and bidirectional associations.

Dependency is another type of relationship expressed between two classes in which one class relies on the other. Dependency also can be used to express dependencies among all the model elements (objects, packages, activities, etc.) included in UML. A dependency is indicated by a dashed line with an arrow from one element pointing to the element on which it depends. *Realization*, shown with a dashed line ending in a hollow triangle, shows that one element is used to realize another element. One class can be a specification or an idea, and another class can implement or detail that specification or idea. Figure 2.8 shows a class Company that is dependent on an Information System that is realized as a Computer-based Information System.

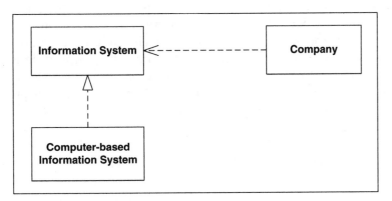

Figure 2.8   Dependency and realization.

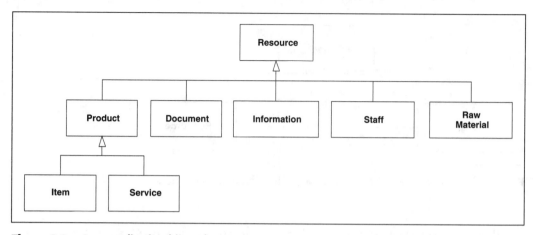

Figure 2.9   A generalization hierarchy.

UML also provides the concepts of *generalization* and *specialization*. The generalization mechanism is used to organize objects in hierarchies. Recall that a class is just a set of objects (e.g., the set of all red cars). A set can be divided into subsets or generalized. For example, a set of all red cars can be divided into subsets of red cars with two doors and red cars with more than two doors. The subset is then a specialization. Specializations are always made upon one or more properties (attributes or operations), such as the number of doors, in this example, or different behavior of red cars. A class can be generalized into a superclass (or in fact, several superclasses if multiple generalization is used) and specialized into subclasses. Figure 2.9 shows an example in which resources are specialized into Products, Documents, Information, Staff, and Raw Material. Products are then further specialized to Items and Services. The line with the hollow triangle shows the generalization; the triangle points at the more general class.

Figure 2.10 shows another generalization hierarchy, this time concerning figures. All figures have a drawing operation, which is redefined for each specialization. The figures also have the position attribute, which is protected (meaning that only those from the class itself and its specializations can use it). The note symbol shown as a rectangle with a "bent corner" in the upper right corner is used in the figure to comment on the subclasses' *draw( )* operation.

The class name, Figure, in Figure 2.10 is italicized to indicate that it is an abstract class. Abstract classes cannot be directly instantiated into objects themselves, but their subclasses can be instantiated (unless the subclass itself is defined as being abstract as well). In *The UML Reference Manual* (Addison-Wesley, 1999), James Rumbaugh writes that "An abstract class may not have direct instances. It may have indirect instances through its concrete descendants." Abstract classes are used to define generic superclasses whose only purpose is to be subclassed and specialized into more concrete classes.

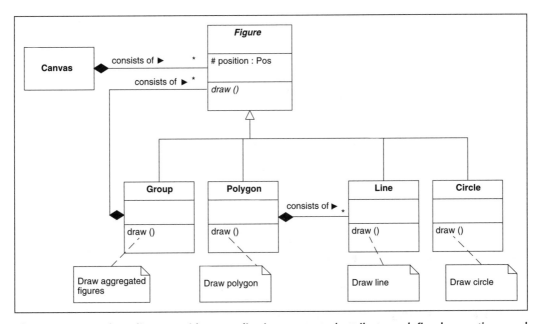

Figure 2.10 A class diagram with generalization, protected attribute, redefined operations and notes.

The draw( ) operation is also italicized to indicate that it is an abstract operation that must be defined in the subclasses. An abstract operation has no implementation in the class in which it is defined, but is a way for a superclass to force its subclasses to implement that specific operation (or again define it as abstract). A class with at least one abstract operation is also automatically an abstract class.

Note that subclasses are not always disjointed. If two subclasses are disjointed, none of the objects belongs to more than one class. In many cases, especially in business modeling, classes overlap (hold overlapping sets of objects). For example, the class Book represents all books in a certain context. These books can be subclassed into management books and software engineering books. However, there is an overlap between the set of all management books and the set of all software engineering books, namely business modeling books. Figure 2.11 illustrates this discussion. The fact that an overlap exists is expressed with the constraint {overlapping}.

A special model element in UML is used to express specifications. This model element is the *interface* and it is denoted by a line with a circle at the end (the "lollipop" symbol). The interface is a specification of a collection of operations that can be implemented by one or more classes. Figure 2.12 shows how the interface concept is used to specify that Microsoft Word and Microsoft PowerPoint both implement the spell-check feature. An interface can't have attributes; it only has abstract operations. Classes that have this interface

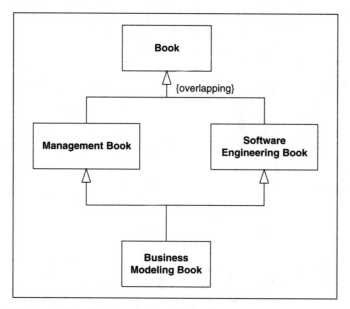

Figure 2.11   Overlapping specialization.

attached to them (that choose to "implement the interface") must implement all the operations defined in the interface. An interface typically describes a generic feature or functionality that different classes or components can choose to support.

Packages

Packages are used to organize and handle complexity in large models. A package groups model elements, such as classes, states and activities, and names that group so that the package can then be referred to as a whole. Dependencies are used between packages to show how the packages are dependent on each other, as shown in the class diagram depicted in Figure 2.13. This type of

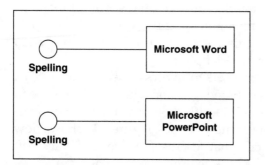

Figure 2.12   An example with interface.

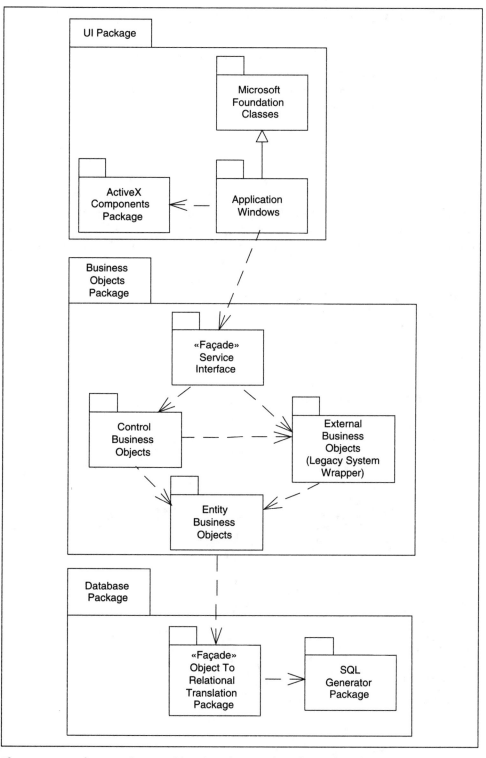

Figure 2.13   Three packages with subpackages. The relationships between the packages are dependency and generalization.

diagram sometimes is referred to as a package diagram, but there is no such diagram type in UML; it is a class diagram that shows packages. It is also possible to draw the packages directly in a model, a class diagram, or a sequence diagram. The package symbol is shown in Figure 2.13.

Powertypes

Often it is desirable to model a system generically, for example, to handle articles, production equipment, or a sales system. A common problem that arises when developing generic models is how to handle new types of objects that are added over time. In a system built, say, for organizing and registering vehicles, it would include vehicle types such as cars, boats, airplanes, helicopters,

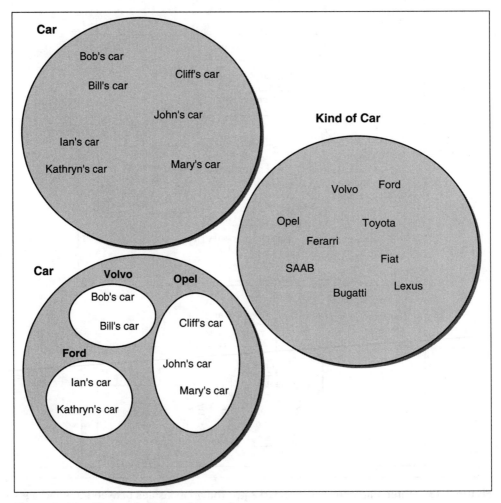

Figure 2.14 Class, subclass, and powertype.

and bikes, to name a few. But what if new types of vehicles were to appear in the future? It is a daunting task to discover and include all object types in a system, not to mention impractical (if not impossible) to model it all beforehand without knowing exactly which types will be required.

Instead, objects and types of objects can be separated. Figure 2.14 shows that the class Car is a set of many cars, such as Bob's car or Bill's car. These cars can be grouped into new subsets such as Volvo, Ford, or Toyota. The subsets (subclasses) are nothing more than objects to the set and class Kind of Car. The class Kind of Car is called a *powertype* to the class Car. The objects to the class Kind of Car (Ford, Volvo, Toyota, etc.) are subclasses to the class Car. Powertypes are used to model types of objects; the objects themselves have no knowledge of all objects of either class.

Powertypes are widely used in more complex business models and in many of the commercial database applications (in databases this entity is often called metadata).

There is a mathematical definition of powertypes as well. In terms of set theory, a class is a set and its subclasses are subsets. The number of objects (elements), let's say X, of the set A can be divided into maximal 2^X (2 power X) subsets. The set of all subsets is the *powerset*. The set of all possible subsets of set A is the powerset of A. For example, if the set Color includes the objects red, green, and blue, there are eight possible combinations of these color objects. The possible combinations (subsets) are: RGB, RG, R, GB, G, B, RB, and $\{\emptyset\}$, where $\{\emptyset\}$ is the empty set. The set that contains these combinations is called the powerset of the set Color.

Figure 2.15 shows how UML powertypes can be visually modeled. In it, the powertype Kind of Car is related to the class Car. The powertype Kind of Car is a class in itself (a stereotyped class; stereotypes will be further explained in

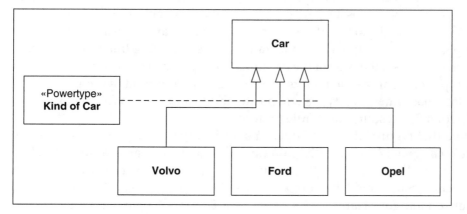

Figure 2.15 The formal way of showing how powertypes relate to classes [Rumbaugh 1999].

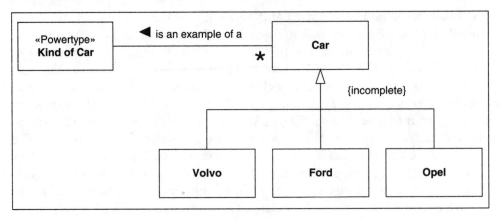

Figure 2.16   A pragmatic way of showing powertypes.

the section on extending the UML). Figure 2.16 shows another, more pragmatic, way of indicating powertypes in UML. It is easy to implement in computer-based systems. The model says that a Volvo, Ford, and Opel are examples (instances) of some kind of cars. Volvo, Ford, and Opel are also cars; they are specializations to the class Car. However, there are more kinds of cars, and that is shown by the constraint {incomplete}.

Figure 2.17 shows a business example in which a powertype is used, specifically, a generic class diagram for an organizational chart. Individual organizational units can be connected to each other to show the relationships among the units (which unit is a subunit to another). For example, the Organizational unit Software Inc. is connected to the units Production, Sales department, and Development, which all are subunits to the Software unit. Each Organizational unit is also linked to an Organization type (which is a powertype). For example, the Organization type Department is connected to the Organizational units Production, Sales Department, and Development, showing that all of these units are departments. Corporation, subsidiary, division, team, and group are other examples of organization types. By being linked to a specific powertype object, the type of the organizational unit can easily be denoted and new types of organizational units can be added later without having to change the class diagram. Powertypes will be illustrated and used in further examples in Chapter 7, "Resource and Rule Patterns."

Note that Figure 2.17 also models a specific organization, Software Inc., as an *object diagram*. An object diagram can be used to show an example of a class diagram. In Figure 2.17, Software Inc. is organized into three departments: Production, Sales, and Development. The Development department is in turn organized into four teams: OOA Team, Java Team, BM Team, and OOD Team. This object diagram shows how powertypes can be used in a simple class diagram. Powertypes also are used to express more complex object diagrams.

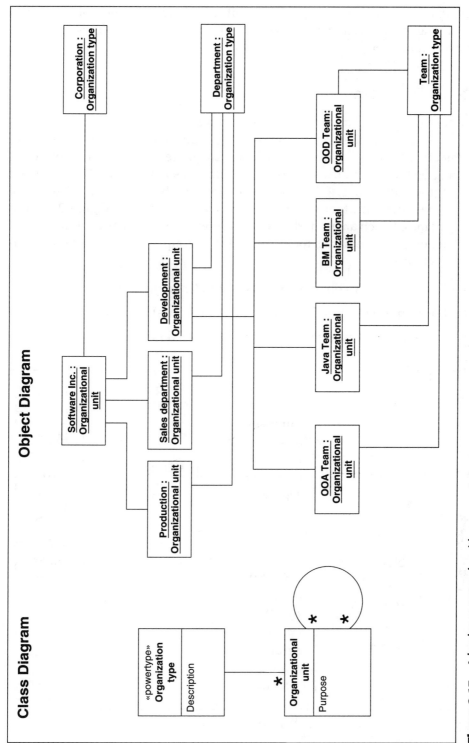

Figure 2.17 A business example with a powertype.

Note that new types of organizational units can be added as new objects, without having to modify the class diagram. The next section explores object diagrams in more detail.

Object Diagram

Object diagrams explain and illustrate complex class diagrams; they are pictures of objects and their relationships at a specific moment in time. Object diagrams are drawn with objects and links. Links are instances of associations and aggregations. Because an object diagram is a snapshot, multiplicity is not shown (the actual links at that moment in time are shown instead). Figure 2.18 is an object diagram that exemplifies the class diagram in Figure 2.10. The object names, which are underlined, are composed of their names, followed by a colon and the class name; for example, G1 : Group. Three examples of naming objects are:

- Ben : Person (An object named Ben of a class named Person)
- Bob (An object named Bob of an unnamed class)
- : Person (An unnamed object of a class named Person)

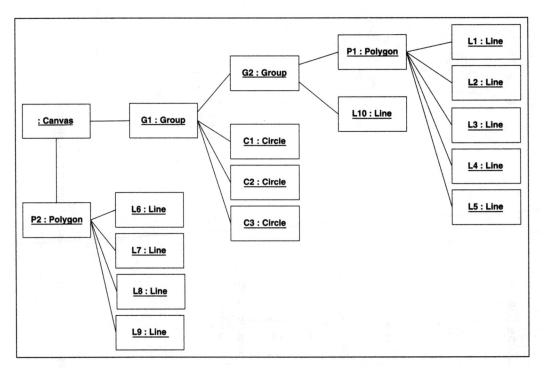

Figure 2.18   An object diagram.

Named objects (e.g., Ben : Person, Bob) are used when the name of an object is of primary interest. The anonymous name form (: Person) is used when only the class is of interest and no specific name is needed for the object.

In addition to object names, the state and attribute values of an object can be shown. The state is shown in brackets after the object name; for example:

Bill's Invoice #34 : Invoice [paid]

Though the attribute compartment is normally suppressed when showing objects, it can be shown, as was the case with class diagrams. If shown, the attribute's value is indicated as follows:

description : string = "this is a sample description"

This technique is often used in combination with activity diagrams and is discussed further in the section about activity diagrams later in this chapter.

Statechart Diagram

A *state* is the result of the attribute's value and links to other objects. It specifies how the object reacts to events occurring around it. Statechart diagrams capture the life cycles of objects, subsystems, and systems. They indicate what states an object can have and how different events affect those states over time. Statechart diagrams should be attached to classes that have clearly identifiable states and complex behavior, but they also can be defined for a subsystem or an entire system. The diagram specifies the behavior of an object and how that behavior differs from state to state. It also shows which events change the state of the objects of the class.

A state is typically represented by the attributes' values and links to other objects. Examples of object states are:

- The invoice (object) is paid (state).
- The car (object) is standing still (state).
- The engine (object) is running (state).
- Jim (object) is playing the role of a salesman (state).
- Kate (object) is married (state).

An object changes state when an event occurs, that is, when something happens. There are two dimensions of dynamics, the *interaction* and the *internal state change*. Interactions describe the object's external behavior and how it interacts with other objects (by sending messages or linking and unlinking to other objects). Internal state changes describe how the object changes state, for example, the values of its internal attributes in different states. Statechart diagrams show how objects react to events and how they change their internal

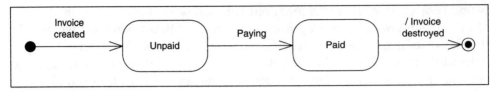

Figure 2.19   A statechart diagram for invoices.

state as a result of the interaction. Interaction between objects is described in more detail later.

Statechart diagrams can have a starting point and several end points. A starting point, or *initial state*, is represented with a solid circle; an end point or *final state* is represented with a small solid circle surrounded by a larger empty circle (to form a bull's-eye). A state is represented as a rectangle with rounded corners. Changes in states, or *state transitions*, are indicated with a line ending in an arrow pointing from one state to another. The state transition is labeled with its cause (the event that generates the state transition). When the event occurs, the transition from one state to another is performed (sometimes spoken of as "the transition fires" or "the transition is triggered"). Figure 2.19 is an example of a statechart diagram.

Figure 2.20 shows a statechart diagram for the Stock Order resource, which represents a stock order placed by a customer. It will be created when an order is received from a customer. At some point, a communication with a marketplace will put this order onto the market. The marketplace will then try to match this order with other orders on the market; that is, match a buy order

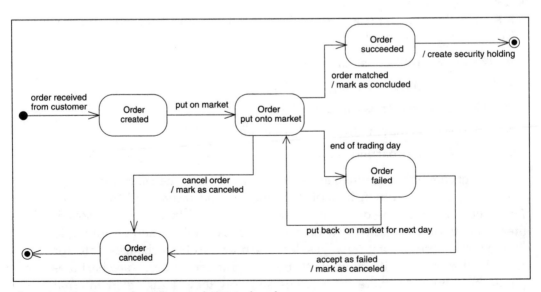

Figure 2.20   A statechart diagram for a stock order.

with a sell order. If a match is reported from the marketplace, the order will be marked as concluded; thereafter, an action will generate a security holding that represents the shares bought. An order can also be canceled and withdrawn from the market; or the trading day can end without making a match. According to the state diagram, there must be an explicit decision to put the order back onto the market for the next day. If it's not put back on the market, it will be marked as a canceled order.

Event Types

There are four types of events that trigger state transitions: *call events, time events, signal events,* and *change events.* A call event is a called operation that affects the attributes and links of an object. An example of a call event is:

withdrawal(amount)

Time events cause a change in time. They are expressed with the keyword **after** and occur at a specific moment in time. An example of a time event is:

after (15sec)

Change events cause a change in a link or attribute value. Change events are expressed with the keyword **when** and occur because of a change in one of the attribute values or links. An example of a change event is:

when (t = 2 days)

A fourth event, called *signal event,* occurs when a signal is received. The signal event is handled and described in the "Activity Diagram" section later in this chapter.

Nested and Parallel States

States can also be *nested* and in *parallel.* A state that contains itself and is divided into other states is nested. A parallel state is when an object has several states at the same time. A car, for example, can be new or old and be moving forward, backward, or standing still.

Figure 2.21 shows a statechart diagram for a production plan that has both nested states and parallel states. Initially, the production plan is proposed and not suspended, which means that the production plan has two states at the same time, namely the state proposed and the state not suspended. Between the time the production plan is started and accomplished, it can be suspended and even abandoned. If the production plan is suspended, it can be restarted; but if it is abandoned, it cannot be restarted (i.e., there is no state transition, trigged by a restart, from the state abandoned to the state suspended or the state not suspended). The production plan has two parallel states at all times,

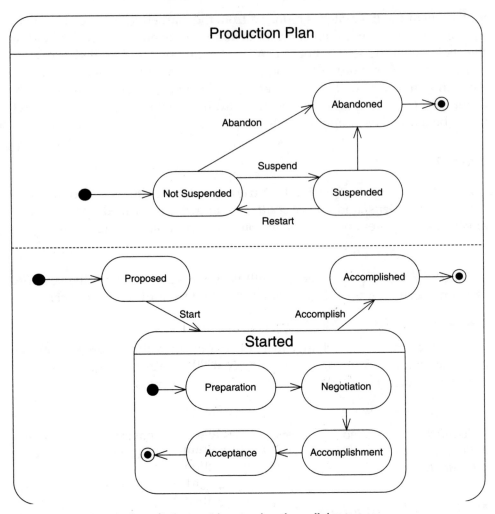

Figure 2.21   A statechart diagram with nested and parallel states.

and it is composed of substates (nested states). The state Started has four internal states (nested states), namely Preparation, Negotiation, Accomplishment, and Acceptance.

State Transitions

A state transition usually has an event attached to it, but it is not necessary to attach one. If an event is attached to a state transition, the state transition will be performed when the event occurs. A *do-expression* within a state can be an ongoing process (e.g., waiting, producing, following some plan, etc.) performed while the object is in the given state. A do-expression can be

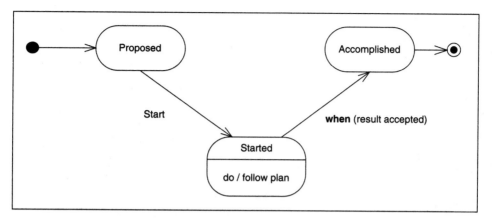

Figure 2.22 A statechart diagram for a plan.

interrupted by outside events, meaning that an event in a state transition can interrupt an ongoing internal do-action. Figure 2.22 shows a state with a do-expression.

If a state transition does not have a specified event, the state will change when the internal actions in the source state are executed (i.e., the do-expressions). When all the actions in a state have been performed, a transition is triggered automatically, without an event.

An *action-expression* can be connected to a state transition. An action-expression is a procedural expression that is executed if the transition fires. It can be written in terms of operations and attributes within the owning object (the object that owns all of the states) or with parameters within the event-signature. It is possible to have more than one action-expression on a state transition, but they must be delimited with a forward slash (/). Action-expressions are executed one by one in the order specified (from left to right). Action-expressions cannot be nested or recursive. It is, however, possible to have a state transition that contains only an action-expression.

An example of a state transition with an action-expression is:

add (n) / sum = sum + n

A special case of the action-expression is the *send-clause,* an explicit syntax for sending a message during a state transition. The syntax consists of a *destination-expression* and a *message.* The destination-expression points out an object or a set of objects. The message should correspond to a state transition in the destination object that is pointed out by the destination-expression. The caret (^) indicates that a send-clause follows.

An example of a state transition with a send-clause is:

out_of_paper( )^indicator.light( )

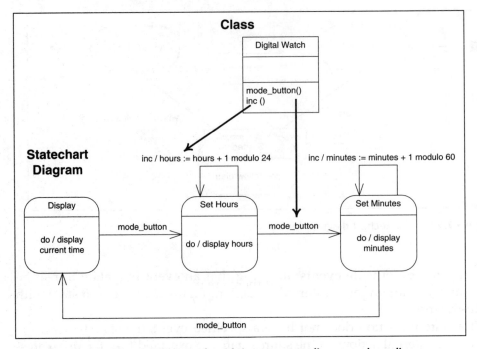

Figure 2.23   The class Digital Watch with its corresponding statechart diagram.

Figure 2.23 shows a class and its statechart diagram. It demonstrates how operations within the class are related to the call-events specified by the statechart diagram. The watch has three states: its normal display state showing the time and two states for setting the clock (hours and minutes, respectively).

Activity Diagram

Activity diagrams are used to explore and describe a workflow, the actions performed in an operation in a class, similar to traditional program flowcharts. In addition, activity diagrams are used to describe business processes, workflows in the context of organizations. They are described in great detail in this section because of their importance to business process modeling. (The term "business process" will be explained and illustrated in greater detail in Chapters 3 and 4, but for the purpose of this discussion, a business process describes a simple flow or sequence of activities.) A workflow can be a simple operation, such as how to place an order in an order system, or it can be more complex, such as how to control production and product development.

Figure 2.24 shows an activity diagram for an order process. The order process begins with the Prepare Inquiry activity and then sends the inquiry. After the inquiry is sent, the Order Process waits for a notice of delivery. When

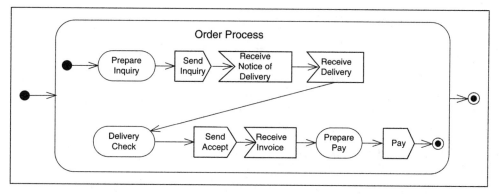

Figure 2.24   An order process.

the delivery is received by the Order Process, it is checked, and an acceptance is sent to the supplier. An invoice is received by the Order Process and the payment is prepared and sent. Note that there are no events specified on the transitions; in an activity diagram there is an automatic transition to the next activity once the preceding activity has been performed.

Activity States

The activity diagram has some similarities to the statechart diagram, but the "states" in an activity diagram are actually activities to be performed, and the transitions are fired by ending activities (i.e., when the activity specified in a "state" has been performed, a transition to the next activity happens automatically; no event is necessary, as is the case in the statechart diagram). The states in an activity diagram are called *activity states,* or more simply, *activities* (states with a do-expression). Activity states are states in which some activity is performed. Activities can be divided into *subactivities*. Subactivities that cannot be further divided are called *actions* (atomic activities); they are indicated with the same symbol, the activity symbol (rectangles with rounded corners). Activities and actions are connected via transitions; transitions in an activity diagram make up the *control flow*.

Control Flow

All syntax used in statechart diagrams (with the exception of events) can be applied to the control flow. A control flow can have guards, actions, and send-clauses. The send-clauses are marked by a special symbol, which is shown in the "Send and Receive" section upcoming. Figure 2.25 illustrates an activity diagram with start, stop, and a set of activities connected with a control flow. The start and stop symbols are the same as in statechart diagrams.

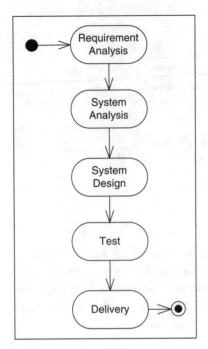

Figure 2.25   A simple software development process without iterations.

Guards can be applied directly to the control flow or in combination with a *decision symbol*. The decision symbol is a hollowed diamond. Figure 2.26 shows an example in which the decision symbol is used to model iterations.

Forking and Joining

A control flow can be *forked* or *joined*. Forking a control flow means that the flow of control is split into several flows, each with its own activities. This technique is used when activities are performed in parallel with some form of *synchronization*. Synchronization means that the control flow is joined, as in Figure 2.27 (which shows a very simplified view of a business process). The synchronization bar, a bold line, is used to show forking (split into several control flows) and joining of several control flows. When flows are joined, if one flow reaches the synchronization bar first, it will wait for the other flows before continuing.

Object Flow

Object flow is a technique used to capture how objects participate in activities and how they are affected by the activities. Figure 2.28 shows an example in which a production activity (a business process) receives an order object and feedback from manufactured products. The production delivers products that

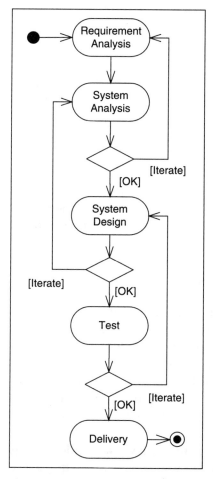

Figure 2.26   An iterative software development process.

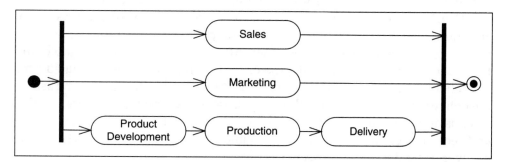

Figure 2.27   Sales and marketing are done in parallel with the activity series product development, production, and delivery. In the automotive industry this is called concurrent engineering; marketing is done in parallel with sales, product development, and so on.

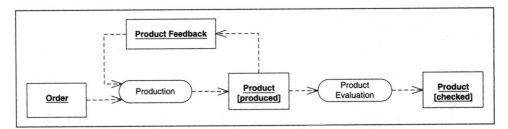

Figure 2.28 An activity diagram with object flow.

are then evaluated in the product evaluation activity. The product evaluation activity delivers checked products. Object flows are shown with a dashed line ending with an arrow. If the arrow points at an activity, it is an input object; otherwise, it is an output object.

Send and Receive

Signals are objects that are explicitly sent or received in activity diagrams. The send symbol corresponds to the send-clause attached to a transition in a statechart diagram. The send symbol is a convex pentagon that looks like a rectangle with a triangular point on one side. The receive symbol is a concave pentagon that looks like a rectangle with a notch in its side. As with the send-clause, both the send and receive symbols are attached to a transition (control flow). The transition is divided graphically into two transitions with a send or a receive symbol in between.

The send and receive symbols are attached to the receiver or sender objects with a dashed line with an arrow from the send or receive symbol to the object. If it is a send symbol, the arrow points to the object. If it is a receive symbol, the arrow points away from the object, to the receive symbol. Showing the objects receiving or sending the signals is optional.

Figure 2.29 shows an example in which signals (i.e., objects) are sent and received. The model indicates that a delivery process begins with the receipt of an inquiry. Once an inquiry is received, the process begins to negotiate with the sender of the inquiry, the customer. After a while, an order is placed and the order is accomplished. While the order is being filled, the estimated time for delivery is sent to the inquiry sender. When the inquiry is accomplished, the delivery is made and the delivery process waits for an acceptance. Finally, it sends an invoice and receives payment. This model shows only the sending and receiving of signals; it is also possible to indicate which objects are the receiver or sender of the signals.

This process can be further detailed; for example, it is possible to add the handling of nonaccepted deliveries. It also might be of interest to see how the delivery process interacts with the order process or to examine how the sup-

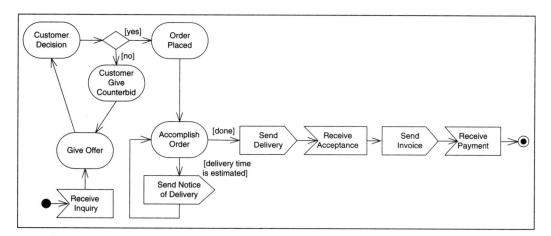

Figure 2.29   A delivery process.

plier and the customer interact. As you probably have guessed, the delivery process does not take place only in the supplier's organization; it also takes place in the customer's organization. This is thoroughly examined in Chapter 3, "Modeling the Business Architecture," Chapter 4, "Business Views," and Chapter 5, "Business Rules." The interaction between the customer and the supplier is discussed in the "Sequence Diagram" section next in this chapter.

Swimlanes

A *swimlane* groups activities with respect to their responsibility. Swimlanes can be used for several different purposes, including to explicitly show where actions are performed (in which object), or to show in which part of an organization activities are performed. Swimlanes are drawn as vertical rectangles in the activity diagram, and the activities that belong to a swimlane are placed within its rectangle. The swimlane is given a name that is placed at the top of the rectangle. In Figure 2.30, swimlanes are used to model organizational units (Product Development, Marketing and Sales, and Manufacturing). The activities are placed in the organizational units in which they are carried out.

Another technique used in Figure 2.30 is *stereotyping*. Stereotypes enable you to create new building blocks in UML based on existing blocks but specific to the problem at hand. All model elements in UML (classes, objects, states, etc.) can have stereotypes. For example, if it is important to denote that an object is an information object holding only information, we can stereotype the object as "information object"; if it is a physical item, then we can stereotype it as "physical item." There are no predefined building blocks for information objects and physical objects in UML, but by defining stereotypes for them based on the standard class concept we can adapt and extend UML to support

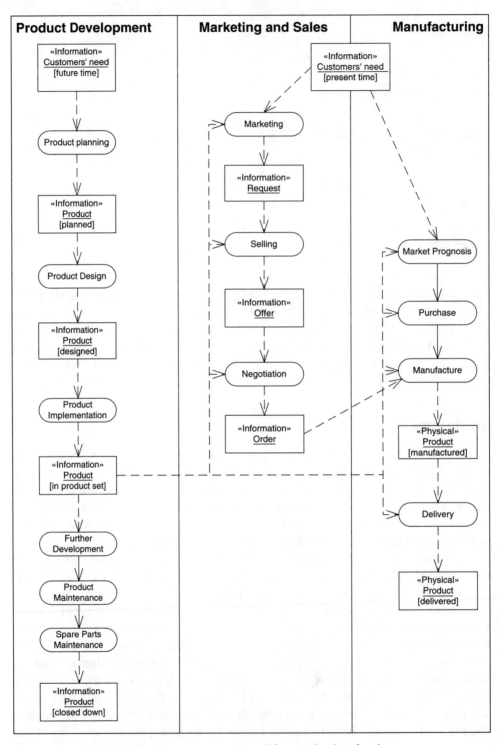

Figure 2.30   A simple business process view with organizational units.

these concepts. In Figure 2.30, the information and physical stereotypes are used. A stereotype name is enclosed in double angle brackets (the guillemet symbol), in the form «stereotype-name». Stereotypes are discussed in more detail later in this chapter and are used in this book to adapt UML for business modeling.

Sequence Diagram

Sequence diagrams are used to explore and visualize the sequence in which objects interact with each other. The objects can be organizational units, companies, computers, people, processes, or mechanical things. Typically, sequence diagrams depict the sequence of messages between a set of objects, where the order and timing of the messages are clearly depicted. Figure 2.31 is one example of such a sequence, the interaction between a customer and a supplier. This figure is based on a repeatable four-phase model for interaction. The first phase, Preparation, consists of two activities: Prepare inquiry and Send inquiry. The Negotiation phase consists of these activities: Prepare offer, Send offer, Prepare counterbid, Send counterbid, Send offer to the customer, Prepare order, Send order, and Obligation. The next phase, Accomplishment, consists of three activities: Confirm, Accomplishment, Notice of delivery, and Delivery. The last phase, Acceptance, comprises these activities: Delivery check, Accept, Invoice, Send invoice, Prepare payment, and, finally, Pay. The figure shows the exact interaction between the customer and the supplier.

Notice in Figure 2.31 that participating objects are placed at the top of the model and *lifelines* are drawn vertically from the objects. The lifelines show when objects are created and destroyed. In this figure, all objects exist from the beginning; Figure 2.32 shows how objects are created and destroyed during the execution of the sequence. The creation and destruction is shown by the lifeline in sequence diagrams.

Activities, such as Prepare Order and Deliver Check, can be shown on the lifelines. The activities are the *connection-point*s to both statechart diagrams and activity diagrams; the objects are the connection-points to the object diagrams and the class diagrams. *Scripts* can be placed on the sides of a sequence diagram, as shown in Figure 2.31 (Preparation, Negotiation, etc.), to clarify the sequences.

Messages in a sequence diagram can have parameters, as shown in Figure 2.32, and guards—just like statecharts and activity diagrams.

Collaboration Diagram

Collaboration diagrams focus on how objects collaborate, and express situations similar to those modeled by the sequence diagram. Sequence diagrams handle sequences and simple selections (with the guards) while collaboration

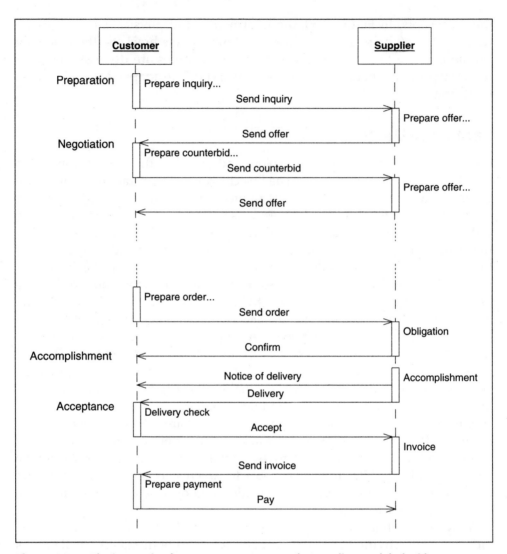

Figure 2.31   The interaction between a customer and a supplier modeled with a sequence diagram.

diagrams handle iterations. Collaboration diagrams make it easier to express more complex interactions and to show the relationships between the collaborating objects. Sequence diagrams are straightforward and easy to read, but because collaboration diagrams are more powerful, they are less readable. Both are useful but in different situations.

Figure 2.33 is a collaboration diagram that shows how to calculate the value of a portfolio. The messages are numbered, indicating the order in

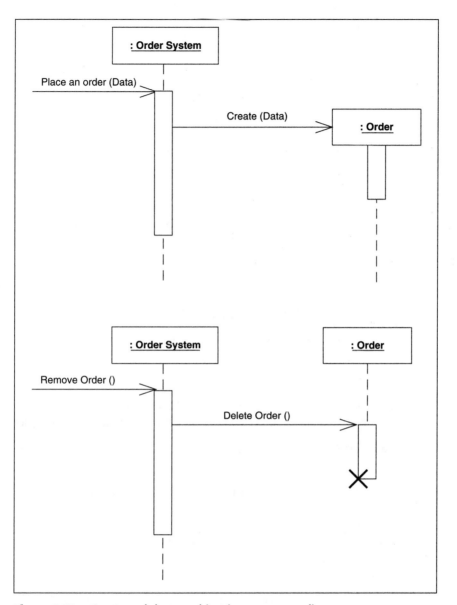

Figure 2.32   Create and destroy object in a sequence diagram.

which they are sent, beginning with 1, followed by 1.1, 1.1.1, 1.2, 1.2.1, 1.3, 1.3.1 and so on.

Figure 2.33 also shows *synchronous messages*, those messages that must be fulfilled before anything else can be accomplished. For example, message 1.1.1 must be sent and accomplished before message 1.2 can be sent.

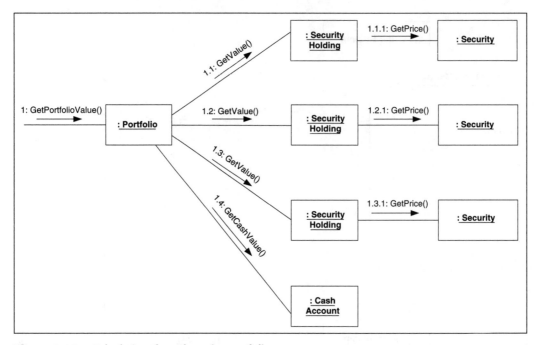

Figure 2.33   Calculating the value of a portfolio.

Iterations are indicated with an asterisk, followed by an iteration clause and the operation that should be called (i.e., the messages that are sent). For example:

* [when there are orders left] get amount ( )

Figure 2.34 shows a complex collaboration diagram for a computer-based information system with a graphical user interface. A sales statistics window is shown (message 1), and the window then creates a statistics summary object (1.1), which will collect the statistics to show in the window. When the statistics summary object is created, it will iterate over all salespersons and get the total order sum (1.1.1) and the budget (1.1.2) for each salesperson. Each salesperson object gets its order sum by iterating over all its orders (getting the amount for each (1.1.1.1) and adding them together), and its budget by getting the amount from a budget sales object (1.1.2.1). When the statistics summary object has iterated over all the salespersons, it has been created (the return of message 1.1). The sales statistics window will then get result lines from the statistics summary object (the result line is a formatted string describing the result of one salesperson) and show each line in its window. When all result lines have been read, the show operation on the sales statistics window returns, and the collaboration is finished. At first, the message-sequence numbering scheme can take some time to get used to, but after a while you will find it easy to read.

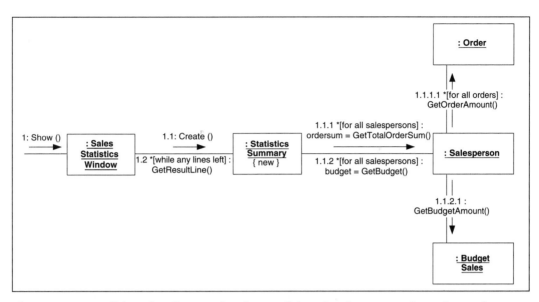

Figure 2.34   A collaboration diagram showing a collaboration that summarizes sales results.

Use-Case Diagram

Use cases capture the functional requirements on a system. They are defined through plain text. The use-case diagram summarizes which use cases are available and their relationships to each other. Use cases and use-case diagrams are formulated in terms of an *actor* and a *system*. An actor is a role that a user or another system has in relationship to the system. An actor always has some interest in using the functionality the system provides. A use case is one use of the system (information system, mechanical system) by an actor.

Figure 2.35 shows a use-case diagram for a computerized insurance system. The actors using the system are the insurance customer, the insurance salesperson, and the claims adjuster.

The customer can sign insurance policies, pay insurance fees, notify the insurance company of damage, and retrieve compensation. Notification of damage also involves the claims adjuster actor. The insurance salesperson can view different types of statistics about customer, insurance policies, and damages.

Use cases are described with textual descriptions, such as:

Signing Insurance Item

- The use case is initiated by the insurance customer.
- Information about the customer (name, address, social security number) is entered.
- Type of insurance is entered.

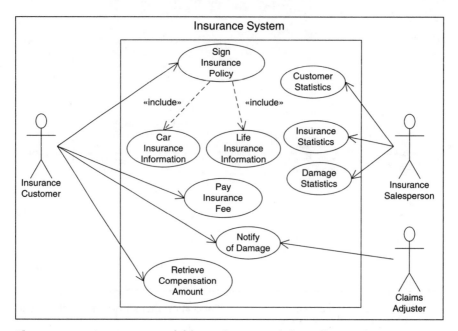

Figure 2.35   A use-case model for an insurance information system.

- Information about the insured object is entered. Depending on type of insurance, either Life Insurance Information or Car Insurance Information is included.

- System calculates the monthly insurance fee.

- A preliminary insurance number, fee, and insurance date are returned to the customer.

Use cases can be linked with three types of relationships:

Include. An include relationship between use cases means that one use case can include and use other use cases in an explicitly defined place in its description. An include relationship is shown as a dependency stereotyped as «include» (see Figure 2.35).

Extend. An extend relationship between use cases means that the base use case (the use case that is extended) is extended with additional behavior by the extending use case. The extensions can be seen as optional functionality added to the base use case, and the base use case does not need to know of the extending use case; it can also be used as-is. An extend relationship is shown as a dependency stereotyped to «extend».

Generalization. Generalization among use cases is the same as generalization among classes. One use case can be specialized to one or several use cases that inherit and add features to it. Generalization is shown with the same symbol as between classes (a line with a triangle).

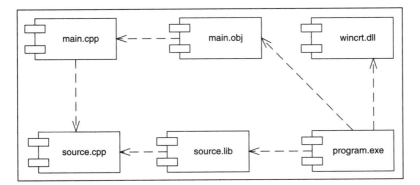

Figure 2.36   A component diagram.

Component Diagram

Component diagrams are used to structure components in software systems. They examine and manage dependencies between components or between interfaces of components. Components in UML are physical, such as source code files, libraries, dynamic components, or executable programs. Figure 2.36 is an example of a component diagram in which six software components depend upon each other. Business modeling does not utilize this diagram directly; it is a part of UML specially designed for software engineering (which in turn could implement the support for a business model).

Deployment Diagram

Deployment diagrams are used to explore different processor configurations for implementing a solution. It is a view of the physical hardware in a system. Figure 2.37 is an example of a deployment diagram with three PCs, a server, a printer, an Internet hookup, and a database server. All of these are viewed as *nodes*, visualized by boxes. The diagram can also be detailed to show the allocation of components or processes to nodes (e.g., show which programs or components execute in different nodes). Business modeling does not utilize this diagram; it is a part of UML specially designed to model the physical architecture of computer systems.

Extending UML

Classes, objects, states, and activities are some of the building blocks that form the foundation of UML. However, there may be situations in which you will want to customize these building blocks to suit your needs. UML provides

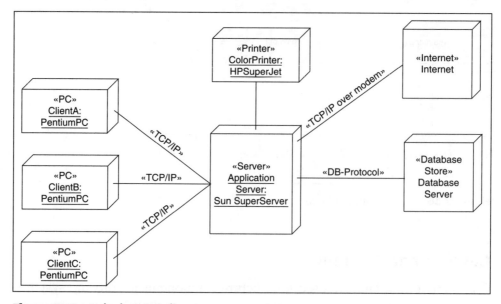

Figure 2.37   A deployment diagram.

three mechanisms for extending UML to apply to your particular modeling requirements: stereotypes, tagged values, and constraints.

Stereotypes

Recall that stereotyping is a technique used to define new kinds of building blocks in UML based on existing blocks. It allows you to customize an existing UML modeling element to suit your particular modeling needs. For example, activities can be used for many things: to specify operations, to specify business processes, and to specify data flow. To constrain activities to just business processes, you can define or stereotype this UML building block as a new type of UML modeling element.

Any UML modeling element can be customized; essentially, you can almost define your own modeling language based upon the UML foundation. Although it is not possible to add new kinds of elements, all existing UML elements can be customized, extended, or adapted by defining and naming the stereotypes. The definitions are textual descriptions; furthermore, a stereotype can have a specific graphical icon attached to it, so that the stereotyped element has a symbol. This new symbol can then be used to identify the new modeling element in the diagrams.

There are three methods for showing and modeling stereotypes. The first, already mentioned, is to show the original model element (a class, an object, a state, etc.) with the stereotype name enclosed within guillemets (double angle

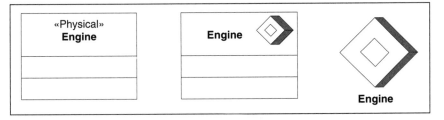

Figure 2.38   Three ways of representing the stereotype «Physical».

brackets): «stereotype-name» (see the left-hand example in Figure 2.38). The second method is to use an optional icon, a symbol that represents the stereotype, inside the original symbol (middle example in Figure 2.38). The last approach is to show the selected icon only, and treat the stereotype as any pre-defined building block in UML (right-hand example in Figure 2.38).

In Figure 2.38, the stereotype «Physical» denotes a special kind of a class that is built upon a normal class; its objects are physical things in the real world.

Figure 2.39 shows another example of a stereotype. Here, an activity is stereotyped to a business process. The icon also includes the stereotype string (which is a part of the icon) in order to make interpreting the icon easier (the string tells us what it is about). The name of the activity, in this case the business process, is shown inside the icon. Handling the process stereotype as shown in Figure 2.39 is practical when modeling large-scale models, especially large-scale business models.

Tagged Values

All model elements can be extended with a *tagged value* that consists of a *tag* and a *value* (it can be a version tag and a version number (value) for a class, etc.). Another example of a tagged value is the modeler (author) of a process and a value that is a text string containing the name of the modeler. Like

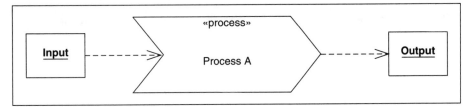

Figure 2.39   A business process, which is a stereotyped activity with object flow (input object and output object).

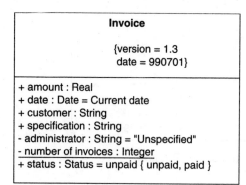

Invoice
{version = 1.3 date = 990701}
+ amount : Real + date : Date = Current date + customer : String + specification : String - administrator : String = "Unspecified" - <u>number of invoices : Integer</u> + status : Status = unpaid { unpaid, paid }

Figure 2.40 A class with two tags: version and date.

stereotyping, this is a technique used to extend UML. All model elements in UML can be extended with tagged values, which are depicted within curly braces—{ }. Figure 2.40 shows a class with a tag for version and a tag for date on the class.

Constraints

A constraint, a term we've used already, is the third way to extend UML. Constraints are rules applied to UML models; they can be applied to just one or to several model elements. A constraint that is applied on several model elements uses a dashed line that crosses the involved model elements; the constraint itself is written within curly brackets. A constraint that is applied to just one model element is defined close to the element, again within curly brackets. Figure 2.41 shows the two different ways of defining constraints.

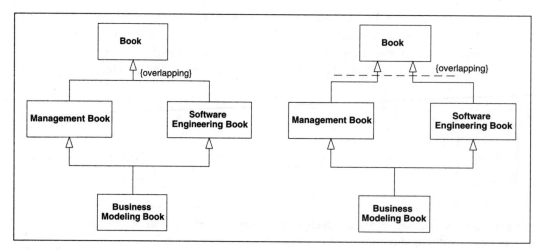

Figure 2.41 Two ways of modeling the same book model.

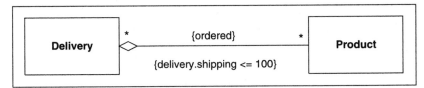

Figure 2.42   A model with both a predefined and a user-defined constraint.

In addition to using the predefined constraints, such as xor and ordered (discussed earlier in this chapter), you can define your own constraints. Figure 2.42 has an example with the predefined ordered constraint and a customized constraint that specifies that the shipping cost of a delivery clip must not be larger than 100. Constraints are often defined using the Object Constraint Language (OCL), discussed in detail in Chapter 5, "Business Rules." In the context of business modeling, constraints and OCL are used to define business rules for the business.

The three extension mechanisms, stereotypes, tagged values, and constraints, can be used to customize and add new functionality to UML. The Eriksson-Penker Business Extensions presented in the following chapters use these techniques to customize UML for real-life business modeling. After a while, you will learn to benefit from customizing UML on your own, but the best way to begin is to use someone else's extensions in some of your projects. You can then try to adjust them and develop your own extensions to suit your line of business and your modeling requirements. Remember, UML should not dominate or constrain you; rather, you should master UML.

Finally, a note on CASE tools that support UML. Some CASE tools on the market have not yet implemented the use of stereotype icons, but most support stereotype strings, tagged values, and constraints. If the tool you use does not support icons, simply use the string variant of stereotypes instead.

Summary

UML is a modeling language that can be used for both business modeling and software engineering. It is a language that can be extended and customized. The following chapters introduce the Eriksson-Penker Business Extension for UML. These extensions make it possible to use UML even in complex and difficult business modeling, all the way to designed and implemented computer-based systems.

UML has nine predefined diagrams; together, they cover structure, behavior, and functionality.

- *Class diagrams are used to describe structures.* The structures are built up from classes and relationships such as associations, aggregate, and generalization. The classes can represent and structure things like information, products, documents, and organizations.

- *Object diagrams are used to exemplify a class diagram.* These diagrams can show objects, the name of the objects, the object states, and links (instances of relationships) among the objects.

- *Statechart diagrams are used to express which states a class object can have.* They also show what triggers the change from one state to another.

- *Activity diagrams are used to describe activities and actions taking place in a system.* These diagrams are used in this book to describe business processes (i.e., to describe the activities taking place in an organizational system).

- *Sequence diagrams show one or several sequences of messages among a set of objects.*

- *Collaboration diagrams describe a complete collaboration among a set of objects.*

- *Use-case diagrams and their attached use-case text specifications are used to describe system functionality.*

- *Component diagrams are a special case of class diagram used to describe components within a software system.* Component diagrams are not used in business modeling.

- *Deployment diagrams are a special case of class diagram used to describe hardware within a software system.* Deployment diagrams are not used in business modeling.

This chapter did not touch upon patterns in UML. Patterns are described in detail in Chapter 6, "Business Patterns." The object constraint language, OCL, is discussed further in Chapter 5, "Business Rules." This chapter also did not address those areas of UML not relevant to business modeling. A more comprehensive description of UML can be found in our previous book, *UML Toolkit* (New York: John Wiley & Sons, Inc., 1998).

The next two chapters provide more detail on how UML can be used and adapted for business modeling. Though the material in these chapters is based on standard UML, the UML extension mechanisms are used to adapt the language to better suit business modeling.

Modeling the Business Architecture

The role of architecture in building any type of structure is well defined. A well-designed architecture makes it possible to thoroughly understand the structure being built, to plan the actual construction, and to estimate costs; it serves as the basis for the blueprints of the structure. Once construction has been completed, a good architecture remains as the documentation of the process and the result, making it possible to understand, maintain and, if so desired, to extend the structure.

Likewise, the importance of architecture in constructing information systems has been acknowledged for some time and is currently the focus of much research. An architecture captures the vital parts of a structure in an organized manner and is a practical tool for managing a complex system, such as a software system or a business. Even though the architecture form of a business is different from that of construction projects, it is an equally important concept. Architecture defines the business structure, so modeling this architecture is key to understanding the business and how it functions.

This chapter discusses the characteristics of a business architecture, the concepts that are used in defining such an architecture, and the set of extensions to UML that will be used in this book to model a business architecture effectively. These extensions, called Eriksson-Penker Business Extensions, have been defined using the built-in extension mechanisms available in UML.

Architecting a Business

Business architecture is the basis for describing and understanding an enterprise: It lists the required parts of a business, how the parts are structured and interact, and how the architecture should evolve. Although it is difficult to clearly define the term, a working definition of business architecture is:

> ...an organized set of elements with clear relationships to one another, which together form a whole defined by its functionality ....The elements represent the organizational and behavioral structure of a business system, and show abstractions of the key processes and structures in the business [Vernadat 1996].

All businesses have some sort of architecture. But because an organizational chart is usually the only description available of the business, many of the situations and structures in it have never been documented or visualized. It is thought-provoking to realize that companies have many drawings for their buildings and/or their products, but none for how their business is conducted.

By defining and documenting how business is conducted, one can capitalize on the business knowledge that is already available. The architecture acts as a knowledge base; it is a strategic asset for the business. Documenting the business system makes it easier to make improvements or innovations to the business, and to identify new business opportunities. Today, with such heavy reliance on information system technology, a business model can also provide the correct requirements of the information system, so that the system best supports the operation of the business.

This book treats a business as a type of system. It is important not to confuse this general term with the more specific term *information system*. There are many types of systems, such as systems in nature and different constructed systems such as a business or a machine. An information system is only one type of system.

Good Architecture

A good architecture allows the modeler to abstract the business into different aspects or views and to concentrate on only one aspect at a time. Achieving abstraction, suppressing the details and irrelevant information, is essential to understanding complex systems and relationships.

A good architecture has the following characteristics:

- *Captures the real business as truthfully and correctly as possible.* It defines an architecture that is realistic and feasible to implement and that achieves the goals of the business.

- *Focuses on the key processes and structures of the business at an appropriate level of abstraction.* The appropriate level is different from case to case and depends on the purpose of the architecture.

- *Represents a consensus view among the people operating in the business.* For example, both managers and workers agree that the architecture correctly describes how the business operates.

- *Adapts easily to change and extensions.*

- *Is easy to understand and fosters communication among the different stakeholders of the business.* An architecture is useful only if it can be understood by its users.

Achieving these characteristics is not simple. It requires several things:

- Modelers that have a high knowledge of the business, or at least access to people with such knowledge who can be interviewed and can participate in the construction of the architecture.

- A modeling language that can capture all the important concepts in the business, along with the relationships between these captures. Both static and dynamic structures must be captured. The language must be simple enough to be understood by many different people, without losing accuracy or power. The language must also be scalable so that things can be described at different levels.

- A capability to organize visual diagrams into different views of the business, where each view illustrates a specific aspect of the business. The complete description of the business can't be defined in a single view.

- A design based on experience, on what works and what does not. If possible, well-defined modeling patterns that have proved to work should be used.

- A development process that ensures the quality and accuracy of the models produced.

Many of these requirements and how to achieve them will be discussed in this book.

Obviously, we need a good technique or language to define the architecture of a business. Although there are several reference architectures (ISO Reference Model, CIMOSA, PERA, etc.) that use different techniques to describe a business, a common factor runs through all of them: the use of models.

If the models are to be effective, they must be expressed in a common language. This book uses process and object-oriented modeling with the Unified Modeling Language (UML) to build business architectures. As stated, UML has already been established as the standard modeling language for modeling information systems. This book shows that it also has the capabilities to express business models. With the techniques presented in the book, a business architecture is based on four views of the business, each of which consists of a number of diagrams that contain the common elements and concepts (e.g., objects) of the business. The views and diagram types show the structure of and interactions between the different aspects of the business. The contents of the views and their internal relationships are defined in Chapter 4, "Business Views."

Business Concepts

A business, an *enterprise*, is a complex system that has a specific purpose or goal. All the functions of the business interact to achieve this goal. The business system also can be interlinked with and affected by the decisions and events that take place in other systems, and so can't be analyzed in isolation. Because of this, defining the boundaries of the business can be difficult. The resources within the organization can also have separate goals that do not always reflect those of the business.

Many of the important elements in a business, such as customers, suppliers, laws, and regulations, are external to the business and are not defined within the business itself. Thus, the business system is an *open system* whose objects and parts are often also parts of other business systems. As such, it cannot be viewed as a *black box* system, which is analyzed by looking only at the input to and output from the system, but as a system whose parts are visible, as shown in Figure 3.1.

Individual businesses have different goals and internal structures, but they use similar concepts to describe their structure and operation: the objects that are part of the system, their relationships and structure, and their dynamic interaction with each other in various situations. A model of the business system describes these concepts. The concepts used to define the business system are:

Resources. The objects within the business, such as people, material, information, and products, that are used or produced in the business. The resources are arranged in structures and have relationships with each other. Resources are manipulated (used, consumed, refined, or produced) through processes. Resources can be categorized as physical, abstract, and informational.

Processes. The activities performed within the business during which the state of business resources changes. Processes describe how the work is done within the business; they are governed by rules.

Goals. The purpose of the business, or the outcome the business as a whole is trying to achieve. Goals can be broken down into subgoals and allo-

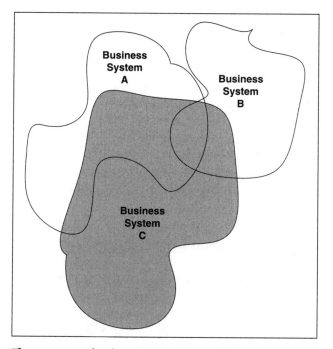

Figure 3.1   A business system is interlinked with other business systems.

cated to individual parts of the business, such as processes or objects. Goals express the desired states of resources and are achieved by processes. Goals can be expressed as one or more rules.

Rules. Statements that define or constrain some aspect of the business, and represent business knowledge. Rules govern how the business should be run (i.e., how the processes should execute) or how resources may be structured and related to each other. Rules can be enforced on the business from the outside by regulations or laws, or they can be defined within the business to achieve the goals of the business. Rules can be categorized as functional, behavioral, and structural.

All of these concepts are related to each other: A rule can affect the way some resources are structured; a resource is allocated to a specific process; a goal is associated with the execution of a specific process. The goal of business modeling is to define these concepts and show the relationships and interactions among them.

A *meta-model* is a model of the basic business concepts and their relationships. The concepts depicted in this model are used to create other models. Figure 3.2 is a meta-model that summarizes the concepts used in business modeling and their relationships to each other. It will be used for the business models developed in the rest of the chapters in this book. This meta-model is a

UML class diagram in which each concept is depicted as a class, and the relationships between the concepts are either an association or a specialization. The meta-model also indicates which factors would hinder or prevent the business from achieving its goals.

The meta-model shows how processes attempt to achieve goals. A goal is established to overcome one or more problems and expresses the desired state of one or more resources. Goals can be expressed as rules that control the process. A process interacts with resources through an interface and can cause the states of resources to change. A process also interacts with other processes by generating or handling events. Resources can be physical (such as people or machines), abstract (such as an invoice or account), or information, holding information about another resource (such as a database record in a information system). The cornerstones of the meta-model are the process, goal, resource, and rule classes. Each of these concepts is explored and discussed in more detail later in this chapter.

The meta-model can appear overwhelming at first, as it is a very strict model of the concepts and their relationships. But by diagramming business concepts, it becomes much easier to grasp and remember them than by reading textual descriptions. This meta-model of the basic concepts demonstrates the power of using models to describe complex structures and relationships, such as the classes and relationships shown in Figure 3.2 and, later, other diagrams that show dynamic behavior and interaction. The concepts in this meta-model are used in the views and diagrams that describe a business. Not all the concepts are used in every diagram; those used are based on the focus and purpose of the diagram.

To a great degree, standard UML symbols and diagrams can be used to create business models. Static diagrams such as class or object diagrams, as well as dynamic diagrams such as sequence, statechart, or activity diagrams, are as valid and appropriate for describing a software system as a business system. However, certain concepts frequently used in business modeling are not part of standard UML. Fortunately, as mentioned, UML has built-in extensions. By using these mechanisms it is possible to introduce and define business modeling concepts in UML. The UML symbols and stereotypes used for each of these business concepts are explored in the discussions that follow.

For the reader who regularly uses UML to describe the code structure of a program, remember that this book uses UML to create high-level business models; the concepts described here are *not* code specifications and should *not* be translated, even mentally, to lines of programming code. Information systems will be designed to support these business models at a later point in the development process, but that step is a long way from the business modeling stage. Attempting to capture reality and business thinking and directly translating it into the syntax of a programming language is very dangerous and subverts the focus of business modeling. Translating the completed business

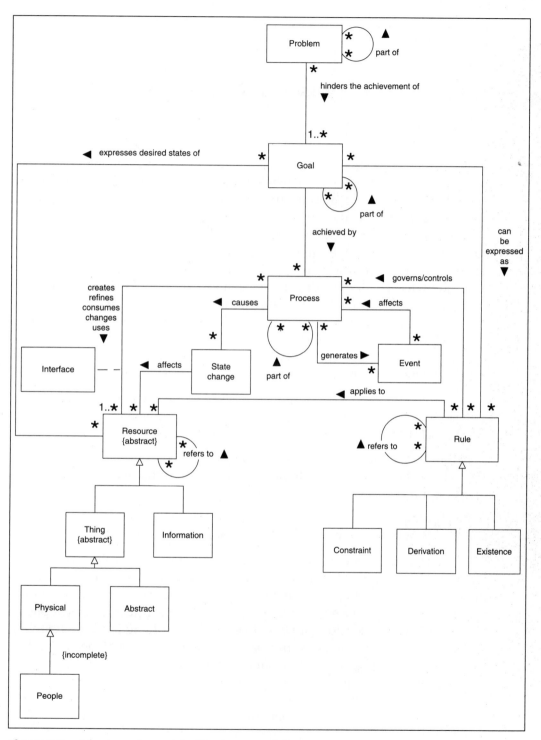

Figure 3.2   A basic meta-model of business modeling concepts.

models to information systems is discussed in Chapter 10, "From a Business Architecture to a Software Architecture."

Eriksson-Penker Business Extensions

Keep in mind that UML was defined to model the architecture of software systems, and though there are similarities between software and business systems, there are also some differences. Business systems have many concepts that are never intended or suitable to execute in a program, such as the people working in the business, manufacturing production equipment, and rules and goals that drive the business processes. Because UML was initially designed to describe aspects of a software system, it had to be extended to more clearly identify and visualize the important concepts of processes, goals, resources, and rules of a business system. To address this issue, we have created a set of extensions based on the existing model elements of UML. We introduced these extensions briefly earlier; they are called, simply, the Eriksson-Penker Business Extensions and provide symbols for modeling the processes, resources, rules, and goals of a business system.

The standard extension mechanisms in UML allow you to adapt UML to accommodate new concepts. The extension mechanisms are:

Stereotype. An extension of the vocabulary of the UML, which allows you to create new building blocks specific to your problem from existing ones [Booch 1998]. Stereotypes may have their own icons.

Tagged value (property). An extension of the properties of a UML element, which allows you to create new information in that element's specification [Booch 1998].

Constraint. An extension of the semantics of a UML element that enables you to add new rules or to modify existing ones [Booch 1998].

The UML specifications contain a five-page document called the "UML Extension for Business Modeling" that describes a set of extensions for business modeling; however, it offers no detailed explanation of how to apply them. It only briefly specifies the extensions with short text descriptions and samples of their icons. These extensions are based heavily on applying use-case modeling to describe business processes and are used as part of the Rational Unified Process, a process product sold by Rational Software Corporation.

Use cases are a common technique for capturing the functional requirements of an information system. They describe the functions provided by a black box system, which is further used to drive the design of the software inside the system. However, viewing a business system as a black box doesn't offer sufficient insight into how the existing or future processes operate. An information system can be characterized by its interactions with a user or a customer, but implementing business process improvement or innovation requires looking at the existing processes and their operation, not just the interactions with a user. Defining the user and the system boundaries is also typically much more difficult since processes from many businesses interact; and if the boundaries are difficult to define, the interactions between the user and the system will also be difficult to capture. Again, a business system is, and therefore must be viewed as, an open system. The fact that a business interacts with its environment is important; describing that alone isn't enough to do business modeling.

The Eriksson-Penker Business Extensions form a basic framework for business extensions to UML to which a business architect can add stereotypes or properties suitable to his or her line of business. Thus, the extensions should not be viewed as a definitive set of business extensions; they are intended to serve as a base upon which further development or adaptations can be made for specific modeling situations or as the use of UML for business modeling advances. The extensions merge UML with process modeling, so that it is easier to use UML for business modeling. Anyone familiar with UML should be comfortable with these extensions, as will those who are knowledgeable in business process modeling. To that end, the extensions have been defined using the standard mechanisms for extensions in UML, and are fully compliant with standard UML. We repeat, they are not in any way an attempt to modify or specify a new modeling language. This means that these extensions can be quickly adopted by those already proficient in UML and can be incorporated into an UML tool that supports the full language (including support for the extension mechanisms) without difficulty. Currently, the Eriksson-Penker Business Extensions are supported in the Qualiware CASE tool; more tool support is expected to become available.

The Eriksson-Penker Business Extensions, described with examples in more detail in the next chapter and summarized in a reference manual in Appendix B, have been designed with simplicity as the highest priority. New icons, although possible in UML, have been avoided in favor of textual stereotypes, extant UML concepts, and symbols. Some adaptations, such as defining a process icon for a UML activity and a special icon for highlighting the information resource objects, have been made to ensure that an experienced process modeler is comfortable using UML for process modeling. Of particular note is the unique use of the activity diagram in the extensions, renamed as *assembly line diagram* when used in this manner. An assembly line diagram is a process model shown in an activity diagram where links are made to objects used during the process. The objects could be information objects in an information system or other resource objects of interest to the process.

Business Processes

The business processes are the active part of the business. They describe the functions of the business, and involve resources that are used, transformed, or produced. A business process is an abstraction that shows the cooperation between resources and the transformation of resources in the business. It emphasizes *how* work is performed, rather than describing the products or services that *result* from the process. A more formal definition of a business process is the following:

> A business process is a collection of activities that takes one or more kinds of input and creates an output that is of value to the customer. A business process has a goal and is affected by events occurring in the external world or in other processes [Hammer and Champy 1993].

Another, more elaborate, definition is this:

> A process is simply a structured set of activities designed to produce a specified output for a particular customer or market. It implies a strong emphasis on how work is done within an organization, in contrast to a product's focus on what. A process is thus a specific ordering of work activities across time and place, with a beginning, an end, and clearly identified inputs and outputs: a structure for action [Davenport 1993].

Michael Porter states that the basis for every enterprise is the process of taking some source materials and manipulating them such that value is added to those materials [1985]. The process is a chain of smaller value-added steps (a value chain). The value of a product is decided by those who consume or use the product, demonstrated by what they are willing to exchange for that product (e.g., money). Thus Porter defines that every enterprise is made up of a number of business processes, each producing value to a customer.

To summarize the similarities between these different definitions, a business process:

- Has a goal.
- Has specific input.
- Has specific output.
- Uses resources.
- Has a number of activities that are performed in some order, depending on conditions and events that occur during the execution of the process. The activities within the process can be seen as subprocesses.
- Affects more than one organizational unit. It is horizontal rather than vertical in regard to the traditional organization of the business.
- Creates value to some kind of customer. The customer can be either internal or external to the business.

A business process has an explicit goal, a set of *input objects* and a set of *output objects*. The input objects are resources that are transformed or consumed as part of the process, such as raw material in a manufacturing process. The input objects also can be refined by the process, in which case the process adds value to them, so that the value of the output of the process is larger than the input. The output objects represent the accomplishment of the goals and are the primary result of the process, such as a finished product in a manufacturing process. The output object is also a resource. An output object can be a completely new object created during the processes or it can be a transformed input object. The transformations made by the process can be physical, logical, transactional, or informational.

During its execution, the process interacts with other *resource objects,* objects other than the input and output objects, that are just as vital. These objects carry information required by the process or they are resources responsible for executing the activities in the process, such as people or machines. In a manufacturing process, it is the people who operate the machines that transform the raw material into a finished product.

Manipulating resources in a process in these ways is not limited to manufacturing processes; it can also be used to describe any type of process, such as a service process or document or transaction processing.

The Eriksson-Penker Business Extensions represent a process in a UML class diagram with the process symbol shown in Figure 3.3. This symbol is used in many existing process modeling techniques (e.g., it is used in all process modeling at the telecommuncations company Ericsson), and it doesn't overlap with

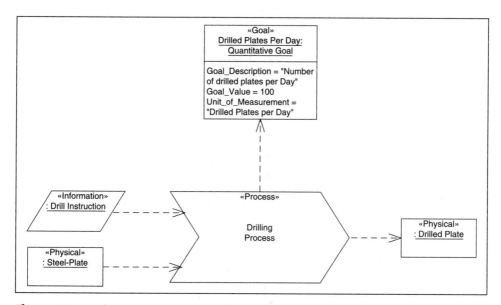

Figure 3.3   Business process symbol, illustrating a goal and the input and output objects.

any existing symbol in UML. In formal UML, the symbol is a *stereotyped activity* (an action state) from an activity diagram; it is also the UML activity diagram that is used to illustrate business processes. A process—that is, an activity stereotyped to process—takes input resources from its left-hand side and indicates its output resources on its right-hand side. The goal of the process is either illustrated as a goal object above the process symbol or, more informally, specified in the tagged value Goal of the process (the tagged value is not visible in the diagram but is available in a tool). Resource objects used as part of the process are shown below the process symbol. A special variant of an activity diagram, the aforementioned assembly line diagram, can be introduced to show how a process interacts with a specific resource (e.g., an information system). The assembly line diagram illustrates resource objects that are affected by the process in one or more assembly lines below the process. The objects in the assembly line are typically information objects from which information is read or written during the execution of the process. Assembly line diagrams are shown and discussed in more detail in Chapter 4, "Business Views."

A process can have tagged values attached to it that contain additional information about the process. The tagged values are not visually represented in the diagram but are a function accessible by double clicking on the symbol in a modeling tool. Although defining all the values of these tags is optional, the goal and the purpose of a process must always be defined. The UML tagged values attached to a process in the Eriksson-Penker Business Extensions are:

Goal. A textual value that describes the goal of the process if a goal object is not explicitly attached to it.

Purpose. A textual value that informally describes the purpose of the process; for example, what the process does and, in the case of a new process, its anticipated effect.

Documentation. A textual value that informally describes the work of the process; for example, the activities completed and the resources involved.

Process owner. A textual value that defines the process owner, the person in the organization who has the overall responsibility for this process and who manages the changes and plans for changes.

Process actors. A textual value that defines actors needed to run the process. Typically, their skill levels are described.

Priority. A textual value that describes the priority of this process; for example, whether it's a core process, a support process, an administrative process, and so on.

Risks. A textual value that describes the risk of the process; for example, what can go wrong either when executing this process or when implementing this process into the business.

Possibilities. Textual values that describe the potential of this process; for example, the opportunities for improving or using this process in the future.

Time. A numerical value that approximates the execution time of the process.

Cost. A numerical value that approximates the cost of executing the process.

The process concept is the center around which business modeling is performed. It is the execution of the process that transforms and refines resources, and in doing so creates value; it is this creation of value that fulfills the goals of the business. The process is also responsible for coordinating and controlling the activities that are performed by the resources that act within the business (e.g., people or machines). A concept called *the Business System Diamond* proposed by Michael Beedle states that the definition of business processes leads to the definition of jobs and structures, which in turn requires management and measurement systems, which in turn reinforce a set of values and beliefs [Beedle 1997].

Process Steps

The process contains a number of steps or activities that are performed as part of the process. Each of these activities can be considered a process of its own and as a subprocess to the containing process. The activities are categorized as follows:

Direct. An activity directly involved in creating the product or the service; that is, the value created by the process.

Indirect. An activity that supports the direct activities; includes maintenance, administration, planning activities.

Quality assurance. An activity that ensures the quality of the other activities; for example, inspections, controls, or reviews.

These categories are not explicitly used during the modeling process.

The processes can also be categorized in other ways, such as development, improvement, or management processes. Processes of different categories typically interact or control each other, as will be illustrated in Chapter 9, "Process Patterns."

The process steps are illustrated as nested activities of the process. Recall that an activity in a UML activity diagram can refer to another nested activity diagram that contains other, more detailed, activity descriptions. The process steps can either be viewed by expanding a process symbol in a tool to view the nested activity diagram or by directly drawing and viewing the nested activities inside the process symbol.

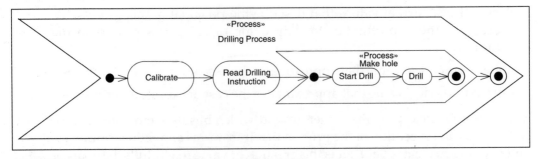

Figure 3.4   A process that contains three subprocesses, consisting of two atomic processes (activities) and one subprocess with yet another two atomic processes (activities).

A subprocess is drawn using the same symbol as for the enclosing process, shown in Figure 3.4. However, if a process does not contain any subprocesses, the standard activity symbol in UML is used. The activity symbol then represents an atomic process, a process that can't further be broken down into more detailed steps. Figure 3.4 shows a process that contains three subprocesses, two of which are atomic processes (activities) and one that itself contains two atomic subprocesses.

Processes can span several organizational borders (e.g., departments or divisions in a business), as shown in Figure 3.5. Therefore, a process is broken down into subprocesses independent of the organization and its structure, and shouldn't be divided just because it crosses an organizational border.

The number of levels between an initial process and an atomic process is arbitrary. Figure 3.6 shows a process with two layers. In some business process methods, the number of levels has been predefined in the method, and each level has a specific name (process, activity, action, task, etc.). This is an artificial and inadequate construction, since different processes have a different number of levels, and a process on a specific level is a process in its own right. The only exception made in these extensions is the atomic process, activity that visually shows that this step has not been broken down into subprocesses. Note that in practice, processes are intertwined and are rarely sequential as in the example shown in Figure 3.6.

A process may be required to hold information about itself, such as how far along in execution it has gone or what accumulated results have been gathered as part of the process. This holding of information is best illustrated by using the stereotype «Information» on one or more resource objects connected to the process. A resource object stereotyped with «Information» is an information object that represents part of the state of the process. Further, a process support object or a business process object is used to implement the handling of a process and its state in an information system. Remember, though, that many parts of the process (people, machines, human judgment, etc.) can't be com-

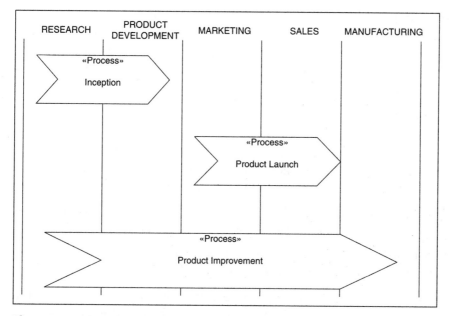

Figure 3.5   Processes span organizational borders.

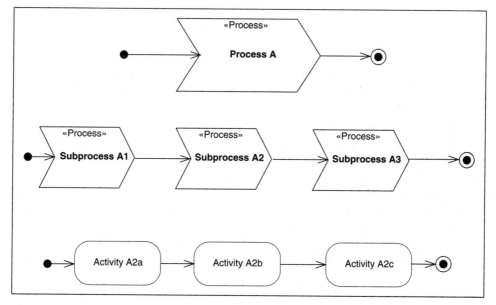

Figure 3.6   A process can be described by subprocesses and finally activities (i.e., atomic processes).

puterized and put into the information system; the objects in the information systems are only representations (i.e., abstractions) of the real process. It is rare that the entire process can be implemented into the information system; typically, some supporting parts of the process are implemented.

Business Events

A process is affected by events occurring in the surrounding environment or generated by other processes that cause a process to be activated. Business events are triggers that initiate activities or that control which activities are performed. A business event can be defined as follows:

- A business event is an external real-world happening that requires certain action [Gale-Eldred 1996].

- A business event represents a record of a change in the business at a particular instant in time [OMG BOCA Proposal 1998].

Several events can occur during the operation of a process to which the process must react, such as a cancelation of an order by a customer, a delivery of material, or the misplacement of a specific resource. A process can also generate events to other processes within the business or in other businesses that will cause these other processes to react in a specialized manner.

An event can:

- Initiate the execution of a process.

- Affect the behavior and execution of the process.

- Conclude a process by generating an event.

Whether the event is generated from the external world or by another process is usually not important, since in a process-oriented view the external world is also defined in terms of processes that generate the events. Some of the most interesting events will come from the external world of the business (i.e., from the processes in that world), such as events generated by customers (orders, payments, complaints), subcontractors (deliveries, invoices), or competitors (product announcements, price cuts).

In the Eriksson-Penker business notation, a business event is represented as a class (the event type) and objects (instances of the event type). The event classes are stereotyped as a business event. Their relationships (i.e., generalization hierarchies) can be illustrated in a class diagram, as shown in Figure 3.7.

The receive symbol (concave pentagon) and the send symbol (convex pentagon) are used in a process diagram to illustrate receiving and sending events, respectively, as shown in Figure 3.8. The receive symbol can be read so that the process waits for this event to occur, or, in case of a decision point with several alternatives, the events that will trigger each of the specified alterna-

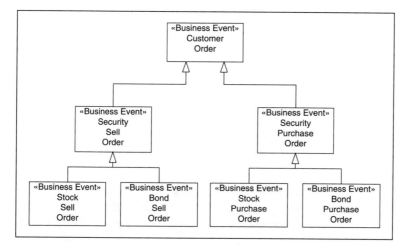

Figure 3.7   Business events are modeled as classes in a class hierarchy.

tives. The send symbol indicates that the process generates and sends the event between two activities. Either of the event symbols (send or receive) can be attached to an object with a dependency arrow, which shows from which object the event is sent or received. If an event symbol is drawn to a process symbol, an expansion of the process symbol shows exactly how and where in the process the event is received or sent. An event symbol can also be attached to its opposite symbol in another process, (i.e., a send symbol to a receive symbol, or vice versa) to indicate how the processes communicate.

Modularizing the Business System

A large system will have many processes. To handle all the processes, they must be grouped, or *modularized* so that a modeler can concentrate on only one set of processes at a time. Processes are modularized using the UML *package*

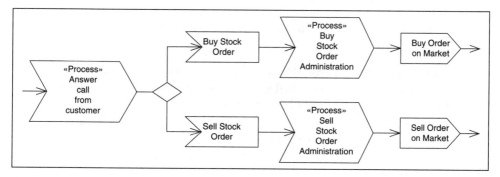

Figure 3.8   Receiving and sending business events during a process.

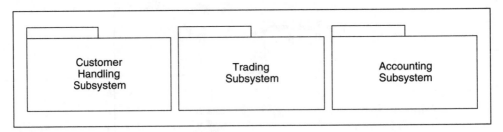

Figure 3.9   Packaging processes together.

mechanism. Processes are allocated to a specific package, sometimes referred to as a subsystem in information systems (see Figure 3.9), each of which contains a set of processes and their subprocesses. A package can in turn also contain other packages.

A package can contain processes that are not directly linked to each other (e.g., by being subprocesses to each other), but are related in some way in the modeler's judgment. This grouping can be based on similar or related functions, shared structure or organization, or related locale. The exact basis for the grouping is up to the modeler, and so cannot be standardized.

Resources

Resources are the objects that act or are used in the business. They are the concepts consumed, produced, transformed, or used by the business processes. Examples include material, energy, products, people, information, and services. Most of the elements normally modeled as a class in object-oriented modeling are resources in business modeling terms. Vernadat proposes a definition of a resource:

> A resource is an entity which can play a role in the realization of a certain class of tasks [1996].

Another definition is:

> A resource is a concept used in the business, and represents anything that we choose to evaluate as a whole.[Darnton 1997]

Resource types are represented as classes. Resource instances are represented as objects. The Eriksson-Penker Business Extensions define some stereotypes to indicate different categories of resource types. A meta-model of these resource types categories is shown in Figure 3.10, in which each class illustrates a specific category of resource types.

Thornton Gale and James Eldred defines four concrete resource types [1996]:

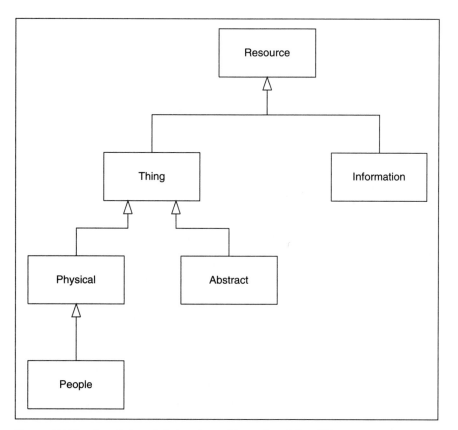

Figure 3.10   A meta-model showing a hierarchy of the different resource types.

Physical. An entity with material reality that occupies a volume of space. It is something that can be seen and touched upon. Commodities, raw materials, parts, or products used in a process are examples of physical resources. A physical object is often constructed from other physical objects.

Abstract. An idea or concept, often a composite of other objects (e.g., a purchase order is a concept relating to a collection of things). Involves things and concepts that aren't physical and cannot be touched upon but are of importance to the business. Contracts, roles, accounts, and energy are examples of abstract resources.

Information object. A representation of a concept, thing, or another information object. It holds information about other resources and works as a surrogate for the resource, for example, in an information system (though not all information objects must be placed in an information system). It is important to separate the information object from the concept or thing it represents; the information object holds facts or knowledge about other objects in the business. An information object can hold information about a bank account, a product, or a contract (i.e., it represents the account or the contract in the information system, but it still isn't the same object as the actual account or the contractual agreement).

People. A human being acting in the process. It's a specialization to the physical resource to emphasize and identify the people in the process (people are, of course, a very important part of the processes). People don't like viewing themselves as physical objects, so they have been given their own class in the meta-model. People are also sometimes more unpredictable than machines (which can be both positive and negative), so they should be highlighted in the process. People could be viewed as a special case of a physical resource and as such are also a subtype to Physical in Figure 3.10.

These four resource types are also the stereotypes used to categorize the resource classes. There may well be room for more stereotypes, such as Machine for a machine or Document to represent a document as part of the business (both subclasses to Physical in the meta-model). To keep the size of the business extensions down, such stereotypes have not been defined. However, it may be appropriate to add stereotypes to a specific domain or business.

Figure 3.11 shows some examples of the different types of resources, where the classes are stereotyped to their respective categories. Note that the information stereotype has a special kind of icon. The icon is a slanted class rectangle. Typically, there are well-defined structures and relationships among resources. A product that has been produced in the business is an aggregate of some parts (i.e., a physical resource is built from other physical resources); the people in the business are organized in a functional organization, such as departments (i.e., a people resource is part of a abstract resource such as an organizational unit), and there are relationships handled by the business between customers and abstract objects, such as orders and contracts.

Goals

A goal describes the desired state of one or more resources. Goals are attached to the entire business and to individual business processes. Goals motivate

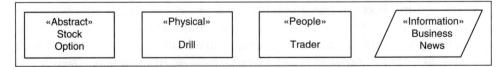

Figure 3.11   Different types of resources stereotyped to their respective categories.

activities leading to state changes in a desired direction. A goal must be measurable in order to track progress. The measure may be defined in quantifiable terms such as profit, volume, time, or quality, or it may be defined in qualitative terms, such as "our company will be regarded as one of the most highly respected firms in this town," or "our company will attract more competent labor." Putting a measure on the goal will make it easier to determine whether it has been achieved. Goals are stated in terms that indicate optimization, such as increase the result, increase the quality, or decrease the time-to-market. The sum of all the efforts of the processes, resources, and rules should achieve the goals.

The business can have an overall vision or goal, such as "we will be the market leader in five years," as well as very specific goals, such as "we will have sales for more than 10 million in Southeast Asia within 12 months." The deeper into the goal hierarchy one gets, the more specific and quantified the goals become. Thus, the vision is typically more loosely specified. The more specific and quantified a goal is, the easier it will be to determine later if the goal has been achieved.

A goal can be broken down into (or composed of) subgoals. Achieving the superior goal is dependent upon achieving the subgoals. Subgoals can also substitute or compensate for other subgoals that have failed or have not been achieved. For example, if the superior goal is "Increase profits by 15 percent," this goal will be achieved if two out of three subgoals make such an increase and the third subgoal makes no profit at all. The two subgoals that were successful compensate for the failed goal.

Dividing goals into subgoals is called *goal modeling*. The basis upon which the goals are divided is up to the modeler. For example, the goal for Southeast Asia can be divided into subgoals for different countries within the region or into subgoals for different products within the region (or into both of these hierarchies).

Goals are closely related to problems, because a problem is an obstacle to a goal. It is a situation or object that stands in the way of achieving the goal. Therefore, it is common to model the attached problems when modeling the goals. By using both the concepts of goals and problems, it becomes easier to accurately describe them. For example, when presented with a goal, one can ask: "What are the problems or obstacles that stand in the way of achieving this?" On the other hand, when presented with a problem, one can ask: "If this is eliminated, what goal has been achieved?" By defining the problems, subgoals can be identified that will eliminate them. The subgoals can then be allocated to business processes in order to eliminate the obstacle.

Representing goals and problems in UML is not simple. The solution used in the Eriksson-Penker Business Extensions is to represent goals as objects, and to use an object diagram to show the dependencies between goals and subgoals. An object diagram is a UML diagram that illustrates object instances. A goal object is indicated as a goal object of a goal class stereotyped to Goal. In the Eriksson-Penker Business Extensions, there are two predefined goal classes: Qualitative Goal and Quantitative Goal, both of the stereotype Goal. A quantitative goal can be described with a target value in a specific unit of a measurement (a quantity), while a qualitative goal is described more loosely, without a specific target value (a quality). There must be a process to determine whether a goal has been fulfilled. However, when using qualitative goals, that process could rely on human judgment rather than a specific value. Objects shown in the goal object diagram are instances of either of these classes, and dependencies between the objects show how they depend on each other.

Problems are shown as notes stereotyped to Problem, and described in plain text. The note is attached to the goal to which the problem relates. In Figure 3.12, the problem "Understaffed Sales Force" indicates a further subgoal, "Increase Sales Force." When the dependencies between a goal and its subgoals are constrained to be complete, the fulfillment of all of the subgoals will guarantee fulfillment of the goal. If they are constrained to be incomplete, the fulfillment of all subgoals will not guarantee fulfillment of the superior goal.

Because it is a vital part of the business vision view, goal/problem modeling and the syntax for it will be discussed in further detail in Chapter 4, "Business Views."

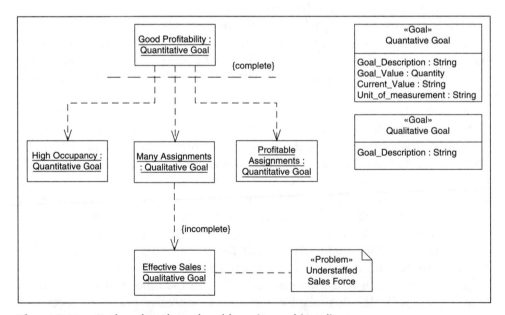

Figure 3.12   Goals, subgoals, and problems in an object diagram.

Business Rules

A business model contains business rules that define constraints, conditions, and policies for how the business processes are to be performed. Business rules can affect all the other concepts; they can constrain the execution of a business process, the behavior of a resource, and the means to achieve a specific goal. Often a rule concerns the relationships among concepts, defining the way the concepts can be related to each other and which conditions must hold in order for a relationship to be valid at a specific point in time. A practical definition of a business rule is:

> . . . a statement that can control or affect both the execution of a business process as well as the structure of the resources in the business. The statement specifies a condition that must be upheld, or a condition that controls which activity should follow next. It can express a business goal, specify the way a process should execute, detail the conditions of a relationship, or constrain the behavior of a resource.

Rules control the business. They are defined either to satisfy external requirements on the system (regulations and laws, or restrictions imposed by other businesses) or internally to safely achieve the goals of the business.

There are three types of business rules:

Derivations. Rules that define how knowledge in one form may be transformed into other knowledge (i.e., how some information is derived from other information). A derivation can be either a computation rule, such as a formula for calculating a value, or an inference rule, meaning that if a certain fact is true, then another inference fact must also be true.

Constraints. Rules that constrain either the possible structure or behavior of objects or processes; for example, the way objects are related to each other or the way object or process state changes occur. The constraints uphold the integrity of objects as they are created and relationships are changed. An operation of an object can be constrained through the use of operation preconditions and postconditions. A precondition must be fulfilled before the operation is executed; a postcondition must be fulfilled after the operation has been executed.

Existence. Rules that define when something may exist and when it should come into existence, that is, when an object is created or destroyed.

Rules can be specified formally in a particular language (that could be executable) or informally in plain English. Sometimes a rule needs to be specified in both ways, using the formal specification for the information systems and the informal specification for the people in the business. Rules complement the diagrams; together they contain all the information about how the business should be run. Rules are used in all of the views, and can relate to other rules; therefore, care should be taken that the rules in each view do not conflict with each other.

Many of the UML diagrams have built-in support for defining rules, using the generic construct of defining a constraint. A class diagram has structural constraints in its relationships (e.g., the multiplicity of an association). A state diagram has behavior constraints in its state and state transitions (e.g., actions to perform when a transition occurs). Derivation rules can be defined as a computational constraint in a UML diagram (e.g., that the value of an attribute is calculated from the value of another attribute). An activity diagram has behavioral constraints in its activity flow (e.g., which activity must take place before another or which condition must be true before an activity is carried out). As noted in Chapter 2, a constraint in UML is expressed within curly braces placed close to the model element that is being constrained (e.g., close to an association that is being constrained). UML has a recommended formal language for specifying constraints, the Object Constraint Language (OCL), which is presented in more detail in Chapter 5, "Business Rules." Business rules specified in OCL can easily be transferred to an information system that supports the business, and in that way become executable.

The Eriksson-Penker Business Extensions use a stereotyped note to define rules. Such a note explicitly connects a rule to a specific element or part of an element in the diagram, and defines more informal *soft rules* that are expressed only in plain text. A soft rule could be an axiom, a principle, or a rule that involves the use of human judgment. Again, rules can be present in all views and in all diagrams. Figure 3.13 shows a class diagram with some built-in business rules (the multiplicity of the associations), a constraint (specifying that a

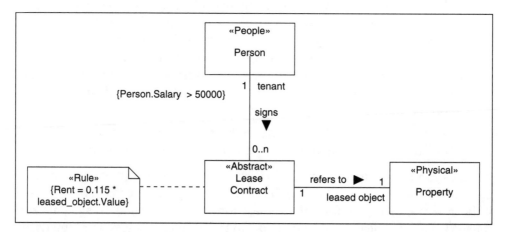

Figure 3.13   Business rules in a class diagram as constraints, rule note, or multiplicity on relationships.

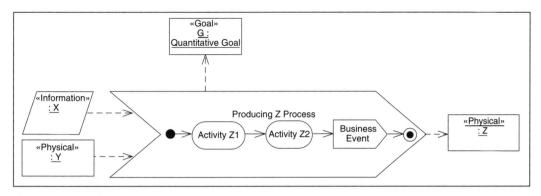

Figure 3.14   An activity diagram showing relationships between processes, resource objects, and a goal object.

Person's salary must be greater than $50,000 in order to get a Lease contract), and a business rule in a note (specifying how the rent is calculated).

Relationships

In addition to relationships and structures within each resource category, there are also relationships between different concept categories. A business process is associated with one or more goals, resources are allocated to a business process, resources can have their own goals, and there can be rules that constrain the possible states of a process or a resource. Since the diagrams used in the different business views are based on standard UML diagrams, the relationships between the concepts are the common object-oriented relationships used in those diagrams.

The relationships most commonly used in UML are:

State/activity transition. A relationship between activities or states, showing which activity or state will follow another. This is called a *temporal relationship*, one that shows the order of activities. See Figure 3.14, where the lines connecting the activities in the process indicate the order.

Generalization. A specialization/generalization relationship, in which objects of the specialized element are substitutable for objects of the generalized element (subtype conformance). Generalization can be used, for example, to show a hierarchy of different resources. See Figure 3.15, where the line with the open arrow shows how an element is a specialization of another element; the open arrow points to the generic element.

Association/aggregation. A relationship that describes a set of links, in which a link is a connection among objects. For example, a customer object has an association to one or more order objects. Aggregation is a special case of association where one of the objects contains or controls the other object; for example, a product is an assembly of some components. See Figure 3.15, where association is the straight line between two classes and aggregation is shown with lines ending with a filled diamond pointing to the controlling class.

Dependency. A relationship between two elements that in some way are dependent on each other. Typically, one object uses the other in some way, and indicates that a change in the object being depended upon will affect the dependent object. A dependency can also be used between an activity and an object to show that an object is consumed or produced by the activity, or between packages to show that packages are dependent on each other. See Figure 3.14. where the dashed line between the process and different resources shows how the process is dependent on the resources.

Refinement. A relationship between two elements where one element is a refinement of the other. For example, refinement describes the same concept but in a more detailed or explicit manner. A refinement is shown using a dashed line with an open arrow. The arrow points to the unrefined element; the refined element is at the other end of the line.

In the Eriksson-Penker Business Extensions, the activity transition has a stereotype «non-causal» that should be read as "the activity at the end of the transition arrow *might* happen." In the world of information systems, no such relationships exist because computers running well-designed programs are reliable and the result is predictable. But in the real world, reliability is less assured. That's the reason for the addition of the non-causal stereotype describing this relationship. An example is when you are driving too fast on the highway. A policeman *might* stop you. Or, if your employees work 16 hours a day for months, they *might* become sick or they *might* resign from the

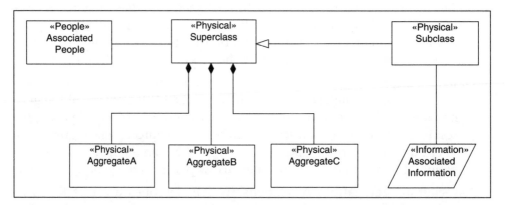

Figure 3.15   A class diagram showing static relationships, such as association, generalization, and aggregation.

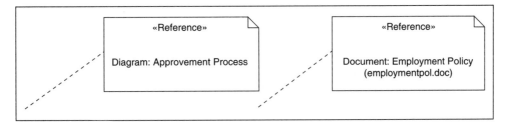

Figure 3.16 A reference note allows the modeler to visually reference another diagram or document in a standard manner.

company. To illustrate those risks and chances, the non-casual relationship between activities can be used in a process model.

General Mechanisms

There is only one new general mechanism in the Eriksson-Penker Business Extensions: the *reference note*. A reference note is a stereotyped note that contains a reference to another diagram or another document (see Figure 3.16). This feature, which is not included in the current UML specification, allows the modeler to refer to another diagram in a standardized manner (sometimes a tool can allow such references, but not in a standard manner). The reference note can also be used to refer to a document; for example, double-clicking or some other user action performed on a note referring to a Word document would start Word so that the document could be read or printed.

Summary

A business architecture is a practical tool for managing the complexity of a system such as a business. An architecture captures an organized set of elements with relationships to one another. The elements and their structure represent the organization and behavior of a business system and show abstractions of the key processes in the system. By clearly defining and documenting the architecture of the business, it is possible to discuss, communicate, adapt, and improve the business. But finding the right level of detail in an architecture can be difficult and is dependent on the purpose of the architecture. The architecture is defined in four different views, each containing a number of diagrams, that will be described further in the next chapter.

The concepts that are used in defining the architecture are:

Process. An abstraction showing a number of activities that form a set of input objects and create a set of output objects that are of value to a customer. The input and output objects, along with objects used during the process, are all resources in the business. A process has a goal and is affected by events.

Events. A change of state that notifies that something has happened in the business. It is generated by one process and received by one or more other processes. Often it will be generated by a process outside the business.

Resources. Concepts or "things" used in the business, such as physical things (e.g., a machine), abstract things (e.g., an agreement), people, or information resources (e.g., information about other resources such as data about an employee stored in a information system).

Goals. The desired state of one or more resources. Goals are attached to the entire business and to processes within the business.

Business rules. A statement that defines or constrains some aspect of the business, and represents business knowledge. It governs how the business should be run (i.e., how the processes should execute).

General mechanism. Mechanisms that can be used in all diagrams. A reference note can contain the name of an external document or another diagram to show where further model information is available.

This chapter explained the UML notation used and the Eriksson-Penker Business Extensions defined for these model elements, along with examples of their basic implementation. The next chapter uses the extensions in diagrams, defines how the diagrams make up the different business views, and explores the relationships among the different concepts and views.

Business Views

Modeling a complex business requires the use of multiple views. Each view focuses on a particular aspect of the business and is described through a number of diagrams, sometimes complemented with a textual document. Links to the information in the views make it possible to navigate from one view to another, thereby providing a more complete picture of the business.

Designing a model is very much like assembling a jigsaw puzzle: At first there are numerous isolated pieces. You begin by putting pieces together, typically by examining the pieces and their structure, form, and appearance. Slowly, a picture evolves until all the pieces come together in a complete image. The same process is done in business modeling: The views are not modeled in isolation one by one, but incrementally as information about the business is collected and understood. The information is modeled in different diagrams, and each diagram is allocated to the view that best captures that particular aspect of the business. This is where the metaphor ends, however, because unlike a puzzle, a business model rarely shows the complete picture of the business, and seldom do all pieces of information fit together seamlessly. Rather, the business model is a picture of a particular aspect of the business.

As a basis for defining a business architecture with these views, it is preferable to have:

- A knowledge of the business, collected from the experience and information of those working in this type of business.

- Previous models of the business.

- Reference models for this type of domain; that is, generic architectural styles or patterns for this type of business.

Frequently it is the case, however, that previous models do not exist, that there are very few, if any, textual descriptions of processes, and that the people in the business openly admit that the current processes are not efficient. Consequently, modeling must begin with group meetings or interviews with the business employees and managers. Rough diagrams are sketched based on the information collected at this early stage. As the modeling process progresses, details are added and the sketches evolve. There is usually one person, the business architect, who is responsible for overseeing the modeling process and envisioning the complete architecture.

A common question asked when defining a model is what level of detail should go into the definition? It is not an easy question to answer. If the model presents a very high-level overview of the business, the description will be too general and only express the obvious. On the other hand, if the model tries to capture everything in great detail, it will be a very complex model that is difficult to use, evolve, or navigate.

The ideal solution is somewhere in between these two extremes. The level of detail included in the model is dependent upon the purpose of the model. If the model will be used for constructing information systems, the definition of the information used and the format of that information should be emphasized. If the model will be used to improve or innovate the business, the interactions in the processes should be emphasized, and possible changes that could improve the overall performance should be identified. Knowing the intended use of the business model is essential to be able to decide the appropriate level of detail necessary for each view or diagram.

Using a tool such as a computer-aided software engineering (CASE) or computer-aided business engineering (CABE) tool to draw these diagrams makes it easier to navigate from a diagram in one view to a diagram in another. The tool stores all information in its internal database and provides links to a specific concept that appears in several diagrams. This makes it easy to find all instances where that concept is defined or used. These tools also make administrating larger models easier than would be possible if they appeared only on paper (smaller models, however, can be handled on just paper). Using a tool allows the modeler or the reader of the model to focus on one aspect of the business at a time, to gradually gain an understanding the business and its architecture. This is not to say that CASE tools should be treated as the miracle tools that they are sometimes marketed to be; what they can do is provide administrative help and simplify the development of complicated models.

This chapter defines four business views using standard UML diagrams and the Eriksson-Penker Business Extensions introduced in Chapter 3, "Modeling the Business Architecture." Recall that these extensions are created using UML grammar and UML's standard extensibility mechanisms that include stereotypes, tagged values, and constraints. The views and the diagrams are illustrated with an ongoing example of a business model for the fictional Sample Business, Inc., a company that markets and sells financial services through the Internet.

Four Common Business Views

The Eriksson-Penker Business Extensions use four different views of a business. We chose the four views as the basis for the descriptions in this book because they are aspects common to businesses in general and blend well with the capabilities of UML. Their incorporation as given here is not mandatory; other views can be defined and used in different modeling processes, such as an economic effects and results view, or a human aspect view that highlights the human role and human goals in the business.

The four views used in this book are:

Business Vision. The overall vision of the business. This view describes a goal structure for the company and illustrates problems that must be solved in order to reach those goals.

Business Process. The view that represents the activities and value created in the business and illustrates the interaction between the processes and resources in order to achieve the goal of each process. The view also demonstrates the interaction between different processes.

Business Structure. The structures among the resources in the business, such as the organization of the business or the structure of the products created.

Business Behavior. The individual behavior of each important resource and process in the business model.

The views are not separate models; they are different perspectives on one or more specific aspect of the business. Combined, the views create a complete model of the business (Figure 4.1).

The following sections discuss each of these views in turn, its overall purpose, the modeling effort required to define the view, the different diagrams within the view, and the techniques for capturing and defining those diagrams using UML. Recall from Chapter 2 that most UML diagrams are applicable for business modeling, but there are three that are not used at all: use case, component, and deployment. These three are used to analyze and

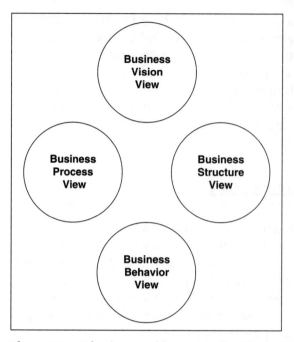

Figure 4.1   A business architecture is described with four views: business vision, business process, business structure, and business behavior.

design information systems, and have a less significant role in business modeling. The use-case diagram identifies the requirements on the information system and links the business models to the information system models. The component and deployment diagrams are used to model software architectures. (Note that there are other opinions on use cases and business modeling, some of which advocate including use cases for business modeling. Our experience is, however, that the most important role of use cases is to specify the requirements on systems, while business modeling requires a more process-oriented approach.)

The four views are presented here in the order in which they are most commonly defined; again this is not a sequential process and order will vary. Chapter 5, "Business Rules," discusses how business rules can be applied in all of the views. Chapters 6 through 9 present business patterns that use these views, and provide additional examples of how they can be used and arranged in modeling different business situations.

Business Vision View

The Business Vision view depicts the company's goals. It is an image of where the company is headed. This view sets up the overall strategy for the business, defines the goals of the business, and acts as a guide for modeling the other views. Many of the goals in this view will not be visible in the other views or in the information systems, despite the fact that they indirectly affect the functionality of the information systems. This is because the goals have been broken down into more detailed goals, or because the information system doesn't actually store information about the goals (the system is part of a larger business process that strives toward the goal). The view guides the modeling process, acting as a point of reference for design decisions when constructing the information systems. The Business Vision view also is used as a motivational tool. It should be shared with the employees of the business, and provide the information and resources, as well as assign the responsibility, to achieve those visions.

Note that the Business Vision view does not contain a detailed description of the goals to be achieved. Rather, it is a basic strategy for moving forward. The vision is often focused on keeping and strengthening the strong aspects of the business and eliminating or improving on the weak ones.

There are some important factors to consider when creating the Business Vision view, according to Geoffrey Darnton [Darnton 1997]:

Company Mission. The overall goal for the company.

Objectives. More specific goals, measurable over a period of time.

Strengths. The specific aspects at which the business excels.

Weaknesses. The specific aspects of the business that require improvement.

Opportunities. Areas of potential growth for the future of the business.

Threats. External conditions that might negatively affect the business (e.g., competitors, changes in technology, etc.).

Critical factors. Elements that are required for the business to succeed or grow (e.g,. a quick time-to-market, good adaption to new technology, etc).

Strategies. Action plans that, if applied, will achieve the objectives.

Core competencies. Areas of the business that are of most importance.

Roles. The specific functions of the people working in the business.

Organization units. Groups into which the business is divided.

Key processes. The key steps to achieving the objectives.

It is also important to look carefully at the customers, competitor companies, and what's going on in the world to identify future changes and trends in the industry among competitors, in the market segment, in technology, or in regulations or policies. These changes can either impose threats or create opportunities for the business, and must be met with changes in business performance. Economic measures such as profitability, solidity, and cash flow must also be studied and benchmarked against similar companies within the same business domain.

The ultimate result of the Business Vision view is a definition of the desired future state of the company, and how that state can be reached. The primary result is expressed in a vision statement, and one or more goal/problem models. A vision statement is a short text document that outlines the vision of the company some years into the future. The goal/problem model is a formal diagram that breaks down the major goals of the business into subgoals, and indicates the problems that must be solved in order to achieve those goals. Thus, the vision statement is the readable form of the vision and the goal/problem model shows the definition of more concrete goals and subgoals that can be attached to business processes.

A member of upper management, such as a CEO, president, or member of the board of directors, is responsible for creating the vision statement and for defining the top-level goals. This person must be able to communicate the vision to all members of the company and act as a leader and mentor for the project. Breaking down the goals and modeling the processes is the responsibility of a business architect or process modeler, but the upper management member acts as a supporter of the modeling efforts, continuously emphasizing its importance to the employees.

There are three techniques used in the Business Vision view:

Strategy definition. Position of the company with regard to the current and future world, and the strategic goals or necessary changes in the business.

Conceptual modeling. Definitions of the important concepts used in the business, along with their relationships to each other.

Goal/problem modeling. Definition of the goals of the company, including the breakdown of goals into subgoals, and the definition of the problems that hinder the achievement of goals.

The results of these techniques are used in other views as well, since they define the goals of the business, the concepts used when describing the business, and strategies that describe necessary changes in the business.

Strategy Definition

Defining an overall strategy for the future means that the business must be viewed in context of its surrounding world in order to identify threats and opportunities that will require the business to change. This also involves decisions about the future direction of the company, raising this question: Does the management or owner(s) want to expand or maintain their position in the market? An expansion normally involves a higher risk, and ultimately it is the owners who decide if they are willing to take that risk.

The strategy is normally based on conclusions that result from evaluating the core processes of the business or by creating new processes that extend the business into new areas or new ways of working. Support processes or administrative processes normally are not considered at this stage, nor are details of how the core processes should be designed or refocused. The strategy shows the direction in which the business is headed; the business processes, as well as the organization, should then be adapted accordingly. The strategy indicates required changes, and presents strategic ideas for the transition. The strategy also looks at previous failures (such as lost deals or product failures) and defines plans that would avoid such failures in the future.

The following are typical considerations and questions for strategy planning:

Customer. Who is the customer and what characteristics does he or she have? How is the customer's interaction with the business changing?

Competitors. Who are the competitors and what are they doing? In what way are they changing their business model?

Size and position in industry. How is the business positioned in the industry? Does it need to expand to increase the market share? How is the industry changing?

Profitability and growth. How do the profitability and growth of the business compare to other businesses in the same domain (benchmarking)?

The surrounding world. What changes (specifically political or technological) are taking place?

Public perception. How does the public perceive the company? In what ways is it desirable to change that perception? Does the company need a new public image?

Service level. What is the customer service level? Could service be improved or extended?

There are two techniques used to define strategy: a TOWS matrix and a vision statement.

TOWS Matrix

One technique used to summarize the business situation is to evaluate threats, opportunities, weaknesses, and strengths. Threats and opportunities are external attributes of the business, and weaknesses and strengths are internal attributes of the business. These attributes are listed in a Threats, Opportunities, Weaknesses, and Strengths (TOWS) matrix [Weirich 1982]. The internal attributes are shown along the vertical axis and the external attributes along the horizontal axis. The matrix then is filled with strategies for handling each intersection between an internal attribute and an external attribute (e.g., one part of the matrix shows how to take advantage of internal strengths and external opportunities, another how to handle internal weaknesses that intersect with the external opportunities). The strategies suggested in the matrix are the basis for a more formal strategy. Strategies that are repeated in several parts of the matrix become especially significant because repetition suggests that those strategies would make a significant impact on the business. The TOWS matrix is often used as a basis for writing the vision statement, the textual document that outlines the future of the business. The TOWS matrix does not use UML, demonstrating our pragmatic view that techniques that don't use UML can also be used when there is no suitable UML diagram available.

Figure 4.2 is a TOWS matrix for Sample Business, Inc. Remember, this is a company that sells financial services via the Internet. Sample Business, Inc. uses the Internet as its primary means of communicating with its customers. Customers use a bulletin board available on the company's Web site to freely discuss different stocks and to read articles about the stock market. The site also shows current stock market prices, offers company profiles, and provides other services of interest to a private financial investor. The company will also act as an online stockbroker, enabling customers to maintain stock portfolios and buy and sell stocks on the markets via the Internet. The brokerage services, along with more advanced services, are available only to subscribing customers who pay a monthly fee. Other services, such as the bulletin board, are available without cost to visitors. Sample Business, Inc., expecting to become a popular site, also gains additional profit by selling advertisement space on the Internet page. Advertisers pay a fee based on the number of visitors to its Internet pages.

Important strategies are identified by analyzing the TOWS matrix for Sample Business, Inc. in Figure 4.2. Again, those that are repeated or are similar are key. Three important parts of a business strategy that can be seen in this figure are:

- Emphasize that it's a complete online financial service provider (the strategy to stress that it is a complete service is mentioned in several places in the matrix).

- Target international customers who want to invest in the American market (the international market is mentioned as an external opportunity).

- Obtain institutional shareholders to secure initial financing (the weakness of not having enough financing must be addressed).

Even though these three strategies are most dominant, many other strategies mentioned in the matrix can and should be used in the vision statement. These strategies are stated as strategic goals for Sample Business, Inc. The means for achieving these goals must be determined. The TOWS matrix is a supporting technique often used prior to the writing of the vision statement.

Overall Business Strategy To become a leading provider of financial services on the Internet, by having a complete range of services offered at competitive prices.	Internal Strengths 1. Good knowledge of Web design. 2. Good knowledge and experience of Internet programming solutions. 3. Knowledge of financial markets and services. 4. Trading knowledge and good contacts with stockbrokers.	Internal Weaknesses 1. Insufficient sales staff. 2. Insufficient financial resources. 3. Company not known— no "branding."
External Opportunities 1. Big interest in financial services on Internet. 2. No complete supplier on market. 3. Inexpensive marketing channel. 4. International market unexplored. 5. Investment interest in Internet companies.	Strategy: 1. Develop easy-to-use and complete financial Web site. 2. Target international customers interested in investing in U.S. market.	Strategy: 1. Sell advertisements through external agents. 2. Find subcontractors that deliver financial information on a royalty basis (based on actual usage). 3 . Attract institutional shareholders. 4. Attract international customers.
External Threats 1. Competition already operating in U.S. marketplace. 2. Economic recession could happen. 3. Only free services are used by customers. 4. Hard to get known on the Internet.	Strategy: 1. Devise slogan and PR campaign about the complete financial site. 2. Advertise site on other Internet sites. 3. Define price strategy that reduces initial cost for customers.	Strategy: 1. Employ good sales manager. 2. Attract institutional shareholders. 3. Launch PR campaign to make site name known.

Figure 4.2 A TOWS matrix example.

Vision Statement

The strategy is summarized in a vision statement, a textual document that outlines the future of the business. It contains descriptions of the current business context (what is changing, what is important), the requirements on the business, the problems that can be visualized, and possible scenarios of what might happen. The vision statement is a description of what the company is to become, how it is going to operate, and what kinds of results are expected. The vision statement should contain clearly stated high-level goals that will later be broken down into operative goals. These operative goals can be linked to goals for individual processes. The vision statement also presents systems or ways to measure whether the high-level goals are achieved.

A vision statement also often contains a plan of the process effort to follow, that is, a description of how to organize the business models that support the vision. The vision statement is not only management's vision of the business, but is also intended to motivate the entire company to be involved in and contribute to the modeling work and, later, the implementation of the business processes. In order to evoke change, the organization must be convinced of the need for change. All too often, the employees are not convinced that the proposed plan will work, or do not support it. Such situations naturally decrease the chances for change. The vision statement should therefore be supported by managers who communicate the ideas and motivate the employees.

Conceptual Modeling

A conceptual model defines the important concepts used in the business. This model establishes a common vocabulary for all the concepts, and demonstrates the relationship among different concepts. Clear definitions of the basic concepts are central for understanding the business or modeling the business in more detail. Without a common vocabulary, individuals may have different understandings and interpretations of the concepts.

It is important to realize that there is a difference between the terms used to refer to an object, the concept that describes the object, and the object in the real world (this theory is called Ogden's triangle). For example, the term "car" is used to refer to an automobile. The concept of a car could be defined as a vehicle with an engine, chassis, and four wheels; and an object example of a car in the real world might be a Toyota Celica 94. Mixing these different views in discussions or models can result in misunderstandings or ambiguity. If several terms are used to refer to the same concept, clear references must be present in a conceptual model to validate all of these terms. If possible, the conceptual model should define one term that will be used consistently throughout all models.

The conceptual model is a high-level model of the concepts that has nothing to do with a database design or with class design in an information system, even though a class diagram is used to create the conceptual model and the concepts are modeled as classes.

Class Diagram for Conceptual Modeling

A conceptual model is presented with a standard UML class diagram. The names of the classes and associations used in the model are important, since they are the concepts being defined. In UML, arrows on association names are used to specify how to read a relationship and to create a clear and understandable model. The classes can have significant attributes attached to them to further describe the concepts, as well as a textual explanation defined in the standard UML property, named Documentation (this text is not visible in the UML diagram but can be retrieved with the help of a tool). Such textual descriptions create a term catalog in which each concept is defined in a few sentences. The name chosen for each concept is then used in other models and documents that describe the business.

Note that this class diagram is not a final diagram describing all possible concepts and all of their relationships. It is a first attempt to define the key concepts used to describe this business. New concepts and relationships can be introduced in this diagram as modeling continues. Also at this stage, the attributes and operations of the classes are not as important as they would be in a class diagram depicting software classes. More important is to capture the concepts as such and their relationships. If adding attributes and operations helps in characterizing the concepts, they also can be defined.

Figure 4.3 is a conceptual model of Sample Business, Inc. The important concepts are modeled as classes, and the relationships are expressed through the UML relationships known as association, aggregation, and generalization. Reading the diagram provides much information about the primary concepts in the business. The customers are divided into three types:

- Ordinary customer, who is anonymous and just visits the Internet site.

- Registered customer, who has registered with name and e-mail address.

- Subscribing customer, who also pays a monthly fee to use some of the more advanced services.

The model shows that a subscribing customer owns one or more portfolios in which both securities and orders to buy or sell securities are stored. Owning a security is modeled as a security holding, where a security holding represents a purchase date, a purchase price, and the number of stocks owned. The Security class represents one individual security on the market and is subclassed into Stock and Stock Option (naturally, other securities could be modeled as well). All securities are associated with price information from the market, and have a grading with a security recommendation (e.g., buy, sell, hold). A security is associated with the company that has issued it and includes a company profile with a detailed description about the company (according to regulations) and news that concerns the company. Finally, all customers can read and write messages on a bulletin board, which is divided into different discussion threads suggested by the customers. The bulletin board also contains articles about stocks and displays paid advertisements.

Each of the classes in the model should also store a few descriptive sentences in the UML Documentation property for the class. The attributes have been suppressed in Figure 4.3, but important attributes should also be defined and shown.

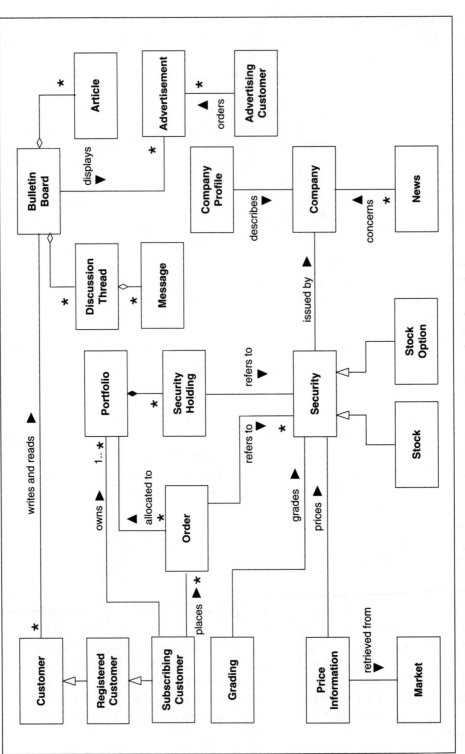

Figure 4.3   The conceptual model of the most important concepts in Sample Business, Inc.

Goal/Problem Modeling

A goal model describes the goals of the business and the problems that stand in the way of achieving the goals. Goals control the behavior of the business and show the desired states of some resources in the business, such as units produced per month, revenue for a specific product, or profit margins. The goal model establishes why the business exists, what the business is trying to achieve, and what the business strategies for achieving these goals are. It does this through a repetitive definition of subgoals, in which each goal is broken down into its subgoals, each of which is in turn broken down to its subgoals. A goal model also indicates ways to improve the business or resolve conflicts between goals. Some of the goals in a goal model can be legacy parts of the business, while other goals might show areas for improvement or entirely new business opportunities.

The goals are achieved by the business processes and the resources that participate in the process. Typically, the more detailed subgoals in a goal model are allocated to individual processes in the business. If the goal is new, a completely new process may need to be designed and implemented in the business.

The goals and problems are modeled in a goal/problem diagram, which is based on a UML object diagram and some stereotypes in the Eriksson-Penker Business Extensions.

Goal/Problem Diagram

A goal/problem diagram is a UML object diagram of objects and their relationships. The complete goal model is actually a number of object diagrams, wherein each diagram shows a specific high-level goal broken down into subgoals. Goals are described as objects of classes that have the stereotype «goal». Such objects are used in this diagram to show goals, the dependencies between goals, and the relationships between goals and the problems they solve.

There are two predefined goal classes in the Eriksson-Penker Business Extensions, though nothing prevents the modeler from defining other, more specialized, goal classes. The goal classes predefined are Quantitative Goal and Qualitative Goal. A Quantitative Goal can be easily measured through some value that is to be achieved. A Qualitative Goal is difficult to describe in measurable terms, and therefore determining if it has been achieved is more complex for than quantitative goals, and involves human judgment. Both of these goal types have a goal description as an attribute. A quantitative goal also has a goal value, a current value, and a unit of measurement.

Modeling goals as classes is required in order to define a goal hierarchy as a set of objects, and doing so also shows the possible implementation of these classes in an information system. Often the goal of a process is not represented in the information system, although the information system provides an excellent opportunity to measure how the goal is being achieved. That is because the information system has all the information necessary to calculate the results of the business (which can be in terms of productivity, economics, quality, etc.) and compare against the goals. By implementing a goal as a class, it is possible to have operations that decide if and to what extent the goal is fulfilled, as well as perform process simulations in an information system.

A specific goal in the business is described as an object of a goal class. The relationships between goals are dependencies and associations. A dependency between two goals shows that one of the goals is a subgoal, or a dependent, of another goal. Associations are used to show links between two goals, such as contradictions between goals.

A dependency is represented by a dashed line from the super-goal to the subgoal, ending with an open arrow. The super-goal is then dependent on the subgoal, which should be interpreted so that the fulfillment of a subgoal contributes to the fulfillment of the super-goal. If a goal can be completely broken down into subgoals, a dashed line is drawn across the dependencies and a constraint is written next to the line, in this form: {complete}. If the goal can't be completely broken down into subgoals, {incomplete} is written (this is also the default if nothing at all is written). A goal that has been completely broken down into subgoals (i.e., the constraint {complete} is specified), indicates that the goal will automatically be filled if all of the subgoals are met. This is what could be seen as a logical AND condition between the subgoals. There is currently no corresponding logical OR condition in the extensions, but the contradictory stereotype, explained later, is used to denote mutually exclusive goals. If a goal is not completely broken down, other events or results might be necessary to fulfill the goal, even if all subgoals are achieved.

The other key concept shown in a goal/problem diagram is a problem. A problem is an obstacle that hinders the achievement of a goal. Identifying the problems is just as important as finding the goals! By finding the problem, new goals or subgoals are discovered that attempt to eliminate the problem. A problem is therefore always linked to a goal. Similar to goals, problems can also be broken down into subproblems. Because problems are linked to goals, this structure is normally only shown indirectly in a goal hierarchy, with the problems attached to their respective goal. In the Eriksson-Penker Business Extensions, a problem is more informally specified in a note with the stereotype «problem» attached to its goal object. A problem can be a temporary problem that can be solved once and for all, or it can be a continuous problem that requires continuous action in order to prevent the problem from reoccurring. Problems are eliminated—solved—by actions.

An action plan can be formulated from the goal model, where temporary problems are resolved as soon as possible, and the goals linked to the continuous problems are allocated to processes in the business (i.e., they achieve the goal through ongoing activities). The action plan contains a list of the problems, the cause of each problem, the appropriate action for each problem, the prerequisites for each action, and, finally, the resource or process responsible for solving it. This can also be shown visually in the goal/problem diagram through the use of stereotyped notes. The stereotypes «problem», «cause», «action», and «prerequisite» specify the purpose of the note. All of these optional concepts are defined through the use of informal notes, because they are normally described in simple text and can't be formally defined. The processes, designed later, that implement the actions and provide the prerequisites are formally defined. The problem note is attached to the goal, the cause-note to the problem note, and so on.

A technique for identifying goals is to ask these questions: Why should we achieve this goal? and "How should we achieve this goal?" The answers to the why question will identify higher goals (goals to which the current goal is a subgoal), and the answers to the how question will identify subgoals. Answering these two questions makes it possible to identify new goals from existing goals, and to reveal additional goals that might not have been discovered by the people in the business.

Figure 4.4 is a generic goal/problem diagram. It shows the Quantitative Goal and Qualitative Goal classes, both of which are stereotyped to «goal», and a number of goal objects of these classes with their dependencies. The goal X is completely broken down into three subgoals (of which two are quantitative and one is qualitative). There is a problem linked to subgoal X1; and the subgoals to X1 (one or both) typically contribute to eliminating that problem. The subgoals to X1 are noted as being incomplete, meaning that other events or results might have to occur to fulfill goal X1. The problem linked to a goal can be used to find new subgoals of that goal.

Subgoals X3-A and X3-B have an association link between them stereotyped to «contradictory», which indicates that the goals are contradictory to each other in some way. Typical examples of contradictory goals are High Quality and Low Cost. Attempting to achieve both of these goals will lead to contradictions or conflicts. For example, a decision to achieve the high quality will lead to an increased cost, which is in conflict with the goal of low cost. Contradictory goals normally cannot be eliminated, but must both be taken into consideration when making the decisions or designing the processes to prevent unnecessary or incorrect steps for achieving the goals.

Figure 4.5 is a more concrete goal/problem diagram from Sample Business, Inc. The overall goal of this diagram is to have many customers. The goal value has been set to 500,000 customers that are known to the business; that is, where the names and addresses of the customers have been registered (an Internet business can also have anonymous customers). This goal has been

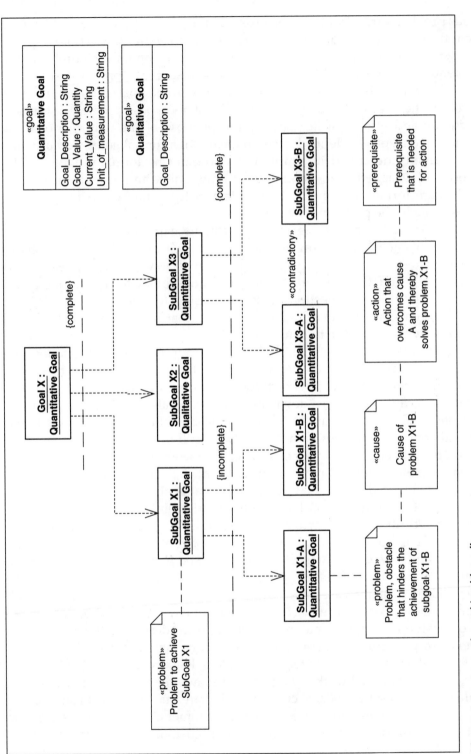

Figure 4.4   A generic goal/problem diagram.

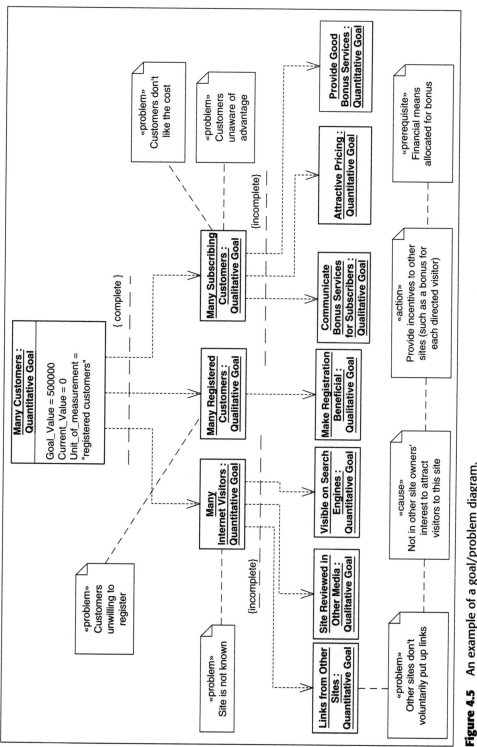

Figure 4.5   An example of a goal/problem diagram.

broken down into three subgoals that also describe the categories of the customers:

- Internet visitors whose names are unknown.

- Registered customers, who have registered their names and e-mail addresses.

- Subscribing customers, who pay a monthly fee to use all the services provided by the business.

All of these categories are considered customers, and the business concept is to provide quality services that will attract as many new subscribing customers as possible.

Problems in Figure 4.5 are linked to each of the three subgoals. For example, the problem attached to attracting more Internet visitors is that Internet users are not aware of the site. This problem could be handled by generating links to the site from other sites within the financial community; by ensuring that the site is visible through the most common search engines; or by mentioning the name of the site in other media. All of these actions have been modeled as subgoals. Again, these subgoals also have problems linked to them that in turn are used to find further subgoals.

The subgoal "Links from Other Sites" also is defined with the optional sequence of a problem, cause, action, and prerequisite definition through the use of notes. Again, these are optional; they don't have to be defined for all problems, or sometimes not all of these notes have to be defined (e.g., often a problem and an action note are enough). They are, however, helpful in visualizing what needs to be done in order to achieve the goals, and what the prerequisites are to an action. This information then is used when designing or changing the business processes.

The goal/problem diagram in Figure 4.5 shows only one of the primary goals of this business. Other goals have their own diagrams. All the primary goals of the business can be summarized in a diagram of their own, where any conflicts between the goals (contradictory goals) are shown. Each of the primary goals then can be described in a diagram of its own, with its corresponding subgoals. For example, the goal of attracting many customers may be contradictory to obtaining high revenue from advertisement since Internet visitors will avoid sites with too much advertising content. This contradiction could be illustrated in the goal model using an association between these goals stereotyped to «contradictory» (an example of using this stereotype was shown in Figure 4.4).

It is important to realize that the goal/problem diagram shouldn't be overformalized or described in too computational terms. The purpose of the goal/problem diagram is to identify and structure the different goals of the business and to break down the goal descriptions to a level at which these goals can be allocated to individual processes.

Business Process View

The Business Process view is at the center of business modeling. The processes show the activities that must be undertaken to achieve an explicit goal, along with their relationships with the resources participating in the process. Resources include people, material, energy, information, and technology; these resources can be consumed, refined, created, or used (i.e., act as a catalyst) during the process. There are relationships between a process and its resources and between different processes that interact, and there is a coupling of processes to goals. The processes have a purpose and a specific goal, and all the processes collectively attempt to achieve the overall goals of the business. The process definitions are used to understand the business, to see threats or opportunities in the business, to improve or innovate, and to act as a basis for other models (such as information system models).

The goals of the company as stated in the Business Vision view are the basis for modeling processes. Existing process descriptions serve as the basis for creating the models, but it is important to note that these must be reviewed with a critical eye. The business processes are modeled by utilizing interviews, discussions with the people in the business, the results of brainstorming sessions composed of carefully selected groups of people, and practical studies of how the business operates. In performing these activities, the modeler attempts to understand and capture how the business operates and how the resources in the company are handled.

The result is the creation of a number of process diagrams that describe at least the *core processes* of the company. A core process is that which has interactions with the external world or is critical for the delivery of goods and services offered by the company. Core processes are normally customer-oriented and horizontal to the traditional organization of the company.

A process description should be a generic description, while an actual execution of a process executes a specific path in the process. This means that the description of a process should contain all the execution alternatives (i.e., including exceptions and error conditions that can occur). A process instance is an example of an execution, a specific way through the general description.

The business architect creates the business process models, possibly with the support of a team of process modelers.

The Business Process view is described with an UML activity diagram. To use the activity diagram as a process diagram, the Eriksson-Penker Business Extensions established a set of stereotypes that define a process and the various resources. In addition, a variant of a process diagram, called an *assembly-line diagram*, is used to more clearly depict how the process interacts with resources during its execution. In the assembly-line diagram, the resources are often information resources (i.e., information objects) in an information system.

It is essential to define the following when modeling businesses in order to identify and specify the business processes:

- *Which activities are required?* These are specified as processes or activities in a process diagram.

- *When are the activities performed, and in what order?* This is specified through the control flow in a process diagram.

- *Why are the activities performed; what is the goal of the process?* This is specified in a process diagram through the attached goal object and a goal diagram that puts the goal into a context with other goals.

- *How are the activities performed?* This is specified in a process diagram, often by breaking down the processes into subprocesses that define the activities in more detail.

- *Who or what is involved in performing the activities?* This refers to the resources that participate in the process.

- *What is being consumed or produced?* This refers to the resources consumed or produced in the process.

- *How must the activities be performed?* This is defined through the control flow in a process diagram or through business rules.

- *Who controls the process?* This refers to the owner of process who runs the process or is responsible for its success.

- *How is the process related to the organization of the business?* This can be shown through the use of swimlanes in a process diagram.

- *How does the process relate to other processes?* This is shown through interaction modeling, which is discussed in the Behavior View section later in the chapter.

As your understanding of the business increases, the answers to all of these questions become apparent, enabling you to accurately model the processes in the business.

Process Modeling

There are several techniques used to model processes, most of which are customer-oriented and require evaluating the products or services produced in the business. By discovering the interfaces to the customer, it is possible to identify the business events that are generated and then analyze them to indicate the appropriate action the business must take for each event. By working backward from defining the product or service, you discover the activities required to produce the product or service. Once the process has been identified, it can broken down into subprocesses. The flow of both control and objects (e.g., resources) are thus captured and described in a process model, in which each step in the process adds value to the resources created or refined in the process.

Processes are modeled first by concentrating on and completely modeling the core processes of the business and then by moving on to the support processes. A business usually does not have more than five to ten core processes, but may have many more support processes. Ideally, all the processes are modeled and integrated into each other, but if that isn't practical, the goal should be to concentrate on the core processes. The core processes have interfaces to the customers and are the processes the customers use to evaluate the business. It is also important to determine whether the indirect support processes in any way constrain the core, direct value processes. That should, of course, be avoided.

Process modeling creates an accurate documentation of the way in which work is performed, perhaps in order to develop better information systems. It is also used to improve or innovate processes to make the business function more efficiently. Process modeling also identifies new opportunities in the business and creates and designs new processes that take advantage of the resources and knowledge present in the organization. Clarifying the purpose before beginning to model more finely aims the focus on what is important in the model. You can better determine if you are on the right track as you model because a clear purpose provides the modeler with a goal to work toward. Knowing the future use of the result makes it easier to decide what is important and what is not.

Process management is an additional area of concern related to process modeling. Because processes aren't strictly allocated to just one organizational unit, but span over several units, a specific process owner within the organization is designated as responsible for that process. The process owner is then given authority over this process across the organization. This is important to ensure that the result of a process is distributed fairly, for example, preventing one organizational unit from profiting if a process goes well while another organizational unit notes a loss by the same process. Ideally, the vertical way of building result units is eliminated and replaced with a complete process organization.

Many books have been written about process modeling, so there's definitely more to say about this subject. To that end the reference list at the end of the book suggests titles to read on the most important work in this area.

Process Diagram

A process diagram is a UML activity diagram with a set of stereotypes that describe the activities performed within the processes and how they interact; the input and output objects; the supplying and controlling resources that participate in the process; and the goal of the process. Figure 4.6 shows a generic process diagram.

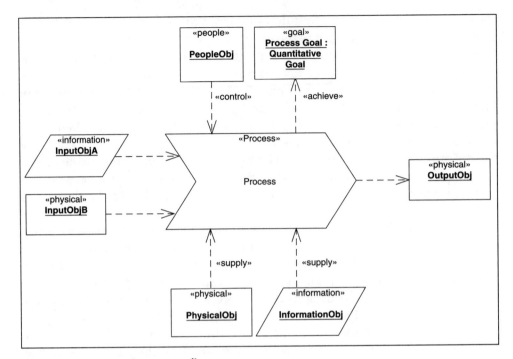

Figure 4.6   A generic process diagram.

A process is an activity stereotyped to «process». This stereotype has the traditional process icon shown in Figure 4.6. A process can contain other processes, or subprocesses, that describe the internal steps taken within the overall process. An activity symbol (a rectangle with round corners) is used to show that a process cannot be broken down further or that doing so wouldn't be meaningful; that is, an activity is atomic. An atomic process should be intuitively understood as specified by the text within the activity symbol, so that the resources that are responsible for performing it can't misinterpret it.

Resource objects and goal objects that are involved in the process are placed around the process. These objects are:

Goal objects. A goal object from a goal/problem diagram that has been allocated to a process. A goal object is drawn above the process diagram and attached with a dependency that is stereotyped to «achieve» from the process to the goal object (showing that the process attempts to achieve the goal).

Input objects. Objects that are either consumed or refined in the process. The input objects are resources, and as such can be stereotyped to «physical», «abstract», «people», or «information». They are connected with dashed lines from the objects to the process (i.e., the activity diagram notation for an input object). Input objects are normally placed to the left of the process.

Output objects. Objects that are produced by the process or that are the results of the refinement of one or more input objects. The output objects are also resources and are connected with a dashed line from the process to the output object (i.e., the activity diagram notation for an output object). Output objects are placed to the right of the process.

Supplying objects. Resources that are participating in the process but are not refined or consumed. These objects are drawn below the process with a dependency (a dashed line) from the object to the process. The dependency is stereotyped to «supply».

Controlling objects. Resources that control or run the process. Such objects are normally drawn above the process, with a dashed line from the object to the process. The stereotype of the dependency is «control».

Refinements by a process to the input objects can change the location of the object, the appearance of the object, or the content of or information in the object. It is difficult to separate an input object from a supplying object because a supplying object can also change its state during the process. An input object represents a key object that is refined or consumed in order to produce the output object. A supply object is one that the process requires (it participates in the process) in order to be able to perform that refinement or consumption. For example, in a manufacturing process, an input object could be raw material, and a supply object could be a machine used in the process. In many cases, the output object is of the same class as an input object, but with additional value resulting from the process.

Note that there is no multiplicity shown in the process diagram. Multiplicity is not shown on dependencies where only one input object of a specific class or one output object is required. Instead, the process is a continuous operation that proceeds to consume input objects and produce output objects. If the number of output objects is required, it should be specified as a goal for the process (e.g., the number of products per day or per month), not through multiplicity as used to specify relationships in UML.

Figure 4.7 is an example of a process diagram that shows the advertisement sales process for selling ad space on Web pages. It has a specific quantitative goal that includes a sales sum, a cost sum, and a yearly budget (note that this goal class is a special class designed for this case). To the left are the input objects: information resources Suspect and Prospect. A suspect is information about a company that may be willing to advertise. A prospect is information about a company that has expressed an interest in advertising. The result of the sales process is Orders. Order is an abstract resource because it is an agreement between a customer and Sample Business, Inc. Participating in the

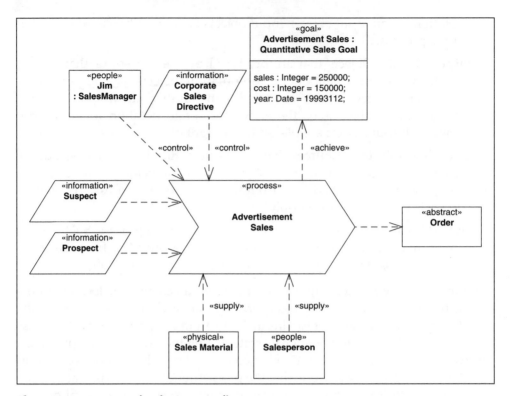

Figure 4.7   An example of a process diagram.

process are the salesperson and sales material resources. The process is controlled by a sales manager and by the corporate sales directives, usually an instruction book on how to conduct sales within this company.

This process, Advertisement Sales, needs to be integrated with other business processes. There could for example be a process to find the suspects and the prospects and an order handling process to handle the order once it has been created. Other possible processes include a sales materials process to produce the sales materials and directives, and a recruiting process to recruit sales staff.

Figure 4.8 is a process diagram in which swimlanes have been added. Recall that a swimlane is a technique used to insert information where a specific process or activity belongs. Normally, swimlanes are used to describe where the activity is performed in terms of the organization of the business (e.g., in which division or department of the company). A swimlane also can show objects other than the organization to illustrate which object is responsible for a specific activity or process. It could, for example, show which machine or person is responsible for performing a specific activity (disregarding the organization to which the machine or person belongs).

A swimlane is indicated by two vertical lines. All processes that are placed between those two lines belong to the organizational unit to which the swim-

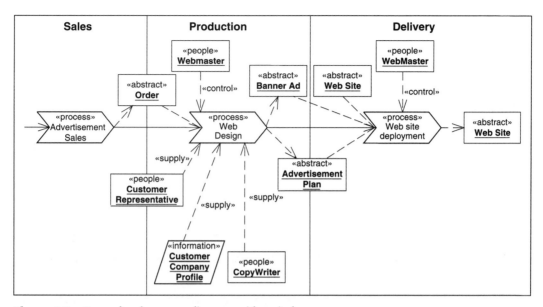

Figure 4.8 Example of process diagram with swimlanes.

lane is named. For example, in Figure 4.8, the Advertisement Sales process is performed by the Sales department. Processes that extend to more than one swimlane span more than one organizational unit, and are performed within more than a single unit. UML specifies that the swimlane lines should be vertical, but when drawing larger process diagrams, it is more practical to draw them horizontally. Swimlanes make it possible to show the integration of processes or how the processes span over several organizations. Showing the input and objects of a process, as previously illustrated, makes it possible to demonstrate how the output objects from one process could either become input objects or work as supplying objects to other processes. A process diagram with swimlanes can then show for each activity the input and the output objects from the activity, as well as which object is performing the activity (shown by placing the activity in a specific swimlane).

In Figure 4.8, the Order object from the sales process is an input object to the Web Design process, where a profile of the company that wants to advertise and a representative for that company are also required as input. The Web Design process, involving a Webmaster and a Copywriter, creates the actual ad and an advertisement plan that describes how often and on which pages the ad should be shown. This then becomes input to the Web site deployment process, the key process in the delivery section of the company. The delivery section, with the Web site deployment process, administers and maintains the Web site, updating the material and making sure the site is available to the customers. The deployment process uses the ad and the advertisement plan to update the current Web site accordingly.

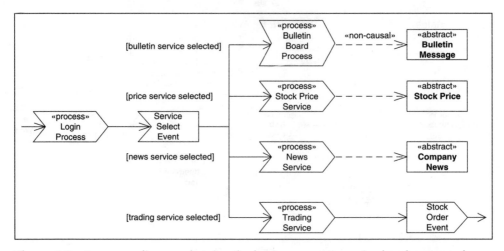

Figure 4.9   A process diagram showing the business events received and generated.

Another technique that can be used in process diagrams is to show the business events that are received or generated by the process. Figure 4.9 shows the customer login process. After login, the process expects a Service Select Event from the customer. These business events are also objects, and are defined in a class diagram, as shown in Figure 4.10. Depending on which business events the customer generates, the process continues to execute one of a set of different alternative processes. This is an example of object-oriented polymorphism, a technique in which the type of an object decides what will happen next. Each process handles a type of request; and by looking at each of these processes, the handling for each request type is detailed. The figure also illustrates the UML symbol for generating a event. The Trading Service generates a Stock Order Event, which is sent to another process (not shown here). This is all standard UML notation for sending and receiving event objects.

The bulletin board example in Figure 4.9 demonstrates yet another stereotype, «noncausal», which when interpreted might cause the process to pro-

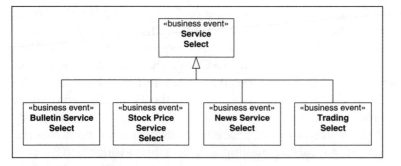

Figure 4.10   A class hierarchy of the business events used in Figure 4.9.

duce the object. The bulletin board process has a noncausal dependency to the bulletin message object, meaning that such an object might be the result of the process (but not always). Relationships and dependencies are usually causal, meaning that the object linked is always used or created as part of the process. In a noncausal dependency, which defines either an object flow or a control flow, the connection might not exist, and there are no well-defined conditions for when it does exist. This is used when there is a noncausal object flow from a process to an object, and the object might become a result of the process (it is impossible to define a clear condition for whether or not the process will produce this object). The noncausal stereotype can also be applied to the control flow lines between processes to indicate that a process might lead to the execution of another process. If this is a result of a well-defined rule condition, a business rule should be defined and specified within brackets to indicate that when the condition is fulfilled, the process will always be executed and no stereotype will be applied. However, often a strict rule cannot be defined and so the noncausal stereotype is used. Remember that here we're trying to describe a complex business that is often very unpredictable, not computer software that, when written correctly, is very predictable.

If a model contains many processes, the processes can be allocated to packages to organize the model, as shown in Figure 4.11. Recall that in UML, a package is a generic grouping of elements. It is up to the modeler to determine which packages are necessary and what they represent. The packages could be mapped to represent the organization of the company, the different types of processes, or a number of abstractions above the process level.

Assembly Line Diagram

The assembly line diagram is a unique diagram in the Eriksson-Penker Business Extensions. As with the process diagram, it is based to a large extent on the UML activity diagram. The assembly line diagram (introduced in the Astrakan method) has been used successfully for process modeling, particularly when the purpose of modeling is the production of information systems that support the processes. It is named assembly line because of the

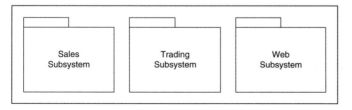

Figure 4.11   Packages of processes.

way it looks—processes that write and read objects placed in an assembly line.

At the top of the assembly line diagram is a process diagram. Below the process diagram are a number of horizontal packages that are called assembly-line packages, each representing a group of objects (the objects in the package can be of one specific class or of different classes; that decision is up to the modeler). An assembly line package is a UML package that is stereotyped to «assembly line» and drawn as a long horizontal rectangle, as shown in Figure 4.12. The purpose of this diagram is to demonstrate how the processes in the upper part of the diagram write and read objects in the assembly line. A reference from a process to an assembly line package is indicated with a dashed line (object flow) between the process and an object within the assembly line package. The type of operation performed on the object is written along the line (as the name of the object flow). The diagram is read from left to right in the sequence of references to the assembly line packages.

Because the objects in the assembly line package are often information objects in an information system, the assembly line diagram shows what information is accessed through the system and how that information is used by the processes. The objects can be other resources as well, and it is up to the modeler to determine what the assembly line packages include. The description of what each assembly line package represents appears in the tagged value "Documentation" of each package, since the packages are all stereotyped to «assembly line». A package could, for example, represent an entire information system, a subsystem in an information system, a special

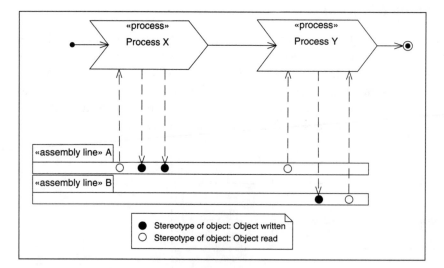

Figure 4.12 Generic assembly line diagram.

category of classes in an information system, or a specific type or group of resources.

The assembly line diagram can be viewed so that the primary activities are shown in the process diagram. The references to the assembly line package are really support activities completed to make the execution of the primary activities possible. Because the UML package mechanism is used, an assembly line package is just a grouping mechanism. The assembly line diagram is an excellent way to show how resources are read or modified as part of the process, and how an object modified (or created) by one process at a later stage is read by another process. The interaction between processes through common resource objects is shown in the assembly line diagram.

Figure 4.13 is an example of an assembly line diagram that shows the processes Stock Order Handling and Trade Handling and their interaction with a number of resources in the assembly line. The first three assembly line packages in this case correspond to classes for Portfolio, Order, and Security Holding, respectively; the assembly line packages Market and Administra-

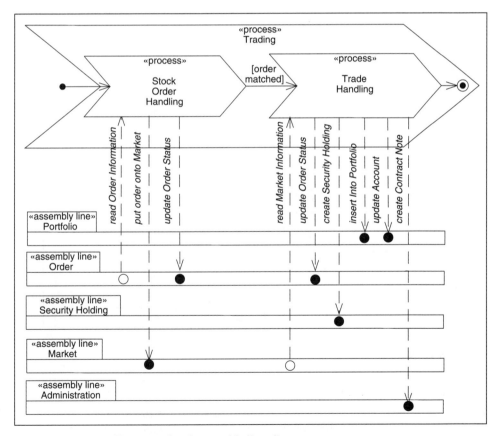

Figure 4.13 Specific example of assembly line diagram.

tion are used more as general grouping mechanisms for a number of classes that represent a market and an administrative unit within the organization. For example, the Trade Handling process creates a Contract Note in the Administration package as its last reference to an assembly line, where a Contract Note (a document that is sent to the buyer or seller as verification of a trade) is an administrative object, that is, an object in the Administration package.

Assembly Line Diagram and Use Cases

Figure 4.14 shows another assembly line diagram in which all the assembly line packages are objects in an information system. The diagram shows how the process interacts with the information system. The references to the assembly line packages comprise information flow to and from the information system and show the interface between the business process and the information system. This interface is described through use cases in object-oriented modeling; and a set of references in an assembly line diagram typi-

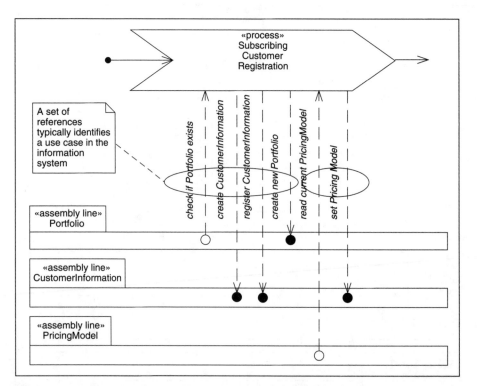

Figure 4.14   The references to the assembly line packages in a assembly line diagram can be mapped to use cases that define the requirements of an information system.

cally become a use case that the information system has to provide. This is very important, because it maps the business process to use cases that describe the functional requirements of an information system; it also identifies the proper actors of the use cases (the roles played by the process that uses the assembly lines). Assembly line diagrams provide the connection between business modeling and software system requirements modeling with use cases. A common question when modeling use cases in a software system is How do I know I have defined the right use cases in terms of the business? The assembly line diagram is a good technique to answer this.

This analysis should start with the assembly line packages at a very high level, such as the system or subsystem level. Once the initial references from the process to the information system are identified, classes in the system can be identified, and the same analysis can be repeated with the packages now defined at a another, more detailed, level. At this more detailed level, the references from the process also become more detailed. A single reference in the initial diagram might be divided into several references. It is also important that each "set of references" that becomes a use case is not chosen in an ad hoc manner, but is selected according to the rules of use case identification (e.g., a use case is a service that brings a specific value to an external actor). The use case should have a clear initiation, a sequence of communication between actor and a system, and a well-defined end that brings value to the actor. If the references from the process to the assembly line packages are randomly put together into use cases, the result will be ill-formed, partial use cases.

Nonfunctional requirements of information systems (such as performance, availability, usability, etc.) can be determined by studying the process descriptions. Factors such as process lead-times will affect support systems, such as information systems, because they define the requirements of the information system. The desired characteristics of the process directly affect both the functional requirements (what should the system do?) and the nonfunctional requirements (e.g., how fast and how reliable must the system be?). There are also factors not directly described in the process that could affect the information systems, such as a change in government or a new law. By deriving all requirements of the support systems from the processes, with the assembly line and the process properties, it is also possible to verify them. Moreover, the processes themselves result from goal modeling, which means that the system requirements can be validated against the overall business goals! Validation is about doing the right things (that achieves the business goals) and verification is about doing things right (so that the goals actually are achieved). This means that by working with goals, processes, and the assembly line diagram, it is possible to verify and validate both functional and nonfunctional system requirements. It is important to point out that the assembly line diagram is not limited to use with information systems; it has also been successfully used to model logistic systems and human resource systems.

Business Structure View

The Business Structure view shows the structures of the resources, the products, or the services, and the information in the business, including the traditional organization of the company (divisions, departments, sections, business units, and so on). It does not show the structure of processes or the breakdown of processes into subprocesses; that is shown in the Business Process view. The Business Structure view is considered supplemental to the Process view, depicting information that can't be shown in the process diagram but that is vital to the operation of the company. It too, is modeled by the business architect, again possibly supported by a team of process modelers.

The traditional organizational charts and descriptions, and descriptions of the products and services that the company provides, are the basis for the Business Structure view. The information from the Process view is also used since it shows which resources are used. Note that, typically, these two views are modeled in parallel, since they contribute to each other and must be consistent. It is difficult to model one of the views completely and then move on to the other, since their development interacts. During your discussions and interviews, you will find that the people in the business will interchangeably present information that belongs in either of the views.

The UML diagrams used to document this view are class and object diagrams. The class diagrams show the principal structure; the object diagrams show an actual configuration of the class diagram (e.g., how an organization looks at a specific point in time). Because the resources are modeled as classes, they have operations and attributes. The operations of a resource are used in a process or assembly line diagram; that is, the processes use the operations to trigger the resource to perform a specific service or action. Recall that a class diagram was also used in the Business Vision view to create a conceptual model of the basic concepts in the business. The class diagrams modeled in the Structure view depict the resources, information, and organization in more detail, in addition to more of the business rules that govern the structure. The conceptual model in the Vision view provides a high-level overview that defines a common terminology.

The interactions among a number of resources can be indicated in a UML sequence or collaboration diagram. Sequence and collaboration diagrams show the interaction among a number of objects, in which both the order in time and the operations performed by the different objects can be shown. (This is further illustrated and discussed in the "Business Behavior View" section later in this chapter.) The more dynamic and flexible the principal structure of the resources is, the more the actual structure can be changed in the future.

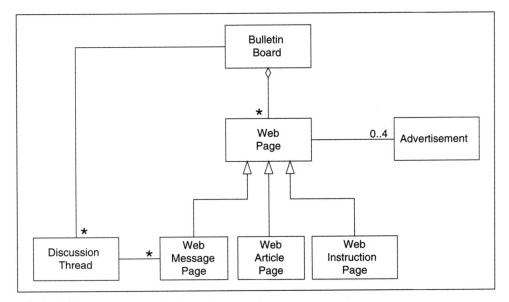

Figure 4.15   Example of resource class diagram.

Resource Modeling

Resource models show the structure of different resources. The generic model is depicted in a class diagram, while an actual configuration of a structure is shown in an object diagram. The inner structure of the resources, which are usually products or services offered by the company, can be presented in a resource model. The difference between a resource model and a conceptual model (as shown in the Business Vision view) is that the resource model concentrates on the more concrete structures of resources, such as products or services, while the conceptual model concentrates on defining the meaning and relationships of important concepts used when defining the business.

Figure 4.15 shows a class diagram of the bulletin board resource structure for Sample Business, Inc. The bulletin board consists of different Web pages that contain messages, articles, or instructions. All messages are organized in discussion threads. A Web page can have up to four advertisements attached to it. This is modeled with traditional object-oriented techniques using class diagrams.

Information Modeling

Information modeling creates models of strategically important information in the business. Even though information is also a resource in the business, it is worthwhile to model it separately using the techniques of class and object diagrams. The information is what goes into the information systems that support the business; it has a very strategic value to the business. Information modeling is an early step in defining the information stored in an information system, even though details such as database issues (e.g., keys, etc.) should not be part of the business model. Such details are defined during the modeling of the software information system.

The requirements of the information are governed by the business, but sometimes the information available also governs the business. For example, the information that the business has can create new opportunities for the business; the more information a business can capture about its customer, the more possibilities it has to adapt and configure its products and services. A very obvious example of this is an Internet business, where numerous commerce sites attempt to learn as much as possible about its visitors and customers in order to customize their Web pages. There are also many examples of companies that have information that is not fully used or explored for the purposes of improving the business or customer relationships.

Figure 4.16 is a class diagram that contains classes for the most important information resources in Sample Business, Inc. Note that a business model can have classes for both Customer and Customer Information. The Customer class represents the actual customer, the physical resource, and how objects of that class behave and interact in the business processes. The Customer Information class represents the information about the customer, which the business stores in an information system (although a simple card file is also plausible). The Customer and Customer Information classes are two separate entities and must be modeled as such. A very common mistake in analyzing and designing information systems is that one class in the analysis model attempts to be both the actual Customer (typically an actor in a use case) as well as the Customer Information.

Organization Modeling

Organization modeling is another special case of resource modeling, in which resources are allocated to organizational units that are related to each other according to specific rules. The allocated resources in an organization include employees, machines, and locations. Processes also can be allocated in an organization, or resources from an organization can be allocated to a process. Remember that a process often spans the borders of several organizational units. This doesn't mean that organization is unimportant. Often the responsibility of running a process is allocated to a process owner who is attached to an organizational unit. This owner manages the process even when it spans organizational units. The organization should strive to make optimum use of the resources within the business, and attempt to avoid internal suboptimization, which, unfortunately, is common in many organizations. The basic functions of an organization model are to show the allocation of resources, the reporting

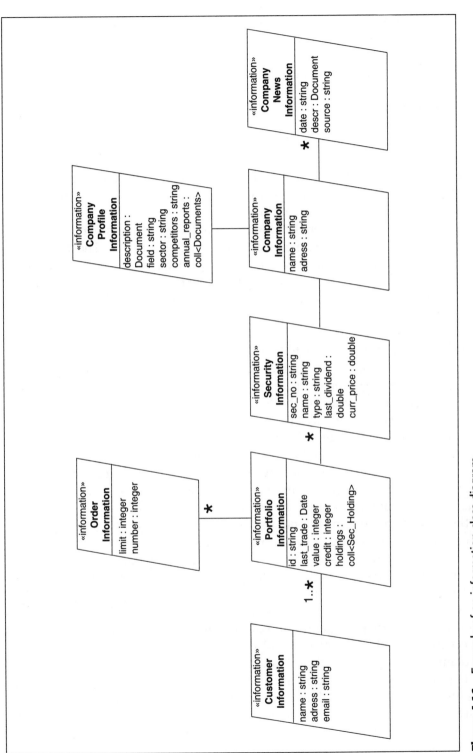

Figure 4.16 Example of an information class diagram.

methods, task assignments, and the way the company is managed. The organization can include several dimensions, such as the organization units, geographical placement, and the allocation of processes.

The overall structure of an organization is expressed through class and object diagrams. A class diagram specifies the basic structure and rules for the organization, and an object diagram shows the actual organization currently in use. The more flexible and well designed the class diagram, the easier it will be to make organizational changes without affecting the business model or its supporting information systems. Resources are typically allocated through an object diagram in which resource objects are linked to organization objects. Processes are linked in an organization through swimlanes in a process diagram, as discussed previously in this chapter.

The trend in organizational modeling is to avoid the classical hierarchical structures in favor of more flexible and dynamic alignments. These organizations can be based on projects or missions in which resources are temporarily allocated to a specific process, and can either be based on a traditional organization from which resources are borrowed or have no organization at all (i.e., all work is done in project form and resources are moved into other projects as soon as a project is complete). The advantage of dynamic organization is that optimal workgroups are created for each task. The disadvantage is that the people in such resources might feel disoriented as a result of not belonging to a traditional organizational unit. Even in very strict hierarchical organizations, informal structures and methods of communication aren't planned for (though in practice they may take place).

Information technology in many situations can be an enabler of more flexible organizations, provided that the information systems aren't designed for a specific organization and can adapt to changes. At worst, if it is impossible or very expensive to adapt the information systems, its construction hinders changes to the organization or the business.

Some advanced organizational patterns and guidelines for creating flexible organizations are discussed in Chapter 7, "Resource and Rule Patterns."

The class diagram describes the names of the organizational units and the business rules for arranging and linking them to each other. Figure 4.17 shows a class diagram for a company with a management team that is organized into divisions. The divisions in turn are organized into sections. This figure depicts a rather static structure that doesn't allow much flexibility. A better solution is to use the concept of powertypes, introduced in Chapter 2, "UML Primer," and explained further in Chapter 7, "Resource and Rule Patterns."

Figure 4.18 shows an object diagram that adheres to the class diagram in Figure 4.17. It shows actual instances of the classes and provides a view of the current organization. A model or a system based on the class diagram in this figure would allow new divisions or sections to be added or removed in the future; but would not allow any changes to the actual structure (e.g., for a sec-

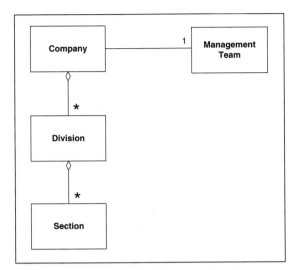

Figure 4.17   Organization model as a class diagram.

tion to have subsections within it or for the addition of new organizational concepts).

Business Behavior View

The Business Behavior view illustrates both the individual behavior of resources and processes in the business as well as the interaction between sev-

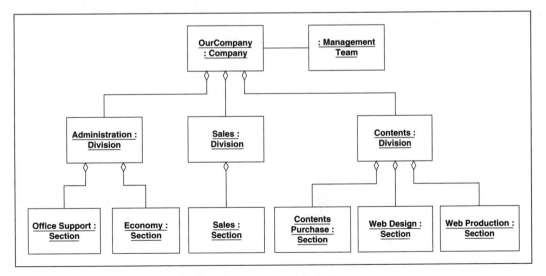

Figure 4.18   The actual organization shown as an object diagram.

eral different resources and processes. The behavior of the resource objects is governed by the Business Process view, which shows the overall main control flow of the work performed. The Business Behavior view looks into each of the involved objects in more detail: their state, their behavior in each state, and possible state transitions. The Behavior view also shows the interaction among different processes, such as how they are synchronized. Used in this way, the Behavior view becomes an important tool for allocating the precise responsibility of the various activities, and for defining the exact behavior of each resource that takes part in each process.

The combined states of the processes and the objects define the current condition of the system. States are changed through the operation of the system, that is, through the processes. Remember that it is actually the resources that perform the work of the business; the process only drives or coordinates the work of many resources. When the state of a process is altered, events are generated to notify other processes about the state change. A state also decides what may happen, which actions will occur if a state changes, and how an object can be made to enter a specific state (i.e., which events must be generated to purposely alter the state of an object). State is thus an important part of the Behavior view, as are actions and events. The Behavior view is defined by the UML dynamic diagrams: statechart, sequence, collaboration, process, and assembly line diagrams.

What is the difference between the Business Behavior view and the Business Process view? The latter illustrates the activities of the system, the transformations and the functionality, while concentrating on the interactions among the resources, goals, and rules in the business. The Behavior view illustrates the dynamic behavior of each of the objects involved in these activities. Some activities are described at a more detailed level, and interactions and responsibilities that are not visible in the Process view are defined. Naturally, there must be consistency between these two views.

The Business Behavior view is fairly detailed and normally is created by the process modelers, with the support of a business architect who ensures that these models are consistent with the business process diagrams.

State Modeling

State modeling shows the behavior of an individual resource by identifying the possible states of a resource and the behavior of the resource object in each state. The behavior of a resource is depicted using UML statechart diagrams with the following key concepts:

  States. The different states the object can have, including its start and end states.

Events. The cause of a state transition, in which the state of the object is changed to another state. The events that can be sent to a resource are shown as operations in the resource class.

Actions. The activities performed either in a specific state or when going from one state to another. The actions performed are modeled as the actions taken within a operation in the resource class.

Normally, the states of resources, not processes, are shown when modeling states. The different states of a process are the activities (i.e., subprocesses) in the process. A statechart diagram for a process is very similar to a process diagram and doesn't add any significant information.

Statechart Diagram

Figure 4.19 shows a statechart diagram for the Stock Order resource, which represents a stock order that is created when an order is received from the customer. At some point, a communication with a marketplace will put this order onto the market. The marketplace will then try to match this order with other orders on the market, that is, match a buy order with a sell order. When a match is reported from the marketplace, the order is marked as concluded, and an action creates a security holding that represents the shares bought. An order can also be canceled and withdrawn from the market; or the trading day can end without making a match. According to the statechart diagram, there must be an explicit decision to put the order back onto the market for the next day. If it's not put back on the market, it will be marked as a canceled order.

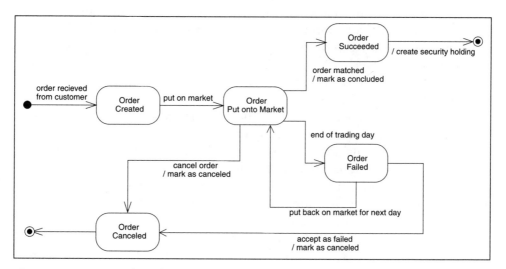

Figure 4.19   A statechart diagram for the Stock Order resource.

Interaction Modeling

The behavior of a business system is also composed of the interaction between processes and the interaction between resources. These interactions can be shown in the dynamic diagrams of UML, such as the sequence or collaboration diagram; this is called interaction modeling. The statechart diagram models the individual behavior of a specific resource, while the sequence or collaboration diagrams show the behavior, the interaction, that occurs among several different resources.

To complicate matters, the interaction between resources is also a part of a process and can be illustrated in a process or an assembly line diagram. Sequence or collaboration diagrams should be used to show only the details of a process, for example, how a specific calculation is performed or how a detailed interaction between specific resources looks. The primary activities and interactions remain in the process diagram.

Sequence and Collaboration Diagrams

The traditional technique for depicting interactions between objects in UML is to draw sequence and collaboration diagrams. Both of these diagram types show how a set of objects interact through operation calls in a specific scenario. Sequence and collaboration diagrams can be used to show the detailed cooperation of a number of resource objects. This cooperation is part of an overall process as well, but is viewed as too detailed to include in a process or an assembly line diagram.

The interaction depicted in a sequence and collaboration diagram is triggered by a reference from a process to an object in an assembly line diagram. The sequence and collaboration diagrams show the detailed interaction between objects placed in different packages. A reference from a process to a assembly line package in an assembly line diagram triggers the interaction among a number of resources in the assembly line diagram. The interaction is modeled by allowing the resources to call operations on each other.

Figure 4.20 is a sequence diagram that illustrates how a security price is updated. This interaction is triggered by the actual trading of securities, a process outside the business. This sequence diagram shows how the price is distributed to the resources within this business. The objects in it might be in an information system, but they might also be resources that interact as part of a process. The sequence diagram, which is read from top to bottom, highlights the order of a specific interaction.

Figure 4.21 is a collaboration diagram that shows how a portfolio value is calculated. Again, this is a detailed description similar to the description of an algorithm; the objects are part of an information system. This interaction can be triggered from all processes that need to know the value of a customer's

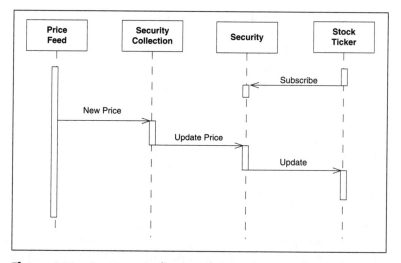

Figure 4.20 A sequence diagram showing how a price update of a security is distributed to other resources.

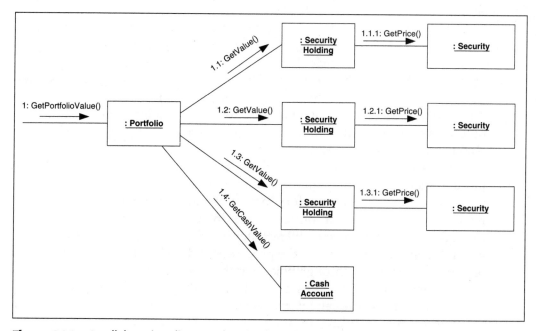

Figure 4.21 A collaboration diagram showing how the total value of a portfolio is calculated.

portfolio, such as a process that allocates credit to a customer or one that produces holding information to a customer.

Sequence and collaboration diagrams both show an interaction, and the modeler can choose which one to use. In general, a sequence diagram emphasizes the sequence in time, whereas the collaboration diagram emphasizes the relationships between the objects (since it is an object diagram in which operation calls between objects have been added). It is also possible to use just one of these diagrams consistently throughout a project, to simplify learning UML syntax and to avoid using too many different diagram types.

Process Diagram

The interaction between processes can be shown in a process diagram, which you will recall is an UML activity diagram with stereotypes from the extensions. The output objects from one process are the input objects to another process. This is the case when the subprocesses of a process are shown, as well as when two independent processes are shown in the same diagram. Note that a process is not modeled as a single class like a resource; it is actually an abstraction of the interaction among and the activities performed by a number of resources. Complicating matters is that a process can have a Process Support class in an information system, but it rarely handles the entire process—the process is not performed entirely within the information system.

Figure 4.22 illustrates how two different processes, A and B, are placed in the same process diagram. Swimlanes indicate the organization of the business. Note that objects created by subprocess A3b are input objects to subprocess B2. Also note the example of how processes are executed in parallel: subprocess A3a and A3b are run in parallel, and objects created by A3a are continuously used as input objects by A3b. The solid lines between the processes show the control flow of the processes and the dashed lines show the object flow between processes.

The assembly line diagram also illustrates the interplay between processes through their interaction with any common resources. One process could create an object that is placed in a particular assembly line package and is later read or used by another process. This interplay becomes clearly visible through the use of the assembly line diagram. Figure 4.23 shows an example in which the interaction between the processes Order Handling and Conclusion of Order is performed through objects in the assembly line packages. The reference from a process to an assembly line package in the assembly line diagram is also what causes an internal interaction between resources, which, for example, are present in an information system. That internal interaction can be depicted using a sequence or a collaboration diagram, as previously discussed in this chapter.

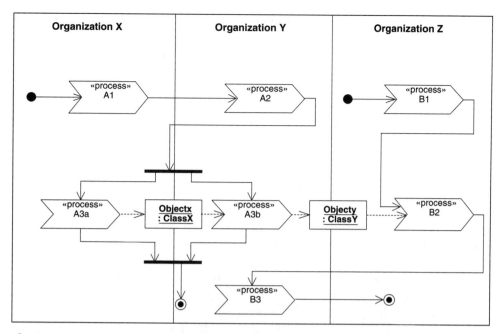

Figure 4.22. A process diagram showing two processes and their interaction.

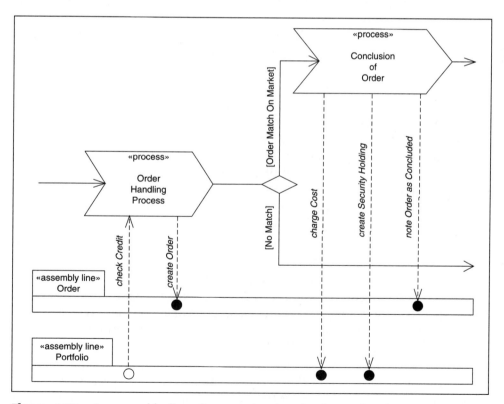

Figure 4.23 An assembly line diagram showing the interaction between processes through common resources in the assembly line packages.

Summary

The Business Vision view shows the future strategy for the business, and is created in collaboration with the upper management or business owners. The company is viewed in context to its customers, competitors, and expected technological and political changes in order to formulate the strategy, a vision of where the business is headed. The strategy is expressed in a textual document, called a vision statement, communicated to all employees in the business and used as input for modeling the views.

The vision statement is supplemented with a conceptual model and goal/problem diagrams. The conceptual model shows all the important concepts in the business and their relationships to each other. The goal/problem diagram set shows the high-level goals in the vision statement broken down into subgoals, analyzed in relationship to each other; it also points out the problems hindering achievement of the goals.

A goal/problem model is expressed in UML class and object diagrams. It leads to an action plan, in which temporary problems can be solved immediately but ongoing problems are allocated to continuous processes in the business.

The Business Process view is at the center of business modeling. It describes the processes in the business along with their goals, resources, and activities. Resources that are consumed, produced, used, or refined during a process include people, material, energy, information, and technologies. A process is described in a process diagram, which is a UML activity diagram with suitable stereotypes to link resources and goals to processes.

The process diagram shows the process and the control flow of how subprocesses are linked to each other (a subprocess is called an activity when it can't be broken down further); it also shows stereotyped object flows to the resources, which are either input, output, or used in the process. A process can also have a dependency to a goal from the goal/problem model. Resource objects that take part in the process can either be supplying objects that feed the process or controlling objects that run the process. The organization of the business can be shown in context to the process through the use of swimlanes, whereby the processes are placed in a swimlane for a specific organization or span several organizational units. A process diagram also contains symbols for receiving or sending business events, where a business event is a means to communicate between processes. A process is triggered by receiving an event; it generates an event when it is finished with its task.

An assembly line diagram is an extended process diagram in which a number of assembly line packages have been added below the process diagram. These packages, represented as UML object packages, can be used to contain a type of information object in an information system. The assembly line diagram can then illustrate the references from the process to the information system—that is, how objects in the information system are used, written, or read during the process and the sequence of those references. This diagram can be used later to define the use cases that depict the functional requirements of the information system. The assembly line diagram is used to link the business models to the use cases in the software models, thus creating the opportunity to trace requirements of a software system all the way to the processes that the system supports. (It also is used to validate the requirements. This connection is discussed in Chapter 10, "From a Business Architecture to a Software System Architecture.")

The Business Structure view shows different structures of the resources in the business. It can be the structure of a product or a service (showing how the product or service is assembled of various resources), of the information in the business, or of the organization in the company. Class diagrams and object diagrams define the structure in each of these cases. A class diagram defines the relationships between concepts and the rules for how they can be assembled. The object diagram shows an actual configuration at a specific point in time (i.e., an object diagram can show the organization as it is right now).

The Business Behavior view describes the behavior of individual resources or the interaction among either resources or processes. A resource is modeled with a UML statechart diagram through its states, the events that affect it, and the actions it performs in a specific state or when it receives a specific event. Interactions are shown with either of the UML dynamic diagrams: sequence or collaboration. These diagrams show how a number of resources interact in a specific situation. These interactions can be viewed as "mini-processes," those not modeled in a process diagram but triggered by a process in a process diagram. Often, the interaction takes place inside an information system and therefore is not shown in the process diagram. Interactions between processes can be modeled in a process diagram in which more than one process is depicted. It is then possible to show the exchange of resources or the synchronization required between the processes. The interaction between processes can also be illustrated in the assembly line diagram in which one process writes objects into an assembly line package and another process uses the same object later.

The next chapter addresses business rules. Business rules are used in all of the views and diagrams presented in this chapter as a way to detail and further specify the information in them. As mentioned, UML has a recommended language, Object Constraint Language (OCL), for defining business rules, and Chapter 5 shows how OCL is used to define different categories of business rules.

Business Rules

Businesses are controlled by rules that regulate how the business operates and is structured. In many cases, these rules are worded in an ambiguous and informal structure, such as "all important customers should have a high credit rating" (without clearly defining which customers are considered important or how to judge what a high credit rating is). Often they are not even considered rules but are referred to as "facts" of the business. Rules ensure that the business is run according to predefined external (e.g., by laws or regulations) or internal (e.g., to make the business run as efficiently and profitably as possible, and fulfill the goals of the business) restrictions or goals. Rules govern policies, terms, pricing, definitions, and configurations, and affect the business processes, organizational structures, and the behavior of the business. Rules can be defined on a high strategic level or they can be formulated to specify the detailed requirements on an information system (a requirement can be specified in terms of rules, or a rule can lead to a certain requirement on the system).

Business rule can be defined as:

- Declarations of policies or conditions that must be satisfied [OMG Analysis and Design Reference Model 1992].
- Units of business knowledge [Odell 1998].

- Statement that defines or constrains some aspect of the business. It is intended to assert business structure or to control or influence the behavior of the business [GUIDE Business Rules Project 1995].

A business rule is a statement that can control or affect both the execution of a business process as well as the structure of the resources in the business. The statement specifies a condition that must be upheld or a condition that controls which activity should follow next. It can express a business goal, specify the way a process should execute, detail the conditions of a relationship, or constrain the behavior of a resource.

Rules are present in both business and software system modeling, and are an integration point between the business and its supporting technology (the information systems). The design of the supporting software can use and implement much information from the rules in the business models. The business knowledge and policies are mapped into rules that are implemented in executable systems, which ensure that the rules are not violated.

This chapter covers how to define business rules using the Object Constraint Language (OCL) in UML. It also describes three different categories of rules—derivation, constraint, and existence—and shows how to use these rules in models. The chapter closes with a discussion about fuzzy business rules, a special type of rule that is based on the technique of fuzzy logic.

Business Rule Syntax

If business rules are defined to their full extent, they govern the entire execution of the processes. That means that when business rules are completely defined, every situation or condition in the business has a rule indicating what should happen next. In practice, business rules rarely can be defined to their full extent; instead they are used to handle specific situations. Rules can be defined to specify the goals of the business, to control the execution of the processes, to specify the behavior of resources, or to regulate the structure of the relationships among resources.

Rules are identified by examining models, evaluating facts, talking with experts within the organization, studying laws and regulations surrounding the business, or studying how the business is run in practice. Rules are typically more business-oriented rather than technically oriented and are expressed in terms of the business.

Rules begin as informal definitions; they often reveal themselves during conversations with employees or experts, in phrases such as:

- "There are two categories of items: standard and nonstandard."
- "When the customer orders a customized item, he or she must make a down payment of 20 percent of the price."

- "Anyone placing an order is a customer and must have one account; optionally, the customer can have up to four additional accounts."

- "Only managers can approve a discount; the maximum discount is 40 percent."

- "Our target group comprises females between the ages of 30 and 40 with a income more than $100,000."

All of these informal statements are, in fact, business rules that can be formalized and expressed in business models. The information systems that follow and uphold the very same rules then can be designed from these business models.

In the past, the implementation of business rules was limited to expert systems. That doesn't mean that ordinary information systems don't support business rules. The code for upholding the business rules often has been diversified into the overall code for the information system.

Direct support for business rules is becoming more and more common in information systems. Business-rule automation "engines" that may be part of information systems handle rules as specific rule objects. In addition to handling the rules, these solutions also allow actions to be attached to rules so that, if the rules are violated, the actions are executed.

With the evolution of component-based development in which systems consist of autonomous components that handle a specific area of functionality, the need to configure and adapt the business rules of each component is important. Components should be able to have their rules specified as properties, or they should be able to handle rule objects that are attached dynamically to the component. The rules adapt and configure the generic component for use in a specific application or business.

In business modeling, it is important to define the business rules in a more formal way than through natural language. A formal language is by nature more specific and less ambiguous than natural language and can be translated into computer programs more easily. A standard rule language is more terse than natural language and reduces the risk of misunderstandings or errors caused by each developer using a different language styles. Some formal rules are expressed directly in UML diagrams as graphical annotations, while others require a more explicit language syntax. These specifications add clarity to the visual models of UML. Formal rules complement diagrams; when used together, they contain all the information about how the business should run.

Sometimes it can be necessary to specify a rule in both a natural, more informal specification and in a formal specification used when designing the information systems. The informal specification is subsequently used to communicate with those in the business who are not fluent in the formal language and shouldn't be expected to learn such a formal language.

Rules in UML

Rules are used in all of the business views and UML diagrams. Many of the UML diagrams have built-in visual syntax support for defining rules. For example, a class diagram has structural constraints in its relationships to depict the multiplicity of an association. UML requires that the multiplicity between classes be defined when defining an association between two classes. The multiplicity is actually a rule that defines how many objects of one class can or must be associated with an object of the other class. In fact, all relationships in a UML class diagram are declarative rules that specify how objects of those classes can be combined and related to each other. Relationships that are not shown in the class diagram are implicitly not allowed.

A state diagram defines *guard rules* to state transitions. A guard is a rule that defines the conditions for when a state transition occurs; that is, when the state of the object is changed from one state to another. There can also be *behavioral rules,* which define the behavior of the object in each specific state. *Derivation rules* are defined as computational constraints in any type of UML diagram (e.g., that the value of an attribute is calculated from the value of another attribute). An activity diagram has behavioral constraints in its activity flow (e.g., which activity must take place before another activity, or a guard condition that must be true before an activity is initiated).

The generic construct in UML for defining formal rules is a constraint. Recall that a constraint is expressed in UML within curly braces close to the model element that it affects (e.g., close to an association that is being constrained). A constraint can be specified either with a formal language or more informally through natural language. The advantage of specifying via a formal language is that it is easier to ensure unambiguous specifications.

The Eriksson-Penker Business Extensions have a stereotyped note for defining rules. This note can be used to more explicitly connect a rule to a specific element or part of an element in the diagram, as well as to define more informal "soft rules" that are expressed only in plain text. A soft rule could be an axiom, a principle, or a rule that involves the use of human judgment. The note stereotype is «business rule»; it is attached with a dashed line to the model element (class, operation, etc.) to which it applies. When it is not easy to place a constraint near the element to which it applies, using a note creates a clearer diagram. There is no other specific support for rules in the Eriksson-Penker Business Extensions.

Again, UML's recommended language for specifying constraints is the Object Constraint Language (OCL); thus, this chapter describes the OCL in some detail. OCL allows constraints to be specified through other languages or more informal specifications. The recommended way to define rules is with a combination of the standard UML syntax and OCL. But note we said

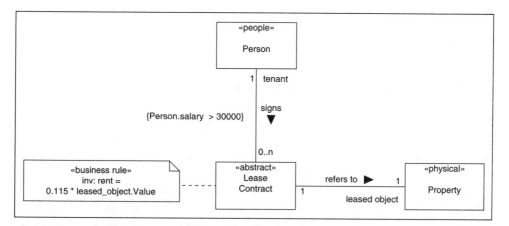

Figure 5.1 An example of some business rules in a class diagram, shown as a constraint, a rule note, or multiplicity on relationships.

OCL is "recommended"; the use of OCL is not mandatory in UML; rules also can be defined more informally or in another rule language (e.g., such as Objective-Z).

Figure 5.1 shows a simple UML class diagram. Some rules in this class diagram use the standard UML syntax. For example, the multiplicity on the "signs" association indicates that exactly one person should sign the contract, and the multiplicity on the "refers to" association specifies that a lease contract refers to exactly one property. This diagram also contains OCL rules. For example, a tenant must have a salary larger than $30,000 (the salary is an attribute in the Person class), and the rent will be 11.5 percent of the value of the leased object. All of these rules are defined clearly and are not ambiguous.

Object Constraint Language

OCL is the language of choice to use in UML to specify constraints and rules. A group led by Jos Warmer and Steve Cook of IBM developed OCL as part of a business modeling project in 1995. It later became part of IBM's UML submission to OMG as the recommended language for defining constraints in models and was officially adopted as part of UML version 1.1.

OCL is designed specifically to be simple yet formal enough to define all types of rules and constraints. Using a formal language such as OCL makes it easier to write unambiguous constraints that can't be misinterpreted. But don't misinterpret the phrase "formal language"; OCL doesn't require a mathematical background and can be understood by most modelers and developers.

A very powerful demonstration of the capabilities of OCL is the UML meta-model (i.e., the UML reference model in which the UML language itself is modeled in UML). Initially, the definition of UML was created with only the graphical annotations of UML itself, which left many subtle issues ambiguous and unclear. By using OCL to define the rules and constraints in the meta-model, the model became much clearer and unambiguous. It also served to illustrate the capability of OCL to fill in the specification gaps that the visual part of UML leaves. It does, however, require the reader of the reference meta-model to know OCL to be able to fully interpret it.

OCL is a declarative specification language. Statements in OCL cannot actually change anything in the model (such as the value of an attribute in an object). They can however specify such a change (e.g., which state change will be the result of a specific operation). OCL expressions are without side effects, which means that evaluating an OCL expression will not affect the object to which the expression is applied (normally referred to as the *context* of the expression). An OCL expression can specify which state changes will occur as the result of calling a specific operation, but it cannot define program flow (i.e., OCL doesn't have any programming language syntax for executable statements such as branches). OCL can only be used to declare OCL expressions that are evaluated, and return a value of a specific type (the type and value is dependent upon the operator and operators used in the expression). OCL is like UML; it is a modeling language used for specifying models, not for writing complete executable systems.

OCL is not an implementation and cannot be used to specify actions, such as what the result is of violating a specific rule or what is performed when a rule evaluates to a specific value. These actions are best depicted in a UML activity diagram or through writing pseudocode.

OCL is a *typed language*, in which all the operators are of a specific type and each operator can only be applied on specific operand types. For example, the operator + (addition) can only be applied on the OCL operand types Integer (an integer number) and Real (a floating-point number, i.e., a double in UML). Types in OCL can be basic, such as Integer or Boolean, collections for representing associations, or classes in the UML model (referred to as model types in the OCL language). All expressions in OCL have a type and evaluate to a value when applied to a specific context.

Using OCL in Models

There are many uses for OCL. Some of the most common are:

Invariants for classes. An *invariant* is a condition that must be true at all times for objects of that class. It specifies a condition that all objects must adhere to. An invariant OCL expression should be stereotyped to «invariant».

Type invariants for stereotypes. A type invariant is an invariant for types. It is used when defining a stereotype to specify a condition that must be applicable to all classes of that stereotype.

Pre- and postconditions for operations. A precondition or a post-condition is a constraint that specifies what must be true before an operation on a class is performed or what will be true after the operation has been performed, respectively. They can be stereotyped to «precondition» and «postcondition» in UML.

Navigational rules in a model. OCL can be used to specify navigation; for example, how to navigate from a specific context to other associated objects in the same model. These associated objects then can be used in computations or constraints.

Derivation rules or constraints. A derivation rule specifies how a specific value is calculated from other values; for example, how one attribute is derived from the values of other attributes (e.g., age could be derived from the birthdate and current date).

Guards. A guard is a condition that specifies whether to perform a specific activity (or process) or, when several alternatives exist, an alternative. Guards can also be used in state diagrams to show under which conditions a state transition occurs, or in sequence or collaboration diagrams to specify when a specific message should be sent. A guard is an OCL expression that, when evaluated to true, indicates that the message, state transition, or activity linked to the guard should be performed or sent.

The next sections provide an overview of the OCL language, and describe its capabilities in defining business rules. For a complete description of the syntax, refer to the OCL reference manual [OMG: Object Constraint Language Specification version 1.3 1999], which is part of the UML documentation, or the book by Jos Warmer and Anneke Kleppe: *The Object Constraint Language: Precise Modeling with UML* [1998]. The version of OCL described here is 1.3, adopted by the OMG in the summer of 1999.

OCL Expressions

The OCL language consists of *expressions*, comprising a statement involving operators and operands, which returns a result value. All expressions are related to a specific *context*, a defined part of a model to which the expression should be applied. The context decides which set of objects the rule constrains

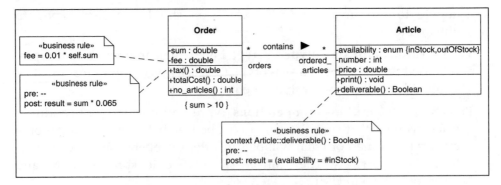

Figure 5.2 OCL expressions always refer to a specific context.

(e.g., typically all objects of a specific class or all objects taking part in a specific association relationship) or defines the place in the model from where navigation through OCL begins. The context is specified with the keyword *context* followed by the name of the context part (e.g., the name of the class to which the expression should be applied):

```
context Order
```

An expression always has a type. When applied on an object, it returns a value. For example, an expression of the type Boolean can return a value of true or false. Figure 5.2 contains a small UML model in which the Order class has an OCL expression:

```
context Order inv:
sum > 10
```

In this example, the OCL constraint is a class invariant on the context Order. Its invariant status is specified with the OCL keyword *inv*: followed by the invariant expression (which always should be a Boolean expression). Here, the Boolean expression must evaluate to true for all objects of that class (all Order objects must have their sum attribute set to a value larger than 10). When writing an OCL expression in text, the context is written on a separate line above the expression. When defining an OCL expression directly in a UML diagram, the expression is placed near the context (sometimes in a note attached to the context); the context specification line does not have to be written in text (see Figure 5.2). The context for an expression can be a class, a relation such as an association, an operation, or an attribute.

Another possible rule on the Order class is:

```
context Order inv:
fee =  0.01 * sum
```

This is an invariant on an attribute, and indirectly specifies how the fee attribute should be calculated (in this example, the fee should be 1 percent of the order sum).

A constraint can be given a name, and be referred to by that name, by specifying the name of the constraint as shown below (the name is feeCalculation):

```
context Order inv feeCalculation:
fee =  0.01 * sum
```

When a property such as an attribute is used in the expression, it is implicit that the property belongs to the Context class. It is possible to show this relationship explicitly by using the *self* keyword. The *self* keyword is a reference to an instance of the current context type. In this example, the context is the Order class, and the *self* keyword refers to an Order object on which the expression is applied. The OCL expression:

```
context Order inv:
self.fee = 0.01 * self.sum
```

is equivalent to the previous expression. The *self* keyword is used in expressions that involve properties from several different classes, to explicitly indicate which properties belong to the Context class. The self reference in the expression here refers to an instance of the Order class.

Two hyphen (--) characters indicate the beginning of a comment in OCL. The comment lasts to the end of that line.

```
context Order inv:
self.fee = 0.01 * self.sum -- calculation of fee
```

An OCL expression also can be applied to an operation instead of to a class or an attribute. Constraints or rules on operations are specified through preconditions and postconditions. For example, the rule specified in the note attached to Article in Figure 5.2 has a postcondition specified.

```
context Article::deliverable( ) : Boolean
pre:  --
post: result = (availability = #inStock)
```

The context of this expression is the deliverable operation in the Article class and, in this example, a post-condition that shows how to calculate the return value of that operation. The type of the expression is the same as the return value of the operation, in this case a Boolean. When a postcondition is specified, the OCL *result* keyword is used in the expression to depict the return value. This rule specifies that the operation will return true if the article in question has the availability attribute set to the value inStock. The availability attribute is an enumerated type with the possible values inStock and outOf-Stock. In OCL, constants of enumerated types must be preceded by a pound, or number, symbol (#) to prevent mistaking them for an attribute.

Another example of a constraint on an operation is:

```
context Order::tax() : Real
pre:  --
post: result = sum * 0.065
```

which specifies how to calculate the returned value (a Real) from the sum attribute.

The types used in OCL expressions are predefined basic types, such as Boolean, Integer, Real, and String; collection types such as Set, Bag, and Sequence; and user-defined types defined in the model (i.e., the classes). The basic types and their operators are listed in Table 5.1.

All of the basic types in OCL can have constant values in expressions; for example, 10 (Integer), 3.14 (Real), true (Boolean), and 'Hello' (String). Most of the operators are well-known mathematical or string operators, and will not be commented upon further here. Two of the Boolean operators—implies and if-then-else—deserve further attention.

The implies operator takes two Boolean operands and evaluates to true when either the first operand evaluates to false or when both operands are true. It should be read that if the first operand evaluates to true, then the second operand must also evaluate to true. If the first operand is false, it doesn't matter what the second operand evaluates to (the result is true). For example:

```
context Order inv:
ordered_articles->size = 0 implies sum = 0
```

should be read that, if the number of ordered articles is 0, then the order sum must be 0. The arrow syntax (->) used on ordered_articles is necessary because size is a property of a collection (collections will be discussed in more detail later in the "Collections" section). If the number of ordered articles is not 0, the expression still evaluates to true, regardless of the sum. The first expression *implies* that if it's true, the second expression must also be true.

The if-then-else construction takes a Boolean expression as its first operand. If the Boolean expression is true, the expression in the then clause is evaluated and becomes the result of the entire expression. If the Boolean expression is false, the expression in the else clause is evaluated and becomes the result. For example:

```
context Order inv:
fee = if (sum < 100) then 2.00 else (sum * 0.01) endif
```

Table 5.1 Basic OCL Types and Their Operators

TYPE	OPERATOR AND RESULT TYPE	OPERATOR DESCRIPTION
Boolean	b1 or b2--Boolean	Logical or
(true, false)	b1 and b2--Boolean	Logical and
	b1 xor b2--Boolean	Logical xor
	not b1--Boolean	Logical not
	b1 = b2--Boolean	Equals
	b1 <> b2--Boolean	Not equal
	b1 implies b2--Boolean	Implies
	if b1 then <expr1> else <expr2> --type of e1 or e2	if then else
Integer	i1 = i2--Boolean	Equals
(natural integer numbers)	i1 <> i2--Boolean	Not equal
	i1 < i2--Boolean	Less than
	i1 > i2--Boolean	Greater than
	i1 <= i2--Boolean	Less than or equal to
	i1 >= i2--Boolean	Greater than or equal to
	i1 + i2--Integer	Addition
	i1 - i2--Integer	Subtraction
	i1 * i2--Integer	Multiplication
	i1 / i2--Real	Division
	i1 mod i2--Integer	Modulo
	i1 div i2--Integer	Integer division
	i1.abs--Integer	Absolute value
	i1.max(i2)--Integer	Maximum
	i1.min(i2)--Integer	Minimum
Real	r1 = r2--Boolean	Equals
(natural real numbers)	r1 <> r2--Boolean	Not equal
	r1 < r2--Boolean	Less than
	r1 > r2--Boolean	Greater than
	r1 <= r2--Boolean	Less than or equal to

(continues)

Table 5.1   Basic OCL Types and Their Operators (*Continued*)

TYPE	OPERATOR AND RESULT TYPE	OPERATOR DESCRIPTION
	r1 >= r2--Boolean	Greater than or equal to
	r1 + r2--Real	Addition
	r1 - r2--Real	Subtraction
	r1 * r2--Real	Multiplication
	r1 / r2--Real	Division
	r1.abs--Real	Absolute value
	r1.max(r2)--Real	Maximum
	r1.min(r2)--Real	Minimum
	r1.round--Integer	Round
	r1.floor--Integer	Floor
String	s1.concat(s2)--String	Concatenation
(sequences of	s1.size--Integer	Size (length)
characters)	s1.toLower--String	Convert to lowercase
	s1.toUpper--String	Convert to uppercase
	s1.substring(i1,i2)--String	Substring
	s1 = s2--Boolean	Equals

The expression in the then clause is a simple constant value and is a calculation in the else clause. Both expressions must be of the same type.

OCL has strict type conformity rules. Operators of different types cannot be mixed randomly; for example, an Integer cannot be compared with a String, and a Boolean cannot be added to a Real. It is, however, possible to add an Integer to a Real, because the Integer can be converted to a Real without losing any information (Integer is a subtype to Real). In addition, the evaluation order has well-defined semantics in OCL, meaning that the order in which the operators in a complex expression should be evaluated is specified.

An OCL expression can use properties of the types defined in the UML model, such as classes. This includes attributes, operations, associations, and enumerated types defined in the class. Operations used in an OCL expression cannot change objects, therefore, only operations that query or calculate a value can be used (this is specified formally in UML so that the operation has the isQuery tagged value set to true).

In the following expression, the operation tax is used as part of calculating the total cost of an order. The tax operation must then be an operation that queries the value of tax without changing the object:

```
context Order::totalCost( ) : Real
post: result = sum + fee + self.tax( )
```

Note that the *self* keyword is used before the tax operation. This is not necessary, but it indicates more clearly that the tax operation is called on the object in context. In addition to operations in the context, operations in associated classes can also be used through navigational expressions.

Sometimes an OCL expression is used in more than one constraint. An example is the OCL let statement, which defines a variable that can be used in several constraints to refer to a specified expression:

```
context Order inv:
let feeCharge : Real =
    if (sum < 100) then 2.00 else (sum * 0.01) endif in
fee = sum + feeCharge + self.tax( )
```

As an alternative to using the let statement, operations can be defined in a class that are only to be used for those OCL expressions. Such operations should be stereotyped to «oclOperation» to visually indicate that these operations are not part of an implementation but are specification operations. The discovery of such operations is, however, often an indication that they also might be of interest as part of the actual implementation of that class; that is, they might have a usage not only in the OCL expressions but also in the executable system. Normally, the let statement is preferred to defining OCL operations in the classes.

The operations oclIsTypeOf and oclIsKindOf return true if the object is of the specified parameter type (oclIsTypeOf) or of a type compatible with the specified type (oclIsKindOf). They can be used to specify expressions that have the context of a superclass but are dependent upon the exact subtype of an object. For example (AirMailOrder and SurfaceOrder are subclasses to the Order class):

```
context Order
inv: self.oclIsTypeOf(AirMailOrder) implies fee = 10.00 + (0.01 * sum)
inv: self.oclIsTypeOf(SurfaceOrder) implies fee = 5.50 + (0.01 * sum)
```

are two invariants that indicate that if the actual object to which the OCL expression is applied is an AirMailOrder object, then the fee must be a base of 10 plus 1 percent of the sum. If the object is a SurfaceOrder, the fee is 5.50 plus 1 percent of the sum. Note that the inv: label must be repeated for each invari-

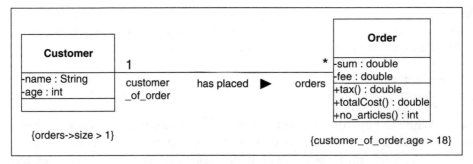

Figure 5.3   Role names in associations are used to navigate from the context to other classes.

ant in the Order context (and that this label can be placed in front of the expression; it doesn't have to be in the same line as the context specification).

Navigation

OCL allows expressions to navigate from their initial context to other related classes. These classes have association or aggregation relationships with the context class. For example, looking at Figure 5.3, it is possible to identify the customer from the Order context and verify with the following invariant that the age of the customer is over 18:

```
context Order inv:
customer_of_order.age > 18
```

This expression navigates from the Order class to the Customer class via the association, and ensures that the age attribute is over 18. In this example, it might, however, have been more appropriate to simply put the invariant in the Customer class to avoid having to navigate, but that is not the case when an expression refers to attributes in several different classes. Putting the invariant in Customer has slightly different semantics. It means that each Customer instance must have an age greater than 18, regardless whether it has a link to an Order. The constraint shown in this above example is only applicable to customers that have a link to Order.

The role name in the association is used to specify a navigational path. In this example, the role name is customer_of_order. If a role name is not present, the name of the class that appears in lowercase at the end of the association can be used instead (in this case, customer). In addition to referring to relationships within the current diagram, it is also possible to refer to model elements in other packages.

Another OCL expression based on Figure 5.3 is:

```
context Customer inv:
orders->size > 1
```

In this expression, the navigation is from the Customer class to the Order class. Because the multiplicity of the association in that direction is more than 1, the expression is a collection of objects (the orders specification results in a collection). The standard size property is referred in that collection, and the invariant ensures that at least one order is attached to the customer (i.e., to be a customer, you must have placed at least one order). Properties such as size can be applied to all collections, (a list of collections properties and operations is given in the next section). The size property returns the actual number of instances in the other end (role) of the association; and in this case, the constraint specifies that there must at least be one instance in that end. The allowed number of instances can also be defined using the multiplicity definition directly in UML. Another way to specify this rule is to change the multiplicity in the association from the asterisk (*), indicating zero or more, to 1..*, indicating one or more. In that case, the OCL constraint would not be necessary.

If the previous example didn't have a role name in the association (orders), the name of the class in lowercase could be used instead (the role name and the class are very similar in this example), as in:

```
context Customer inv:
order->size > 1
```

When a model uses qualified associations, as illustrated in Figure 5.4, a specific object can be referred to in an OCL expression. This is done through the following syntax:

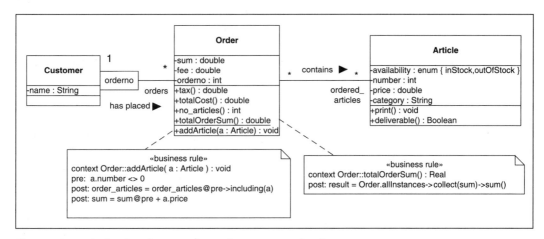

Figure 5.4   Navigational expressions often return collections.

```
context Customer inv:
orders[12589].totalCost( ) > 0
-- order no 12589 must have totalCost > 0
```

But note that the use of a specific order number in this example is rather uncommon, because rules are typically applied to all objects of a specific class rather than a specific instance. The point is, the possibility of identifying a specific object in a collection through the use of qualified associations does exist.

Collections

When navigating with associations to other classes in the same model, the result is often a collection of objects, as demonstrated in the previous section. OCL has a number of operations that can be applied to collections to perform more advanced operations, such as iterating through the objects in the collection, creating a new collection that is a subset of a collection in which the objects satisfy some condition, or combining collections into new collections. A property or operation of a collection is referred to with the arrow syntax (e.g., collection->property/operation). Note that this is different from referring to a property or operation of a single object, which uses a dot instead (e.g., object.property/operation).

Examples of common, simple operations that can be applied to collections are (using Customer as the context):

```
self.orders->size -- returns the number of associated objects
self.orders->isEmpty -- returns true if no objects are associated
```

The role name is used to refer to an association and evaluates to a collection of objects. As already mentioned, if a role name is not defined, the name of the associated class in lowercase can be used instead.

Collections can also be used when defining pre- or postconditions:

```
context Order::addArticle(a : Article) : void
pre:   a.number <> 0
post: order_articles = order_articles@pre->including(a)
post: sum = sum@pre + a.price
```

These expressions specify the precondition that the article number of the parameter must not be 0. It also specifies that the order_articles collection will include the article object after the operation and that the sum will have been increased with the price of the article. Note the pre: and post: labels specify pre- and postconditions on an operation.

OCL has two specific keywords that can be used only when specifying postconditions: *@pre* and *result*. The *result* keyword has only been used to show the return value of the operation (the previous expression doesn't return any value and doesn't use the *result* keyword). The *@pre* keyword is used to indicate the value of an attribute or an association before the operation is executed. This keyword then can be used when the same attribute or association is on both sides of the equal sign in an expression. This is the case with the first postcondition in the previous example, which specifies that after the operation the order_articles collection will be the same as before the operation, but with the article argument included.

There are certain properties for all model types (classes) in OCL. For example, the name property returns the name of the type, the attributes property returns a collection of attribute names, and the operations property returns a collection of operation names. An invariant that always evaluates to true would be:

```
context Order inv:
Order.name = 'Order'
```

Such an invariant would not be specified in practice. A more practical example is that for all classes there is a property allInstances that returns a collection with all existing objects of that class. The class Order has a class operation that returns the total sum of all orders and then makes use of this operation:

```
context Order::totalOrderSum( ) : Real
post: result = Order.allInstances->collect(sum)->sum( )
```

The allInstances property returns a collection in which the collection operator collect is applied. This operator, which will be described later in this chapter, creates a new collection that consists only of the sum attribute. Finally, the sum operator is applied to this collection to add all orders (do not confuse the sum attribute in the Order class with the sum operator; they are two different things). Using the allInstances feature is sometimes dangerous, because the existence of all objects of a class must be considered within an overall global context (all Orders in a system, or all Orders in the world). OCL does not define such a global context, though it's reasonable to define the system in operation to be that global context. Also, applying allInstances to a predefined type such as Integer would result in an infinite set of objects.

There are three types of concrete collections: Bag, Set, and Sequence. These collections are all subclasses to an abstract collection type, which contains operations common to all collections. The relationships among the different collections are illustrated in Figure 5.5. A Bag is an unordered collection that can contain duplicates of the same element. A Set is an unordered collection in which duplicate elements cannot occur. Sequence is an ordered collection that can contain duplicate elements. Unless otherwise specified, a normal association in a UML diagram evaluates to a Set and an ordered association evaluates to a Sequence. The operations supported by each type are summarized in

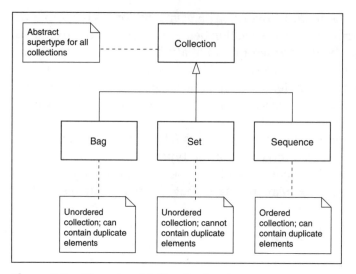

Figure 5.5   Hierarchy of OCL collection types.

Table 5.2. Note that the operations listed for the abstract collection type are available to all collections. Also note that no operations change the contents of a collection; operations such as append return a new collection in which an element has been added, but it doesn't change the original collection.

Table 5.2   Collection Types and Their Operators

TYPE	OPERATOR AND RESULT TYPE	OPERATOR DESCRIPTION
Collection	size : Integer	Number of elements.
	count(Object) : Integer	Number of elements of Object.
	includes(Object) : Boolean	True if collection includes Object.
	includesAll (ObjColl) : Boolean	True if collection includes all objects in ObjColl.
	isEmpty : Boolean	True if collection has no elements.
	notEmpty : Boolean	True if collection has elements.
	sum( )--Integer or Real	The sum of adding all elements in collection.
	= -- Boolean	True if two collections are identical.
	union(Collection)--Collection	Combines two collections.
	including(Object)--Collection	Returns a collection with element added.

Table 5.2 Collection Types and Their Operators (*Continued*)

TYPE	OPERATOR AND RESULT TYPE	OPERATOR DESCRIPTION
	excluding(Object)--Collection	Returns a collection with element removed.
	intersection(Collection)--Collection	Returns a collection with common elements.
	iterate (InitExpr; Expr)--Expr Type	Iterates over collection and performs expression.
	select(Expr)--Collection	Returns a subset of collection where all elements fulfill Expr.
	reject(Expr)--Collection	Returns a subset of collection where all elements do not fulfill Expr.
	collect(Expr)--Collection	Returns a collection with type Expr.
	exists(Expr)--Boolean	Returns true if at least one element fulfills Expr.
	forAll(Expr)--Boolean	Returns true if all elements fulfill Expr.
Bag	asSet( )--Set	Returns as a Set collection.
	asSequence( )--Sequence	Returns as a Sequence collection.
Set	s1 - s2--Set	A set with elements in first set but not in second.
	s1.symmetricDifference(s2)--Set	A set with elements that are in either set but not in both.
	asBag( )--Bag	Returns as a Bag collection.
	asSequence( )--Sequence	Returns as a Sequence collection.
Sequence	first--Type in Collection	First element.
	last--Type in Collection	Last element.
	at(Integer)--Type in Collection	Element at given position.
	append(Type)--Sequence	Returns a collection with element added at end.
	prepend(Type)--Sequence	Returns a collection with element added at the beginning,
	asBag( )--Bag	Returns as a Bag collection.
	asSet( )--Set	Returns as a Set collection.

Some very powerful operations can be used on collections. Examples of the most common operations (iterate, collect, select, reject, forAll, exists) follow.

The iterate operation is the generic operator for iterations in OCL. This operation iterates over all elements in the collection and applies an OCL expression to each element in the collection. The iterate expression contains a specification of the iterator used in the expression, an optional declaration of an accumulator, and, finally, the expression that is applied on each element and assigned to the accumulator. The generic syntax for the iterate operation is:

```
collection->iterate(i : <IteratorType>; acc : <AccType> = <initialexpr>
| <expr-with-i-and-acc>)
```

where the iterator type is the same type as the collection, and the accumulator type is of any type. The following iteration can be used to calculate the sum of all ordered articles:

```
context Order inv:
sum = ordered_articles->iterate(a : Article; result : Real = 0
| result + a.price)
```

This iteration assigns the value of each element in the ordered_articles collection to the iterator a. It then evaluate the expression result + a.price and assigns the result to the result accumulator, which accumulates the total price. The type and value of the entire expression will then be of type Real containing the sum of all prices.

An alternative to the iterate operator is the collect operator. The collect operator creates a new collection based on the original collection. The new collection is of the type specified in the argument expression. The collect operator is used to create a collection of the type Real that contains all the prices. The sum operator is applied to this new collection to sum all the prices:

```
context Order inv:
sum = ordered_articles->collect( price )->sum
```

The select operation creates a new collection that is a subset of the original collection, and thus has the same type. The operation contains an expression that specifies which objects in the original collection also should be in the new collection. To create a collection called tools_articles that is a subset of all elements, where the category is 'Tools', use:

```
context Order inv:
tools_articles = ordered_articles->select(category = 'Tools')
```

The reject operation performs an operation similar to the select operation, with the exception that those objects that match the expression are rejected from the new collection.

The forall operation tests an expression on all elements in a collection. In order for the operation to return true, the expression must be true for all elements. The following example of the forall operation also shows that more than one object can be referred to in an expression. It uses two iterators, a1 and a2, that iterate over all the objects in the entire collection. The expression then specifies that if a1 differs from a2, the number attribute must be different for the objects. This is equivalent to specifying that the number attribute must be unique for all Article objects, as shown next:

```
context Article inv:
Article.allInstances->forAll(a1, a2 : Article | a1 <> a2 implies
a1.number <> a2.number)
```

Another feature for collection is called isUnique. This feature can be used more conveniently to describe the previous constraint:

```
context Article inv:
Article.allInstances->isUnique(a : Article | a.number)
```

The exists operation also tests an expression on all objects in a collection, but in order for the operation to return true, only one of the objects has to satisfy the expression. The following expression returns true if at least one article of the category 'Tools' is in stock:

```
context Article inv:
Article.allInstances->exists(category = 'Tools' and availability =
#inStock)
```

Collection operators never change the contents of a collection, because OCL is free from side effects. They either return a new collection or a specific value, such as a Boolean (true or false).

Business Rules Categories

In practice, OCL is used to define different types of business rules. James Odell [1998] divides business rules into derivation rules and constraint rules. Derivation rules define how knowledge or information in one form may be transformed into another form, that is, how conclusions can be made based on information. A derivation can either be a computation rule (e.g., a formula for calculating a value) or an inference rule (e.g., if some fact is true, then another inference fact must also be true).

Constraint rules constrain either the possible structure or the behavior of objects or processes, that is, the way objects are related to each other or the way object or process state changes may occur. The constraints uphold the integrity of objects as they are created and relationships are changed. An operation in an object can be constrained through the use of operation preconditions and post-conditions. A precondition must be true before the operation is executed. A postcondition must be true after the operation has been executed. Constraint rules can be *stimulus/response* rules, *operation constraint* rules, or *structure constraint* rules

An additional category of business rules not mentioned by Odell is *existence* rules. Existence rules define under what circumstances something can exist (the lifetime of an object) and when it should come into existence (i.e., when an object is created or destroyed).

This section defines and provides examples of each of these categories of rules, using UML and OCL. It is important to note that many rules can't be placed in a single specific category; sometimes a rule fits in several of these categories. Also, in many cases, rules are connected to and interact with each other.

The basis for the examples in this section is the UML example in Figure 5.6. It shows a class diagram depicting a finance business. A Customer owns one or more Portfolios where each Portfolio contains a Cash Account, zero or more Orders, and zero or more Security Holdings. A Holding is a representation of a number of a certain Security. There are different types of securities, such as Stocks, Bonds, and Options. An Order is an instruction to buy or sell a specific security at a maximum or a minimum price.

Derivations

Derivation rules define how information in one form may be transformed into another form, that is, how one piece of information can be derived based on another. They are used to link information together and show dependencies between different pieces of information. Derivation rules can be divided into two subcategories: inference rules and computation rules.

Inference Rules

Inference rules specify conclusions that can be made when certain facts are true. For example, from the generalization specification in Figure 5.6, you can conclude that if an object is a Bond, then that object is also a Security and, as such, has a name and a price. This inference rule is specified directly in the diagram.

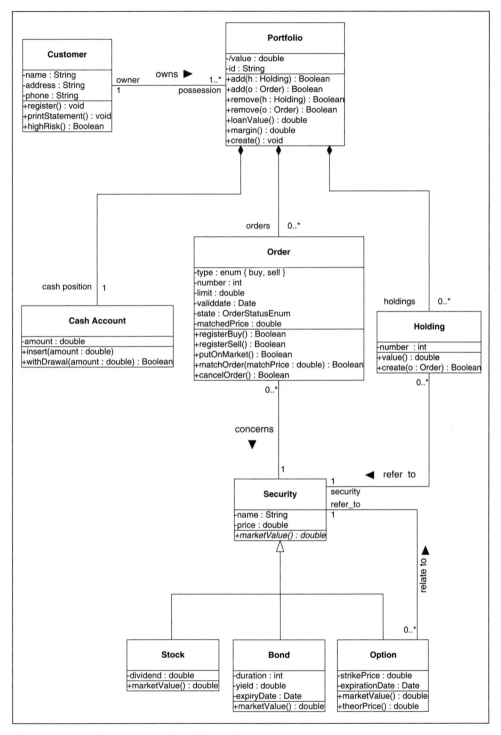

Figure 5.6   A class diagram describing a finance business.

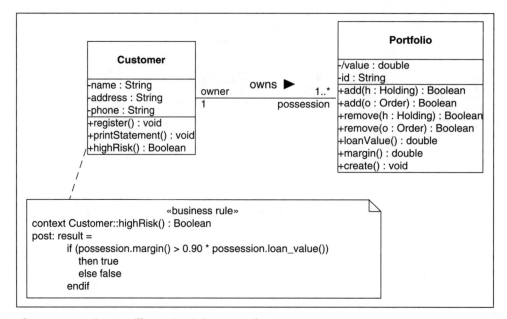

Figure 5.7   Diagram illustrating inference rules.

Another inference rule shown in this diagram is that a customer is considered highRisk if the margin is higher than 90 percent of the total loan value of the portfolio. That is specified in the postcondition in the highRisk operation in the Customer class in Figure 5.7 as:

```
context Customer::highRisk( ) : Boolean
post: result =
      if (possession.margin( ) > 0.90 * possession.loan_value( ))
            then true
            else false
      endif
```

The *implies* operation is often used for inference rules. For example, for a buy Order, the matched price must be less than or equal to the limit of the order (while for an Order to sell, the matched price must be larger than the limit).

```
context Order
inv: type = #buy implies matched_price <= limit
inv: type = #sell implies matched_price >= limit
```

Another more elaborate expression is that for a sell order, the customer's Portfolio must contain a holding with the same security that is being sold, which is expressed as:

```
context Order inv:
type = #sell implies (portfolio.holdings->exists(
security.name = self.security.name))
```

Computational Rules

Computational rules are mathematical in nature and are expressed as an equation. They are similar to inference rules in that they derive their result from some other information. Computational rules derive their results by processing an algorithm, and are used to specify derived attributes or how operations behave.

For example, the following computation rule can be used to calculate the total value of a Portfolio (see Figure 5.8):

```
context Portfolio inv:
value = holdings->iterate(h : Holding; result : Real = 0; result +
(h.number * h.security->price));
```

This expression iterates over all holdings and accumulates the value of all holdings in the result accumulator. The value of each holding is calculated by multiplying the number of securities by the price.

Another computational rule defines how to calculate the loan value of a Portfolio. In this example, the select operator is used to identify those holdings containing either a Bond or a Stock (because Options have no loan value). An iteration is performed on the resulting collection, which calculates the loan value to 90 percent of the value of a Bond and 60 percent of a Stock. Though a rather complex rule, it is very clear and compact in OCL.

```
context Portfolio::loanValue( ) : void
post: result =
     holdings->select (
          security.oclType = Bond or security.oclType = Stock )
     ->iterate( h: Holding; value : Real = 0;
          if (h.security.oclType = Bond)
          then value + (number * security->price * 0.90)
          else value + (number * security-price * 0.60)
          endif
     )
```

The @pre keyword in OCL is used when the same property is both part of the result and the expression. This happens when the value of a property is specified to be changed by the postcondition. For example, the add operation in the Portfolio class adds a Holding object to the holdings association, which can be expressed in OCL as:

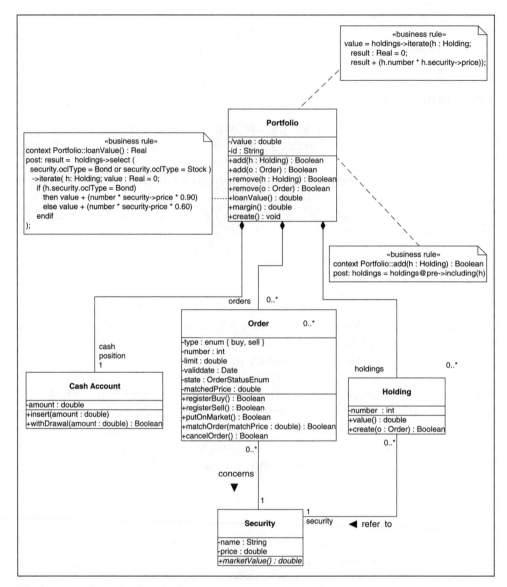

Figure 5.8   Computational rules.

```
context Portfolio::add(h : Holding) : void
post: holdings = holdings@pre->including(h)
```

The expression should be read such that the holdings collection preceding the call to the operation will add the argument to its collection, and the holdings collection will contain that element after the operation has been performed.

Constraints

Constraints govern the possible structure or the behavior of objects or processes; that is, the way objects are related to each other or the way object or process state changes may occur. Constraints are used to uphold the integrity of objects as they are created and their relationships are changed, and to control the behavior of objects and processes. Constraints can be divided into three categories: structural, operational/behavioral, and stimulus/response.

Structural Rules

Structural rules are applied on types and associations, and specify that some conditions that regulate the structure must always hold (i.e., be true). They are typically specified as invariants on classes. They help to define the structure of the enterprise or to relate different terms to each other, and express the static aspects of the business.

The structural rules are often inherent in the class diagrams, through the definition of associations and multiplicity. For example, Figure 5.9 states that a Security object can be associated to zero or more options, but one option can only be associated with one specific Security object. There are many more structural rules in the class diagram or in any class diagram expressed with UML's visual annotations for multiplicity.

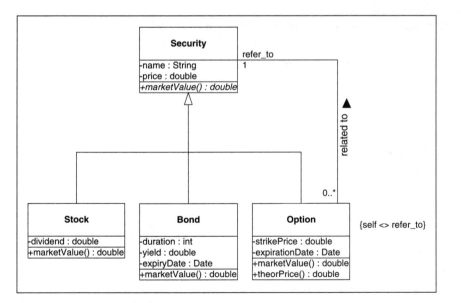

Figure 5.9   Structural rules.

Other structural rules cannot be expressed in the diagrams, and must be specified in OCL. For the example in Figure 5.9, let's say an Option cannot refer to another Option (i.e., be an option to an option). There is no visual way to depict this in UML, but it could easily be defined in OCL as:

```
context Option inv:
refer_to.oclType <> Option
```

If options were in fact allowed to refer to other options, and if one then wanted to state that an option never should be able to refer to itself (it can't be an option to itself), this would be expressed as:

```
context Option inv:
self <> refer_to
```

Operational/Behavioral Constraints

Operational or behavioral rules define pre- and postconditions that constrain what must be true before or after an operation is performed. They limit the way state changes can occur and how the object on which the operation is performed is affected by the operation. A precondition expresses constraints under which an operation will perform correctly (what must be true before the operation); a postcondition guarantees the result of the operation (what will be true after the operation).

For example, the operation putOnMarket in the Order class in Figure 5.10 requires that the state be "created" before the operation is called and guarantees that the state will be "onMarket" after the operation has been performed.

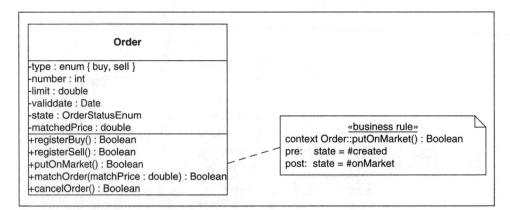

Figure 5.10   Operational/behavioral rules.

Figure 5.11   A statechart diagram with an operational/behavioral rule.

```
context Order::putOnMarket() : void
pre:    state = #created
post:   state = #onMarket
```

There doesn't have to be an explicit state attribute in the class, as in this case; the state can be represented by one or more ordinary attributes as well. OCL also has a operation called oclIsInState that returns true if the object is in the specified state.

```
context Order::putOnMarket( ) : void
post:   if (oclIsInState( #prepared))
            state = #onMarket
        else
            state = #incorrect
        endif
```

The same rule could also be expressed in a UML statechart diagram in which each state would be represented with its own UML state symbol (see Figure 5.11). The operation is defined as an event that causes a transition from one state to another, and shows the effect of the operation when performed after the Order is in the created state.

Stimulus/Response

Stimulus/response rules specify that certain actions should be performed when certain events are generated in the business. They are of the form "when this happens, do this." They can't be fully defined in OCL because OCL is a declarative language, thus can't be used to define actions. This type of rule is better defined in UML as an activity or statechart diagram, which can show actions. The event (or stimulus) part of the operation can be specified as guards in OCL, and the actions can be specified either as action states or as action specifications of the state transitions.

Figure 5.12 shows three guards defined in OCL that define conditions that will move the object into a specific state or make the object perform a specific action (in an action state).

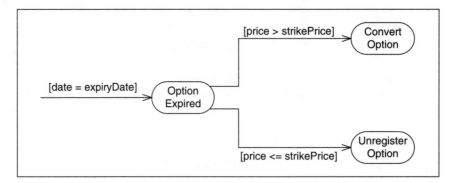

Figure 5.12   An activity diagram illustrating stimulus/response rules.

Existence

Existence rules govern when a specific object may exist. Again, this type of information can be inherent within the class model (such as an aggregated object that can only exist when its surrounding object exists). It can also be expressed as an OCL invariant, for example as in Figure 5.13, where an Option object may not exist if its expiration date is older than the current date.

```
context Option inv:
not Date.now.isAfter( self.expirationDate )
```

In this example, Date is a class that represents dates. It is not part of the standard OCL definition, but can be defined in the model to be used in rules such as this.

The OCL operation oclIsNew returns true if, used in a postcondition, the object is created during the performance of the operation (i.e., it didn't exist at precondition time). It can be used to specify conditions in which the creation of an object is involved and integral.

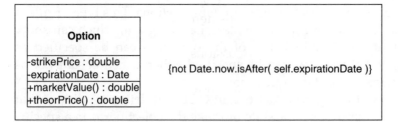

Figure 5.13   Existence rules.

Fuzzy Business Rules

Business rules defined in OCL or by the ordinary syntax of UML are based on the logic used to write computer programs. The definitions created with this logic can be strictly interpreted; they have well-defined boundaries. For example, if a business needs to decide if a person is to be considered young, middle-aged, or old, the rules would be very clear: if the person has an age between 0 and 35, the person is young; between 36 and 55, the person is middle-aged; and if older than 56, the person is old. With such strict rules, a person who is 34 years and 364 days old is considered to have the same status as a newborn baby one day, but not the next. Clearly, strict binary rules are not always effective and can, in fact, put limitations on a business rather than support the business. Often, more flexible rules are required.

Fuzzy logic (i.e., logic that isn't based on strict computational operations or values), defined in the late sixties, established a new means of expressing more complex logic than was possible with ordinary logic. Fuzzy logic has been used in areas such as cancer diagnostics, health control, earthquake warning systems, and stock analysis. It is used in cases in which complex logic is difficult or impossible to describe in ordinary binary logic. It is most common in decision-making systems where the decision has to be based on a number of complex factors. The classical illustration of fuzzy logic is the following: If you take a grain of sand from a heap of sand, the latter is still considered a heap of sand. Take away another grain of sand and it is still a heap of sand. If you continue to remove the sand, one grain at a time, until there is only one grain of sand left, is it still considered a heap of sand? If not, when did it stop being a heap of sand? A binary rule has trouble handling such paradoxes.

Using fuzzy business rules is a technique that implements the ideas behind fuzzy logic to describe business rules. By combining fuzzy logic and business rules theory, rules that have been difficult or impossible to express as traditional business rules now become possible. Whether something is true is not stated in binary terms, true or false, but through a function that returns the veracity of a specific statement. Whether someone is considered young or not is expressed as the veracity between 0 or 1. A newborn baby is young with the veracity 1, while a 30-year-old could be considered young with the veracity of 0.5. Figure 5.14 shows plotted functions for being young, middle-aged, or old (the actual values should be based on discussions and opinions of the one who defines the rules, that is, the business modeler).

Fuzzy logic is based on well-established mathematical set theory. The veracity describes to what extent something belongs to a specific set (the fuzzy set). In the example in Figure 5.14, a 30-year-old belongs to the set Young with the veracity 0.5 and to the set Middle-aged with the veracity 0.75. Note that the

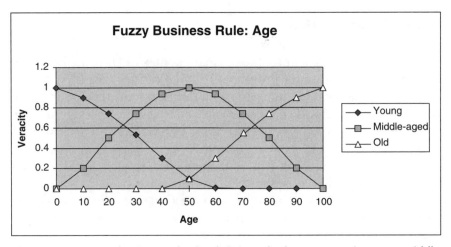

Figure 5.14   Fuzzy business rules for defining whether a person is young, middle-aged, or old.

number specifies veracity, not probability (to what extent is it true that a 30-year-old is young or middle-aged?). The sum of the veracity doesn't have to be 1. For example, a 35-year-old could be considered young with the veracity 0.6, middle-aged with the veracity 0.4, and old with the veracity 0.1. The formal mathematics for defining the veracity is a function, called the *fuzzy set function*, which returns the veracity for a specific value (e.g., the veracity for a person being in a specific set for a specific age). The function could be defined through a mathematical formula, a table, or a plotted graph.

When several fuzzy set functions are defined, they can be combined to evaluate the veracity of a compound statement that contains several fuzzy business rules. If they are combined with an *or* operation, the result shows to what degree it is true that an object is in either of the fuzzy sets. If the fuzzy set functions are combined with an *and* operation, the result shows to what degree it is true that an object is in both of the fuzzy sets. There is also a *not* operation that negates the fuzzy sets, the veracity of not being in a specific set.

If there are the fuzzy business rules for being middle-aged and for having a good salary, as shown in Figure 5.15, they can be combined to define to what extent a specific person object is both middle-aged and has a high salary. It is then possible to use this rule to define whether a specific person or a customer is in the desired target customer group for a company (e.g., Sample Business, Inc. may very well target its financial services to middle-aged people with a high salary). Using traditional logic, a person who is between 35 and 55 years of age and has an annual salary of more than $80,000 would be considered the target group. However, someone who is 34 years old and has an annual salary of $100,000 is not among the target group, which isn't a sound business con-

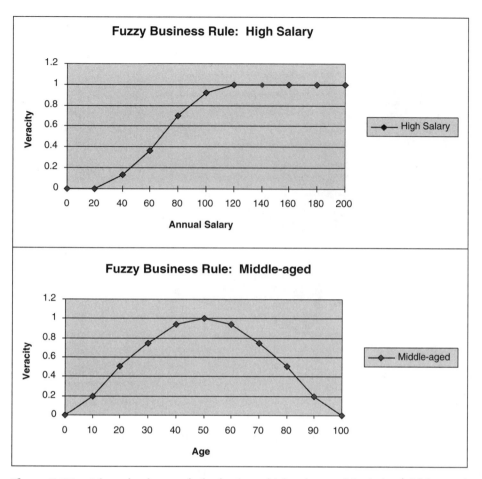

Figure 5.15 A fuzzy business rule for having a high salary and for being middle-aged.

straint. Using fuzzy business rules, the veracity for such a person would be very high for "being middle-aged and having a high salary" and would then fall within the category. By applying an AND operation between the fuzzy business rule for being middle-aged and the fuzzy business rule for having a high salary, a new fuzzy set is constructed showing people who are both middle-aged and have a high salary. The graph for that fuzzy set is shown in Figure 5.16.

It is also possible to combine more than two fuzzy sets. There are well-established mathematical rules for doing this. Drawing graphs of such fuzzy sets becomes increasingly complex as the dimensions that are combined increases. By using fuzzy business rules, very complex rules can be defined and then used to capture and describe facts about a business that are very difficult to describe with traditional binary logic.

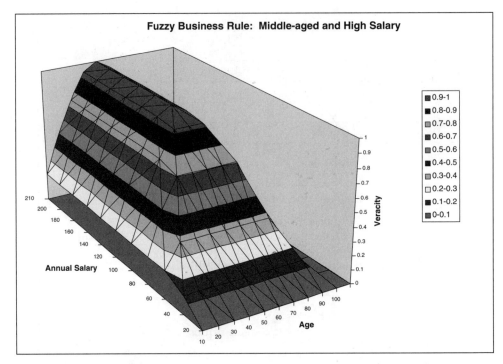

Figure 5.16   A combined fuzzy business rule showing the target group of the company: middle-aged people with a high salary.

Though further description of the mathematical foundations for combining fuzzy sets and the technique for implementing fuzzy business rules in an information system is beyond the scope of this book, the subject of combining fuzzy logic and business rules is a new and innovative idea that should be further explored. It is introduced in this book to inspire further research in this area.

Summary

Business rules are used in all of the business views. Rules are constraints that define how the business can operate or how the resources of the business can be structured. Rules can affect both the execution of processes—that is, which process or activity should be executed next—or the relationships between resources—that is, how two types of resources are related to each other. Rules are defined through the built-in visual syntax and semantics of UML or formally expressed as constraints in OCL. A constraint, shown within curly brackets in UML, can contain an expression that defines a constraint on the type to which it is attached. An OCL expression can also be placed in a note and attached to the model element to which it applies. The Eriksson-Penker Business Extensions use a specific stereotype, «business rule», on such notes.

OCL, which was originally developed as a business modeling language at IBM, is a declarative, formal language wherein constraint expressions can be specified free from side effects. OCL has a number of constructs to specify invariants, pre- and postconditions, and navigational expressions. It is not a programming language and has no support for specifying the actions that should be taken if a rule is violated or if a guard condition is fulfilled. Such actions are instead shown using statechart or activity diagrams.

Rules that cannot be expressed simply using traditional logic can be defined as fuzzy business rules. A fuzzy business rule is expressed as a function that decides the veracity in a certain statement (it precludes specifying only binary logic in which something is true or false). Fuzzy business rules, based on fuzzy logic, avoid strict boundaries and thus can be used to express rules that are in better accordance with the real world. Fuzzy business rules can be combined with each other to create very complex statements.

With the groundwork laid by explaining business modeling and business rules, the next four chapters move on to describe a set of common and reusable patterns that show practical use of the techniques learned.

Business Patterns

Many problems that recur when modeling business systems have been solved before. So why solve them all over again? Patterns make it possible to capture and describe these business-modeling problems and their corresponding solutions so that the solutions can be reused. Solutions, in the context discussed here, are not program code. They comprise a realization that is used to structure or model the business. A solution cannot be directly translated into code.

A pattern is a generalized solution that can be implemented and applied in a problem situation (a context), and thereby eliminate one or more of the inherent problems in order to satisfy one or more objectives. Patterns can be considered prototypes for production. The architect Christopher Alexander defines the term pattern in his book, *The Timeless Way of Building* [1979] as follows:

"Each pattern is a three-part rule, which expresses a relation between a certain context, a problem, and a solution.

- As an element in the world, each pattern is a relationship between a certain context, a certain system of forces, which occurs repeatedly in that context, and a certain spatial configuration, which allows these to resolve themselves.

- As an element of language, a pattern is an instruction, which shows how this spatial configuration can be used, over and over again, to resolve the given system of forces, wherever the context makes it relevant.

- The pattern is, in short, at the same time a thing, which happens in the world, and the rule which tells us how to create that thing, and when we must create it. It is both a process and a thing; both a description of a thing which is alive, and a description of the process which will generate that thing."

Patterns are established generalized solutions that solve problems that are common to different business situations. They can be reused repeatedly and can be combined and adapted in many different ways. It is important to realize that patterns are not "invented"; they are found in existing models that describe real-life business systems. In other words, patterns are really the result of experienced modelers who have identified general solutions to common problems. They also serve as a means to improve business vocabulary; modelers who understand the underlying pattern can use the pattern name to describe and communicate complex business structures and relationships.

Patterns are found in all phases of development, from business modeling to the actual coding and testing stages. Patterns found in business models are referred to as *business patterns;* patterns found in system design are known as *architectural patterns* (high-level system patterns); patterns closer to the programming level are called *design patterns.*

Be aware, however, that patterns do not solve every problem. In order to benefit from patterns, the context in which the pattern is intended to be used must be fully understood. The solution to a problem presented in the pattern applies within the context described in the pattern. When applied incorrectly, patterns can *cause* problems, such as ill-structured models. There is also an obvious risk for *pattern overload*; that is, routinely using patterns without considering the problems at hand or just for the sake of using patterns. Again, patterns are not solutions to all problems; a pattern should be used only for the type of problem that it is meant to address.

Types of Patterns

There are numerous types of patterns. We have already mentioned business patterns, architectural patterns, and the most well-known, design patterns. Different types of patterns have different purposes, are used in different phases, and address different sets of problems.

- Business patterns address problems within the business domain, typically analysis situations such as how to model and structure business resources that include invoices, organization, information, and so on. Business patterns also address how to organize and relate business processes, business rules, corporate visions, and goals.

■ Architectural patterns address problems that occur in the area of the architectural design of information systems, such as how to organize subsystems within a system or how to define system implementations at the highest level of abstraction.

■ Design patterns are used for situations in which the analysis is already mapped and described, and the focus is on producing technical solutions that are flexible and adaptable. Numerous design patterns have been documented, for building parsers, for translating objects to relational databases, for creating flexible class hierarchies, and for changing or extending code structures.

The focus of this chapter and Chapters 7 through 9 is on business patterns: how they can be used, when they should be used, how they are described and documented, and most important, why they should be used.

How Business Patterns Are Used

The first stage in all types of problem solving is to understand the area of concern. This can be achieved using an analysis method, such as induction and deduction in theory of science, Polya's Problem Solving Method in mathematics, Rational Unified Process in software engineering, or Gareth Morgan's metaphors in the theory of organization. Business patterns can be used as tools to help you, first, understand a problem situation in the context of business modeling and, second, how to deal with the problems in that situation.

Understanding a problem situation is not solely dependent upon the analysis method used; it is also dependent on the modeler's knowledge and experience, existing models and frameworks, the perceptual process—how you perceive and understand things in the world around you—and learned patterns. Patterns are thus a complement to analysis methods and are useful in analyzing business situations—the business modeling stage. Analysis can be focused on understanding an existing business situation through modeling; it can also be an attempt to model a new business or an improved business in order to implement it.

As we mentioned before, it is important to realize that business patterns are not directly transferable to program code. They are used to create understandable and flexible business models that describe the structure and behavior of a business; these models can later be used as the basis for creating information systems to support the business, thus at a later stage be transformed into program code (and indirectly be the basis for program code). The design of the information system then can implement architectural or design patterns. Business patterns are also handy for remodeling an existing business model. Likewise, unstructured models can occasionally be remodeled and improved through the use of patterns. In fact, business patterns are not just a tool to produce or improve models, they are also an excellent way to teach good modeling techniques.

Business patterns are often combined with each other or adapted to the situation at hand. However, it's important to keep the patterns' principal purpose in mind when combining or adapting them. When combined incorrectly or misused, they lose their usefulness in solving problems. Changing a pattern too radically can dilute or eliminate the advantage of the pattern; in fact, doing so could change the pattern to a totally different, unproven, and untested pattern (which might be useful, although that will not be known at the time).

You can also "mine" patterns on your own, especially if you work a lot in a particular business domain and find yourself solving the same problems over and over again. Patterns evolve from structures or interactions that occur frequently in that domain, and an experienced modeler can see those structures and interactions. The patterns can be more or less generic to the domain; some will be very specific to the domain while others may also be used outside the domain. Patterns that are very generic can be found in different problem situations or contexts that contain similar problems with similar solutions. In other words, when you have learned how to use patterns, you will also start to find them in your own work.

Pattern Categories

Patterns are often organized and classified into a set of categories independent of the problem domain they describe. There are different possibilities for categorizing patterns, but a common delineation is as follows [Gamma 95]:

Functional. These patterns represent solutions to functional problems, such as how to describe the functionality of information systems and business systems.

Structural. The structural category is composed of patterns that deal with structural issues, such as how to structure resources.

Behavioral. These are patterns in dynamic descriptions that capture behavioral aspects, such as how something changes over time or how things react to stimului.

It is important to note that the fact that a pattern is placed in a specific category doesn't mean that it contains only the aspects associated with that category. For example, a structural pattern also contains behavior. Categorizing the patterns is simply a way to organize, catalog, and refer to them.

The business patterns presented in this book have another categorization, more suited for business modeling:

- Resource and rule patterns
- Goal patterns
- Process patterns

These categories will be discussed in more detail shortly.

Pattern Form

Patterns are described based on the intent of the pattern. We call this the *pattern form*. If the intent of a pattern is to help create high-quality models that are implemented to accomplish some business effect, the pattern form should be a generic model or model example. For instance, if a business wants to cut its lead-time by modeling its delivery process, the modelers can use a Time-to-Customer Process pattern (discussed in Chapter 9, "Process Patterns") to help them structure the delivery process. This Time-to-Customer Process pattern is most beneficial if it's expressed as an example model or as a generic model. As a matter of fact, the Time-to-Customer Process pattern is expressed as a generic model and exemplified with some model examples.

If the intent of the pattern is to implement a model component in a modeling language, the pattern form should be a meta-language. A UML model component can be an extension to UML, in which case the meta-language is UML itself.

A third pattern intent might be to suggest an aspect on which to focus during a modeling session, in order to achieve a goal. In this case, the pattern form comprises metaphors. In business-modeling sessions the customer's needs and desires are normally the focus, thus the customer focus is a frequently used pattern in business modeling. The customer is a metaphor for a receiver of the business services; this is easily realized by modeling the police authority. Begin by asking how the customer is related to the police authorities. If the customer is the society, then all the criminals, who also are part of society, are also customers to the police—though it is unlikely they would agree. The metaphor, customer, is extremely powerful in most situations; but in this example, it is better to model the receiver of services, which is the society, and model the product received by the receiver, which is legal security.

The business patterns discussed in this book are concerned with the production of high-quality models that help solve common business problems (they are not concerned with the business modeling process, such as modeling sessions, project management, etc., or the business modeling language). Therefore, these patterns are expressed in a generic model and then exemplified through one or more model examples that illustrate possible implementations.

The Patterns in This Book

As mentioned, we use three categories to organize and classify the business patterns discussed in this book: resource and rule patterns, goal patterns, and process patterns. The resource and rule patterns are structural. We combine them into one category because rules are not easily separated from the resources that they constrain or affect. Goal patterns are also structural, while process patterns are both functional and behavioral. As previously discussed, the fact that a pattern belongs to a certain category doesn't mean that the pattern can only possess characteristics for that category. Placing the pattern in a particular category means that the pattern is based more on the category under which it falls.

There are many business patterns that only have structure; they are patterns that organize resources such as organizations, people, documents, and so on. The structure can be used in many different ways, so it's better not to define just one specific interaction when capturing the pattern.

The reason for classifying business patterns in those categories and not just as structural, behavioral, and functional has to do with the use and intent of the patterns. As mentioned, business patterns are concerned mainly with the concepts of resources, rules, processes, and goals; therefore, these concepts are used as a foundation for categorizing the business patterns.

Chapter 7, "Resource and Rule Patterns," covers 13 such patterns; Chapter 8, "Goal Patterns," describes 3 goal patterns; and Chapter 9, "Process Patterns," describes 10 patterns in that category. In Chapters 7 and 8, the patterns are presented in alphabetical order. In Chapter 9, the process patterns are described in the order used since they are related to each other and are easier to understand when presented in sequence. The patterns are described using UML and the Eriksson-Penker Business Extensions presented in Chapter 3, 4, and 5, which contain stereotypes for concepts such as processes, resources, and goals.

At the end of this book in the Appendices, you will find an overview that summarizes all the patterns. To truly understand these patterns in detail, the detail in text should be read, but once done a quick glance at the "Business Patterns Table" should help you find the appropriate pattern for the problem at hand.

Resource and Rule Patterns

Resource and rule patterns provide guidelines for modeling the rules and resources within the business domain. All businesses have to deal with products and documents; therefore, one of the most important resource and rule patterns addresses this domain. Other resource and rule patterns address finding and separating the core business concepts from their representation and modeling types, objects, and values. Organizational structures and contract definitions are also examples of resource and rule patterns.

Goal Patterns

Goal patterns are found in goal modeling. Goal modeling is a very critical issue; a validated and verified goal model supports all other modeling work. Goal models affect the entire modeling process—how the system is built and how it's used when built. For example, consider a library with the overarching goal to serve the nation and its citizens with information. If all the subgoals related to this main goal are about how to serve the nation and its citizens with information based on how libraries work today, nothing will change dramatically. On the other hand, if one of the related subgoals says that it shouldn't be necessary or even desirable to visit the library to borrow a book or a magazine, the architecture, design, and implementation will be greatly affected and significantly different. Though the initial analysis will probably be the same in both cases, the architecture, design, and implementation will be different depending on the subgoal: in this case, to be able to borrow items without visiting the library. A possible architecture that satisfies the mentioned goal would be an Internet-based solution, where the customer could order the items and pick them up at a specified location (at the post office, etc.), or, an even more radical option, via Adobe Acrobat files posted as e-mails.

Process Patterns

The third kind of business pattern is the process pattern. Process patterns are behavioral and functional patterns whose intent is to increase the quality in workflow models and other process-oriented models. Process models normally refer to resources, and are restricted by rules in order to satisfy the process goals. One can say that the processes are descriptions of how to achieve specified goals with a set of predefined resources and rules, where the rules express possible states of the resource and the goals express desired resource states. Process Layers, Time-to-Market, and Work Order are some of the patterns presented in this category.

The Business Patterns Template

Each business pattern in this book is described using the following business pattern template:

- Name
- Intent

- Motivation
- Applicability
- Structure
- Participants
- Consequences
- Example
- Related Patterns
- Source/Credit

The following sections describe each heading in the template and demonstrate its use, with references to the Employment pattern that is discussed further in Chapter 7, "Resource and Rule Patterns."

Name

Every business pattern has a short, distinct Name, which is a metaphor for the pattern. The name should be one that can be easily associated with the structure of the pattern; just hearing the name should be enough to recall the pattern. Thus, the name initiates a common vocabulary for discussing and using the pattern to perform modeling on a higher abstraction level. Business modelers can discuss possible solutions or model constructs by simply using the names of documented patterns. The pattern name we'll use here as an example is:

Employment

Intent

The Intent section describes and summarizes the general purpose of the business pattern, answering the questions: What does the Business Pattern do? What problems does it solve?

The Employment pattern is a resource and rule pattern whose purpose is to help structure employment. In this case, employment is defined as a contract between a person (employee) and an organization. If the employment is not separated from the organization and the employee, problems can arise, such as defining the employment in terms of responsibility, contract of employment, and so on.

Motivation

The Motivation section exemplifies the use of the pattern by describing the recurring problem in a concrete problem situation (a context) and shows how the pattern can be used to solve that problem. The motivation leads to an understanding of what the pattern community refers to as the forces that lead to the solution. The Motivation section is a guide through the rest of the pattern description, which is explained in more generic terms.

Suppose that persons are employed by an organization where the construct of employment is expressed as start and end dates in a contract of employment. Furthermore, the employment has working instructions, sometimes many different such instructions. If the relationship Employment is expressed just as an association between the person and the organization, it is not possible to express the start and end dates of the employment; it will also cause problems when connecting the employment relationship to the contract of employment and the working instructions.

The solution is to model the employment as a concept, a class, that is, the connection between the persons and the organizations. The reason to model Employment as a separate class is because it is an important concept within the problem domain, therefore it is possible to express factors such as start and end dates of the employment and relations to other concepts such as contracts and working instructions.

Figure 6.1 illustrates the employment of a person, with name, address, and birthdate. In this model, a person can have one or more employments, each of which refers to an organization and is expressed in a contract of employment. The organization referred to by the employment has name, address, and purpose as attributes. Each employment has several work instructions.

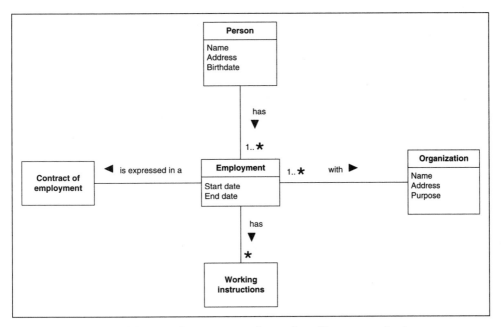

Figure 6.1 The model shows how a person is employed in an organization.

Modeling important concepts as separate classes can significantly improve the quality of business models because the classes can be extended with attributes and relationships to other important concepts. Furthermore, when expressed as separate classes, temporal aspects—those having to do with time and changes over time—can easily be expressed, as we did here with Employment, which has two attributes—start and end dates—that describe its temporal rules.

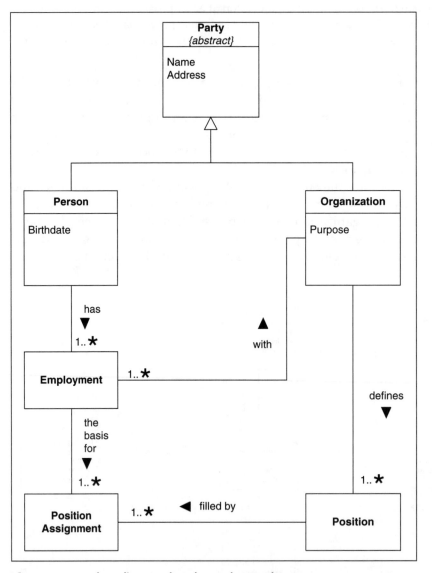

Figure 6.2   A class diagram that shows the Employment pattern structure.

Applicability

The Applicability section defines in which problem situations the pattern can be applied, and which problem it solves. The Applicability section also tells you how to recognize problems that can be solved with the pattern.

> The Employment pattern solves problems in the domain of employment; it provides a backbone where you can put all information about the employment without the risk of a low-quality model that cannot be changed or managed in the future. The Employment pattern can be implemented and used just to understand the employment structure within an organization or it can be used to build an information system that can organize all information about the employment.

Structure

The Structure section contains a generic visual representation of the pattern in UML. The visual models used to describe the pattern can be class diagrams (see Figure 6.2), object diagrams (see Figure 6.3), sequence diagrams, or activity diagrams.

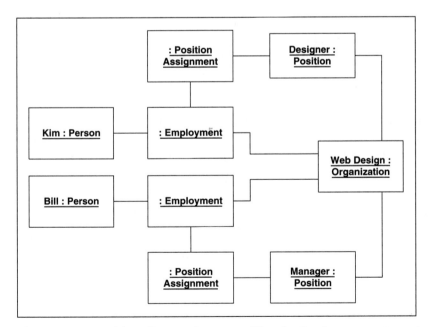

Figure 6.3.   An object diagram that exemplifies the Employment pattern structure.

Participants

The Participants section defines and describes the model elements that participate in the pattern, as visualized in the Structure section. The responsibility for each participant is listed in the Participants section. The name of the participants is shown in italics the first time it is mentioned so that it is easy to identify the participating classes in the text description.

Party is the abstract class that describes both persons and organizations in the Employment pattern. The Party class can be extended with general attributes such as name, address, and so on. The purpose of the Party class is to describe properties in common to the persons and organizations

Organization is a subclass that specializes the Party class. In this context, the Organization is a means by which to structure and group resources (such as people) in a company, so that responsibilities and goals can more easily be allocated and supervised. Note that organizations are normally composed of suborganizations or divisions, but this is not shown here because it's not the organization's structures that are described in the Employment pattern. We describe a separate pattern structuring organizations.

Persons are the second element in the Party class. Persons are human beings. Human beings are organic systems, as opposed to organizations, which are artificial systems. Persons are also active systems. This means that they act on their own.

Employment is the relation between the persons (employees) and the organizations. Employment is its own class and can have several attributes including start date, end date, kind of employment, and so on.

A *Position* held by a person is itself something of significance, with attributes such as pay grade, working instructions, and so on. A Position is typically defined by one organization (but it can be more than one) and is normally held by more than one person, at least over time. A person can also have more than one position at a time. All this argues for specification of a position assignment, where the start date, end date, and so on can be specified.

Position Assignment specifies the relationship between the person and the position.

Consequences

The Consequences section describes how the pattern supports the earlier defined goal, and eliminates the perceived problems within the problem situation. The Consequences section also outlines the necessary trade-offs of using the pattern.

The pattern helps to structure the relationship between a person and the organization where the person is employed. The advantage in using the pattern is that the concepts of significance, such as position assignment and employment, are modeled; therefore, further changes are possible. Further changes could be the addition of new concepts or the definition of new rules. These changes are easier to implement when all concepts are modeled in a consistent way.

The disadvantage, or trade-off, can be that the pattern implementation may turn into an unwieldy and unclear model. On the other hand, if terms from the problem situation are used to name the classes and relations, this will facilitate the interpretation.

Example

The Example section provides a concrete model, an implementation example, where the pattern is used to solve a problem.

Figure 6.4 is an example of an implementation of the Employment pattern, where the organization is composed of other organizations. The organization can be a department, subsidiary, or a parent company. The persons are employed within an organization, where the employment is the basis for the position assignment. The position assignment is an assignment to the position. Positions are defined by an organization, and contain things such as pay grade, and so on. The employment is expressed in a contract of employment, and both the employment and the position assignment have start and end dates. The position has working instructions and a pay grade. The model is an example of how the pattern can be used and implemented to fit a special problem situation where organization and sub-organizations, employment, contracts, and positions should be expressed.

Related Patterns

Patterns can be related to other patterns, alternative patterns, or complementary patterns. Alternative patterns are similar to each other and are used to solve similar problems. Complementary patterns are used as additional complements and often are combined with the described pattern.

The Party pattern, for example, can be combined with the Employment pattern to express how parties are built up and where employment fits in. The Contract pattern has similarities to the Employment pattern, but is a more general pattern that can be used together with the Employment pattern to express contracts of employment and so on.

Source/Credit

The Source/Credit section lists the source of or gives credit to the inventor of the pattern. Patterns do not always have a single source; a pattern may evolve and be improved by several people over many years. The source and credits given in this book are complete to the best of our knowledge at the time of this writing, and are given in this form.

The Employment pattern is described in Hay 1996.

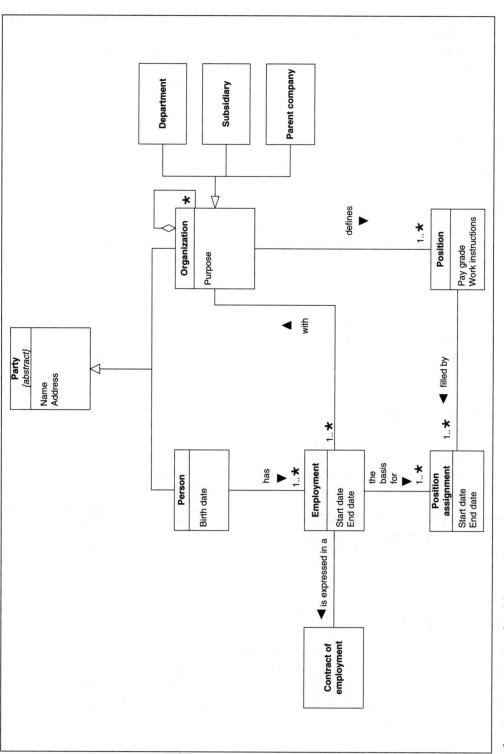

Figure 6.4 An example of the Employment pattern.

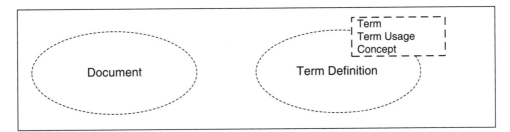

Figure 6.5   The collaboration symbol represents a pattern.

Patterns in UML

There has been an increasing interest in patterns, and UML is the first modeling language to provide a specific, visual symbol to represent a pattern. This UML symbol, called a *collaboration*, is used to represent both the structure (typically a class diagram) and behavior (typically a sequence or a collaboration diagram) in a pattern. The collaboration symbol is an ellipse drawn with a dashed line and the name of the pattern inside the ellipse, as shown in Figure 6.5. The ellipse represents a pattern. If a user wants to study the structure and behavior of the pattern (i.e., see its class diagram and possibly also a sequence diagram) he or she should expand (or "zoom into") the pattern (typically through a command in a modeling tool). When the pattern symbol is expanded, the diagrams that describe the generic pattern are shown. If the Term Definition symbol in Figure 6.5 were expanded, it would show the structure of that specific pattern. In this case, the class diagram in Figure 6.6 would be shown, where the classes in the pattern are shown with their relationships to each other. If the pattern also had behavior, a sequence diagram would also be shown when the pattern was expanded.

A pattern (or collaboration in more generic UML terms) also can be parameterized, whereby the classes in the pattern are listed in a rectangle in the right-hand corner of the ellipse. By listing the classes in the pattern, it's possible to show how the pattern is used in a concrete implementation, or use of the pattern. A parameterized pattern can be used in other diagrams, as shown in Figure 6.7. The pattern symbol is shown along with a list of the classes that are

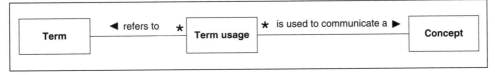

Figure 6.6   When a pattern is expanded, the structure of the pattern is shown; in this case the Term Definition pattern is shown as a class diagram.

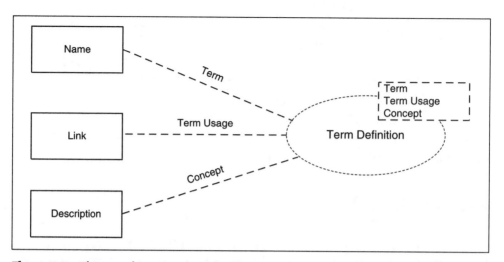

Figure 6.7   The use of a pattern in a specific case, where the concrete classes have dashed lines to the collaboration symbol and to the role name they have in the pattern.

part of the pattern (the formal parameter classes of the pattern). The dashed lines lead to the concrete classes used in this implementation of the pattern. On each dashed line is the role name the concrete class has in the pattern. In Figure 6.7, the Name class takes the role of the Term class in the pattern. When the pattern is expanded, the concrete classes replace the parameter classes in the pattern, as shown in Figure 6.8.

Because UML has a specific symbol for patterns, it's easy to model and use patterns with a modeling tool that supports this. Remember that not all UML tools support the pattern symbol. In Chapters 7 through 9, a number of patterns are shown through class diagrams and sequence diagrams, and all of these patterns can be represented by UML collaboration symbols and easily used in business models.

Other Work in Patterns

The area of patterns has prompted a great deal of work, both past and ongoing. The set of business patterns contained in this book represent only some of

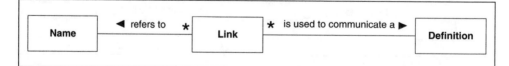

Figure 6.8   When the pattern is expanded, the concrete classes are shown in their role in the pattern.

that work. Therefore, we list here a number of references that contain recommended additional reading on patterns, which in many ways have inspired the patterns defined in this book. Not all of the patterns described in these references are business patterns (or they're not always referred to as business patterns); some of these sources describe architectural patterns, design patterns, or even patterns in other areas such as project management, or Alexander's work, which is directed toward house and city architectures.

Christopher Alexander. *Timeless Way of Building*, Oxford University Press, 1979.

Christopher Alexander. *A Pattern Language*, Oxford University Press, 1987.

Scott W. Ambler. *Process Patterns: Delivering Large-Scale Systems Using Object Technology*, Cambridge University Press, 1998.

Michael A. Beedle. "cOOherentBPR – A pattern language to build agile organizations," PLoP-97 Conference, 1997.

Frank Buschmann, Regine Meuiner, Hans Rohnert, Peter Sommerlad, Michael Stal. *Pattern-Oriented Software Architecture: A System of Patterns*, John Wiley & Sons, Inc., 1996.

Martin Fowler. *Analysis Patterns: Reusable Object Models*, Addison-Wesley, 1997.

Erich Gamma, Richard Helm, Ralph Johnson, John Vlissides. *Design Patterns*, Addison-Wesley, 1995.

David C. Hay. *Data Model Patterns: Conventions of Thought*, Dorset House, 1996.

James Coplien and Doug Schmidt (eds). *Pattern Languages of Program Design*, Addison-Wesley, 1995.

John Vlissides, James Coplien, and Norman Kerth (eds). *Pattern Languages of Program Design 2*, Addison-Wesley, 1996.

Robert Martin, Dirk Riehle, Frank Buschmann, and John Vlissides (eds). *Pattern Languages of Program Design 3*, Addison-Wesley, 1998.

Important, ongoing contributors to the work of patterns are the annual patterns conferences, such as PLoP, EuroPLoP, and ChiliPLoP. Each year, new papers on patterns of different types are presented and workshopped, and the state-of-the-art in pattern development is described.

Summary

Many of the problems that arise when modeling businesses have arisen before and have been solved before; there is no reason to solve them all over again. A pattern is a description of a common solution to a recurring problem that can be applied to a specific context. A pattern is described with a structure through a class diagram, that shows the participating classes in the pattern. It can also have behavior, which is illustrated with a sequence diagram that shows how the classes communicate in a specific situation.

There are many types of patterns, such as architectural patterns that show the high-level architecture of a system, design patterns that are more oriented toward programming, or even patterns that are used for project management. The patterns presented in this book are business patterns that describe common modeling solutions to use when doing business modeling: modeling resources, organizations, goals, processes, and rules. There are three categories of business patterns: resource and rule patterns, process patterns, and goal patterns. Each of these categories addresses problems in their specific context. The next three chapters present a number of business patterns organized according to the business pattern categories introduced in this chapter.

CHAPTER 7

Resource and Rule Patterns

The patterns described in this chapter will help you to identify, represent, and structure business resources. Resource modeling is an important issue in business modeling. All businesses use resources, which include, but are not limited to, people, material, or information, and products, which act, are used, or are produced within the business.

> **NOTE** To understand and use the patterns described in this chapter, you need to familiarize yourself fully with the business extensions to UML, described in Chapter 4, "Business Views"; you should also review the concept of *powertype*, discussed in Chapter 2, "UML Primer."

Business resources are arranged in structures (modeled in the Business Structure view, explained in Chapter 4) and have relationships with each other; they take an active or passive part in the business processes, to achieve the goal of those processes. The 13 patterns defined in this chapter are used in that view.

As mentioned in Chapter 3, "Modeling the Business Architecture," rules affect processes, resources, and goals. Most commonly, rules are used to define how to organize resources. Rules are an inherent part of the resources, and, in particular, the structures and relationships among the resources, which means they cannot be easily separated. Therefore, there are no separate "rule patterns"; instead, rules are part of the resource patterns.

The patterns in this chapter establish rules for structuring and representing resources. The patterns are subsequently used for modeling the resources in a business. Without them, a modeler must define classes for some or all of the concepts found in the business, then attempt to connect all of the concepts without benefit of an overall plan or structure.

These patterns enable you to:

- Express a core business concept separately from the representation of that concept (Core-Representation), handle information about a resource in the business separately from the resource itself (Thing-Information), or represent a title separately from items of that title (Title-Item).

- Depict and organize the business events that occur in a business (Business Event-Result History).

- Model common business concepts and situations, such as contracts (Contract), documents and document copies/versions (Document), employment of persons in an organization (Employment), and addresses that might become obsolete (Geographic Location).

- Separate an individual actor resource in the business from the different roles in the business (Actor-Role).

- Structure the definition of common business terms used in the business (Business Definitions).

- Define and represent a flexible business organization (Organization and Party).

- Represent a complex product and all information about that product or parts of it (Product Data Management).

- Model the relationship among a type, objects of that type, and values that those objects can have (Type-Object-Value).

Though most of these patterns have been used for more than 20 years in business process modeling, rarely have they involved object-oriented concepts; and, of course, they have not been modeled with UML. They have proven to be essential in the structure and representation of business resources. When resources are well structured and well represented in the business model, it's easier to connect and use these resources in the process patterns (presented in Chapter 9).

Resource and rule patterns are often used when a client or employee describes an organization or a resource structure in terms of what that organization or structure looks like right now. For example, the names of the departments or the names of a product structure (which could be captured in a UML object diagram). Using these patterns, you, the modeler can abstract this information into a more generic model that isn't applicable to the organization or structure as it looks today, but allows for future changes and extensions, such as a well-designed UML class diagram.

Example implementations of these patterns include:

- Car manufacturing systems, to describe a very complex product structure and to link all related documents to the product part to which they refer.

- Financial systems, to define abstract and complex financial instruments and to separate the core meaning of an instrument from a variety of representations.

- Document handling systems to administrate document originals, different versions of those documents, information about the documents, and copies of those documents

As you can see from these examples, these resource and rule patterns are generic enough to be used in almost any kind of business.

The 13 patterns defined in this chapter are presented in alphabetical order. References that describe common combinations and relationships among the patterns can be found in the Related Patterns section for each pattern.

Actor-Role

Intent

The Actor-Role pattern provides guidelines for using actor and role concepts, including how they should be separated and how they can be combined.

Motivation

An *actor* is someone or something that functions on its own, such as a machine or a person. You can employ actors within a company. A *role* describes an action taken by the actor. You cannot employ the role; it is defined and owned by the company or organization that uses it. For example, IBM employs Eric as vice president of training; thus, Eric is an actor playing the role of VP of training.

An actor can have more than one role at a time, and the same role can be played by more than one actor. For example, one person can play the roles of a switchboard operator and receptionist at the same time; conversely, a number of different people (actors) can play the role of switchboard operator and receptionist. There are also situations in which two or more roles can be played by one person, though not simultaneously. For example, one person may play the role of a manager, whose job it is to confirm incoming invoices. That same person may also play the role of a bookkeeper whose job it is to book the invoices. However, this person, who can and is allowed to play both roles, cannot play them at the same time because he or she should not be responsible for both booking and confirming incoming invoices. The Actor-Role pattern makes it easier to model and describe the rules for such occasions, which can be very hard to model if the actor and role are not properly separated.

Another example is a system that handles sensitive data (such as strategic or military information) where the roles of system operator and system administrator need to be separated, because a system administrator adds or removes user accounts to the system, whereas a system operator has access to the data within the system. In this case, an actor that has had the role of system administrator can never take on the role of system operator, because one would like to avoid the risk of a system administrator who creates an account for him- or herself and thus gains access to sensitive data. In this example, separating the roles eliminates a security risk.

A third use for the Actor-Role pattern is when an actor needs to be matched to different roles. Roles and actors have different attributes. Actors have attributes that describe competence, knowledge, and experience. Roles have attributes that describe operational directions (such as responsibility or the security level attached to that role) and, often, requirements for the actors who play those roles. These requirements can be based on the actor's defined attributes—his or her competence, knowledge, and experience. This pattern helps to identify which actors are most qualified or even permitted to have certain roles.

If rules are assigned to different roles and there is no separation of actor and role, the rules are difficult or even impossible to express because a single entity involves both the actor and the role. If the actor has several roles, there is a big risk that the roles will be simply lost in the model, or that the actor will be defined as having an aggregated role that may become very specialized for that actor and be intermingled with the actor's attributes. The distinction of different roles becomes lost because the roles are not separated from the actors that play them. As stated, if in a military system that handles sensitive information the roles of system administrator and system operator are not separated, a system administrator can give him- or herself access to sensitive data and become a serious security hazard.

Applicability

The Actor-Role pattern can be used in all problem situations in which there is a need to separate actors from roles. For example, a business rule for a bank could be that all large withdrawals must be approved by the bank's office manager. But if the roles of office manager and bank clerk are not separated, and an actor is defined as just "employed in a bank," it would be hard to express precisely which actors are allowed to approve large withdrawals. The Actor-Role pattern separates the bank employee actors from the roles of office manager and bank clerk.

Consider this example: In the healthcare industry, it may seem inappropriate for a surgeon to be also an assistant surgeon. Nevertheless, there may be situations in which an actor who is a surgeon may also work as an assistant to another surgeon. The actor in this case has several roles, which are mutually exclusive. The Actor-Role pattern models the actor (the Actor class), the different roles (the Role class) and the business rule to ensure that they are mutually exclusive (Actor-Role connection rule).

Structure

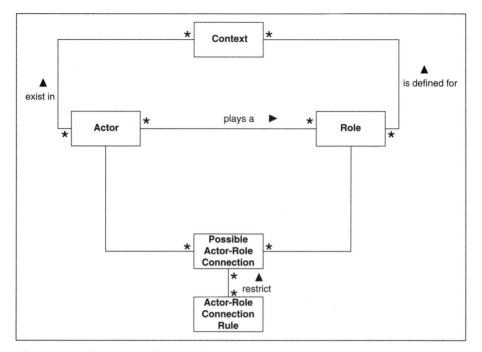

Figure 7.1   The Actor-Role pattern's structure.

Participants

Context is the situation in which the actors exist and for which the roles are defined. The context in some way describes the situation, for example, with attributes such as working pace, work environment, or obligation of confidentiality.

Actor class describes the actors. It can be people, machines, or similar items. The Actor class can have attributes such as competence, knowledge, skills, age, and culture; it can also be specialized into subclasses.

Role is a description that tells the actor how to function in a particular context. Typical characteristics associated with role are degree required and competence required. Role can also be specialized into subclasses.

Possible Actor-Role Connection expresses possible or allowed connections between actors and roles. Though there may be connections or combinations of connections that are prohibited, the Possible Actor-Role Connection class expresses only those connections that are allowed.

Actor-Role Connection Rule is the basis for the Possible Actor-Role Connection class. Objects can be defined as regular logic, that is, XOR and AND. The XOR rule means that only one of several possibilities is allowed at a certain point in time; AND means that all associated roles must be played at the same time.

Consequences

The Actor-Role pattern enables the easy separation of actors and their attributes from the roles that they play. The roles are defined for a certain context, usually by a specific organization. One advantage of using the Actor-Role pattern is that you can identify roles that cannot be played at the same time by the same actor, along with certain actor requirements that are dependent upon the roles played. Using this pattern also makes it possible to locate and define certain connections, such as that a certain actor can play a set of roles in one context but not in another.

NOTE **If the Actor-Role pattern is always used in situations where a one-to-one relationship exists between the actor and the role, then using the Actor-Role pattern will lead to the definition of more classes than necessary and possibly make the model more complex.**

Example

Figure 7.2 shows an object diagram in which the context is a lottery. The lottery is an object of the Context class; there are three actors within the context: Miller, Smith, and Mellborn. The possible roles within the context are lottery cashier (selling lotteries and handling payment), lottery participant (buying lotteries), and lottery manager (the person who arranges the lottery).

There are potential connections between Miller and the roles of lottery cashier, lottery participant, and lottery manager, meaning that Miller at some point in time can perform one or more of those roles. However, the Actor-Role Connection rule (XOR) states that the roles of lottery participant and lottery manager cannot be played simultaneously—only one of the roles referenced can be valid at a time. This rule expresses the important constraint that a lottery manager cannot participate in his or her own lottery, a constraint that can possibly be enforced upon the model by legal means. This object diagram shows that the actor Smith can play the roles of lottery cashier or lottery participant and that the actor Mellborn can only have the role of lottery participant.

Object diagrams are used to exemplify a class diagram (in this case, a class diagram that shows a pattern at a certain moment or in a specific use); they express a snapshot of a real situation. Figure 7.2 is an object diagram for the

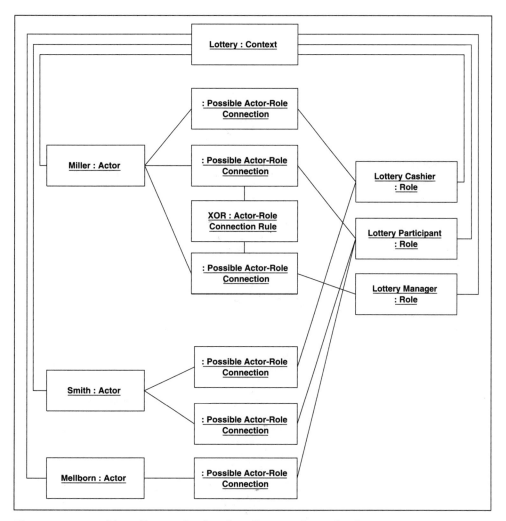

Figure 7.2   An object diagram for the class diagram shown in Figure 7.1.

pattern structure depicted in Figure 7.1. It contains only the rules that are the objects of the classes—Possible Actor-Role Connection and Actor-Role Connection rule—and not the links between the actors and the roles. In other words, this object diagram shows a situation in which actors and roles *can* be but are not yet connected to each other.

In Figure 7.3, another object diagram, the actual connections between the actors and the roles have been added. In it, the actor Miller now plays the role of lottery manager, actor Smith plays the role of lottery cashier, and actor Mellborn has the role of lottery participant.

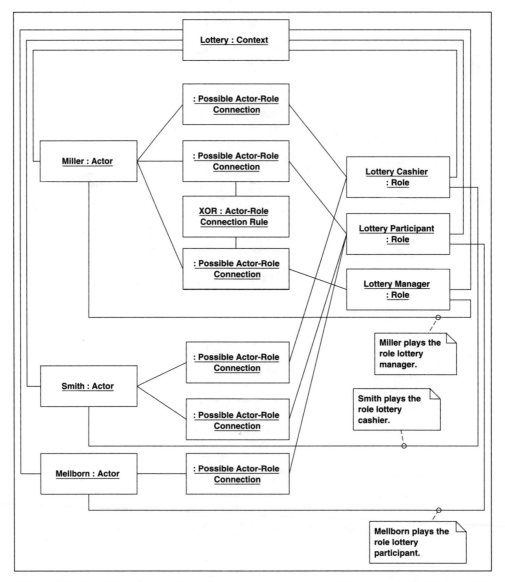

Figure 7.3   An object diagram that shows how actors and roles are connected at a certain moment in a certain context.

Related Patterns

The Actor-Role pattern can be combined with the Organization and Party pattern, discussed later in this chapter, typically by creating an association from the Role class in the Actor-Role pattern to the Organization Unit class in the Organization and Party pattern, then by connecting and defining the role so it's a specific part in the organization. For instance, in the lottery example, the role of lottery manager can be assigned to the Power Ball, Lotto, or Keno organizational units; each unit handles a specific type of lottery, and each lottery manager is connected to one of these units.

The Actor-Role pattern can also be combined with the Employment pattern (also described later in this chapter), in which case the Person class in the Employment pattern would be exchanged with the Actor class in the Actor-Role pattern. For instance, the actor/person Smith could have the role as lottery cashier, be employed in the International Gambling Company, and have a position assignment that specifies when he started his full-time employment as lottery cashier. The role would be modeled in the Actor-Role pattern and the employment and position information would be modeled using the Employment pattern.

Source/Credit

Its origin is unknown, but this pattern has been invoked to model mine-clearance systems used by the United Nations. A description of the concepts underlying this pattern can be found in Murray R. Cantor's book, *Object-Oriented Project Management with UML* (John Wiley & Sons, Inc., 1998).

Business Definitions

Intent

The Business Definitions pattern captures and organizes business term definitions, then creates systems for managing them.

Motivation

All businesses have many critical concepts that must be communicated clearly, accurately, and easily via terms—that is, words. The important terms for these concepts, called *business definitions,* must be defined unambiguously. According to Tony Buzan, the inventor of the mind-mapping technique, if you ask a group of four people to associate a word with a given concept such as "car", none of the first 10 associated words will be the same. This is not surprising. That associations we make to the same concept are very individual is well known in other fields as well, such as conceptual modeling. Therein lies the need to rigorously define critical terms used to describe concepts within a business. It is not sufficient to just define the concept that the term represents. As Buzan's research proves, people will undoubtedly use the same term differently, so it is also necessary to demonstrate the various uses for the term; in short, it must be carefully defined for each potential situation or group of users.

Business definitions are composed of a term (the actual word or words), a description of how it's used, and a concept (the semantics of the term, the actual meaning of the word).

In the field of object-oriented modeling the term *multiplicity* is widely used to describe the number of instances allowed at the end of an association. In the world of data modeling, another term, *cardinality,* stands for the same concept. This is an example of two terms used to describe the same concept, but in different contexts (object-oriented versus the data-modeling community). This clarifies the need to differentiate the use of the term and its concept. Figure 7.4 shows a simplified model for capturing business definitions.

Figure 7.4 A simplified model that can be used to capture business definitions with terms, concepts, and the different ways to use the terms.

Consider this example: Within the healthcare industry, it is not always obvious what is meant by the term "patient." If you visit a doctor twice, are you one and the same patient? The answer is probably yes. However, if you visit two different hospitals, are you then considered one and the same patient? That might not always be the case, if there is a lack of communication or shared information between the hospitals. The lack of communication is a result of the term "patient" not properly being defined. The hospitals do not realize the need to share their information about "patient." If you are not seen as one and the same patient, there is a risk that the instructions from the two doctors won't be coordinated (such as prescribing medicines that shouldn't be used simultaneously). Your health insurance company, however, considers the patient definitely as one and the same, since they trace all the patient's treatments. This shows that the term patient can have different uses and meanings in different contexts, the health insurance company considers the patient to be one and the same, while the two different hospitals do not. Further consider that a pharmacy has customers while a hospital has patients; when a hospital sends a patient to a pharmacy he or she then becomes a customer. This is an example that shows that the same concept can have two different terms (patient/customer). This is referred to as the *term usage*. Clearly, then, to define a healthcare business process, it is vital to define the various terms, the correct use of those terms, and the concepts that those terms represent. This is where the Business Definitions pattern comes in.

Applicability

The Business Definitions pattern can be used to analyze and document terminology for large enterprises. It can also be used to specify and build terminology servers (that serve an enterprise with term definitions and operate as an encyclopedia to be referenced when writing documents about the business or its information systems).

Structure

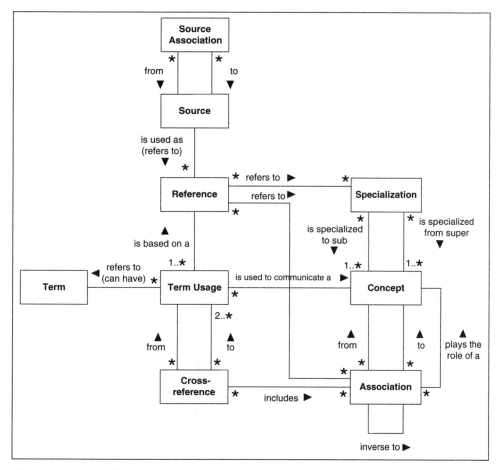

Figure 7.5   The full description of the Business Definitions pattern.

Participants

Term is represented with words and has a name, which can be a text string or an equivalent. Term is used to communicate one or many concepts. The terms and concepts are connected to each other through the Term Usage. Terms that are spelled and pronounced alike but have different meanings (refer to many concepts) are called *homonyms*. For example, in general, the term *method* means a structured way of doing things. But to people in the UML community, method can also mean an implementation of an operation in a class. Different terms that have the same meaning (refer to one and the same concept) are called *synonyms*. As described previously, multiplicity and cardinality can be synonyms. As used within the UML and most object-oriented communities multiplicity is used to indicate that an association can link a specified number of class objects to each other, whereas cardinality is used within the entity-relationship modeling community to denote the same concept.

Term Usage class is the connection between the terms and the concepts, or how the term is used by a specific group of users. Typical attributes can be a description of the term's users. The usage itself is not expressed as an attribute; it is expressed through the associated classes Reference, Term, and Concept. In some cases, it is useful to connect the Term Usage to an explicit user or group of users. This may be achieved by adding a user class and associating it with the Term Usage class.

Concept is an understanding or interpretation of something in the real world. Concepts are used to structure thoughts about ideas of the world. Terms are used to communicate concepts among people. The terms refer to objects and ideas in the world that people wish to communicate. The concept name or label is the term used. And in some way, the concept must be identified, especially in an implementation. A Concept class may have an attribute such as an ID to solve this problem. Typically, the Concept class has attributes such as description and definition. However, a concept is defined through its relationships to other concepts. The relationships can be of two kinds: *Association* or *Specialization*.

Association is used to combine or relate concepts to each other. An association can also be considered a concept; therefore, the associations are said to play the role of a concept. Associations also exist between the instances (objects) of the concepts, meaning that associations have multiplicity. As with concepts, associations do not have names, and thus terms are used to describe them. An association exists among instances of concepts and therefore also has multiplicity. The typical attributes for an association are multiplicity and description.

Specialization is another potential relationship between concepts. As opposed to Association, Specialization is used only between concepts; it cannot be instanced and does not have multiplicity.

Cross-reference is used to specify terminology servers that must support many different terminology applications, such as journal systems, intranets, dictionaries, encyclopedias, and spell checkers. One term usage is used in one terminology server or other cross-reference mechanism, and therefore the Cross-reference class is from one term usage (the server's use of the term) to at least two other term usage (the terminology applications like journal systems, intranets, encyclopedias, and so on). The Cross-reference class can have attributes such as rule and access rights, and can include associations to several concepts, which is necessary if one term in one usage is equivalent to several terms in another usage.

Source is the point of origin from which the different kinds of term usage are generated and described. Typical attributes are name, source category, status (preliminary, fixed, and so on), version, and date.

Reference class is between the Source and the Term Usage. The Reference uses a Source with references to both specialization and associations between the Concept referred by the Term Usage and other concepts to present a picture of how to use a Term that references a Concept. The usage is the Term Usage, which is based on a Reference. The Reference can have attributes, such as kind of usage (own, refer, use, etc.) and recommendation for use (yes, no).

Source Association. Sources may be connected to each other, and these connections can be specified in the Source Association.

Consequences

The Business Definitions pattern makes it possible to maintain and provide business definitions for many different professions and domains in one model or system that is built on the principles of term, term usage, and concept. The discussion of healthcare in the Motivation section is one example where different disciplines must interact and communicate, even though they have different terminology and interpretations for common words.

For the person responsible for capturing and defining the business terms, the Business Definitions pattern clarifies the differences between a term, its use, and the concept. The pattern is implemented by instantiating it into an object diagram, where each object represents a term, the term use, or a concept (or relationships between these things, as defined in the Participants section). It is then possible to define such things as two term objects for the same concept, or to define one term object that can refer to two different concepts.

This pattern, however, only works if the people defining the meaning of terms can agree; if they can't, this causes a locked situation from which the business model or system development can't evolve. More important is that such a situation indicates that confusion and different interpretations of the terms used in the business exist, and this pattern alone can't resolve this dilemma.

Example

The example in Figure 7.6 was developed with Term, Term Usage, Source, and Concept. As shown earlier in this section, concepts must always be communicated via terms; the figure shows both how to define and use concepts through terms. A concept is defined through one term usage object, which also relates the definition of the concept to a corresponding term for that definition. The definition is also related to some source. The defined concepts in the model are

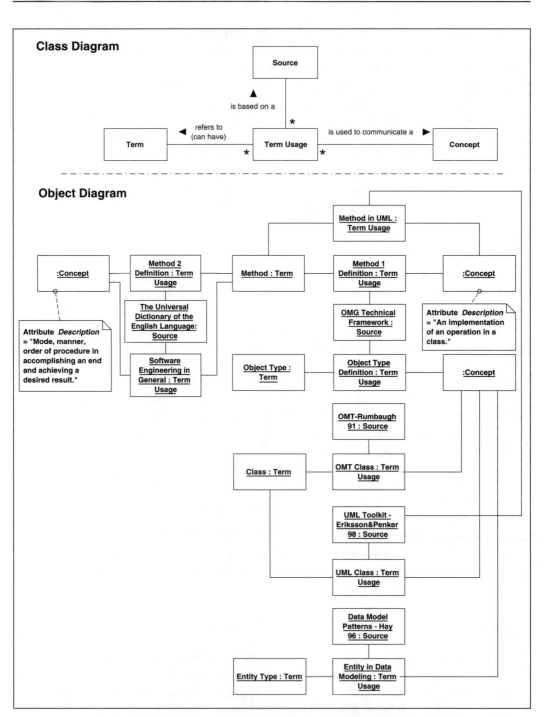

Figure 7.6   The model shows a class diagram—a terminology model for object-oriented terms—which is an application based on the Business Definitions pattern. The object diagram shows how the class diagram can be instantiated.

Method 1, Method 2, and Object Type. The defined concepts Method 1 and Method 2 have the same term, namely Method, but are different concepts (one refers to the concept of software development method and the other refers to the method that is part of a class definition). The term Method is a homonym (can refer to two or more different concepts). The terms Class and Entity Type are synonyms for the concept defined for the term, Object Type; that is, there are three different terms that refer to the same concept.

The model in Figure 7.6 also shows sources for these definitions and other uses for these terms. For example, the term Class in UML means an Object Type (defined in OMG Technical Framework) according to the source *UML Toolkit* [Eriksson 1998].

A recurring problem that we've noticed is the definition of the term Customer, raising the question does someone become a customer after placing the first order or is someone who showed an interest in the offered product or service a customer, too? Especially when merging enterprises and business processes, it is vital to synchronize and define the term Customer, sometimes dividing it into several different terms, use of terms, and concepts. Otherwise, in particular with sales and marketing processes, the definition becomes unfocused and thus badly controlled.

Related Patterns

None.

Source/Credit

Sven-Bertil Wallin at Astrakan formalized this pattern. The pattern is widely used in Scandinavian healthcare services and county councils.

Business Event-Result History

Intent

The Business Event-Result History pattern is used to track significant business events and then to connect these events to their results. Capturing the different business events, along with their results—such as decisions, contracts, statements, or products, will help you to make better business decisions. The goal of this pattern is to enable you to keep a record of all important business events, which are typically described with attributes such as description, purpose, and result.

Motivation

Decisions are made in every business based on significant business events that occur. Business events cause decisions to be made, and decisions, in turn, cause something else to happen. For example, if an invoice is received (a business event), a decision is made whether or not to pay. The decision to pay the invoice is the result—the invoice is paid.

A business is driven by events inside or outside of the business in a set direction that is a result of the business goals, visions, and strategies. The historical record, coupled with the goals, visions, and strategies drawn up for the business, provide the information you need to make better decisions and/or more accurate predictions about the business. Examples of different types of business events include:

- Offer to sell
- Sale
- Purchase
- Negotiation
- Delivery
- Complaint
- Payment
- Confirmation of payment
- Invoice

Figure 7.7 shows the key concepts required to record the business events and their significant effects, which are usually one of following:

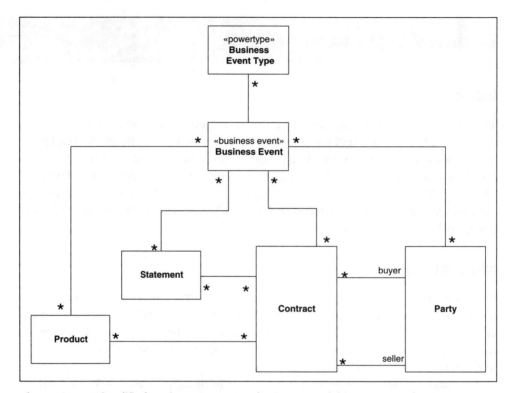

Figure 7.7 A simplified Business Event-Result History model for capturing business events.

A contract that represents a decision. The contract rules the circumstances of a delivery, when the delivery is a product. The contract is usually between a seller and a buyer; for example, someone who delivers and someone who receives and pays.

A statement that expresses the contract. A statement can express many contracts and a contract can be expressed many times. Remember not all contracts are written. The written contract is considered a statement; the statement is the written object—on paper or in electronic form. Contracts can also be oral, some of which become written and are published in a statement.

A product that represents the deliverables. Products can be abstract entities such as a service, business effort, or market share, or tangible, such as software and hardware.

All businesses need to record their business events. For instance, not knowing which customers are late with their payments creates the risk that the business may continue to sell products to these delinquent customers. Also, by studying the buying patterns of customers, it is possible to increase the sales to these customers or to adapt or develop the products and services of the business to better satisfy customer needs. Resource planning is another example where a record of business events is needed. If a certain group of employees are always overworked, this signals to the organization a need to increase allocated resources or head count in that category. The same applies to other types of resources. The Business Event-Result History pattern offers a solution to the problem of recording business events and their consequences, without knowing beforehand which events and consequences will occur in the business.

Applicability

The Business Event-Result History pattern is suitable for problem domains in which you need to maintain a history of business events and their results. It is most often used to model financial systems and enterprise resource planning (ERP) systems.

Structure

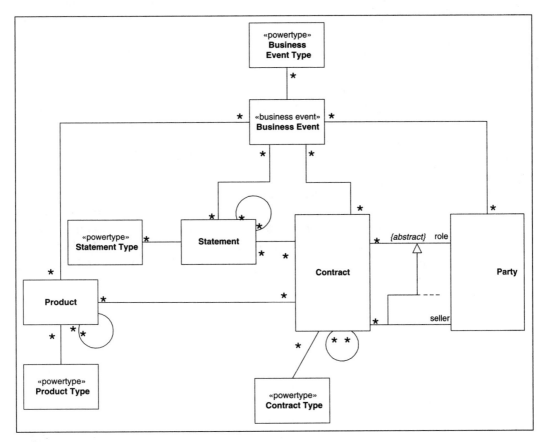

Figure 7.8   The structure of the Business Event-Result History pattern.

Participants

Party is a class that represents both people and companies. The parties play a role in the context of a Contract. Typical roles are seller and buyer. Party typically has the attributes name and address.

Business Event describes occurrences of significance. Examples of Business Event attributes include date, priority, and description.

Business Event Type describes the Business Event. Common instances of the Business Event Type class are delivery, contract signing, and purchase.

Contract represents a deal or a decision. The Contract rules the circumstances of a delivery, where the delivery is a Product. The Contract is usually between a seller and a buyer, but it can also be between other parties. Common attributes are description, date, and until-date. Contracts can be associated with each other; for example, one contract can be complementary to another contract. This is also shown with the recursive association.

Contract Type describes the type of a Contract. Two common examples of the Contract Type class are skeleton contract and lease contract.

Statement expresses a Contract. A statement can express many contracts and a contract can be stated many times. Typical attributes are description and date. Statements also can be associated with each other. This is shown with the recursive association.

Statement Type describe the type of Statement. Common instances are written and verbal statements.

Product is a class that represents the deliverables. Products can be abstract objects, such as a service, business effort, market share, or physical objects such as software and hardware. Common attributes are ID and name.

Product Type describes types of products. Instances of the Product Type class are computer program, support, consulting, and installation.

Business events are connected to their results in terms of Product, Contract, Party, and Statement. The models produced in accordance to the pattern should be integrated with the models used to describe the business goals, rules, and processes. Furthermore, the recursive associations at Product, Contract, and Statement can be replaced advantageously with a class that represents and describes the recursive connection.

Consequences

Using the Business Event-Result History pattern ensures that models produced to track important business events and their causes are extensible. Extensible means that new kinds of events and causes can be added at a later date to the same overall structure.

Using this pattern makes it possible to record business events and, at a later point in time, analyze these events and draw conclusions. These conclusions typically lead to activities or decisions in the business, such as to discontinue a relationship with a customer or vendor because of poor payment history. If no record of business events is maintained, no history is available to learn from, and the same mistakes may be repeated over and over again.

One potential problem with this pattern is that if too many low-level business events are recorded, the amount of detail will make the record hard to analyze and draw conclusions from. Events should be defined so that they are easy to understand in a business context; for example, order placed, product delivered, invoice paid, and so on.

Example

The employees at the Jackson & Co. consulting firm have problems tracking their contracted work. They don't know how many requests for offers really turn into actual contracted work, nor do they know what percentage of contracted work is performed as planned (quality of delivery, delivered on time, and so on. The absence of this information makes it hard for them to optimize the sales process. They don't know how much effort to spend on producing offers and, conversely, which requests for offers should be acted upon. Clearly, Jackson & Co. needs to automate the process for recording business events and to produce a model for this based on the Business Event-Result History pattern.

Figure 7.9 shows the Business Event-Result History pattern used in a model for the Jackson & Co. consulting firm in which the following business events occur:

Request for offer

Signing contract

Delivery

Signing skeleton contract

Partial account

Delivery on call

Each business event causes a different effect. A business event may cause an invoice to be sent (which in turn creates a debt), a contract to be written, an offer given, an acceptance of delivery, and possibly a product delivery. The delivery is of a product, which can be a Service, Hardware, or Software. The Services might be one of the following: Support, Consultancy, Training, or Installation. Usually, the contracts are between a buyer and a seller, though sometimes a broker is involved as well.

Let's say Jackson & Co. (a Party) receives a request for an offer (Request for Offer is a subclass to Business Event) from International Insurance (another

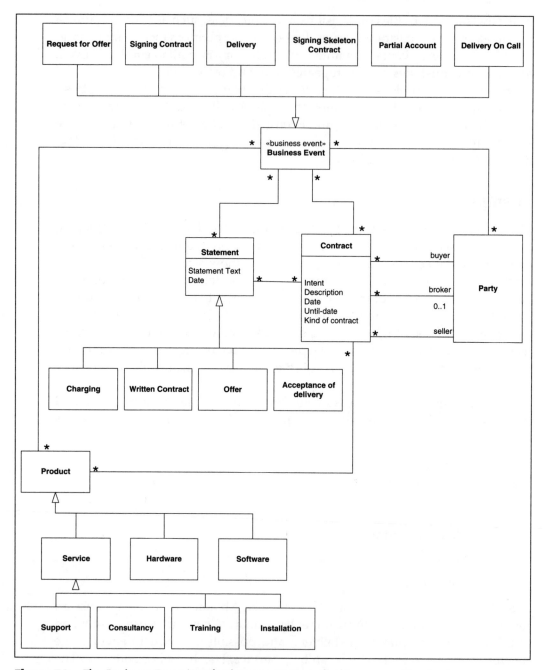

Figure 7.9   The Business Event-Result History pattern applied to a consulting business.

Party). This requests leads Jackson & Co. to send an Offer (Offer is a subclass to Statement) to International Insurance that is valid for two months. International Insurance accepts the offer and signs a written contract (Signing Contract is yet another Business Event), which leads to a Contract between the two parties. Jackson & Co. delivers a Product (Delivery is a Business Event) according to the contract, and the customer then signs an Acceptance of Delivery. You can describe all types of business events and the effect that the events cause, such as statements written or products delivered; in this case, the effect is the contract written between different parties (see Figure 7.9).

Related Patterns

The Contract pattern (described next) is used to model the contract element in the Business Event-Result History pattern. The Contract pattern replaces the Contract class in this pattern and models the Contract in a more elaborate manner.

The Business Event-Result History pattern can be combined with the Product Data Management pattern (described later in this chapter) to extend the functionality of the Product class in the Business Event-Result History pattern. For instance, if the product delivered is software, you might want to model the documents (such as manuals and installation guides) that are delivered with the software, and they are described with the Product Data Management pattern.

The Statement class in the Business Event-Result History pattern can be combined with the Document pattern to handle versions and copies of statements. If a statement occurs in several different languages, the Document pattern (also described in this chapter) can be used to model the different language versions of the document.

Source/Credit

Similar thoughts are expressed in the "Inventory and Accounting" chapter in *Analysis Patterns,* by Martin Fowler (Addison-Wesley, 1997).

Contract

Intent

The Contract pattern provides guidelines for modeling the important and very common concept of contracts.

Motivation

Contracts are core objects that are expressed and represented in some way, usually in written agreements. The contract connects one or more sellers with one or more buyers, both of which can be people, governments, or companies. The contract should also reference a mutual agreement, usually the acceptance of the rendering parameters of a product or service of some sort. Examples of products include a bank account, a car, or a boat; examples of services include consulting, legal, and accounting.

It is important to understand that the contract is not the same as its representation. The contract's representation can be a written or verbal agreement or an Internet application where a signature is not possible. As to the latter, be aware that banks and insurance companies have started to run into problems with electronic agreements. In the past, companies in these business arenas dealt with one kind of contract—written agreements with signatures—and existing support systems and business processes were designed to handle only this type of contract. Today, many people demand and expect Internet functionality, in lieu of or in addition to paper-based written agreements with signatures. Companies that don't provide these types of services will probably be out of business in a couple of years. That is why bank and insurance company systems modeled without separating the contract as a concept from its representation, such as written agreements and electronic signatures, need to be restructured to support a variety of representations. The point is, when contracts are modeled separately from their representation, it is easier to add new representations with less cost and a faster turnaround.

To create high-quality models in businesses that use contracts, it is essential to separate the agreement itself—the contract—from its representation, whether a written or verbal contract, an Internet site with fields for passwords and user names, or something else.

Applicability

The Contract pattern can be used in all businesses that utilize contracts to design flexible business and supporting systems. Banks, insurance companies, retailers, and e-commerce companies are just some examples of businesses that can benefit from this pattern.

Structure

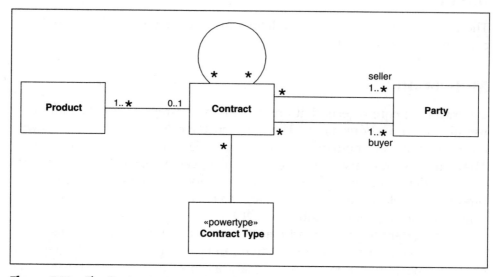

Figure 7.10 The Contract pattern structure.

Participants

Product is the item agreed upon and to which the contract refers. *Contract* is the agreement between one or more buyers and one or more sellers. The buyer and seller are the parties that participate in the deal. Typical contract attributes are description and date. *Contracts* can be related to each other. A *skeleton contract* is one type of contract that is usually related to other contracts. It defines the general terms for contracts between two companies. For instance, a company that purchases consulting services initially can write a skeleton contract containing general terms and agreements; then when hiring a specific consultant a smaller but more detailed contract can be written to include the terms specific to that hire.

Contract Type specifies the kind of contract. Skeleton and lease contracts are two examples of contract types. Different representations of *Contract* are not modeled here. Instead this can be done via the Core-Representation pattern (in which case, the *Contract* class presented here is equivalent to the Core class in that pattern).

Party class specifies a buyer or a seller that is a person, a government, society, club, or company. Common party attributes are name, address, telephone, fax, and other descriptions and identifiers.

Consequences

The Contract pattern facilitates the design of flexible business processes and support systems to handle changing contract terms and representations.

Example

Twenty years ago John Doe (Party1) bought a homeowner insurance policy (Product1) from the Alpha Insurance Company (Party2). The insurance contract (Contract1) was then renewed every year. Five years ago, John took out an additional insurance policy (Contract2) for life insurance (Product2). Three and a half year ago, John decided that the life insurance policy (Product2) should run six months at a time, so the contract for that (Contract2) was rewritten; the contract for the homeowner insurance (Contract1) was not changed and continued to run a year at a time.

Figure 7.11 is a model used by the Alpha Insurance Company implementing the Contract pattern. The model shows that a person (a party) can be a policyholder who has an insurance contract with an insurer (also a party). The insurance contract refers to the insurance itself (the product), which could be car insurance, life insurance, or homeowner's comprehensive coverage. The Insurance contract can be expressed in an insurance policy.

Had Alpha not used this model, it would not be possible to handle the different insurance policies independently. The company would have to rewrite the contract entirely if a change in just one of the policies occurred.

To continue with John Doe: Two years ago, he decided to start doing all of his business on the Internet. In terms of his insurance coverage, this was not a problem because the Alpha Insurance Company had separated its contracts from their representations (using the Core-Representation pattern), meaning that an insurance contract could as easily appear on the Web as on paper.

Related Patterns

The Contract pattern is used to model the Contract element in the Business Event-Result History pattern. We described how to use these patterns together under the Related Patterns section for the Business Event-Result History pattern.

The Product Data Management pattern can be used to extend the concept of a product specified in the Contract pattern, for example, if there are different documents attached to the product to which the contract pertains. The Product class in the Contract pattern and in the Product-Data Management pattern becomes the same class; the Contract pattern describes the modeling of contracts, while the Product Data Management pattern handles the documents attached to the product.

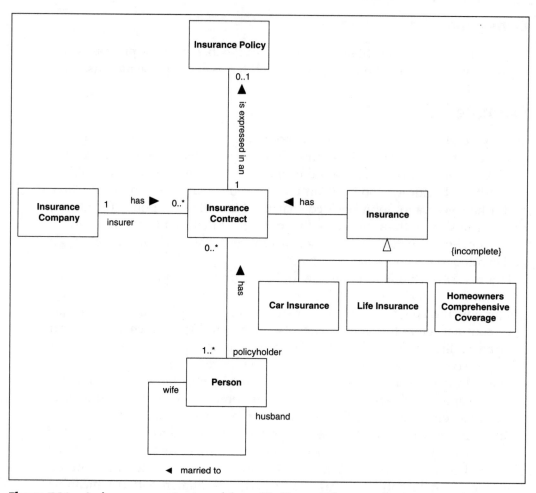

Figure 7.11   An insurance contract model specified in accordance to the Contract pattern.

The Core-Representation pattern, described next, can be combined with the Contract pattern to express the representation of the contract; for example, to shown the same contract on a Web page, in a written document, and so on.

Source/Credit

Contract patterns are covered in the "Derivative Contracts" chapter in *Analysis Patterns* by Martin Fowler (Addison-Wesley, 1997).

Intent

The Core-Representation pattern structures the essentials in a problem domain with the purpose of building well-structured and easily changeable models. The core objects of a business, such as debt, agreement, customer, product, delivery, and order, are objects that rarely change fundamentally; conversely, the representations of these objects often change or are extended. A modeler should take this into consideration and separate the core objects from their representations. This process is aided by the Core-Representation pattern.

Motivation

Core objects are items of importance, and are portrayed by representations. All businesses have both core objects and different representations for these core objects. Common examples of core-representation pairs are:

- Debt – Invoice
- Insurance contract – Insurance policy
- Business Object – GUI
- Country – Country code

To demonstrate the types of problems that can occur when a core object is not separated from its representation, we'll consider the common business concept of an invoice. Modeling an invoice as one single entity typically leads to several problems. The first is that invoices are normally written and printed on paper, although more often now, companies are using other media to transmit their invoices, such as via the Internet. A paper-based invoice and a Web-based invoice do not have equivalent properties, but the debt that they represent has the same properties, regardless of the representation. If the invoices are separated from the debt that they account for, it is much easier to add, remove, or change the different ways of settling the debts as well as changing their representation. A number of companies that want to implement e-commerce solutions can't currently because their billing systems do not allow for it. These systems are structured based on business rules that involve credit invoices, that is, written orders with signatures. These rules make it hard or impossible to introduce new types of invoices such as electronic invoices and orders with digital signatures. If, however, these systems had been based on models that separated the concept of Debt (the Core concept) from different representations of that debt such as different types of Invoices, this would not have been a problem.

A second problem that can be solved by separating a core object from its representation is that one or more invoices can replace one or many other invoices, whether the debt has actually changed or not. This can happen when invoices are consolidated for a company.

Invoices, obviously, are just one example of a representation of a common core business concept—debt. In fact, it is the debts themselves that are the important business concept; the invoices are a medium used to request payment and so are of no real importance.

Applicability

The Core-Representation pattern can be used in all situations where one or more representations occur of the core objects in the business, and when new or altered representations are expected in the future. Typically, contracts, orders, deliveries, or products are involved.

Structure

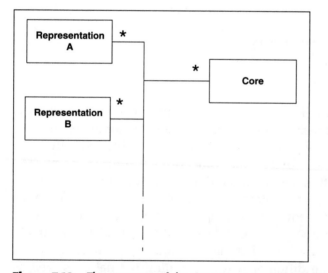

Figure 7.12 The structure of the Core-Representation pattern.

Participants

Representation is a class that expresses an aspect of the core object. One business object representation within an information system might be a GUI object, such as a window or a graph. Another possible representation for a business object within an information system might be a mechanical item such as a robot.

Core class is an object of importance within the business, such as debt, position, or contract.

Consequences

Models that use the Core-Representation pattern can handle changes in the representation without redefining the core object. It is also possible to add new representations at a later date without affecting the definition of the core.

This pattern helps modelers create adaptable systems, in which the structure can easily be altered to work in new situations. An adaptable system is less expensive to maintain.

Example

Mac's Foodstore has a number of checkout counters with cash registers, all of which are connected to the store's computer system. The receipt that is printed from these cash registers for each customer contains sales slip strings, where each article has a specific sales slip string with the article's price, name, and so on. Note though that the names that appear are specific for sales slips because there is very limited space (for example, "6-p Coke"). Each article also has a specific order code that is used when Mac makes gross purchases.

Not too long ago, Mac's customers made it clear to him that they wanted to be able to use the Web to order deliveries from the store. This meant Mac had to meet special requirements, since customers could not browse the actual store aisles or review the sales slip strings or order codes; they needed more information, both in terms of figures and descriptive text describing the articles.

The Web system also generated another significant difference: When a customer shops in an actual store, he or she has all the articles in hand before paying; shopping via the Web, that same customer would not, for example, be able to see that a particular item was sold out. And because Mac doesn't want dissatisfied customers, he had to be able make alternative articles available as substitutes, for the same price. Mac was able to institute this new Web capability easily, because his systems had kept separate the Article (Core) from Article Representation (Representation). Thus it was possible to add full name, description, picture, of a suggested substitute for a given item. Had this not been the case, the quality of Mac's Web shopping system would have been inferior and frustrating to the shopper; or it would have required a total redesign of the existing system. Figure 7.13 shows Mac's model, wherein Article and Article Representation are separated.

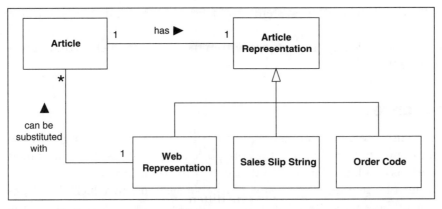

Figure 7.13   An example in which the Core-Representation pattern is used to separate Article from Article Representation.

Related Patterns

Core-Representation can be combined with the Contract pattern to represent the Contract. Thus the Contract pattern can be seen as a specialization of the Core-Representation pattern. An example of this was included with the Contract pattern discussed in the preceding section.

Source/Credit

This technique has been widely known since the sixties, when it was used to implement systems that handle concepts represented or presented in several different ways. This pattern is also apparent in user-interface frameworks, such as the well-known Model-View-Control architecture.

Document

Intent

Documents are used in all businesses, and they can cause a lot of confusion for modelers. One common problem is when a copy is made of a document. This raises the question: Is the copy another document, the same document, or a "copy document" linked to the original document? Also, a document might exist in several different versions; the basic content and purpose of the document may be the same but the details are different.

When information systems are used to handle documents, other problems can raise additional questions, such as: If I copy my Word file, does it become two documents? If so, which is considered the original? What happens if I switch the names on them; which then is the original and why? The intent of the Document pattern is to provide a practical way to approach the issues inherent in the modeling of documents, including different versions and copies of documents.

Motivation

Our previous book, *UML Toolkit*, is a document. A document always has one or more authors (who in turn can also be authors of other documents). This reasoning is illustrated in a class diagram shown in Figure 7.14. The document (in this case, *UML Toolkit*) can exist in many copies around the world and in several versions, such as in English, Dutch, Japanese, and Finnish. All of these versions are related in that they contain the text of the *UML Toolkit* (they are all versions of one and the same document). Each copy of this document has been distributed in a geographical place in the world; there are, for example, several copies of the English version of *UML Toolkit* in Sweden and there are many copies of the Japanese version in Japan.

Since the invention and subsequent widespread use of such media as copy machines, computers, and the Internet, the definition of the term document has changed—really, expanded—from something written or printed to also include things such as audio and video. This raises the question what happens when it is impossible to distinguish the original document from its copies? To answer the question, it is necessary to separate the concept document from the representation copies. By using the term document for the concept, and copy for its representations, the confusion disappears. But that's not the end of it: The copies can have further designations, such as the first copy and the signed copy. Furthermore, documents exist as physical copies, and all copies have a location, such as a directory in a computer's hard drive, a postal address, or

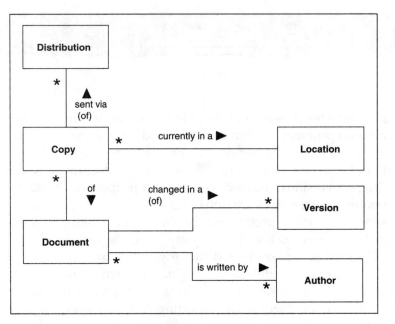

Figure 7.14   A simple model for handling documents and copies in many versions.

just a geographical position. And a document's copies can distributed from one location to another via e-mail, an intranet, the Internet, or by so-called snailmail.

Applicability

E-mail systems, libraries, configuration management (CM) tools, and product-data management systems (PDM) are all problem domains where the Document pattern can be useful. In fact, though, because documents are used in all businesses, this pattern can serve as a starting point and either simplified or extended as necessary to fit the situation.

Structure

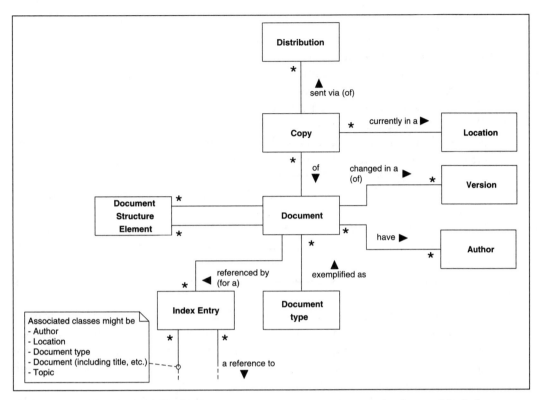

Figure 7.15   The structure for the Document pattern. It captures motivation, and includes index, document type, and document structure elements.

Participants

Document is a class who defines to the concept of a Document, not the physical documents (i.e., copies). The Document class has attributes such as title and ISBN. You could model Document with the attribute author, but if an author has written several documents, Author should become a class of its own, because UML and most object-oriented modeling language do not support reverse multiplicity on attributes (the multiplicity on the opposite end of an association).

Author represents the generator/creator of a document. There can be several authors for one document or one author for several documents. Common attributes are name and age.

Copy represents the physical items, such as all the printed copies of a book. One document might exist in several copies.

Location is where a copy exists (an instance of the Copy class). The Location class is used to structure information about copies from a user's point of view. If the location is an Internet site, for example, the attribute would be a URL.

Version. A document can be an amendment to another document or can exist in several formats or in several languages. It is a matter of debate whether a document containing the same information but published in a different format, language, or medium is a different version of the same document or is a different document entirely. In the Document pattern, documents that contain identical content are considered different versions of the same document. Documents that contain variations in the contents, such as amendments or edits, are considered different documents; in this case, the documents are connected through the objects of the Document Structure Element class. The Version class is used to show that one document exists in several versions but with identical content.

Document Structure Element is a class that describes the objects used to connect documents to each other. The connections can be versions, such as amendments, or collections of documents.

Document Type specifies the type of a document. Typical instances are book and report.

Index Entry is a class used to index documents. A document can be indexed on version, document type, or author, for example. Each index entry is a reference to one or several objects, such as author, title, or topic, and is an index for just one document. The index is a strategy for identifying documents through a set of information associated with the document.

Distribution is a class that represents the distribution of a copy. A copy can be distributed several times, each time to a separate location. The distribution can be via electronic mail, an intranet, or the Internet, or via a more conventional method such as a ground delivery service. Typical attributes are sender, recipient, and method of distribution.

Consequences

The advantage of using the Document pattern is that it helps you to understand and structure documents in an organized way. There are, however, two drawbacks. The first is that you must determine how to decide when something is a new version of a document or an entirely new document. The Document pattern as such does not solve this problem. The second drawback is that, in many cases, Index Entry is connected to all other classes in the model, which does complicate the model.

Example

Figure 7.16 illustrates how to use the Document pattern to model a bookstore. Here, the Document class represents the different book titles in the bookstore. The Copy class represents the physical items placed at certain locations in the bookstore. The copy locations are modeled with the Location class. The Author class represents the document's author, and the Document Type class is used to classify the books in the store. Examples of classifications are mystery and science fiction. The Distribution class is used to handle and document different kinds of distributions, such as snailmail, e-mail, or an overnight

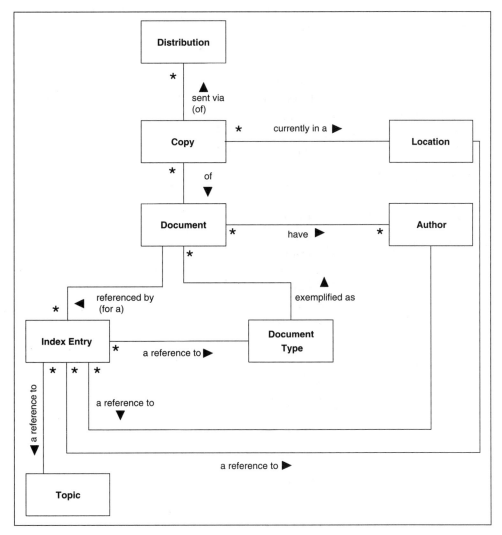

Figure 7.16 An example using Document pattern.

delivery service such as Federal Express. The Topic class represents different subjects to which an index entry can be connected, such as travel, automobiles, environment, and healthcare.

As an example, let's take the book titled *The Cuckoo's Egg: Tracking a Spy through the Maze of Computer Espionage,* authored by Clifford Stoll; its type is nonfiction. The topic of the document is computer security. It exists in 54 copies at the A+ Computer Bookstore. These copies have been distributed to the store via Federal Express.

Related Patterns

The Document pattern can extend the Product Data Management pattern by replacing the latter's definition of the Document class with that in the Document pattern. For instance, if the different Office software packages from Microsoft were organized with the PDM pattern, one product would be Word 97 and another document would be the English user manual. The Document pattern comes into the picture because several translations (versions) of the Word 97 manual exist.

The Geographic Location pattern (described later in this chapter) can be combined with the Document pattern to specify the location of a document's copy in more detail. This can be done by replacing the Party class in the Geographical Location pattern with the Document class from the Document pattern.

Source/Credit

This pattern was inspired by the document patterns found in *Data Model Patterns: Conventions of Thought* by David C. Hay (Dorset House, 1996).

Employment

Intent

Employment is a contract between a person (employee) and an organization that indicates factors such as assigned responsibilities, contract of employment, and start and end dates. The Employment pattern breaks down and then organizes these underlying concepts with the purpose of describing and representing that information to handle both present and future forms of employment.

Motivation

Suppose that John Samuels is employed at XYZ Corporation. His employment has start and end dates, and the parameters of the employment are expressed in a contract of employment that includes work instructions. If he's still employed, the end date is not used.

If the Employment relationship is expressed only as an association between a person object, in this case John Samuels, and an organization object, in this case XYZ Corporation, you cannot indicate additional information such as start and end dates, work instructions, or contract of employment, because none of this information is relevant to either a Person class or a Organization class; it is information attached to the relationship between a Person and a Organization. The solution is to consider employment as a concept that connects the person and the organization, and model employment as a class. Employment is an obviously important concept to an organization, and to model employment as a separate class allows for additional links to other concepts, such as start and end dates, contracts, and work instructions.

Figure 7.17 shows how employment can be modeled. Here, the Employment class has the attributes start and end dates; of course, more attributes could be added. The Employment class associates a class with work instructions and an organization. The terms of employment are expressed in a contract. By modeling employment in this manner, you avoid the problems that might occur if it had been modeled only via an association between a person and an organization. One problem occurs because it is impossible to attach work instructions to employment; instead, these instructions must be associated with either the person or the organization. If one person does two jobs for the same organization, it's impossible to separate which work instructions go with which job. Another problem would be if the person changes jobs within the organization and another person takes over the first person's previous job. Such as situation can be dealt with more easily when employment is handled as a separate class.

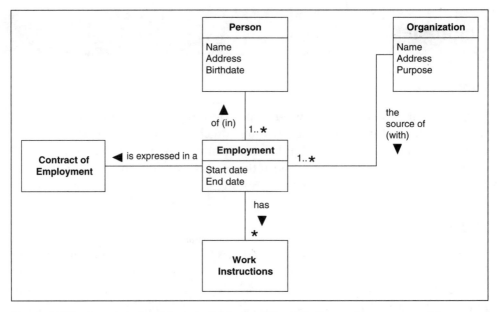

Figure 7.17   An example of how individuals with attributes such as name, address, and birthdate can have more than one job in the same organization, where the employment is expressed in an employment contract and includes work instructions.

Applicability

The Employment pattern lays the foundation for all information about the forms of employment within an organization in a flexible and high-quality model. The Employment pattern can be implemented to clarify the employment structures within an organization, or to build an information system that organizes information about employment and its structure. Enterprise resource planning (ERP) systems, such as SAP R/3 and Movex, are typical candidates for this pattern since they are often used to administer and organize information about employment, work instructions, contracts, and so on.

Structure

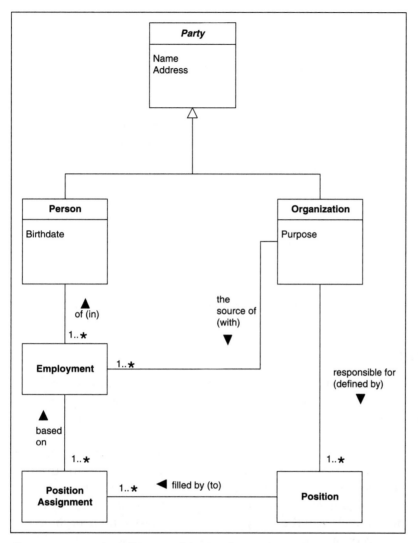

Figure 7.18   A class diagram of the Employment pattern structure.

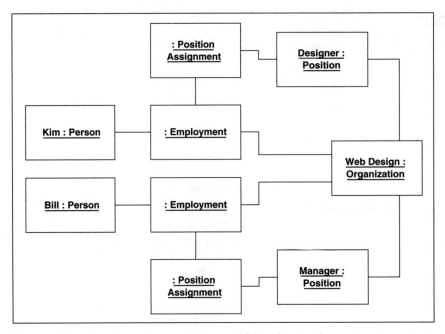

Figure 7.19 An object diagram that exemplifies the Employment pattern structure.

Participants

Party is the abstract class that describes both persons and organizations. It can be extended with general attributes such as name and address. The purpose of Party is to describe the properties that persons and organizations have in common.

Organization is a subclass of the Party class. The organization is an artifact, meaning it is created by people. The purpose of an organization is to structure the resources (including people) within a business. Suborganizations are not shown because the organization structures are not described in this pattern.

Person is another subclass of the Party class. Persons are human, organic systems, as opposed to organizations and suborganizations, which are artificial systems. Persons are also *active* systems, meaning that they can act of their own accord.

Employment is the relationship between the Person and Organization. Employment is its own class, and can have several attributes, such as start date, end date, and employment type.

Position is held by a Person and is typically defined by one Organization (but it can be more than one) and has attributes such as salary and work instructions. A position is held by more than one person over time; similarly, a person can also have more than one position at a time.

Position Assignment specifies the relationship between Person and Position, including the start and end dates.

Consequences

The Employment pattern structures the relationship between a person and his or her employer. By defining specific classes for the Employment, Position, and Position Assignments, it is possible to model attributes that are not appropriate to attach to the Person or the Organization between which the employment is contracted. Work instructions can be defined in the Employment class; a person can have two different jobs for the same organization; different persons within the company can switch positions with each other; and so on. Adding new concepts to employment or defining new rules for administrating employment also becomes much easier using the Employment pattern.

Example

The Big Burger restaurant is an Organization divided into the parent company, Big Burger, and its subsidiaries, Big West, Big East, and Big City, which are located in different parts of town. Each subsidiary is divided into three departments: Cashier, Lobby, and Grill. Management is planning to change the organization, but they have not yet decided on the new structure.

A total of 150 people are employed at Big Burger; 50 are employed at Big East. At Big East, there are three managerial positions (Position) and a manager assigned (Position Assignment) for each department—Cashier, Lobby, and Grill. There are also a number of employees in the three departments; each has a position (Position) with pay grade and work instructions. Each Position is filled by a Position Assignment that is based on Employment. All employees have a contract of Employment.

Bill, for example, has been employed for five years, and has only one Employment but several different Positions. At first, Bill was a cashier assistant in the Cashier department, then he was manager of that department, now he is the top manager for Big East.

Figure 7.20 illustrates what a model for Big Burger's employments might look like, based on the Employment pattern. Note that the Organization is divided into Parent Company, Subsidiary, and Department, and that the model allows for more subsidiaries and departments than are currently part of the makeup of Big Burger. It is always important to produce models that are flexible, that allow for future changes; models should not just show a current structure. In the case of Big Burger, the planned restructuring might lead to new subsidiaries and additional departments. The model is designed to accommodate that, as well as new positions, new people, and new jobs.

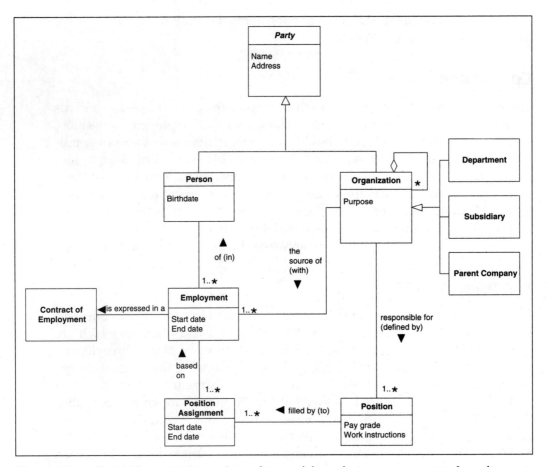

Figure 7.20 The Employment pattern is used to model employment, a contract of employment, and position.

Related Patterns

The Employment pattern can be combined with the Organization and Party pattern, described shortly, in which case the definition of the Party class in the Employment pattern would be replaced with the definition of the Organizational Unit class in the Organization and Party pattern, to express how parties are built up and where employment fits in.

Source/Credit

The Employment pattern is described in *Data Model Patterns: Conventions of Thought*, by David C. Hay (Dorset House, 1996).

Geographic Location

Intent

The intent of the Geographic Location pattern is to prevent the modeling of addresses or locations using formats that may become obsolete in a short period of time.

Motivation

An address is one of the most vital components in all businesses. Despite its importance, it is usually very poorly modeled. The purpose of the Geographic Location pattern is to define the concept of an address. But before delving into that, it's important to understand the problems involved with addresses. Address has historically been interpreted as defining a specific physical, geographic location. Consider the definition of address used by the post office: An address specifies a house or building number, a street name, a city and state, a zip code, and a country name and code, if necessary, where the mail should be delivered.

However, the emergence of the Internet has changed the traditional interpretation of the concept of an address. An Internet address does not contain the information just described as used by the post office; at most, it contains the country where the recipient resides. Looking at an Internet address then does not give any indication where the owner lives; it is a logical address that at some point is translated into a physical address. Consequently, it is also impossible to produce statistics from a set of Internet addresses, as you could from a traditional customer list, to determine where customers reside or to do other common computerized tracking tasks. As a result of the widespread use of the Internet, most postal systems worldwide have been reevaluating their definition of address, and have renovated, or, more precisely, tried to renovate, old systems.

The problem caused by assuming that an address refers to a specific geographic location is not new. Consider a sailor on a ship that's out to sea. We'll delve into this example in more detail shortly. But first, let's look closer at the definition of an address.

One way to approach the task of defining address is to split it into site and geographic location. Most addresses have a geographical reference, either explicitly stated—such as United States—or implicitly stated, as in international Internet addresses, which end with the country code such as .se or .uk. Addresses can also contain a logical part (a site); the site can be an apartment number or a street number. An address always refers to the specific location of a party: a person, a company, a department, or a government.

It is not always obvious which part of an address is the geographic location and which part is the site, but a number of cases clearly demonstrate this split. Let's get back to our sailor at sea. We'll assume his girlfriend wants to address a letter to him. She cannot specify the exact geographic location or coordinates of the ship, which are subject to change as the ship moves. Instead, she specifies a site—the name of the sailor, the ship, and the shipping company. The sailor in this case is the party placed at a site, (ship X at shipping company Y), which has a reference to a geographic location (normally the geographic location of the shipping company's headquarters). Using a site and geographical location is much more effective than referring to the exact geographic location of the ship, which is constantly changing while at sea.

A *placement* with an effective start and end date is used to represent a unique position within a *site*. A site is a logical (not physical) location of the *party*, used to organize placements of parties. *Geographic locations*, physical references, are hierarchical, and point to some site where the party is located. When a party's address is just a geographic location, the site is used as a direct reference to the placement of the party in that geographic location. These concepts and their relationships are modeled in Figure 7.21. The Geographic Location pattern

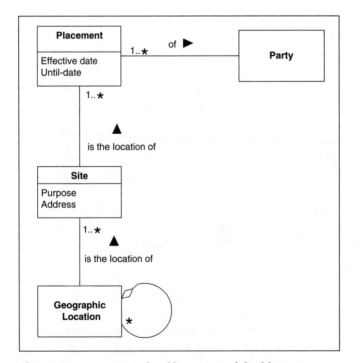

Figure 7.21   An example of how to model addresses.

allows for different formats, logical or physical, to be used in defining addresses; it also enables the translation between different formats. Therefore, if the format of an address becomes obsolete, models and systems based on this pattern can accommodate that change.

Applicability

The Geographic Location pattern can be used whenever you need to model an address. Examples of problem domains are mail-order companies, the post office, shipping agencies, and accounts receivable departments.

Structure

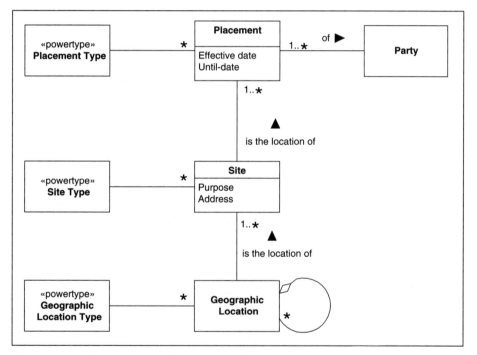

Figure 7.22   The structure of the Geographic Location pattern.

Participants

Party is the class that describes the entity with a location. *Party* can be a person, a governments, or a company.

   Geographic Location is the geographical position of a Party. The geographical position can be a country, a city, a street, or anything that has a geographical connection of some sort. A common attribute is name. Geographical locations are built as hierarchies. For example, the geographical location Los Angeles is located in California, which is located in the larger country of the USA.

Geographic Location Type indicates a specific type of geographic location. A geographic location type can be a country (an instance of the Geographic Location Type class), such as United States (an instance of the Geographical Location class connected to the instance "country," which is an instance of the Geographical Location Type class). Geographic location types can also be cities, streets, or states.

Site is a logical concept, rather than a geographic location or physical concept. A site is a delimitation. A Web page, a telephone area code, or a department within a company are all examples of sites. The Site class describes the sites. Typical attributes are purpose and address (the address is a text string).

Site Type specifies the type of an instance of the Site class, such as file location or Web page.

Placement represents a unique position within a Site. Each Party may be subject to one or more Placements at a Site; for instance, a telephone number within a specific area code or a position of an employee in a department. Typical attributes are effective start and end dates. Placement type describes the kinds of placements, such as within a Web site specifying, for example, the "first page" or "upper right corner" or an organizational designation.

Consequences

The Geographic Location pattern precludes the use of fixed structures that don't allow for changes in the format structure of an address or for new types of address definitions. The structure involves new site types, placements, and geographic locations. Many post offices made the mistake of building systems based on a fixed structure of addresses that wasn't valid even at the time (recall the sailor example). In the object-oriented world, an address is often modeled with just an address string attribute with no well-defined structure of its contents, which often leads to problems.

Example

This example shows how two different types of addresses, an Internet address and a postal address, can be represented with the Geographic Location pattern. Using the same pattern to represent both demonstrates that a system based on this pattern can handle the translation from one address format to the other.

Internet mailing addresses can be divided into geographical location, site, and placement. The Internet address

bob.smith@ibm.uk

has the Geographical Location United Kingdom, the Site IBM, and the Placement of the person, Bob Smith (Party).

An example of a postal address is:

John Wiley & Sons, Inc.
605 Third Avenue
New York, NY 10158-0012
USA

In this address, John Wiley & Sons, Inc., is the Party that is placed at the address 605 Third Avenue, New York, NY, 10158-0012, USA. The address can be interpreted as a Site, with the address text "605 Third Avenue"; and the Geographic Location zip code 10158-0012, which is a part of the geographic Location City, New York, which is a part of the Geographic Location State, NY.

In practice, most addresses are put into Geographic Location with the most detailed elements (street, apartment number, Social Security number, and so on) defined in Site.

Related Patterns

The Geographic Location pattern can be combined with all patterns that require addresses or locations to be modeled.

Source/Credit

The Geographic Location pattern is based on a pattern of the same name presented by David C. Hay in his book *Data Model Patterns: Conventions of Thought* (Dorset House, 1996) to split addresses into placement, site, and geographic location.

The Geographic Location pattern is similar to the Place pattern by Scott Ambler in his book *Building Object Applications that Work* (Cambridge University Press/SIGS Books, 1998).

Organization and Party

Intent

The Organization and Party pattern is used to create flexible and qualitative organizational charts in object-oriented models.

Motivation

Companies are structured in order to better control their management. A company can, for instance, consist of a parent company, three subsidiaries, and one to six departments within each subsidiary. By dividing a company into smaller units and spreading the responsibility for specific activities to various units, it is easier to manage production.

Organizational structures are rarely static, however; they change as needed to adapt to market shifts or to become more effective.

If the organizational model for a company consists only of a class for a company, such as J&S Company, and a department, say Manufacturing, it will be difficult to describe the parent company and its subsidiaries because neither was specified in the model's original organizational structure. Even if other kinds of organizational units are later introduced, there will always be units or possibilities that are not covered by the model. Figure 7.23 models a consortium that consists of many parent companies and subsidiaries (subsidiary is a specialization to a parent company). The figure also shows that a subsidiary consists of many departments and that the departments consist of many teams. Not covered by this model is the concept of an organizational unit such as government or virtual company.

One of the points of this discussion is that it's hard to model all types of organizational units in advance, particularly today when there are many new types of organizations that are not hierarchical in nature; for example, process organizations based only on processes used by subsidiaries to General Motors or matrix organizations used by the telecommunications company Ericsson.

That said, note that there is an effective and flexible way to include the functionality that enables adding or removing new kinds of organizational units such as department, consortium, parent company, and so on, and at the same time organize and combine the different kinds of units to fit various problem domains. The solution is to add an organization *type,* which we describe in the next sections.

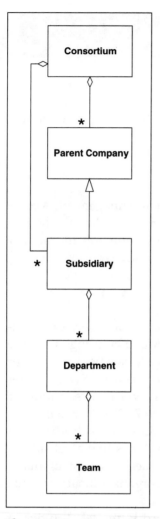

Figure 7.23 An example of an organization.

Applicability

The Organization and Party pattern can be used to model all organizational structures, as far as we know. It is particularly powerful for organizations that change regularly over time or where many different kinds of organizations must be captured in the same model or system.

Structure/Description

There are two structures for this pattern: basic and extended. The basic structure is used to model hierarchical organizations. The extended structure is used to model more complex structures (network structures) that include organizations comprising teams that span departments, divisions, or virtual companies.

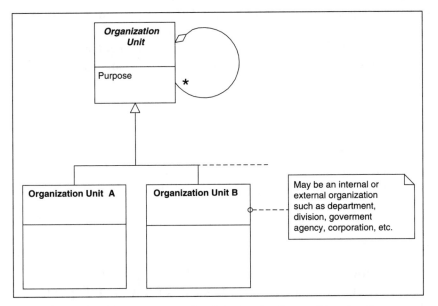

Figure 7.24   The basic structure for the Organization and Party pattern.

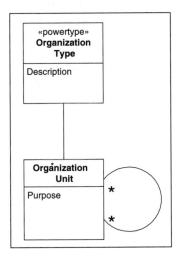

Figure 7.25   The extended structure for the Organization and Party pattern.

Participants

Organization Type is a class whose instances are different kinds of organizations, such as process organizations, matrix organizations, hierarchical organizations, parent companies, subsidiaries, departments, teams, projects, or groups. A typical attribute is a description of the organization type, such as assignment of responsibilities and ways of control.

Organization Unit is a class whose instances are the units of some type, such as parent company, subsidiary, or department. A typical attribute is unit purpose, such as trying to get a specific market share within a region.

Organization Type and Organization Unit could be substituted with Party Type and Party to model parties with this pattern (typical parties are people, society, government, and company).

Consequences

Organizational models produced using the Organization and Party pattern are built upon a solid foundation that allows for changes in the organization over time without causing structural problems or alterations to the original model or system.

Example

Let's take a look at how C&A is organized (modeled in Figure 7.26). Note that this figure is an object diagram that is an instance of the class diagram that describes the Organization and Party pattern in the Structure section. The object diagram demonstrates the use of the pattern. C&A has a board composed of the president and other shareholders; the company is divided into seven departments, and one of them, the Sales Department, consists of two additional departments: Telesales and Web Sales. C&A also includes the following organization units:

- The Financial Department is responsible for the firm's finances, including credit references, credit card checks, and accounts receivable.

- The Production Department produces items, either by assembling those they manufacture or by relabeling those purchased from subcontractors.

- The Purchase Department is responsible for buying outside products and developing subcontractor relationships.

- The System Department is responsible for the technical infrastructure and information technology of the business. It comprises systems analysts, programmers, systems architects, operators, and support staff.

- The Sales Department, divided into Telesales and Web Sales, is responsible for selling products.

- The Product Department develops new products and product sets.

- The Marketing Department is responsible for implementing the marketing plan.

By using the Organization and Party pattern, C&A can easily add, change, or remove organization units when necessary. Typical applications based on C&A's organization are time reporting systems, wager systems, sales systems, and order systems. If C&A had chosen to model its organization with a more static class diagram, which only allowed for certain types of departments, it would not be possible to later alter the units in these applications. It would also be expensive to adapt these applications in case of such a change.

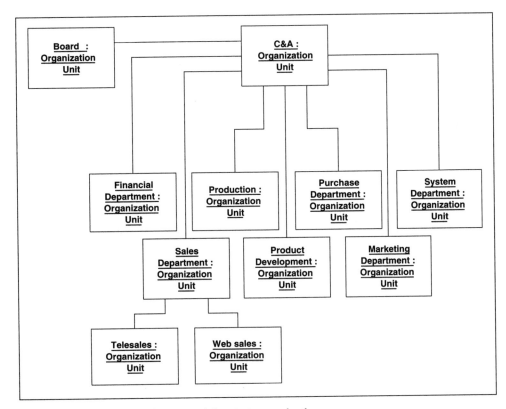

Figure 7.26 An object diagram of the C&A organization.

Related Patterns

The Organization and Party pattern has similarities to the Product Data Management pattern, and it can be extended in that direction, which would imply classes named Organization Connection, Assignment, Contract, and others similar, which would specify the connections between the different organization units. Furthermore, it is possible to add rules for how organization types can be combined, just as with PDM.

The Employment pattern can be combined with the Organization and Party pattern, in which case, the definition of the Party class in the Employment Pattern would be replaced with the definition of the Organization Unit class in the Organization and Party pattern to express how parties are built and where employment fits in.

Source/Credit

The Organization and Party pattern is described in *Analysis Patterns: Reusable Object Models,* by Martin Fowler (Addison-Wesley, 1996).

Product Data Management (PDM)

Intent

All businesses have many products and/or documents that must be organized and structured. Capturing the structure of the relationship between documents and products is a difficult but common problem in all businesses. The Product Data Management (PDM) pattern is used for that purpose.

Motivation

Let's take for an example the production of computer-aided software engineering (CASE) tools—program tools that support the development of software systems. If a business produces several CASE tools, it is necessary to organize the following:

- *Different kinds (types) of CASE tools, such as requirement CASE tools, analysis and design CASE tools, and business modeling CASE tools.* Each kind of CASE tool has its own description and pertinent data.

- *All of the actual CASE tools—a UML tool, UML Enterprise, Business Modeler, BPR++, and so on.* These are different tools, or products, of the tool type CASE tool.

- *The data about the different CASE tools.* Data can be manuals, analysis specifications, architecture, and source code.

In addition, it is also necessary to model how these classes (product type, document, etc.) are related to each other. An example of a relationship is a CASE tool developed in many versions, all of which must be compatible with each other.

All documents have a document type. The document "UML Tool Manual" has the document type manual, and the document "UML Tools Requirement Specification" has the document type requirement specification. Similarly, all products have a product type. The product UML tool is an example of a CASE tool, where the CASE tool is a product type.

Product types are related to document types. For example, all CASE tools must have a requirement specification, analysis document, and manual. Moreover, products are related to documents; for example, the Rational Rose CASE tool is linked with the Rational Rose manual. Document types can also be related to each other. For example, all analysis specifications should be made within the context of a specific requirements specification. Documents can be connected to each other in the same way as document types. This structure also applies to products, which can be related to each other as well. For example, the CASE tool product UML Enterprise consists of executable code, manuals, packing, and free support, all of which can be considered as products of some kind. Figure 7.27 shows a simple model of document types, documents, product types, products, and their relationships.

Structuring different things in an enterprise in this manner enables the handling of these things and thing types, and the relationships between them without maintenance problems—a big advantage. The structure is stable and adjustable, allowing for the addition or removal of new types of things during the business life cycle.

When implementing an information system that supports the business during its life cycle, it is very important that the system be dynamic, and allow for additions, removals, or changes to concepts to accommodate the business it supports. Fixed structures without this capability cause problems when the business changes and new requirements are introduced. The PDM pattern makes a dynamic system possible, and the code of the information system does not have to be changed; therefore, new products or product types can be added dynamically.

NOTE You probably noticed the similarities between this pattern and the Organization and Party pattern. The difference is that they are used in different contexts. PDM is used to model products and documents; the Organization and Party pattern is used to model organizations.

Applicability

Product data structures are used in most businesses to organize different items, documents, and products, but the reasons for structuring and organizing resources vary from one business to another. One common reason is to support planning, manufacturing, or sales. A typical situation in which the PDM pattern can be used is one in which resources have to be handled, structured, and organized without prior knowledge about all the possible kinds of resources. The PDM pattern makes it possible to avoid static system implementations where all the concepts are programmed once, without flexibility allowing for change.

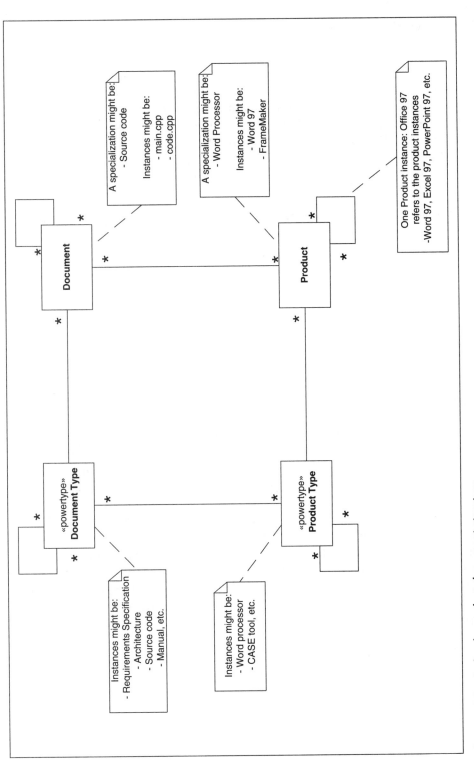

Figure 7.27   A simple product document structure.

Structure/Description

Figure 7.28, a generalization of Figure 7.27, shows the general PDM structure which may be applied to problem domains, in addition to products and documents; for example, to handle the organization of business rules, assets, knowledge, or information. The Resource class is the generalization of the Product and Document classes shown in Figure 7.27. Resource type is the generalization of Product and Document types in Figure 7.27.

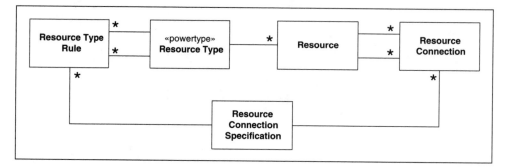

Figure 7.28   The general structure of the Product Data Management pattern.

Participants

Resource class captures and describes the resources used in the enterprise. The resources can be products, services, or documents. Examples of the Resource class are "my document," "your bike," "item #567." The Resource class can have attributes such as name, purpose, ID or serial number, and age.

Resource Type is used to define the type of resources. Examples are product and document. The Resource Type is a powertype to the class Resource, meaning that instances of the Resource Type class are subclasses to the Resource class. For example, an instance of the Resource Type class can be document, and an instance of the Resource class can be the document LTB-823v6, where LTB-823v6 is an instance of the document. The Resource Type can have attributes that contain knowledge about the corresponding resources. Resource types can have attributes such as a unit of measurement (gallon, inch, kilo, and so on).

Resource Connection Specification states and describes the allowed resource connections. It is connected to one or more resource type rules that act as the basis for defining the Resource Connection Specification. An object of the Resource Connection Specification class specifies which object of the Resource Type Rule class a specific Resource Connection object reflects. It combines a specific connection between resources and the rule that specifies that such a connection is possible and allowed. An object of the Resource Type Rule class describes how objects of the Resource Type class can be related, and thereby how resources of one type can be connected to resources of another type.

Resource Connection is the class that captures connections between actual resource instances. It is referenced in the Resource Connection Specification class. The *Resource Connection Specification* makes it possible to specify and describe the connection between two resources, that is, between two actual resource instances. A Resource Connection object must adhere to the rules specified by the Resource Type Rule objects.

Consequences

The advantage of using the PDM pattern is that you can always handle new types of resources and new types of rules in a flexible and dynamic way. The disadvantage of this powerful pattern is that is does make implementation in a programming language somewhat more complicated than simply defining each resource as its own class.

There are three ways to implement this pattern:

- *Instance new classes in run-time, which requires the support of meta-classes in the programming language.* The new classes are the objects of the Resource Type class or the Resource Type rule, which are both meta-classes whose instances in turn are classes. Not all languages support meta-classes (classes whose instances also are classes).

- *Instance a type class to an object, where that object represents a type (class).* This is the method shown in Figure 7.28.

- *Prohibit the instantiation of new types during run-time; instead define all resource types statically as subclasses to the Resource class.* This means that new resource types cannot be added during run-time. Though this will simplify the programming, it is a poor, and the least flexible, solution, and does not use the full power of the PDM pattern.

Example

The PDM pattern can be specialized to handle products and documents, as shown in Figure 7.29 where all the relations have also been inherited. The Document Type rule, Document Type–Product Type rule, and the Product Type rule are all specializations of the Resource Type rule. The same circumstances are valid for the Resource connection, which is also specialized. Finally, the Document Connection Specification, the Document-Product Connection Specification, and the Product Connection Specification are specializations of the Resource Connection Specification.

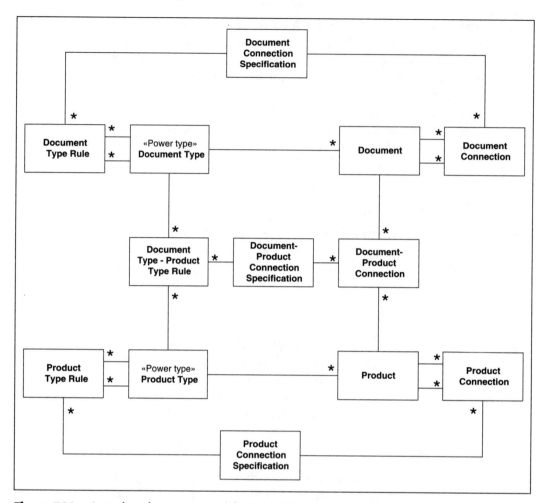

Figure 7.29   A product-document specialization of the generic PDM pattern.

Complex models like the one shown in Figure 7.29 can be more easily understood by using one or more object diagrams that illustrate the use and benefit of the model in the class diagram. Figures 7.30 and 7.31 show two possible object diagrams that do this.

Figure 7.30 shows the object structure for Microsoft Office 95: Office 95 is an Office product, and an Office product is a type of product. Office products consist of office parts, where an Office part is also a type of product (a Product type). The Office package is a Product Type rule that connects an Office product with its Office parts. The Office package is specified with Office package products, which are Product Connection Specifications. The Office 95 product is connected, in accordance to the Office package products, to the PowerPoint 6.0, Word 6.0, and Excel 7.0 products, which are all of the Product type Office Part.

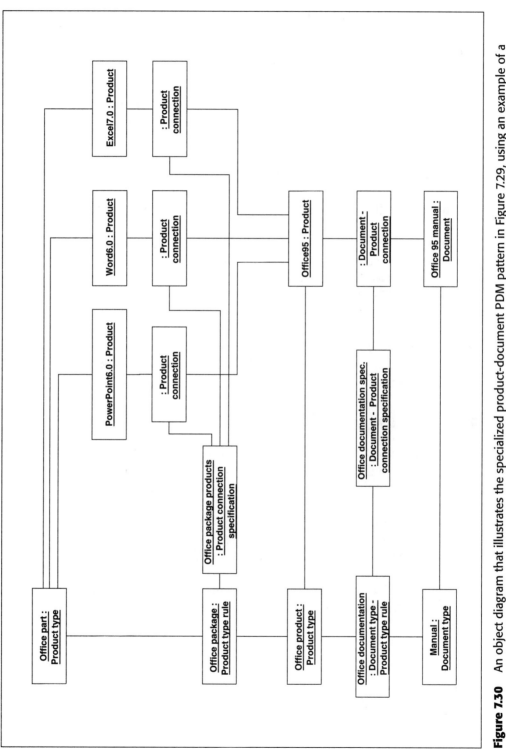

Figure 7.30 An object diagram that illustrates the specialized product-document PDM pattern in Figure 7.29, using an example of a structure for Microsoft Office 95.

The Office products are also connected to manuals. The Office Documentation rule (which is an object of the class Document Type–Product Type rule) points out that an Office product should be connected to a manual. The rule is specified within the Office documentation specification, which is a Document–Product Connection Specification. Office 95 is connected, in accordance to the Office Documentation Specification, to an Office 95 manual.

Figure 7.31 is another object diagram that shows objects instantiated from the class diagram in Figure 7.29, but differs in the number of office products listed. Figure 7.31 contains two office products, Office 95 and Office 97. This is achieved by adding new objects without changing the static structure or adding new classes. Objects that belong to Office 97 are added, but their corresponding types (the object Office product: Product type) are the same as in Figure 7.30.

The specialized PDM pattern for products and documents can be extended further by representing copies of documents and items related to products. Figure 7.32 shows the PDM pattern extended with both Document copy and Product item. The document copy is concerned with representing the actual copies. One document, the "UML Tool Requirements Specification," might exist in several copies. Products can also exist in several copies, that is, the actual instances of that product. Product copies are called items. It is particularly important to organize and handle copies and items if they are sold, lent out, or booked.

Related Patterns

Title Item, described shortly, is one pattern that can be combined with the PDM pattern, as shown in the example in Figure 7.32. When this is done, the PDM definition of Document is replaced with the Title definition in the Title-Item pattern.

Another pattern that is closely related to PDM is Contract, because the rules, connections, and specifications can all be viewed as types of contracts. We described how to combine these patterns under the Related Patterns section for the Contract pattern.

PDM can also be combined with the Business Event-Result pattern, described in the Related Patterns section for the Business Event-Result History pattern.

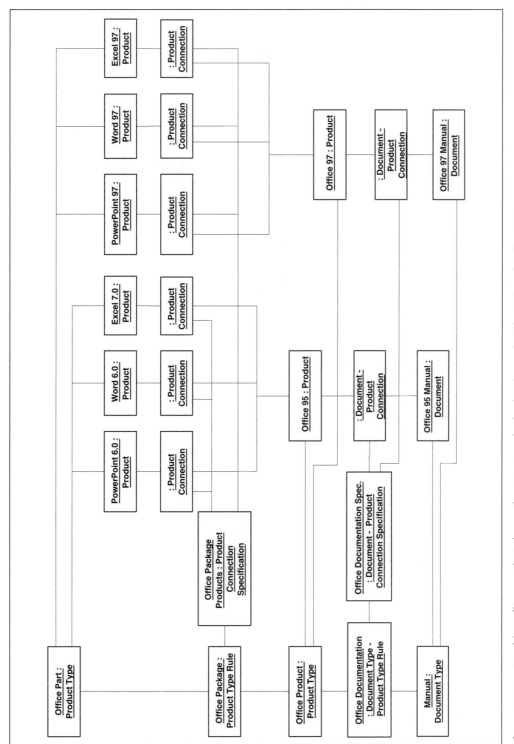

Figure 7.31   An object diagram that shows the structure for both Microsoft Office 95 and Office 97.

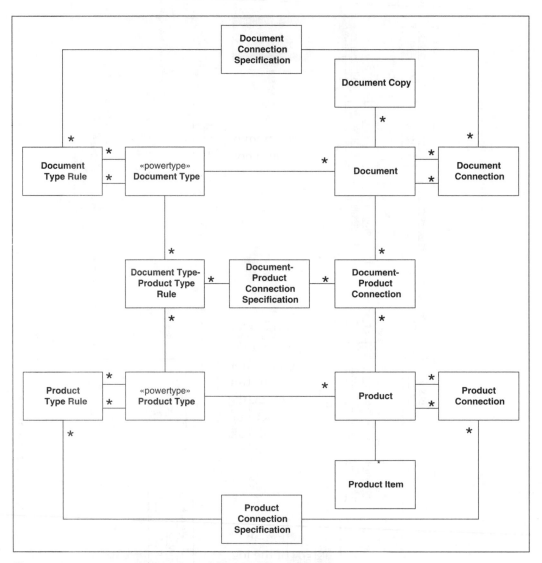

Figure 7.32   An extended version of the specialized PDM pattern.

Source/Credit

Sven-Bertil Wallin at Astrakan, and Andreas Rüping at Software Design & Management GmbH & Co have formalized PDM in their work. Andreas Rüping published his formalization of this pattern in the paper "Project Documentation Management," presented at EuroPLoP '99 [Rüping 1999].

Thing-Information

Intent

The Thing-Information pattern eliminates the focus-shifting that occurs during the modeling process by referring to two frequently used foci (thing focus and information focus) in business modeling and how they are related to each other.

Motivation

When performing information analysis in a business, it is important to keep in mind that the information can be about something outside the information system itself or about other pieces of information. Because information is named according to what it represents, it is not always easy to distinguish between the information and the thing, especially when both appear in the same model.

During construction of a business model it is common to analyze and structure both the resources and information about those resources. For instance, logistics in a company comprise both the actual transportation of goods and information about those goods and their transportation. The goods have attributes such as size, color, and form while the information about the goods has attributes such as delivery address, price, and delivery date. If the resource and information about the resource are modeled in the same class, these concepts are intermingled, making it difficult to determine which attributes describe the physical resource and which attributes provide information about the resource. This causes problems when maintaining and updating the information. Simply put, the resource and information about the resource are two different things, and need to be modeled as such.

Both the resources and the information about them should be modeled in the same model, because both are part of the logistics. However, because often the information about the resource is named after the resource, the information can easily be confused with the actual resource. The solution is to clearly state what the information is and what the information is about.

Some examples of typical Thing-Information pairs are:

Product/information PDM systems can handle information about products and product documentation. Systems that implement PDM do not contain the products or the documents; they store information about the products and the product documentation.

Customer/information. Many systems, especially business support systems, handle customers. However, information systems do not handle or store the actual customers, only information about them. Similarly, models contain classes with operations that are not concerned with the information about the class, but rather with the operations directly aimed at the class. For example, "the borrower goes to the shelf and picks up the book" is an operation directed at the actual customer; it's not an operation in the Customer class in an information system that contains information about the customer.

Applicability

The Thing-Information pattern can be applied to all business modeling situations in which it is of interest to separate the information about a thing, from the thing itself. This is a very generic need and this is also a generic pattern that is widely usable. By separating the information from the thing that can be modeled and defining it separately, misunderstanding and confusion can be avoided. The information is often stored in an information system, while the thing itself is outside the information system but part of the business model. For example, information systems such as client databases, business intelligent systems, and e-business systems would use this pattern to separate and model both the resources and the information about the resources.

Structure

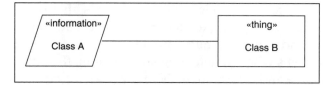

Figure 7.33   The Thing-Information pattern structure.

Participants

Thing is an object that can be concrete and physical, such as a customer, or abstract, such as mathematics. Things form the building blocks of an enterprise, and can be specialized to several types of things such as products, documents, people, and machines.

A formal definition for information and information system is as follows:

Information is the knowledge increment brought about by a receiving action in a message transfer; i.e., it is the difference between the conceptions interpreted from a received message and the knowledge before the receiving action. [FRISCO 1996]

Consequences

The consequence of not using this pattern when modeling systems that involve both information and the concept the information represents is that they become intermingled and result in a model that is hard to maintain and use as the basis for the information system. By using the Thing-Information pattern, the resource and the information about it are clearly separated, meaning that future maintenance of the models and the building of information systems based on the models will be easier.

Example

B2B Agency is a company that performs market analysis for other companies. B2B collects information about companies, including who their customers, subcontractors, competitors, and potential clients (prospects) are. The market analysis B2B performs is based on this information. B2B Agency then sells and distributes the market analysis report to actors in the marketplace, who may also be companies that B2B Agency collects information about. The market analysis contains information gathered for the purpose of increasing sales for B2B's customers. These customers are also operating in the marketplace, meaning that information about them is also present in the market analysis report. The customers can study the collected information about other actors in their marketplace and compare this with the information that B2B Agency has collected about them—sometimes referred to as *benchmarking* (see Figure 7.34).

Note that B2B Agency collects *information;* it doesn't collect companies. Though this seems obvious, we've seen several cases where the actual resource (in this case, the company) is modeled instead of the information. Here that would mean that the information in the market analysis report would be based on incorrect information. A company has attributes such as name, business vision, employees, capital, products, and knowledge, while information about companies contains attributes such as turnover, revenue, stock value, number of employees, number of clients, client categories, and so on. Also note that the marketplace in which B2B Agency's customers operate comprises the actual companies, not the information about those companies. Clearly, when modeling both resources and the information about them, they must be cleanly separated.

Related Patterns

All patterns that are used to structure information or resources can be combined with the Thing-Information pattern because this pattern models both resources from the real world and the information about these resources (typically stored in information systems that support the business model).

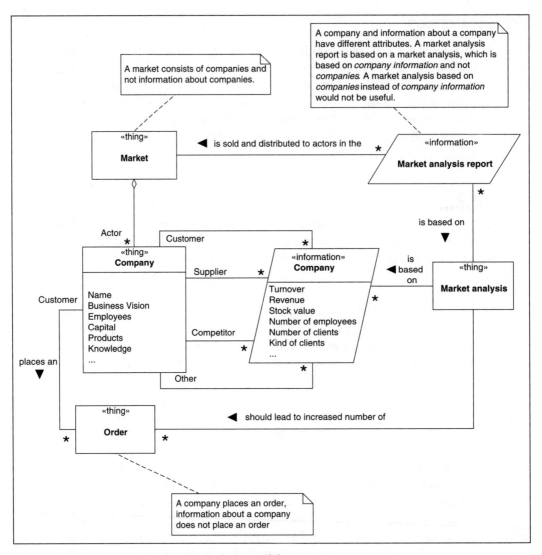

Figure 7.34   B2B Agency's market analysis model.

Source/Credit

The Thing-Information pattern is similar to Peter Coad's Item-Item Description pattern, which was first presented in Communications of the AMC (September, 1992) and modified in his book, *Object Models: Strategies, Patterns and Applications* (Yourdon, 1996).

Title-Item

Intent

The Title-Item pattern helps modelers to simplify the design process for systems that involve objects that exist in multiple copies or instances. It separates the information about the title from the information about individual instances of that title.

Motivation

A title is a concept that typically refers to an item. A book title, for example, might be *Business Modeling with UML*; the item would be the actual copy of the book that you are holding in your hands.

One concrete example is the problem domain of a library. In a library, both the book titles and actual books (items) have to be organized and handled. A popular book is represented as one title in the library, but it is represented by several items, assuming because of its popularity that multiple copies of it have been purchased. Each copy, or item, can be borrowed by different people. At a library, searches are performed for titles, not the items they represent. However, a borrower checks out an item—a physical copy of the book, not the title. Figure 7.35 shows a simple library model where titles and items are modeled together with reservations, loan, and borrower information. Title is specialized to book and magazine titles.

The model captures these core concepts: Title, Item, Loan, Reservation, and Borrower (stated as Borrower Information), as is the case with all other classes. However, because people and information about them are commonly confused, it is a more practical approach to model people either as physical people or information about them.

If, in this library example, you don't separate a book's title from the copies of the book (items), it would be impossible for a borrower to reserve a book that hasn't been bought by the library (since the object doesn't exist yet). But a borrower should of course be able to reserve a book title before it is purchased; then, when the actual book copy (item) is bought, that copy can be loaned to the borrower who has reserved the title (if there are several reservations to that title, a waiting list must be maintained). Similarly, when a borrower wants to reserve a book that has been purchased but all copies are lent out, a request can be made to reserve the title. The reservation is made on the title, not on the actual copies (and no copy must be bought before a reservation can be made, as long as the title object exists).

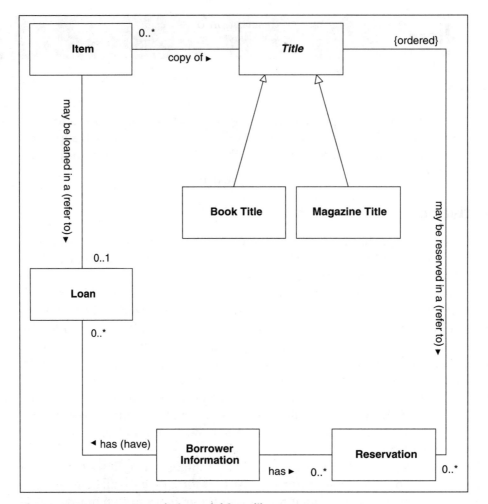

Figure 7.35 A system analysis model for a library system.

Another problem that arises when title and items are not separated is that it is difficult to search for a book title. The search is for a title, and a title can exist without a physical book being present on a shelf in the library. As an example, let's say Jim wants to borrow a book on business modeling from a library. The librarian helps Jim to search for a suitable book and suggests the title *Business Modeling with UML*. But then the librarian notices that all copies of that book are currently checked out. To help Jim decide whether he wants to reserve the book, the librarian gives him a printout containing a description of the book (which is an attribute of the title object). After reading the description, Jim reserves the book. If the library hadn't separated the title *Business Modeling with UML* from the 10 copies it owns, Jim would have had problems searching for a suitable title; he wouldn't have been able to reserve the title, and he wouldn't have been able to get a description of the book (the description is attached to the title, not to a specific book item).

Applicability

The Title-Item pattern can be used for all problem domains where it is imperative to separate the concept title from the item it represents. These include stores, wholesale dealers, and retail outlets.

The pattern can be extended with powertypes, such as Kind of Title and Kind of Item, to handle more complex structures. This is explained in the Structure and Participants sections.

Structure

Figure 7.36   The basic structure of the Title-Item pattern.

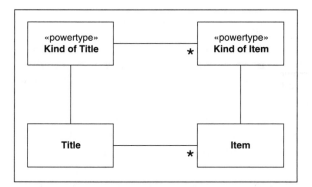

Figure 7.37   The extended version of the Title-Item pattern.

Participants

Title is the class that represents the title concept. Objects of the Title class might be book titles such as *UML Toolkit* and *Business Modeling with UML*. The Title class can have several attributes, such as name, ISBN, publisher, and edition.

Item represents the actual object that corresponds to a title. This book is an example of an Item, which corresponds to the Title object *Business Modeling with UML*. The Item class can have attributes such as current borrower and due date.

Kind of Title is a class that categorizes the different types of titles. One object of the Kind of Title class might be Biography and another Mystery. The objects of the Kind of Title class reference specific titles. For example, the object Computer Literature is an object of the Kind of Title class and references objects of the Title class, such as *UML Toolkit* and *The C++ Programming Language*. Typical attributes are description and rules. In a library application, one rule would be the lending parameters. Different kinds of titles will have different lending times; for example, magazines might have a lending time of one day while novels might have a lending time of three weeks.

Kind of Item is used to categorize the items themselves. The item that corresponds to the movie title *Terminator 2* could be a videotape, a laser disc, or a DVD. Videotape, laser disc, and DVD are examples of objects of the Kind of Item class.

Consequences

Using this pattern ensures that title and actual items of the title can be handled separately. By not separating titles from items, there is a risk of, for instance, jeopardizing sales of a product because the actual items of that product are temporarily out of stock.

Example

Let's say the New York City Library wants to handle its many titles and many copies of each title (some might be hard cover, others paperback). Furthermore, some of the copies are reference versions that are not allowed to be taken off the premises. The library also has online books that can be read via an Internet browser on the library's on-site computers. The titles in the library are organized into categories such as novels, fiction, nonfiction, biography, and so on; the items are also categorized into hard cover, paperback, reference copy, online version, and so on.

A slightly extended model of the Title-Item pattern is shown in Figure 7.37. A specific adaptation of this extended version is shown in Figure 7.38, where Title, Title Category, Loan Item, and Loan Item Category are modeled. The Title class comprises the book titles, such as *Business Modeling with UML*; the Title Category contains categories including Computer Science; the Loan Item is a specific copy of the book title; and the Loan Item category might be something like Reference Copy (not to be borrowed from the library) or Online Copy.

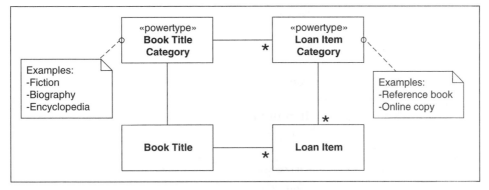

Figure 7.38   An example based on the extended version of the Title-Item pattern.

Related Patterns

The Title-Item pattern can be combined with the PDM pattern, in which case, the PDM definition of Document would be replaced with the Title definition in the Title-Item pattern. An example of this combination was shown in Figure 7.32.

Source/Credit

No sources known.

Type-Object-Value

Intent

The Type-Object-Value pattern models the relationships between a type, its object, and value.

Motivation

In some cases, a modeler may only be interested in the types (classes) and their objects. Recall that a type is a description that can have corresponding objects in the real world (or at least in our understanding of the real world). These objects have values that are also objects. Two or more objects can have the same value, but remain different objects (they are similar but not the same).

There is a difference between type, object, and the set of valid values that objects of a type can have. For example, the type Country (in this pattern, type is an equivalent with class) can have the objects Ireland, Sweden, and France. The countries can have different values, dependent upon the meaning of the objects. Values can be strings such as Ireland, Sweden, or France; letters such as I, S, or F; or country codes such as 353, 46, and 33.

In most languages used for business modeling, "semantics" refers to what an object actually represents. For example, the class Country can have an object Ireland that represents the country and island of Ireland, but the value of the object Ireland can be 353, which is the country code. The value can also be the text string Ireland. Neither of these values is the actual country.

The values assigned depend on the purpose of the model. A model of a phone system would probably use the country code as a value. If the system were for geographical information, the values might be composed of geographical coordinates; the values would be independent of the country objects. Several objects can use one value simultaneously. This raises the question: Why aren't the values represented as attributes in a class? For example, the class Country could have the attribute Country Code or Country Letter. The answer is that Country Code and Country Letter are not properties of a country; they are values used to represent countries. Valid properties of a country are population, area, and currency.

Figure 7.39 illustrates the differences between type, object, and value. The figure also provides an example where the same object, a country such as Sweden or France, can have different types of values that represent it (different types of values are used in different contexts). One type of value to represent a country is the country letter code S or F. This is used in Europe to mark the license origin of a car. Another type of value is the telephone country code

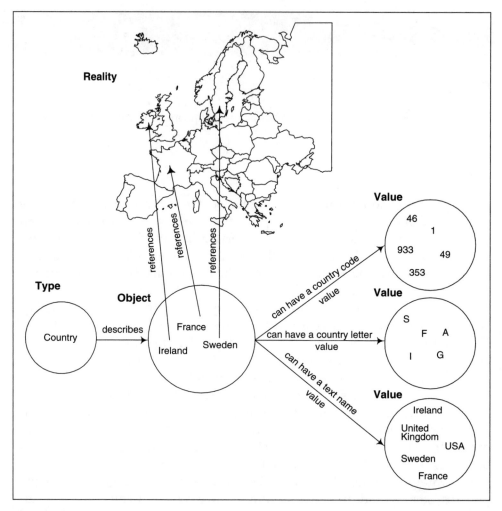

Figure 7.39   Why and how to separate types from objects and values. (This is not a UML diagram.)

used when calling different countries. Interestingly, the same value, say the letter S, can be used in different situations and mean different things depending on the context. The potential contexts are based on the object that the value represents.

If a country code letter or country code number is modeled as an attribute in a type such as Country and the type is then used in other contexts, the type will contain incorrect information. This problem can be prevented by modeling a country only with the relevant attributes, such as number of residents, geography, and so on. The problem caused by a value meaning different things in different contexts can be solved by having a separate class for type (Country), object (Sweden), and value (46).

Applicability

The Type-Object-Value pattern is applicable for all problem situations in which it is important to clearly distinguish between what the objects refer to (in this case, actual countries) and the values the objects can have (for example, 46). You can use this pattern in geographical and diary systems to model physical information about countries or cities or to model the values used to communicate and represent this physical information.

Structure

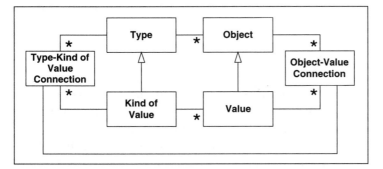

Figure 7.40   The structure for the Type-Object-Value pattern.

Participants

Type is the class that describes a set of objects.

Object is a subclass that is a collection of all possible objects of the Type class. The objects (the instances of the Object class) represent an object found in the real world. All objects have some value; for example, the object United Kingdom has the value of the string United Kingdom.

Value is the class that captures valid values for a certain kind of value. For example, one kind of value might be color; and allowed values (that is, the objects of the Value class that are connected to the object Color of the Kind of Value class) can then be red, yellow, orange, black, white, and so on. A set of values is also referred to as a *value domain,* meaning that the Value class represents a value domain. The Value is a special case (specialization) of an Object.

Kind of Value specifies the type of Value. The Kind of Value class is a specialization of a Type.

Type-Kind of Value Connection specifies which kind of values a Type has and in which types the Kind of Value is used.

Object-Value Connection represents the connection between an object (an instance of the Object class) and a value (an instance of the Value class) that is allowed in the specification Type-Kind of Value class.

Consequences

A model based on the Type-Object-Value pattern will precisely define and handle what is modeled and how is it represented with objects and values. Using this pattern will ensure that types and objects of types are separated from the values used to represent and communicate them. This separation prevents the misinterpretation of attributes—interpreted differently based on the context—and makes it possible to reuse values for different objects (you don't have to define the same values over and over in the model or in systems based on the model).

Example

A marketing company called MoneyMaker works with different types of market communications. MoneyMaker has global clientele and so uses different techniques such as telemarketing, direct mail, and e-mail advertising to communicate with them. It also plans to implement other channels in the future. Depending on the type of market communication it is working with, Money-Maker uses different systems. These systems are based on information from different countries. Thus MoneyMaker needs to represent a country in a num-

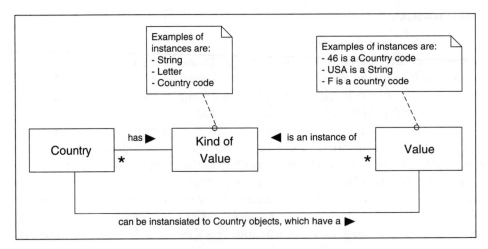

Figure 7.41   An example of using the Type-Object-Value pattern.

ber of different ways depending on which system is being used. For instance MoneyMaker wants to represent Ireland with the postal text string Ireland, with telephone country code 353, or with the e-mail suffix .ie. The Type-Object-Value pattern enables this, by representing the type Country and its various objects such as Ireland with different values (Ireland, 353, .ie) depending on the application context. Figure 7.41 is a model that structures MoneyMaker's approach to handling countries and values.

Related Patterns

The Type-Object-Value pattern can be combined with all other resource and rule patterns to extend them with the functionality of handling both objects and values at the same time.

Source/Credit

No sources known.

Summary

The resource and rule patterns describe typical business problem situations and solutions and provide guidelines for handling these problems. From a structural point of view, resource and rule patterns help to describe the right problem, in the right form, and from the right view. Because this collection of patterns is based on practical experiences, they give insight into the world of business problem and domain analysis.

Today, business systems cannot be easily described and built; they must be flexible and create high value to their users. Business systems must focus on usability, flexibility, and cost-effectiveness. The patterns presented in this chapter, together with those in Chapters 8 and 9, lay a strong foundation that both business analysts and architects can work from to achieve those goals.

CHAPTER

8

Goal Patterns

As discussed in Chapter 3, "Modeling the Business Architecture," goal modeling is a critical issue in business modeling. Business goals are what the business models and the resulting business process strive for. They establish the foundation not only for the business-process design, but also in the definition of business resources and rules. Therefore, a well-validated and verified goal model supports the rest of the business modeling work.

Goal models affect the entire process for developing and improving businesses, from designing the very first process models to implementing information systems to setting up training programs for end users to, finally, establishing product structures.

There exist some fundamental patterns in goal models. This chapter describes three such powerful goal patterns, all of which use the business extensions to UML described in Chapters 3 and 4. The Goal patterns help to:

- Assign business goals to a business process, and indirectly to the resources and rules attached to the process (Business Goal Allocation pattern)

- Break down a higher-level goal into sub-goals, where the sub-goals can be more concrete and easily assigned to a business process (Business Goal Decomposition pattern)

- Identify and structure the problems that can hinder the achievement of goals, and to model the causes, actions, and prerequisites attached to the problem (Business Goal Problem pattern)

These patterns are highly related to each other. Typically, the Business Goal Decomposition pattern is used first to break down high-level business goals into more concrete and measurable sub-goals. These sub-goals are then allocated to individual business processes using the Business Goal Allocation pattern. When defining a goal hierarchy with the Business Goal Decomposition, it is often suitable to use the Business Goal Problem pattern in order to find the problems that can prohibit the achievement of goals. These problems often lead to the identification of sub-goals that help avoid the problems.

Goal patterns are used in the early stages of Business Modeling, when a vision statement issued by the owners, top management, or Board of Directors is transferred into a more concrete business model. The diagrams produced are part of the Business Vision View in the framework described in Chapter 4, "Business Views."

Establishing business goals has always been a very important part of Business Modeling, because the goals not only direct and drive the business process but also make it possible to measure the success of the business at a later date. Occasionally business developers perform goal modeling only, without modeling the business further. Doing so ensures that the decision makers within a business are able to focus and agree on essential business goals. We have used these patterns in many situations and projects within the manufacturing, finance, banking, and consulting sectors. It's amazing to see how goal modeling can help to identify the often neglected or ignored business sub-goals that are imperative to achieve the high-level business goals. These patterns can be used in virtually any business, since all successful businesses must describe and understand their goals.

The patterns outlined in this chapter have traditionally been used without UML, that is, just documented informally on a whiteboard or with notepads. The Business Goal Problem pattern, for example, utilizes UML's informal Note model element to describe the business goals. As you can see the business goals are often described informally in one or two sentences, but it's recommended to use as much detail as possible. Although goal diagrams can be done informally, it is well worth using UML to model them. When all of the business models are expressed in UML, you can track the goals back to the goal diagram as they're assigned to business processes. This allows the process goal to be viewed in terms of the higher-level business goals. It's also important to document and update the goal diagrams, which is easier to do if they are captured in a modeling language and tool.

Business Goal Allocation

Intent

The Business Goal Allocation pattern is used to assign goals to specific business processes, resources, and rules in order to facilitate the description and validation of those business processes, resources, and rules during business modeling.

Motivation

A business process exists for a reason: it strives to achieve a set business goal. Any business process without a corresponding goal should be eliminated. The more clearly a business goal is stated, the easier it is to define and design the corresponding business process so that the goal can be achieved. Goals can either be expressed in a quantitative way (using a number in a specific unit of measurement) or in a qualitative way (whereby the goal is described in natural language and focuses on the qualitative aspects rather then the quantitative aspects). (Even though this pattern links goals to business processes, it also assigns a goal to a specific business resource or rule.)

Goals are the best way to validate a business process; they help us determine whether the appropriate steps are being performed within the business process. By allocating goals to the business processes, we also simplify the work involved to describe the processes, because the allocated goals become part of the business process description. In addition, goals can be used to achieve other goals. We show an example of this in the Business Goal Decomposition pattern discussed later in this chapter.

As the example in Figure 8.1 shows, a goal can express a desired state. In this case, the desired state is a high rate of return for the selling and delivery

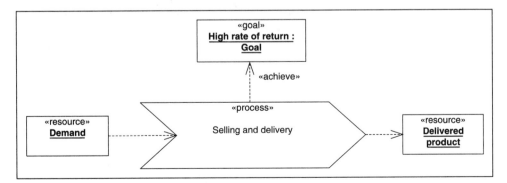

Figure 8.1 The process of selling and delivering products should result in the goal: high rate of return.

process. The selling and delivery process receives demands as input and delivers final products to customers. The goal in this case means that the process should result in a high rate of return by selling and delivering products. Goals can also express a desired direction for the organization, such as "our business should continuously improve in terms of profitability and turnover rate." Two other goal examples are: "Of all sold and delivered products, only 1 in 1000 should have any defects." and "Balance of trade should be kept."

Applicability

This pattern can be applied in all situations in which it is necessary to validate any type of business model, including design or other technical models. One example might be a space shuttle telescope that was specified and constructed in small parts, or subsystems. Though each part worked properly on its own, when the engineers assembled all the parts, problems appeared. The telescope was too slow, and it could not zoom in on objects when the space shuttle was in motion. How could this happen? Because the overall goal—that the telescope should zoom in on objects while moving in space—was not explicitly stated, the engineers were concentrating on their individual subsystems. If the overall goal for the system had been stated, it could have been broken down and allocated to the different subsystems and used to specify and validate the constructed subsystems.

Another example might be working with purchase processes, where it is very important to clarify the goals and allocate them to the purchase process. Typical goals are that the purchases should be as close to the sales and as inexpensive as possible. If a purchase process only focuses on purchase, without a clear goal, it might end up with a large inventory of nonsalable products and a huge amount of restricted equity.

Structure

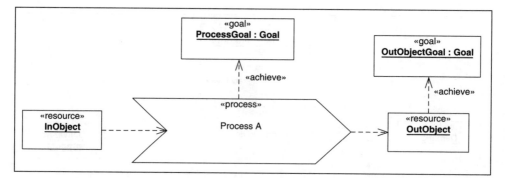

Figure 8.2   The structure shows that a goal can be allocated to a process or an object.

Participants

ProcessGoal is a goal that is allocated to a business process, in this case to Process A. This goal states the desired business process state or direction. Many times the goals are formulated in terms of the OutObject; however, the OutObject can have an explicit goal as well, such as an OutObjectGoal.

Process A is a business process that has a goal, ProcessGoal, that must be achieved. Process A takes on an object, InObject, as input and delivers an object, OutObject, as output.

InObject is the object that is refined through Process A.

OutObject is the output from Process A. The OutObject has a goal, OutObjectGoal, which indicates a desired state for the OutObject.

OutObjectGoal is the goal of the OutObject. It expresses a desired state or direction.

Consequences

Using the Goal Allocation pattern, business processes, resources, rules, and other business goals can be validated during business modeling. For instance, if a process is motivated by a goal, the goal should also be used when validating the process. Ask: "Will running the process achieve the goal?" If not, the process has to be reworked. If the goal will be achieved, the process can be validated, that is, shown to be correct. The same holds true for resources, rules, and goals. For example, if a goal is allocated to an OutObject, ask if the object will achieve the allocated goal? If not, the process of producing the object must be remodeled.

Example

Jim & Co. is an advertising agency whose ultimate goal is to be the leading advertising agency selling and producing advertising material by the year 2005. It has several business processes: a sales process, a marketing process, an advertisement production, and a managing process. The sales process receives prospects (hot leads) and suspects (probable leads) as input and output orders. In order for Jim & Co. to achieve its overall goal, all processes, including the sales process, must be managed effectively. Jim & Co. manages the sales process by empowering the sales staff, defining sales directives, and establishing clear goals for the sales process. The financial goal for 1999 was to reach a sales budget of $250,000,000 and a 25 percent profit margin. However, it was also important that the placed order result in customer satisfaction, otherwise the overall goal to be the leading advertising agency year 2005 would be difficult to reach. Note that while it is possible to fulfill the sales budget for one year without satisfied customers, dissatisfied customers will negatively affect future sales.

To fulfill Jim & Co.'s overall goal, the sales process should result in satisfied customers and meeting the sales budget. Note that at some point the goal of satisfying customers could conflict with meeting the sales budget, that is, the goal of the sales process. If the budget is difficult to reach one year, it might be tempting to sell and deliver products without considering the customers' needs and satisfaction, thereby obstructing the overall goal. Why set up contradictory goals (goals in conflict)? In most businesses, goals may be contradictory by nature. It is better to address both goals at the same time instead of suppressing or ignoring one or several of them.

Figure 8.3 illustrates Jim & Co.'s sales process, which corresponds to ProcessA in the Goal Allocation pattern. The ProcessGoal is the quantitative SalesGoal with a Sales Budget, Profit Margin, Monetary Unit, and Budget Year. The OutObject Order has the qualitative OutObjectGoal Satisfied Customers, and the SalesProcess takes the InObject Prospects. The SalesProcess is supplied by SalesMaterial and SalesPerson, both of which are necessary when executing the sales.

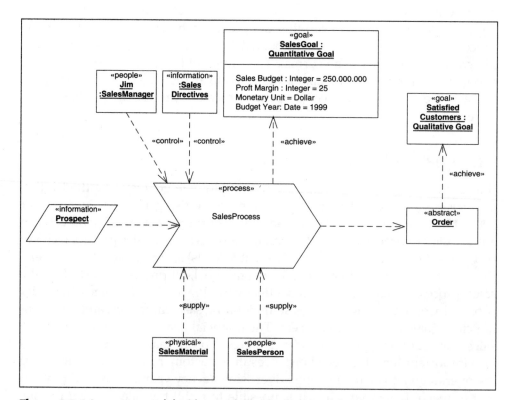

Figure 8.3   A process model with a goal allocated to the Sales Process for Jim & Co.

Related Patterns

If goals are allocated to other goals, the Business Goal Allocation pattern turns into the Business Goal Decomposition pattern where goals are composed and/or decomposed.

Source/Credit

The Goal Allocation pattern has been formalized by consultants at Astrakan, the Swedish method company. It has also been described in the book *Perspective on Business Modeling,* by Professor A. G. Nilsson, C. Tollis, and C. Nellborn, Springer-Verlag 1999. It has also been described in the EuroPLoP'98 paper titled "Capturing and Structuring Goals: Analysis Patterns," by Dr. Elizabeth A. Kendall and Dr. Liping. Moreover, the Euro project F3 (From Fuzzy to Formal, ESPRIT III Project 6612) also formalized this pattern and documented it in "From Fuzzy to Formal," Technical Annex II, ESPRIT Project 6612, 1991, and in *The F3 Requirement Engineering Handbook*, SISU, Sweden, 1994.

Business Goal Decomposition

Intent

The Business Goal Decomposition pattern is used to streamline the goal-modeling process by breaking down the business goals into hierarchies. In this way, high-level business goals can be divided into more concrete sub-goals that are then allocated to specific business processes.

Motivation

As the Business Goal Allocation pattern demonstrates, goals can be allocated to processes, resources, rules, and even other goals. Goals are used to motivate the establishment of processes, rules, resources, and other goals, as well as to validate processes, rules, resources, and other goals. To identify goals for allocation, the overall goal for the business is broken down in smaller pieces called subgoals.

For example, suppose that the overall goal for a library is to provide the public with information and to encourage people to read quality literature. Though praiseworthy, this overall goal is too general; it needs to be broken down into subgoals in order to be able to identify and validate the business processes. One subgoal could be that the library should provide information by complementing its book content with Internet access. Another subgoal could be for the library to establish competent and personal customer service to encourage reading. A third subgoal could be that the library needs to supply books that more accurately reflect the needs of the people, while providing quality literature. If it is difficult to access information, or if service is poor, visitors might stop borrowing from that library. Likewise, if the books in the library don't meet the needs of the readers, they will stop coming in to the library. Finally, if the books are not considered quality literature, the overall goal cannot be achieved.

Once the goals have been identified, it is possible to define the library's business processes. One important process is the lending process, which achieves the goal of supplying literature by providing access to information and quality service. The library also has a procure process, to acquire books that meet the needs of the people and are considered quality literature.

By breaking down an overall goal into subgoals, it is easier to identify the business processes. Moreover, the subgoals are helpful for validating processes. When the processes are run, the results should be compared with the subgoals and the overall goal. If a discrepancy exists, the processes must be remodeled.

Examining how goals are achieved, as in the library example, helps to break down goals. How should a library achieve the overall goal to serve the public with information and to encourage reading of quality literature? The answer to this question are the following subgoals:

- The library should provide information by complementing its books with Internet access.

- The library's books should meet the people's needs.

- The library should have competent and personal customer service to encourage reading.

- The books should be considered quality literature.

Another way to identify subgoals is to ask why something is done. This enables identifying the goal for it. In practice, goals are broken down by asking how things should be achieved at the same time asking why things are done, in order to identify goals. For example, you can ask why a company should have an Internet site. The answer could be because the company works with Internet technology and must demonstrate its knowledge in the area. Why must the company demonstrate its knowledge in the area? The company could be a startup with few existing references and thus needs the Internet to lure clients. Another reason for the company to have an Internet site could be because it is a cost-effective way of distributing manuals and patches for the software that it develops.

By repeatedly asking why, high-level goals are identified. In this example, both answers have a tremendous influence on the development of the Internet site. If the goal is to demonstrate the company's skill in Internet technology on an Internet site, it is important that the site make an impression on new and potential customers. If the site is to be used for distributing manuals and patches for software, it is important that the customers are able to find and get what they are looking for.

Applicability

The Business Goal Decomposition pattern can be utilized in all situations where the business goals are not fully understood. This pattern helps to better define the overall goal and its corresponding subgoals.

Structure

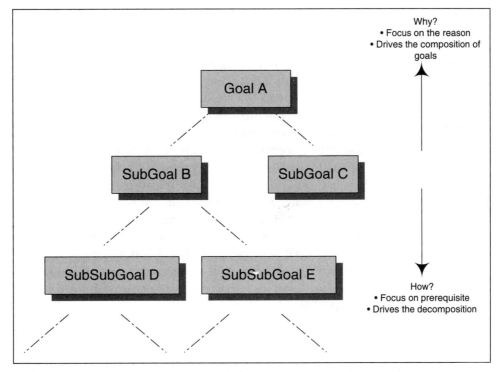

Figure 8.4   A principal sketch (not in UML notation) that shows how business goals are created and broken down.

Participants

Goal A is the overall goal. It is decomposed into subgoals: SubGoal B, C, and so on. Recall that goals can be either qualitative or quantitative, as is the case for Goal A and its subgoals. *SubGoal B* is a subgoal to the overall goal, Goal A, and can be decomposed into further subgoals such as SubSubGoal D and SubSubGoal E.

SubGoal C is also a subgoal to Goal A. SubGoal B and SubGoal C can be composed into Goal A.

SubSubGoal D is a subgoal to SubGoal B.

SubSubGoal E is a subgoal to SubGoal B.

Consequences

When you compose and decompose business goals, you help to facilitate the validation of the overall business goals. If a goal cannot be decomposed, and if it cannot be allocated to a business process, resource, or rule, the business goals should be eliminated. By composing goals, they are also questioned (by asking why) which is a kind of validation; however, the overall goal cannot be composed further and is also difficult to validate. The best way to validate the overall goal is to compare it with the business idea.

When decomposing goals, contradictory goals may appear. The goals of high-quality production, rapid production, and low-cost production can all be a decomposition of the same goal—high rate of return—but they are all contradictory. If production is rapid, it is hard to make it low-cost as well because the machinery necessary to reach high speeds is probably expensive. Rapid production is also contradictory to high-quality production, because achieving high quality demands more time. High-quality production also requires more sophisticated machinery and staff, which means that it, too, is contradictory to low-cost production since more sophisticated machinery and staff also mean increased expenses. The Business Goal-Problem pattern provides guidelines for handling this type of problem.

Example

A concrete goal hierarchy from the Internet company Internet Business, Inc. is shown in Figure 8.5. The overall goal is to attract many customers (Goal A). The desired goal value has been set to 500,000 customers. This goal has been broken down into three quantitative subgoals (corresponding to SubGoal A and B in Figure 8.4) that also describe the different customer categories:

Many Internet visitors. Internet visitors whose names are unknown.

Many registered customers. Customers who have registered their names and addresses.

Many subscribing customers. Customers who pay a monthly fee to use all of the site's services.

The sum of these three subgoals can lead to the overall goal of 500,000 registered customers. As Figure 8.5 shows, the subgoals can be broken down further into more specific goals (SubSubGoal D, E). For example, the subgoal Many Subscribing Customers can be broken down further into the sub-subgoals Communicate bonus service for subscribers, Attractive pricing, and Provide good bonus services. As mentioned in Chapter 3 "Modeling the Business Architecture," and Chapter 4 "Business Views," goals should not just be named; they should also be described. In Figure 8.5, the quantitative goals have the attrib-

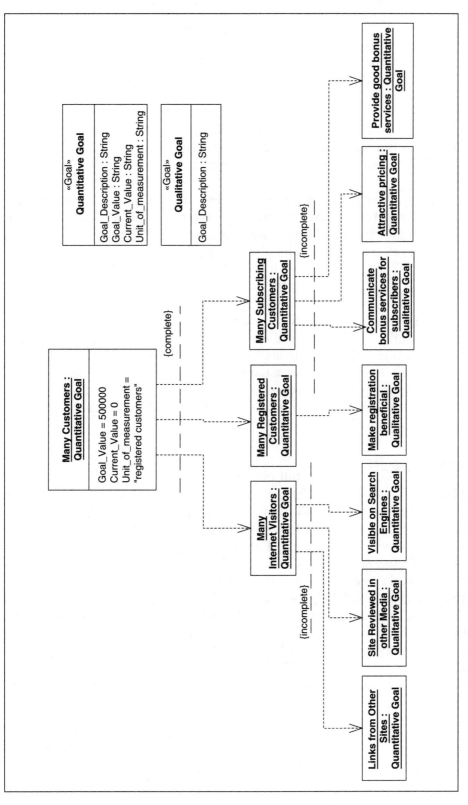

Figure 8.5 A goal hierarchy.

utes Goal_Description, Goal_Value, Current_Value, and Unit_of_measurement. The qualitative goal has only the attribute Goal_Description. The quantitative goal Attractive pricing could be described with the Goal_Description attribute: "Internet Business, Inc. should offer attractive pricing for all Internet-based services such as the daily newsletter, banners, and more." A goal value for the goal Attractive pricing could be: "5 percent lower than the five largest competitors," which also means that the unit of measurement would be a percentage.

Both the goals of getting many subscribers and getting many Internet visitors are not fully broken down, which is also shown by the constraint {incomplete}. As in the case with Internet Business, Inc. and Figure 8.5, it is difficult, sometimes even impossible, to break down goals fully.

Related Patterns

The Business Goal Decomposition pattern is a special case of the Business Goal Allocation pattern. If goals are allocated to other goals, it's considered goal composition or goal decomposition. The Business Goal Decomposition pattern is also related to the Business Goal-Problem pattern. When decomposing goals, contradictory goals are sometimes identified and may lead to problems. These problems could then be modeled and handled by using the Business Goal-Problem pattern.

Source/Credit

The Business Goal Decomposition pattern has been formalized by consultants at Astrakan, the Swedish method company. It has also been described in the book *Perspective on Business Modeling*, by Professor A. G. Nilsson, C. Tollis, and C. Nellborn, Springer-Verlag, 1999. The Euro project From Fuzzy to Formal, ESPRIT III Project 6612 has also formalized this pattern in "From Fuzzy to Formal," Technical Annex II, ESPRIT Project 6612, 1991, and in *The F3 Requirement Engineering Handbook*, SISU, Sweden, 1994. It has also been described by John Mylopoulos, Lawrence Chung, and Eric Yu in the article "From Object-Oriented to Goal-Oriented: Requirements Analysis," *Communication of the ACM*, January 1999, Volume 42, Number 1, pp. 3–37. Finally, it has been described in the EuroPlop'98 paper "Capturing and Structuring Goals: Analysis Patterns," by Dr. Elizabeth A. Kendall and Dr. Liping.

Business Goal-Problem

Intent

The Business Goal-Problem pattern is used to identify the connection between business goals and their related problems in order to correct the problems and achieve the goals.

Motivation

Problems can hinder the achievement of business goals and therefore must be identified and then removed. Modeling goals helps to locate problems; conversely, modeling problems helps to identify goals; they are the flip sides of the same coin. This discussion is meant to demonstrate that identifying goal problems helps to achieve goals and vice versa.

For example, a company requires more funds so it can continue to meet its growth goal. To achieve this goal, it wants to increase its earnings potential. In this example, the goal is to continue to grow and the related problem is the lack of funds. To achieve the goal and eliminate the problem, the company's earnings potential must be increased. The earning potential can be increased by organizational rationalizations such as closing down, merging, selling, or buying organizational units (i.e., departments and subsidiaries). Many times, rationalizations also include training programs, new strategies, and new business policies. Figure 8.6 shows another example of a goal with a corresponding problem, namely that of a company that wants to attract many Internet visitors, which is hindered because the site is currently unknown.

Applicability

The Business Goal-Problem pattern can be applied in any context where problems and goals need to be identified and handled. The pattern is appropriate not only for finding goals and their related problems, but it is also useful for eliminating those problems.

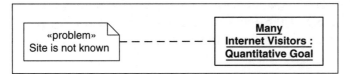

Figure 8.6   A problem associated with a corresponding goal.

Structure

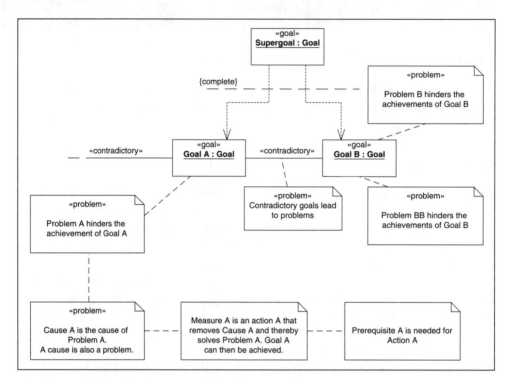

Figure 8.7 The structure for the Business Goal-Problem pattern.

Participants

Supergoal is the overall goal.

Goal A is a subgoal to Supergoal. Problem A hinders the achievements of Goal A. Problem A also contradicts Goal B, which leads to problems, Contradictory Problems.

Goal B is a subgoal to Supergoal. Problem B and Problem BB hinder the achievements of Goal B. Goal B also contradicts Goal A, which leads to problems, Contradictory Problems.

Problem A hinders the achievements of Goal A. It is caused by Cause A.

Problem B hinders the achievements of Goal B.

Problem BB hinders the achievements of Goal B.

Contradictory Problems hinders the achievements of Goal A and Goal B. As with the other problems, there is a cause; in this case, the goals themselves are the cause. One or several actions can be taken to eliminate the problem, but only under certain circumstances (prerequisites). One prerequisite might be that the goals cannot be changed, thus limiting the possible actions. Another prerequisite might be that one of the goals could be changed or removed in favor of solving the contradictory problem.

Cause A causes Problem A. Cause A can be removed if Measure A is taken and Prerequisite A is valid.

Measure A is an action that can be taken to remove Cause A.

Prerequisite A must be valid if Cause A is removed through Measure A.

Consequences

Using the Business Goal-Problem pattern is an effective way to structure and handle goals and their associated problems. By identifying causes, possible actions, and necessary prerequisites, problems can be eliminated and the goals can be achieved.

Example

Figure 8.8 shows the business supergoal of an Internet-based company trying to increase its number of customers. The supergoal is broken down to subgoals, which are to attract customers to the company's Internet site, to encourage them to become registered users, and, finally, to become full subscribers. Here are some of the problems the company faces:

- Internet users currently are not aware of the company's site because the company has not advertised the site. The unawareness is the problem and the lack of advertisement is the cause. This cause can be removed by linking the site to other sites (this is the measure). The prerequisite is that there be other sites that are interested in linking to this company's site.

- Customers who are unwilling to register hinder the goal of encouraging visitors to become registered customers. The unwillingness is the prob-

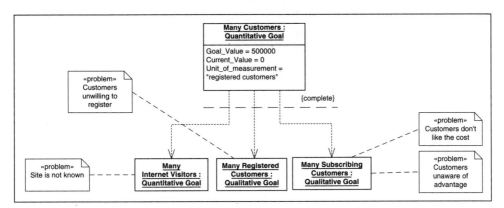

Figure 8.8   Goals and problems connected to each other.

lem; the cause is that the registration is not beneficial. The measure is to make registering beneficial by offering free products and free Internet magazines to registered customers. The prerequisite is that it be possible to make the registration beneficial and that visitors access the site.

■ The risk that the customers may be resistant to paying the cost can hinder the goal to attract site subscribers. The problem is the risk of customers not wanting to pay the cost, and the cause may be that competitors offer less expensive alternatives. The measure is composed of attractive pricing and bonus systems. The prerequisites are that Internet visitors come to the site and that it is possible to cut the prices.

■ When customers aren't aware of the site's advantages, the goal to attract subscribers is hindered. The problem is the unawareness of advantages. The cause may be that visitors do not have much time to investigate the site, and a measure is to restructure the site and highlight the advantages. The prerequisite is that visitors come to the site.

Related Patterns

The Business Goal-Problem pattern is related to the Business Goal Decomposition pattern. When decomposing goals into subgoals, new and contradictory goals can appear that requires the use of the Business Goal-Problem pattern.

Source/Credit

The Business Goal Allocation pattern has been formalized by consultants at Astrakan, the Swedish method company. It has also been described in the book *Perspective on Business Modeling,* by Professor A. G. Nilsson, C. Tollis, and C. Nellborn, Springer-Verlag, 1999. The Euro project F3 (From Fuzzy to Formal, ESPRIT III Project 6612) also formalized this pattern; it has been documented in "From Fuzzy to Formal," Technical Annex II, ESPRIT Project 6612, 1991 and in *The F3 Requirement Engineering Handbook*, SISU, Sweden, 1994.

Summary

Business Goal patterns describe typical problem situations and solutions within the context of analyzing and handling goals and their corresponding problems. This collection of goal patterns is based on practical experiences, and provides insight into the world of analyzing, describing, improving, and validating businesses and business models.

Process Patterns

In this chapter, we address three types of process patterns, each of which focuses on different aspects of process modeling. The first and, perhaps, the most intuitive type of process patterns are the *Process Modeling patterns*. As their name indicates, Process Modeling patterns focus on how to model processes to achieve high quality for the model, and the execution of that model, which is the actual work carried out in accordance to the process description. Most of the patterns discussed in this chapter are Process Modeling patterns.

The second process pattern type comprises the *Process Instance patterns*, which address the differences between the business process descriptions and the execution of those descriptions. A process can execute in several parallel instances, as is the case with production. For example, a car production process does not output one car at a time; it produces thousands of cars simultaneously, and each batch can be considered a process instance.

Process Support patterns make up the last type of process patterns. These patterns describe common problems and solutions inherent to business process deployment, which are normally implemented in some sort of application system that supports the business process.

Basic Process Structure

Intent

The Basic Process Structure pattern falls under the Process Modeling pattern category. It shows how to form the business process concept in terms of supplying business resources, goals for the process, and the transformation or refinement of input and output resource objects. It provides the basic structure for describing a business process.

Motivation

A business process always has a goal, so to design a business process, you must first describe the goal that motivates that process, then connect it to the process described. As stated previously, a goal expresses the desired state for or result of a business resource. A business process refines incoming resources and delivers refined resources that should meet the desired state or result described in the connected goal. To deploy a business process, a *supply* is necessary. The supply consists of the business resources that are furnished to the process to refine the resources that enter into the process. Let's look at an example. The process of refining metal into tools such as hammers or screwdrivers requires resources such as electricity, machines, and labor. This results in tools that meet the demand of the market. The incoming resource to the tool production process is the metal; the supplying resources are the electricity, machines, and labor; the result is tools. The goal of the process it to deliver tools that meet the demand of the market.

Numerous problems can occur if the different resources involved in a process are not kept separate. For example, if the resources are not separated in the model, it is difficult or even impossible to distinguish between those that should be refined and those that should be used or consumed. Let's expand on the tool production process. The metal is refined, the electricity is consumed, but what about the labor—the people who actually design and manufacture the tools? Are they consumed? People are considered assets in terms of intellectual capital and physical capabilities, and therefore are refined as well as consumed. Skilled people will design and produce not just better tools, but also tools that meet the customers' demands.

The Basic Process Structure pattern shows how business processes should be modeled and structured to produce high-quality process models that distinguish incoming resources from consumed, used (some resources are just used and not consumed, such as tools), or refined and produced resources.

Applicability

This pattern is a de facto standard pattern for how a business process is defined in terms of its resources and goals. The pattern can be used in all situations where there is a course of events or actions that need to be defined and described.

Structure

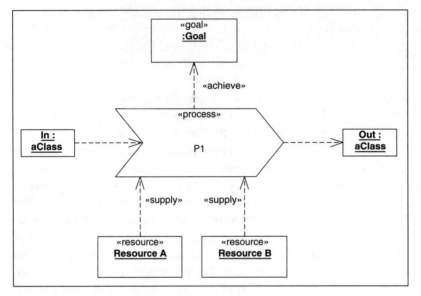

Figure 9.1 The Basic Process Structure pattern.

Participants

Process represents a set of related activities that can be performed.

Goal is an object of a goal-stereotyped class that provides the motivation for the process and expresses the desired output.

In is some object that should be refined. Note that the object is not explicitly named. It is sufficient to say that it is an object of a specified class that should be refined through the process.

Out is an object that is the result of the process, or the product (the refinement).

Resource A and *Resource B* are resources supplied to the process. Typical resources that supply a process are knowledge, information, machines, information systems, or people.

Consequences

The Basic Process Structure pattern provides a proven and clear architecture for process modeling that facilitates the modeling of business processes by separating and structuring resources that are used, produced, consumed, or refined.

Example

Software Inc. develops software on contract, but the company has had problems in the past satisfying its customer base and with internal planning. Poor project planning has led to a shortage of developers, purchases of tools that don't meet the project's requirements, and unmet customer needs. Software Inc. has decided to improve its project planning skills by implementing the Basic Process pattern to control a project's goals, specifications, deliverables, work output, and developer and tool requirements. By describing the project as a process, *software development process*, with the overall goal of achieving *customer satisfaction*, the work activities, work sequence, and goals can become clearer for all Software Inc. employees. By defining that every software development process must start with a specification and end with a working and documented software system, both the project leaders and project members will know the rules for how a project should start and finish. In order to coor-

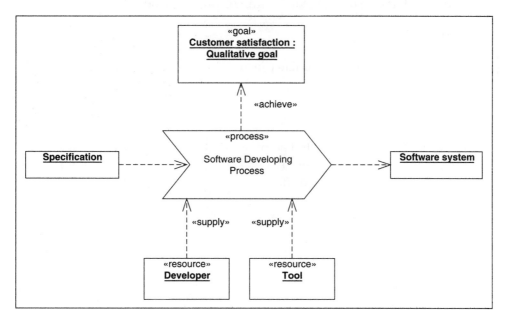

Figure 9.2   Using the Basic Process Structure pattern.

dinate developers and tools among different projects, every project must be run according to this process and specify its developer and tool requirements.

Figure 9.2 is a graphical representation of how Software Inc.'s software development process can look at its highest level: It starts with a specification (a requirement specification) of what to model and build. This specification is the In object. The Out object is a software system. The software development process is a Process whose Goal is customer satisfaction. Moreover, the software development process requires developers and tools, which are supply resources that correspond to Resource A and Resource B in the basic pattern structure.

Related Patterns

The Basic Process Structure pattern is the generic pattern for defining and describing the concept of a business process. It forms the basis for all other Process patterns.

Source/Credit

IDEF0 (Integration Definition for Function) is a standard that describes functions in enterprise modeling; it is also the source for the structure described in this pattern. The IDEF0 approach is used in most process modeling methods and with CASE tools such as Qualiware, Vision, and Cool.

Process Interaction

Intent

The Process Interaction pattern is another Process Modeling pattern; it shows how to model and organize the numerous interactions that occur between different business processes.

Motivation

All business processes interact with other business processes, typically via the transmission and exchange of resources or information (which is a kind of resource) between the processes. For example, a business process can be a sales process whereby the interaction between them occurs by transmitting resources such as orders, price information, material, products, statistics, and so on. A sales process can also transmit orders to a production process or receive marketing material from a marketing process. Regardless of what and how it is transmitted, the interaction between business processes is often difficult to model because of its complexity. In addition, the vast number of potential resource combinations and exchanges can make these types of interaction difficult to model. Also, details of the interaction's configuration are usually not interesting; the focus should be on the resources exchanged between the processes. The Process Interaction pattern offers a simple way to model a complex interaction through the use of an assembly diagram.

Let's invoke the car industry example again, this time to examine the marketing process. To model the marketing process completely, we have to consider how the process interacts with the market—the consumer base and the car designers. The consumer base is in a constant state of change; the demand of the market changes according to the economy, trends, and new technologies. The car design process is also continually changing. Car models must be developed that can keep up with the market's new and changing demands (not present demand, since those car models are already in production). Therefore, we have a marketing process that interacts with both a fickle and everchanging consumer and with a production process that must continually adapt and try to predict the market's future demands.

Can we model a business process, like our car marketing process that interacts with two separate processes that are difficult to predict and in a constant state of change? The answer is no. It would be impossible to specify every possible interaction between these processes, because the potential interactions are extensive.

The solution to this problem is to model both the abstract and the physical resources that connect the business processes, instead of attempting to specify every possible interaction between them. In our car marketing example, we would first determine the business resources that are exchanged between the marketing process and the consumer, the consumer and the marketing process, the marketing process and the car design process, and, finally, the car design process and the marketing process. For example, the consumer delivers reactions, demands, needs, and wishes to the marketing process. The marketing process delivers product data sheets, advertising material, visions of car ownership, and specific feelings associated with a particular car to the consumer. The marketing process delivers information about the market's behavior, current demands, and predictions about future demands to the car design process. The car design process then delivers ideas about new models, upcoming buzzwords, and so on.

The key to capturing complex interactions between business processes is to design them so that they handle the resources transmitted among them, instead of trying to capture every single interaction such as sequences, iterations, and selection. The resources are placed in assembly line diagrams. As you may recall from Chapter 4, "Business Views," a business process communicates via assembly lines. As the example here shows, it is better to model the resources exchanged by the processes rather than all possible combinations of detailed interactions among the processes. The assembly line diagram has been constructed for the explicit purpose of highlighting the exchange of resources between business processes.

Applicability

The Process Interaction pattern can be used wherever complex interactions between business processes are modeled. Customer relationship management (CRM) is a typical complex interaction that has benefited from this pattern, and Amazon.com is a Web site that has implemented the CRM. Amazon engages in a personal dialog with its customers to be able to recommend products—books, CDs, electronics, toys, and so on—based on a specific customer's behavior or profile. And because the interaction between Amazon and its customers is difficult to predict, it is a typical candidate for the Process Interaction pattern.

Structure

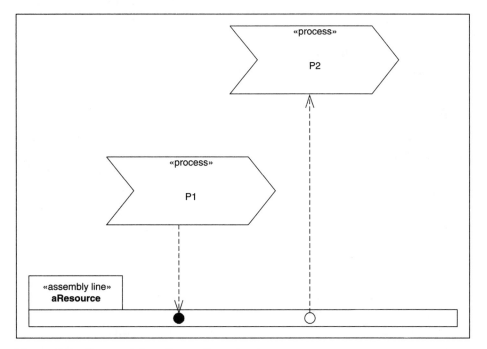

Figure 9.3 Process Interaction pattern structure.

Participants

P1 and *P2* are business processes that interact with each other. The P1 process delivers an object, which is shown as a filled circle, which is a stereotyped object (refer to Chapter 4, "Business Views," for more information on modeling with the assembly line diagram). The P2 process receives an object, which is shown as a open circle, also a stereotyped object. Both objects are resources placed in the assembly line aResource.

The *aResource* is a stereotyped package. The stereotype is an assembly line. The P1 and P2 processes can communicate with each other through the assembly line.

Consequences

The Process Interaction pattern can be used to model and organize very complex interactions between business resources. However, this pattern should not be used for every interaction–especially those that don't add any value. For example, a company that models its business processes to implement a new computer-based math system would not necessarily benefit from modeling the interaction among employees, because the relationships among employees would have no bearing on how the system will eventually be used. On the other hand, modeling, or at least analyzing, the interaction among employees, their attitudes, and employee culture might be of interest if the goal is to encourage integration between companies newly merged.

Example

HandySam.com is a new online hardware store. It sells tools and materials and offers tips for how to fix or improve consumers' houses, cars, boats, and so on. Sam doesn't believe it's enough just to start the portal on the Internet and wait for customers to find it, so it advertises in specialty magazines targeted at his customers. When a customer arrives at the Web site for the first time, Handy Sam has made sure it not only highlights interesting products but also offers nuts-and-bolts advice. This demonstrates that the company behind the Web site knows its stuff.

After a while, Handy Sam also realizes that it can show new and old customers what others with similar interests or needs have purchased. This is perceived as a value-add by Sam's customers, and is a strong marketing tool for the site. Sam has also set up chat groups where customers can share ideas and experiences. This further emphasizes to the target audience that HandySam.com is the site for all their hardware needs. To increase the number of visitors to the site, Sam also recently started to send e-mail to the existing customer base, notifying them when popular tools are back in stock or when new tools hit the market.

Handy Sam realizes that to successfully interact with the customers, they must analyze this process. At first, Sam tried to model in detail what happens from the first time a customer comes to the site to later visits, including making several purchases or exchanging tips. Then Sam recognized that the number of all possible interactions was too high to analyze and document, and decides instead to concentrate on what is sent between the site and their customers. Sam discovers that the interaction really consists of: Tip, Customer Information, Notification, Product Information, Product, and Order.

Figure 9.4 shows how Handy Sam's customer interaction process, with the goals of generating new customers, satisfying current customers, and producing more orders, interacts with the customers purchase process through assembly lines in an assembly line diagram. Note that a customer's purchase process is not always completely controlled by the customer; sometimes the customer must get approval from his or her boss, or he or she buys things based only on recommendations from friends or other customers. Thus the customer purchase process must be modeled separately from the customer.

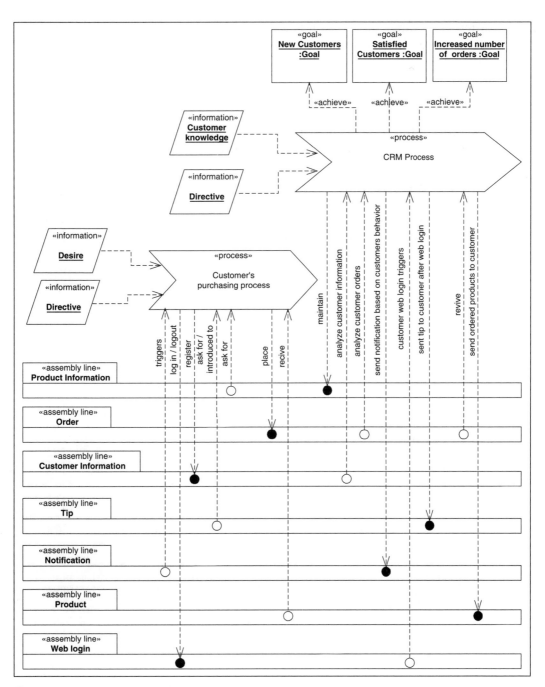

Figure 9.4   An example of the Process Interaction pattern.

After some time, Handy Sam is told that his ideas are called CRM, and that others have thought along the same lines, among them an online book seller called Amazon.com.

Related Patterns

The Process Interaction pattern can be combined with all of the Process Modeling patterns to detail and explore the business process interaction.

Source/Credit

The Process Interaction pattern and the assembly line diagram are a part of the Astrakan Method, whose inventors are Hans Willars, Marianne Janning-Andéhn, and Clary Sundblad.

Process Feedback

Intent

Process Feedback is a Process Modeling pattern that evaluates the business process results, and, based on those results, adjusts the process accordingly to achieve the business process goal.

Motivation

As mentioned earlier, a process starts with input and ends with an output. The process uses and consumes resources to create and refine other resources that become the output. A process has a certain goal to achieve such as to produce a certain number of mobile phones per hour. To achieve the desired quality on the mobile phones, you can also define other goals for the manufacturing process; for example: If less than 1 percent of manufactured phones have a defect, the goal has been met. But for a manufacturer of mobile phones to be profitable, these goals are not enough. The manufacturing process must consume and use as few resources (energy, material, people, and so) as possible. If the effective use of resources is not achieved, it can become too expensive to manufacture the phones, thus potentially enabling competitors to gain market share that will be hard to recover.

How can this be handled? The solution is to measure and evaluate the manufactured mobile phones to improve the production process. For example, a decision may be made to switch to a cheaper material for the mobile phone chassis, the theory being that the quality of the phones themselves would be unchanged. Unfortunately, the new material gets scratched while the chassis are being manufactured, causing even more defective phones. When the mobile phone process is evaluated properly in a controlled situation, this problem can be easily pinpointed to the new material being used in phone chassis, revealing to the manufacturer which material works and which doesn't.

Another example could be a new factory production line being tested for its efficacy in increasing productivity. What is revealed is that although productivity increases, quality is decreased, because personnel were not trained properly. When such a mistake is made, evaluated, and documented, it can be used the next time a production line is changed. The principle is that an evaluation of a process result is fed back into the process, enabling it to work more effectively in the future. If this is not done, the risk is that all changes to a process will cause degradation.

Applicability

The Process Feedback pattern can be applied to all situations where the business process results must be evaluated to provide competitive edge. Manufacturing, marketing, and sales processes are examples of the different business processes that must be evaluated each time they are executed. For example, if the sales process is evaluated each time it is executed, the sales budget can be increased or decreased based on feedback from the sales channel.

Structure

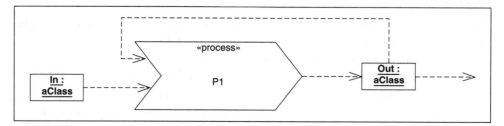

Figure 9.5 The structure of the Process Feedback pattern.

Participants

In is the object that *enters* the P1 process.

Out is the object that *results* from the P1 process. The Out object should have an increased value, and provide feedback to the beginning of the P1 process.

P1 is the process that refines the In object to the Out object. The Out object is returned for analysis, and the process is adjusted based on the results of that analysis. An example is a process that outputs products of which 10 percent are rejected. The process must be adjusted (e.g., in terms of temperature, pressure, humidity of the atmosphere; material defects; and so on). The adjustment occurs at the beginning of the process, and is based on the knowledge from the latest execution of the process. For example, if there are many scratches in the mobile phone chassis, the process must be adjusted, in this case, to use another material for the chassis.

Consequences

When the evaluation of the process result is fed back to the process, there is a risk that the process may overreact and make changes that are so dramatic that the next evaluation causes even more reaction. Overreacting to feedback (self-oscillation) is, of course, a potential problem that must be addressed. The standard approach is to apply some kind of filter to the feedback, which can be tuned to block the feedback that causes self-oscillation. There are many different types of filters. The *linear filter* is a simple type; a simple algorithm is applied to the feedback. For example, a linear filter is one in which the feedback is divided by 25. More complicated filters that use integration and derivation are beyond the scope of this book.

Example

Phonz 'R Us manufactures and sells mobile phones. The mobile production process is its manufacturing process that starts with an order from the sales process; that is, manufacturing is controlled by the number of mobile phones sold. The number of orders is rarely constant; during some parts of the year, there is limited need for phones, while at other times (such as before the holidays) large volumes are required. Because of the changes in the number of orders, the manufacturing process also changes; sometimes personnel work in two shifts, other times in three shifts. When the demand is really high, additional personnel are needed, and parts of the manufacturing process are then outsourced to other factories. Furthermore, ongoing attempts are made to use cheaper material in the phones and to automate the production. In summary, Phonz 'R Us works with a varied volume in production and with a process that is continually changed to manufacture mobile phones with the defined company goals. The goals that concern mobile phone manufacturing are: a maximum of 0.5 percent of the phones may have a defect; and no phone may cost more to manufacture than 25 percent of the reseller's sales price.

Since the production process is continually changing, occasional problems arise, in the form of production stoppages, increases in cost, or degradation in quality of the phones. To handle these problems, Phonz 'R Us documents every change in the process with a description and the time the change was introduced. It is then possible to evaluate the produced mobile phones and to trace production and quality problems to the changes made in production. In this way, the company, one, learns to prevent mistakes in the future, and, two, has the opportunity to correct any defects in the phones before they reach the market.

Figure 9.6 shows the Phonz 'R Us process for producing mobile phones; it takes orders as input and produces manufactured phones. The manufactured phones are examined in the evaluation process that delivers feedback on the manufactured phones to the mobile phone production process. The evaluation process also delivers the mobile phones for shipment to resellers and retailers, and, ultimately, to consumers.

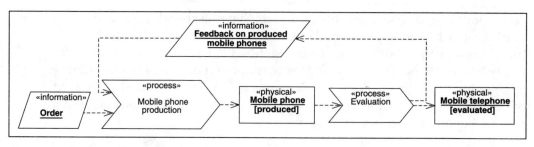

Figure 9.6 A sample process model with feedback.

Related Patterns

The Process Feedback pattern can be combined with all Process Modeling patterns to evaluate their results, and based on those results, to adjust the process accordingly to achieve the business process goals.

Source/Credit

No sources known.

Time-To-Customer

Intent

The Time-To-Customer pattern is a Process Modeling pattern that demonstrates how to describe a business with two main processes: Enable and Available, in order to shorten the lead time from customer demand to customer satisfaction.

Motivation

The business of training people is one whose practitioners recognize that their services must be updated on a continuous basis if they are to remain competitive. Many training companies have attempted to develop courses they thought appropriate, only to discover they could not be sold. Other training companies have chosen not to develop courses until their customers explicitly request them.

Neither of these company strategies can compete with the approach of training companies that market their courses as "just-in-time" for demand. Note, these just-in-time courses might only be in the planning stages; that is, not yet produced. The courses have been assigned authors, reviewers, and the other resources needed for production. Being able to market products on a just-in-time basis, when the demand takes off, means it is possible to gain market share, specifically to catch the first wave of customers (the early adopters). Early adopters are also usually willing to pay more to get the first available product, in this case, a training course.

But these advantages come at a price: Such a business strategy requires thought and planning. It's necessary to structure two important processes: product-to-market and product-to-customer. The product-to-market process (also called an available process) governs which products are planned, which marketing materials are produced, when the products are developed, how and when the resources for development are planned and allocated, and how the development is done. The product-to-consumer process (also called an Enable process) starts with an order that predicts future orders, and communicates with the product-to-market process so that the products are ready in time for delivery to the end customer. Structuring the business in available and enable processes precludes spending resources on unnecessary product development, yet does not delay getting products to market. And the products produced should already have or will have a demand in the marketplace.

Applicability

All situations where the main business processes are modeled in terms of production, sales, or delivery are applicable to the Time-To-Customer pattern, for example, the automobile industry, mail order firms, and the telecom industry. These are all businesses where the importance of delivering the right product at the right time is crucial.

Structure

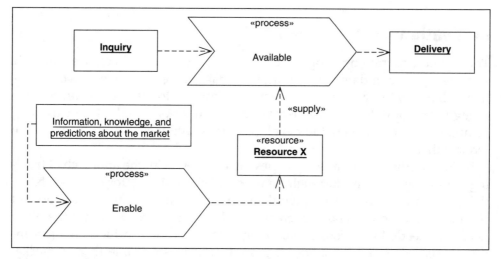

Figure 9.7   The structure of the Time-To-Customer pattern.

Participants

Inquiry is an object that represents an inquiry. This object initiates the Available process.

Delivery is the product delivered from the Available process. Note that the delivery doesn't have to be a physical product; it can be a service, information, and so on.

Available process is responsible for making a delivery after an inquiry. The process is supplied with Resource X, which can be people, knowledge, concepts, or a sales prospectus. The resources that supply the Available process are produced by the Enable process.

Resource X is the resource that supplies the Available process.

Enable is the process that equips the Available process by supplying Resource X.

Information, knowledge, and *predictions about the market* are the input to the Enable process.

Consequences

Applying the Time-To-Customer pattern should result in shorter lead-times and reduced restricted equity. With an efficient enabling process in place, businesspeople can stay one step ahead of the market demand, which in turn shortens the lead-times. Not buying and procuring items before selling and marketing them can reduce the restricted equity.

Example

The example shown in Figure 9.8 presents a business that's modeled with the two important processes: product-to-market and product-to-customer, in this case, a pharmaceutical company, Pharmatica. Pharmatica develops it prescription drugs based on predictions for customers' future needs. For quite some time, it has been working on a drug called Sniftron, for the common cold. Although Sniftron was planned several years ago, and Pharmatica was certain that there would be a large demand for it, the company waited to release it to the public because production wasn't possible at a cost that would result in a product that could be priced at an amount the customers would be willing to pay.

Later, however, Sniftron was put into the product stage, and marketing and sales processes were initiated. Still, production was kept on hold until the first orders for the product were placed. As orders started to come in, Pharmatica managers saw that the demand for Sniftron was large, and so they gave the go-ahead to production to buy the raw materials necessary to manufacture Sniftron on a large scale. (Of course, Pharmatica could not manufacture Sniftron based only on orders placed; it also makes predictions based on orders received and on raw material inventories.) The purchasing and manufacturing departments must also cooperate so that the purchasing department doesn't buy raw materials at too high or too low a rate in terms of what the manufacturing department actually needs. Pharmatica then delivers drugs, such as Sniftron, and performs a quality assurance check for any defects and informs manufacturing.

Once a product has been moved into the product stage, and sales and marketing processes have been launched, the products will be further developed, until they are replaced by newer and better drugs. And where the products that Pharmatica develops are medical equipment of some sort, the maintenance and spare parts handling is also part of the process.

The product-to-customer process comprises marketing, selling, purchasing raw materials, manufacturing, and delivery. This process has the goal to sell as much product as possible with as high a profit, while ensuring that customers get quality products in a timely manner. The product-to-market process is concerned with market predictions, the development of new prod-

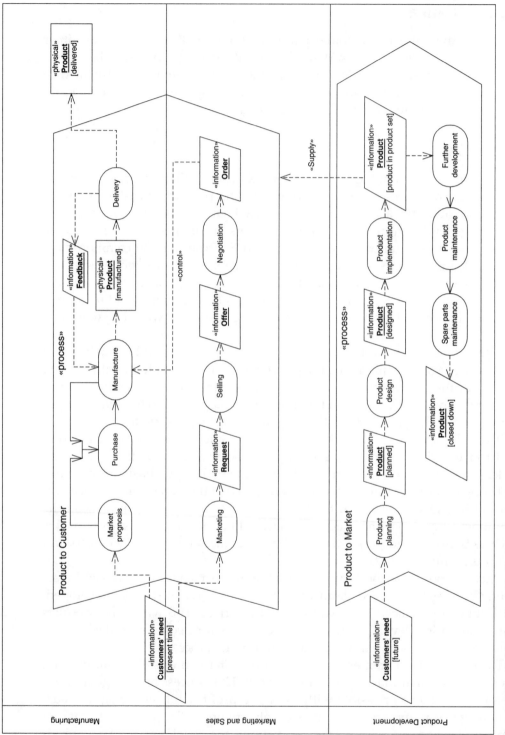

Figure 9.8   Using the Time-To-Customer pattern.

ucts, and the handling of maintenance and spare parts. The purpose of the product-to-market process is to make sure that the right products reach the market at the right time, while preventing the development of products that might never sell. Pharmatica's two processes, product-to-market and product-to-customer, show how the company can succeed in launching the right products at the right time, with low development and production costs.

Related Patterns

The Time-To-Customer pattern is related to the Process Layer Supply pattern, described next, which is the more general idea behind this pattern.

Source/Credit

This pattern is documented in the book, *Process Management* by Gösta Steneskog, published in Liber, Sweden, 1990.

Process Layer Supply

Intent

The Process Layer Supply pattern is a Process Modeling pattern that organizes the structure of complex organizations into primary and supporting business processes. Breaking the organization down into primary and supporting processes allows for a better understanding of the entire organization and provides a stable foundation for future reengineering efforts.

Motivation

To state the obvious: A business must create value for its customers or it will not survive. Customer value is created by performing a series of activities that the customer perceives as valuable. These activities are called a *value chain*. The customer will be in direct contact with some value chain activities, while others will be invisible to the customer. Typically, the activities that the customer sees are sales activities, the delivery of products, product support, and so on. They are called *primary activities*. Examples of activities with which the customer has no direct contact include planning, recruitment, purchase of raw materials, and so on. These are called *support activities*.

In his book, *Competitive Advantage: Creating and Sustaining Superior Performance*, New York: Free Press, 1985, 1998), Michael E. Porter looks at an organization's chief business as a single process and then divides it into several subprocesses. He then examines how each subprocess contributes value to the overall process. To help establish value chains in complex organizations, Porter has defined these two key activity categories as follows:

- *Primary activities*. Inbound and outbound logistics, operations, marketing and sales, and service.

- *Support activities*. Procurement, technology development, human resource management, maintenance of infrastructure for planning, accounting, finance, legal matters, government liaison, and quality.

As discussed in the Time-To-Customer pattern, many businesses can be described with a product-to-market process and a product-to-customer process, where the product-to-market process supplies the product-to-customer process with a product set. The product-to-market process is a support activity to the product-to-customer process, which is the primary activity. These two processes are both supplied with knowledge, people, machinery, and so on. But there must be another process that supplies them, a process that maintains the infrastructure, called the maintain infrastructure process. This means that the product-to-market process supplies the product-to-customer process, but the new process supplies both. As you can see, it is possible to divide processes into primary processes that are supplied by supporting processes. The division can be made in several layers where one process can supply and be supplied at the same time.

There are several layers of processes; among them are primary activities and supporting activities. The intent of this pattern is to clearly identify and organize the primary and supporting business processes. By structuring the organization into primary and supporting processes, you can achieve a better understanding of the entire organization and establish a solid foundation for the future.

Figure 9.9 illustrates this discussion. Note that the maintain infrastructure process is a supporting activity to the other processes—product-to-market and product-to-customer. Product-to-market and product-to-customer are pri-

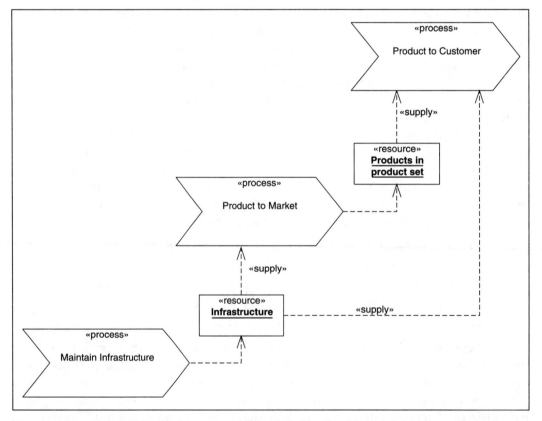

Figure 9.9   The maintain infrastructure process supplies the product-to-market and product-to-customer processes while the product-to-market process supplies the product-to-customer process. Here, the product-to-market process can be considered as both a primary and supporting process.

mary activities in relation to the maintain infrastructure process. The relationship between product-to-market and product-to-customer is that product-to-market is a supporting activity to product-to-customer, which is a primary activity.

Applicability

The Process Layer Supply pattern can be used wherever the business being modeled is complex and must be structured or understood before building information systems, such as sales automation and product-data management systems.

Structure

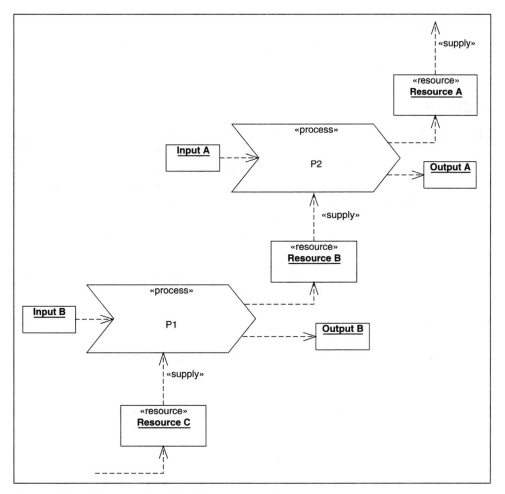

Figure 9.10 The structure of the Process Layer Supply pattern.

Participants

Input A and *Input B* are the objects that are refined to output.

Output A and *Output B* are the objects delivered from the processes supplied by Resources B and C. Resource A is supplied to some other process, not described here because the structure is recursive—there can be any number of layers of processes.

P1 and *P2* are both processes supplied with resources—Resources B and C. Both processes deliver resources to supply some other process.

Resource A, Resource B, and *Resource C* are objects used to supply the processes; they can be people, machines, or information.

Consequences

Applying the Process Layer Supply pattern reorganizes a business into a target-oriented enterprise that is motivated by goals, and where the business processes are layered in a hierarchy in which each layer creates the conditions required for the layer above.

Example

The boat appliances business Sailor Inc. sells appliances to pleasure boats and commercial boats. It quickly established itself on the West Coast, then wanted to expand both in the United States and internationally. The Sailor Inc. concept is to create networks with partners; and through these partners, establish a brand name for its line of appliances. Sailor Inc. also sells directly to the end customer, but makes sure to keep the list prices and by that give their partners the opportunity to look like they are a bit cheaper or at least not more expensive.

Sailor Inc. discovers that it is difficult to expand, in particular because management hasn't formalized how to create a network of partners, how to get to know and understand their partner's customers, how to create a brand name through their partners, and so on. In a simple business or manufacturing process, it is easy to identify what is valuable to a customer—product characteristics, good service, the sales environment, and so on. It's more difficult in a business such as Sailor Inc. that rarely meets its end customer. How can they ensure that the end customer recognizes that Sailor Inc. products provide higher value? To scale up and become more global, this knowledge must be formalized in order to spread it to new managers, personnel, and partners.

Sailor Inc. uses the Process Layer Supply pattern to identify which of its processes can provide value directly to their end customer and which processes provide value by supplying resources to the processes that directly create customer value. The end customer directly relates to the selling and delivery process, which starts with outlining customers' needs and leads to delivery of products to the end customer. The goal of the selling process is to maximize the return of invested capital. To sell and deliver, the product set must continuously be developed, in part through working with current partners but also by getting in touch with new partners—or, in some cases, by ending some partnerships.

The establishment process handles the sales network and the product set. Its purpose is to enable selling and delivery. The establishment process starts with customer profiles and partner profiles. To establish the business and build a network, a product set based on goodwill in the market is needed. This is achieved through the marketing operation process, whose purpose is to enable the establishment process. The marketing operation process influences the market and delivers goodwill to the end customer to support the establishment process. To influence the market, an infrastructure is needed, one that comprises the Internet; an intranet and extranet; and fax, telephones, videoconferences, and other technological capabilities. This infrastructure is developed and maintained in the keep-up-infrastructure process. The infrastructure provided by this process is also used by the establishment and selling and delivery processes.

Figure 9.11 illustrates Sailor Inc.'s main processes. Selling and delivery, establishment, marketing operation, and keep up infrastructure correspond to the P1, P2, processes and so on in the generic structure of the pattern. The infrastructure in the figure corresponds to Resource C; goodwill corresponds to Resource B; and the product set and sales network correspond to Resource A. Demand, customer profiles, partner profiles, and market are all input to the processes. Delivered products are output from the process.

Related Patterns

The Process Layer Supply pattern is related to the Process Layer Control pattern, up next, which is also organized in a hierarchy of layers. In the latter pattern, each layer controls the layer below, whereas each layer in the Process Layer Supply pattern supplies the layer above. We show how to use these patterns together next.

Source/Credit

Early adopters of this pattern were Björn Nilsson (Astrakan), C.G. Lövetoft (Astrakan), and Gösta Steneskog (Institute V, in Sweden). The pattern is used in some of the largest Scandinavian companies in the electrical power industry, as well as retail chain stores. It is also frequently used in the Astrakan

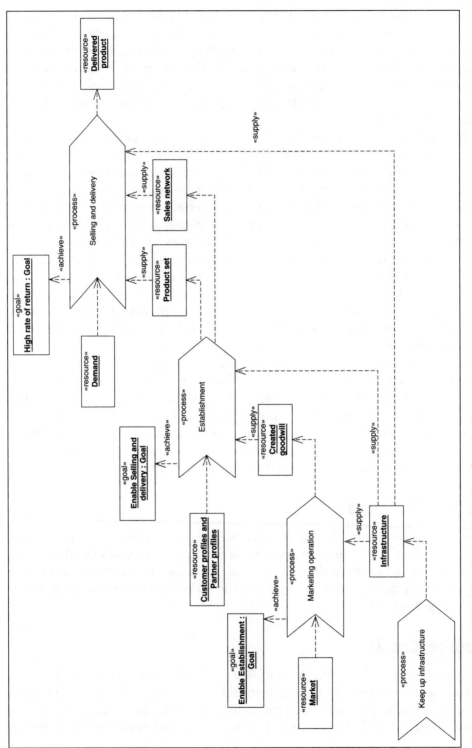

Figure 9.11 An example of the Process Layer Supply pattern.

method. The international standard language IDEF0 is also built upon these theories and principles. In addition, the paper "Dependent Demand: A Business Pattern for Balancing Supply and Demand" (PLoP'97 conference) deals with patterns in supply change management, which is a special case of the Process Layer Supply pattern.

Process Layer Control

Intent

Process Layer Control is a Process Modeling pattern that helps to structure complex businesses for the purpose of reengineering or understanding them. The fundamental principle is that all businesses can be layered into processes, where each layer controls the layer underneath.

Motivation

A business can be considered a system, motivated by one or more goals that activate the processes. Typically, the overriding goal is to improve profitability, return on capital, or political and social efforts.

A business can be studied and modeled from several perspectives, two of which are very useful when modeling business processes:

- *Target-oriented perspective.* Layers the processes for organizing the business into a hierarchy. Each process enables the process above it; the process at the top is motivated by the overall goals of the business. This perspective is used in the Process Layer Supply pattern previously described.

- *Control-oriented perspective.* Leads to a layered business with a process hierarchy. The difference is that the process on top, which is directly motivated by the overall goal, controls the process underneath, which in turn controls the next process, and so on.

These perspectives either focus on enabling the process above or on controlling the process below.

The Process Layer Control pattern focuses on controlling the process below. The business development process shown in Figure 9.12 is an example of a process that is directly motivated by the overall goal. This process results in strategies. The strategies control the management process, which results in goals, tactics, incentives, and so forth. The output from the management process controls the execution (the operative work), which results in effects that are in accordance to the overall goal. The effects are normally expressed in terms of customer satisfaction.

If a business and its processes are not well structured, the company management will lose control of the business. The Process Layer Control pattern is a way of describing businesses or parts of businesses from a control-oriented perspective. (Note: This pattern should not be used to describe businesses

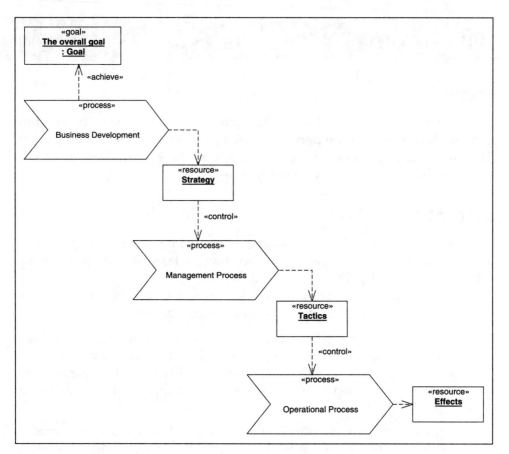

Figure 9.12   A business development process.

from a target-oriented perspective. For that, the Process Layer Supply is recommended.

Applicability

The Process Layer Control pattern is suitable for modeling control-oriented businesses, e.g., where the top business processes control the processes underneath, which in their turn control the next processes, and so on. Typical situations are when building control systems, such as CAM (computer-aided manufacturing), quality control, and accounts receivable and invoicing systems.

Structure

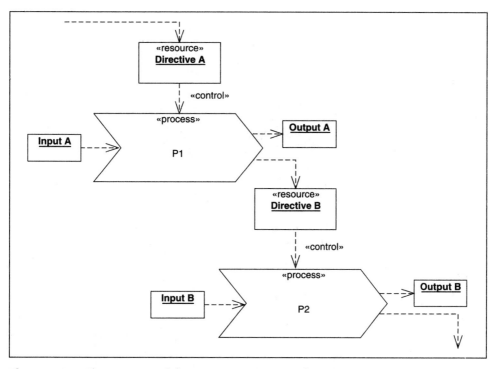

Figure 9.13   The structure of the Process Layer Control pattern.

Participants

Input A and *Input B* are the objects that are refined to output.

Output A and *Output B* are the objects delivered from the processes controlled by the directives.

Directive A and *Directive B* are objects that contain directives to the processes to which they refer.

Process P1 and *P2* are controlled by *Directive A* and *Directive B*.

Consequences

Applying the Process Layer Control pattern reorganizes a business as a control-oriented business, one governed by goals and directives, and whose business processes are layered in a hierarchy in which each layer controls the layer below it.

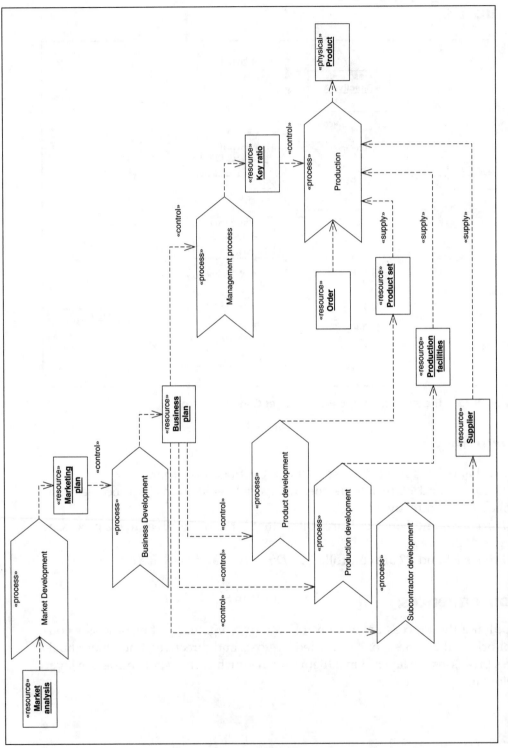

Figure 9.14   The Process Layer Control pattern in use.

Example

The example in Figure 9.14 uses the Process Layer Control pattern together with the Process Layer Supply pattern. It is built based on the principles of the Process Layer Control pattern. This means that the entire business is controlled in several layers. Market development (a process in the pattern structure) is the top-level process, which takes a market analysis as input (Input object in the pattern structure) and delivers a market plan (Directive in the pattern structure). The market plan controls the business development process (a process in the pattern structure) for the entire business, which is concerned with creating the business plan (directive). The business plan controls management , product development , production development, and subcontractor development processes (all processes in the pattern structure). The management process controls the production via the key ratio (Directive in the pattern structure; for example, production targets and allowed quality variance). The production process is supplied with a product set (not the actual products but design and material requirements and so on), production facilities (robots, turning lathes, and so on), and suppliers that deliver raw material, electricity, and so on. The supply is called resources in the process layer supply pattern. The production process delivers the manufactured products (Output object in the pattern structure). The supplier is delivered from the subcontractor development process; the production facilities are delivered from the production development process; and the product set is delivered from the product development process. The supplier, the production facilities, and the product set are all called resources in the Process Layer Supply pattern structure.

Related Patterns

The Process Layer Control pattern is related to the Process Layer Supply pattern; it is their respective focus that distinguishes them.

Source/Credit

Early adopters of this pattern were Björn Nilsson (Astrakan), C.G. Lövetoft (Astrakan), and Gösta Steneskog (Institut V, in Sweden). The pattern is used in some of the largest Scandinavian companies in the electrical power industry, as well as retail chain stores. It is also frequently used in the Astrakan method. The international standard language IDEF0 is also built upon these theories and principles.

Action Workflow

Intent

The Action Workflow pattern is a tool for analyzing communication between parties, with the purpose of understanding and optimizing this communication.

Motivation

Communication refers to how two or more parties transmit and receive information and how they react to this information. Whether the parties are people or computers is of no importance in this context.

Customers have various needs, such as the need for products. Depending on the need, one organization plays the role of a customer by ordering a product to satisfy a specific need, while another organization plays the role of a supplier. The customer and the supplier interact with each other, as shown in Figure 9.15.

What Figure 9.15 does not reveal however, is the real interaction—the preparation, the negotiation, the deal, and the acceptance. Very few customers, for example, would place an order without going through a bidding procedure or a negotiation. The point is, actual interactions between the customer and the supplier are rarely documented or detailed in systems or process descriptions. For instance, many e-mail systems cannot automatically confirm that a recipient has actually received and opened a message; this should be an obvious part of the process, to preclude the need for the sender to confirm whether the mail reached its destination.

A great deal of study has been done in the area of communication that directly affects how we model interchanges. In the early '80s, F. Flores, M. Gaves, B. Hartfield, and T. Winograd introduced the Action Language perspective, based on Searle's Speech Act theory; it has proven to be a new paradigm for information systems analysis and design. In contrast to the traditional views of data flow, the Action Language perspective emphasizes what people do while communicating, that is, how they create a common reality by means of

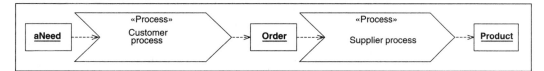

Figure 9.15 A customer places an order that results in the production and delivery of a product.

language, and how communication brings about a coordination of their activities. F. Flores, M. Gaves, B. Hartfield, and T. Winograd's work resulted in a wave of software applications, called action workflow systems; examples include Coordinator and many other workflow systems such as Lotus Notes and Metro. One of the most popular models in the area of action workflow is the repeatable four-phase Flores model for interaction, outlined here:

1. *Preparation*. Consists of two activities: prepare inquiry and send inquiry.

2. *Negotiation*. Consists of these activities: prepare offer, send offer, prepare counterbid, send counterbid, send offer until the customer prepares order, send order, and fulfill obligation.

3. *Accomplishment*. Consists of these activities: confirm, accomplish, send notice of delivery, and make delivery.

4. *Acceptance*. Consists of these activities: confirm delivery, accept delivery, prepare invoice, send invoice, prepare payment, and pay.

Flores's four-phase model is very helpful when structuring interactions like the one shown in Figure 9.15, because it is an established way of structuring communication. Figure 9.16 shows an interaction analysis based on the Flores model; in particular, note the interaction between the customer and the supplier, which is not shown in Figure 9.15. By basing the interaction analysis on the Flores model, a more detailed process description that shows how both the delivery process (labeled supplier process in Figure 9.15) and order process (labeled customer process in Figure 9.15) can be created (see Figure 9.17).

Notice that the two main business processes have been renamed during the interaction analysis. Both the delivery process and the order process have an explicit goal and a clear customer value. The goal of the delivery process is to deliver the product agreed upon. The goal of the order process is to order the correct product, at the correct price, and deliver it on the correct delivery date.

The interaction analysis based on the Flores model also verifies that the activities performed in each process are carried out by the parties involved (the supplier organization and the customer organization).

Applicability

The Action Workflow pattern is helpful during the process of structuring and for understanding interactions among organizational units, people, or processes. It can be used with interaction analysis to specify exactly how objects interact, why they interact, and when they interact, in order to detail the description of the studied objects. Typical applications are action workflow systems such as Lotus Notes, but include business reorganizations during which departments are merged, closed down, or launched.

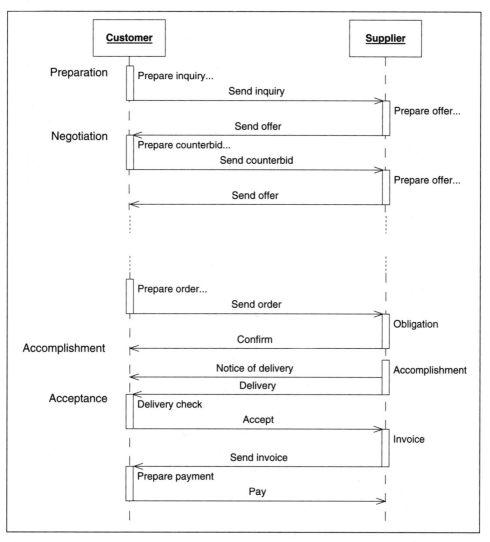

Figure 9.16   An interaction analysis of the organizations involved in the process model shown in Figure 9.15.

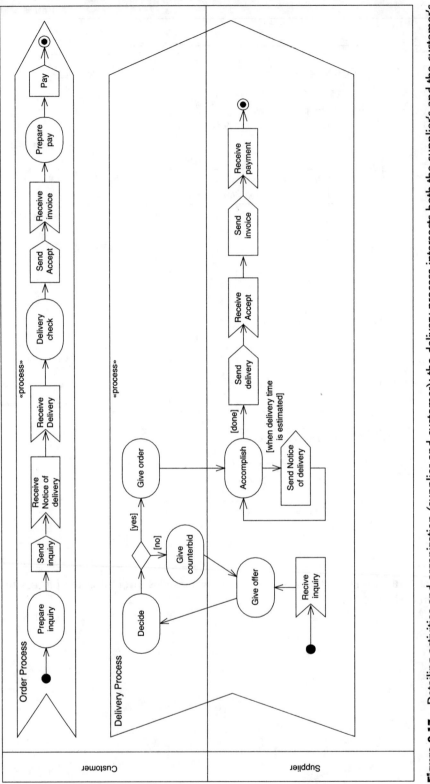

Figure 9.17 Detailing activities and organization (supplier and customer); the delivery process intersects both the supplier's and the customer's organizations.

Structure

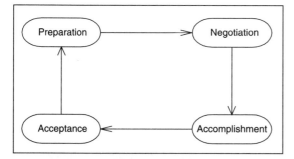

Figure 9.18   The Action Workflow pattern structure.

Participants

Preparation is when one party prepares an inquiry, then contacts the second party.

Negotiation is when the parties discuss and revise the conditions until both are satisfied.

Accomplishment is the follow-through on commitments made by one or both parties during the Negotiation.

Acceptance is when both parties agree on the accomplishment. They are then ready to move on to the next Preparation.

Consequences

Using the Action Workflow pattern enables the exploration, and subsequent understanding, of interactions between objects such as processes and organizations. In many cases, this leads to a reorganization of the process descriptions as well as the organizational structures and responsibilities.

Example

The Action Workflow pattern can be applied on both the macro level (interactions between two business processes) and the micro level (actions inside a process). Figure 9.19 shows one process where the actions taken inside the process are captured, structured, and described with the Action Workflow pattern. Specifically, a product development process is delineated; here, the input is information about market analysis and the output is products (again, not the actual products but the product under development; therefore, the stereotype «abstract» is used). The process goes through preparation, negotiation, accomplishment, and acceptance.

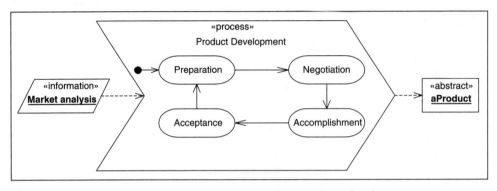

Figure 9.19 The activities performed during the product development process are modeled according to the Action Workflow pattern.

Product development involves communication with both customers and internal organizational units, such as the sales, production, and the marketing departments. A company that manufactures car accessories, for example, must have a product development process; and in order for that process to work, it is important to define the steps the process entails. Modeling a product development process without communicating with customers and internal organizational units will result in a process that fails in practice. Again, product development is about communication, and so the Action Workflow pattern can be used to model it. A product development process must follow the same steps that all communication does: preparation, negotiation, accomplishment, and acceptance, as detailed here:

Preparation. The product development process begins by determining where to use information from the market analysis to plan new products —that is, the preparation of product definitions.

Negotiation. The process actors (those following the process descriptions) begin to negotiate with the sales department and the production. The process actors also are concerned with preparing the products for the market; they must determine whether their customers are willing to pay for the product and who their competition is. This means that the actors working in the product development process have to negotiate with the market, production, and sales departments.

Accomplishment. Following the formulation of and agreement to the ideas, a product design is accomplished.

Acceptance. With the product defined and designed, it is possible to produce, market, and sell it. Note that it is not necessary to have the product in hand before selling it; only a product definition is required. Acceptance can occur several times; for example, first the marketing process may be accepted; and later, when the product definition has been polished, acceptance might be a go-ahead for the sales and production departments.

The entire process is highly iterative and incremental. The iterations are completed in the sequence listed previously: preparation, negotiation, accomplishment, acceptance. Typical increments for each iteration are: a future product, a well-defined product, a product that can actually be manufactured, and a further-developed product.

Related Patterns

No sources known.

Source/Credit

Speech Act scientists Searle, F. Flores, M. Gaves, B. Hartfield, and T. Winograd are the founders of this pattern. Their Action Language perspective has had a tremendous impact on the business modeling discipline and in systems analysis and modeling fields. These ideas were initially published in the article "Computer Systems and Design of Organizational Interaction," by F. Flores, M. Gaves, B. Hartfield, and T. Winograd, in *ACM Transactions on Office Information Systems* [Flores 1988].

Process-Process Instance

Intent

Process–Process Instance is a Process Instance pattern that clarifies the distinction between a process and a process instance, and the impact that clarification has on process models and process thinking.

Motivation

As we've mentioned previously, a process is a graphical or textual description for possible executions. But the process does not perform the actual execution; the execution is an instance of the process. The same relationship exists between a process and a process instance as between a class and an object of that class (see Chapter 2). Moreover, a process can execute in several parallel process instances, as in production. For example, an automobile production process does not produce one car at a time; it produces thousands of cars simultaneously. Each batch of cars can be considered a process instance.

Without separating the process from instances it's not possible to describe properties that are only connected to the process; furthermore, it's not possible to describe properties that are connected to each instance of the process. Typical properties for instances are time and space; typical properties of a process are characteristics, description, and so on. Not being able to tell when and where an individual process instance executes, of course, causes problems. An international automobile manufacturer will have its manufacturing process executed in many different factories all over the world; but even if the end product is the same in all cases, if employees were not able to track where a certain car was manufactured, it could become problematic—for example, if a defect were discovered and had to be rectified. Clearly, in addition to being able to define each process instance, the process itself needs to be described, because it contains the generic description upon which all instances are based.

Applicability

The Process-Process Instance pattern is applicable to all situations where the execution of a process is of interest; for example, when modeling production processes that can execute in multiple instances or at several places simultaneously.

Structure

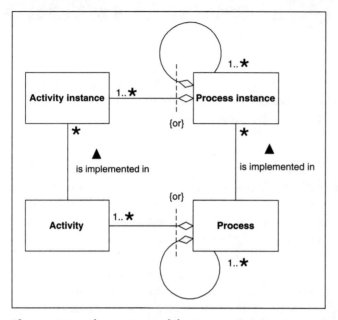

Figure 9.20   The structure of the Process-Process Instance pattern.

Participants

Process describes all the Process Instances. A Process contains other Processes or Activities. At the bottom level is at least one Activity.

Process Instance is an instance of a Process; it is the execution of a Process. Just as the Process contains other Processes and Activities, the Process Instance contains Process Instances and Activity Instances.

Activity is an atomic Process.

Activity Instance is an instance of an Activity.

Consequences

The Process-Process Instance pattern distinguishes between the process descriptions and the execution of a process. This results in higher quality, and eases the implementation of process models in a business and of information systems in that business.

Example

A software development process can be documented in a book as well as online (formatted in HTML and "published" on the Internet). A person can read one of the document copies that describe the software development process and follow it step by step to build an application or system. A week later someone else could read one of the document copies describing the software development process and begin the development process. Now there are two people who are following the same process, but are in different phases of development. The first person might have already formulated his or her system requirements and started the analysis, while the second person has just started the requirements phase. Thus, a process can be in progress in several executions at different locations and in different phases (processes or activities). This illustrates how one Process (the development process) exists in several Process Instances (the work performed by the two people). Each Process also consists of Activities such as formulating requirements and analysis, and these Activities exist as Activity Instances.

Related Patterns

The Process-Process Instance pattern is related to the Resource Use and Process Instance State patterns, which are described next.

Source/Credit

No sources known.

Resource Use

Intent

Resource Use is a Process Support pattern that structures the resources used in process instances in order to model and implement their use in a supporting information system.

Motivation

As stated, production processes begin with an order and end with a delivered product. The process is dependent upon resources that are produced, refined, consumed, and even used as a catalyst. For example, car production requires a factory with production facilities and employees, raw materials, blueprints, and electricity. Raw materials such as sheet metals are refined into chassis parts by consuming electricity. Catalyst resources, on the other hand, such as product sets and visions, and are not consumed, produced, or refined in a production process, but rather in business or product development processes.

It is important to understand that resources can be used in one way for one process, and in a totally different way in another process. Product sets, too, may be used as catalysts in one kind of process, then refined in another kind of process. A resource can also participate in several processes at the same time, regardless if the use is different. This pattern provides a way of structuring the many uses of resources.

Neglecting to account for the fact that a resource can be used in different processes in different ways will in many cases lead to processes that don't make optimal use of the resources. A typical negative result would be production stoppages if, for example, machines were upgraded at the same time those machines were planned to be used for production. The only way to circumvent such a dilemma is to study the resources and their use in the different processes until there is complete understanding of their design; then it will be possible to configure both the processes and the resources in the appropriate way.

Applicability

The Resource Use pattern is applicable to all situations where the resource use within a process must be explicitly modeled. One example is during the modeling and building material planning systems.

Structure

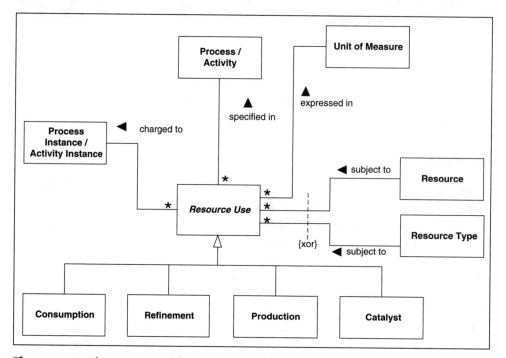

Figure 9.21   The structure of the Resource Use pattern.

Participants

Process/Activity represents the process or activity that consumes, produces, or refines the resources and resource types.

Process Instance/Activity Instance represents the actual execution of the processes and the activities.

Unit of Measure specifies in which unit the resource use should be measured. It is typically gallon, inch, ampere, and so on.

Resource Use is the use of the resources or the resource types. A Resource is typically produced, consumed, or refined, or acts as a catalyst. A Resource Type is typically produced or refined, or acts as a catalyst. However, a Resource Use object refers to only one Resource object or (xor) one Resource type object.

Resource represents the objects and information used in a Process or an Activity.

Resource Type represents the type of objects and information used in a Process or an Activity.

Consumption refers to the use of a Resource or Resource Type. Electricity, oil, and food are consumed, for example.

Refinement refers to the improvement of a Resource or a Resource Type. For example, a piece of metal can be refined into a cable.

Production is when a Resource or a Resource Type is created. Computers, printers, and mobile phones are examples of objects that are produced.

Catalyst is a Resource or a Resource Type that is used to initiate another event. A catalyst is not affected by but is necessary for production, consumption, or refinement. For example, production tools are necessary to produce products, but the tools themselves are not necessarily affected by the production process (e.g., a laser measuring instrument is normally not affected by the object it measures).

Consequences

The Resource Use pattern connects the actual use of the resources to the process and its instances. This connection eliminates the gap between process orientation and object orientation. The resources are modeled as objects, both outside and inside information systems.

Example

The production process at Phonz 'R Us uses raw materials and production equipment to deliver phones. The production process takes an order as input and delivers a product (one of phones in Phonz 'R Us product line). By studying in detail how the different resources are used, it is possible to establish that what is consumed are raw materials and what is refined are also raw materials. Similarly, the order initially placed is refined as a completed order. What is produced are products, and the production equipment is the catalyst; but note, the production equipment could also be viewed as being consumed, depending on the type of equipment being used.

The reason to perform such a detailed study in the case of Phonz 'R Us is to understand how the products are made from raw material. This in turn helps to specify the purchasing process. For example, it would be very cost-ineffective to purchase at a low cost material that that is to be refined, if the material consumed to refine the cheap material is very expensive. The point is, it may be more cost-effective to buy expensive material that is cheaper to work with and refine. Take electricity for example. If a certain plastic requires extreme pressure to mold it, the result will be high costs, both in electricity and in production equipment. The overall cost might be lower if more expensive plastic was bought that needed less pressure to mold it. Phonz 'R Us might also want to study the process it uses to maintain its production equipment. Figure 9.22 illustrates this reasoning.

The process diagram contains the process production process that is supplied with the resources, raw materials, and production facilities. The process

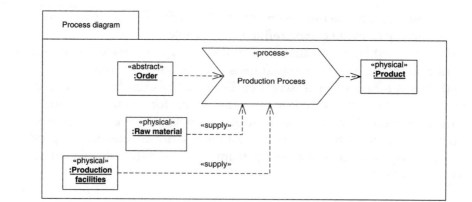

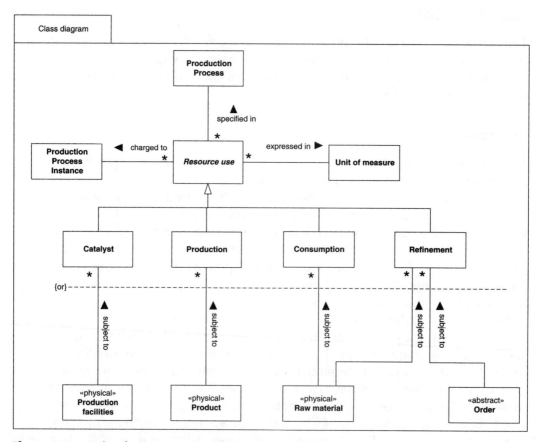

Figure 9.22   Using the Resource Use pattern.

takes an order as input and delivers products. The class diagram demonstrates how the process uses resources. The model indicates that the resource use is specified in the production process and charged to the instance of the production process—the process instance. Each resource use is expressed in a unit of measure.

The use of the production facilities is the catalyst, meaning that the production facilities are used, not consumed, produced, or refined. The products are produced in the production process; the raw material is consumed and refined to produce products; and the order is refined from a placed order to a filled order.

Related Patterns

The Resource Use pattern uses the Process-Process Instance pattern to define the concept of process and process instance. It can also be used with all other business process patterns to specify their resource use in detail.

Source/Credit

No sources known.

Process Instance State

This pattern is also known as the State Design pattern. Our intent here is to show how a well-known design pattern can be used to improve the quality of business modeling—not to reinvent the pattern wheel, so to speak.

Intent

The Process Instance State pattern is a Process Support pattern that shows how the state of a process instance can be used to create both well-designed processes and support systems, such as for computer systems.

Motivation

As with the Process-Process Instance Pattern, this pattern focuses on process instances. A process instance goes through a number of activities and/or subprocesses during its execution. If an activity or a subprocess is executed more than once, it is unclear whether the process instances remain in the same state after the first and second executions. A counter that tracks something—for example, number of items produced—is an example: Every time the counter increases it number, it enters a new state. The counter is defined in the process, and each counter that actually counts is in a process instance that is affected by the activity "increase." This means that a process instance can go through several states during its lifetime.

In addition, a process instance or activity can be suspended, or it can be abandoned. This means that a process instance within a product development process, for example, can be in the state "product planned," "product designed," "product in product set," or "product on market"; or the instance can be suspended for some time. Furthermore, a process instance can be proposed and accomplished.

The risk of not modeling the states of a process is that the process won't work in practice. Consider a sales process in a telemarketing company that specifies that an employee should call a certain customer to try to sell him or her a product. That process might not work if it hasn't specified how to determine whether someone else at the telemarketing company has already called the same customer; the result would be a customer who is annoyed and so definitely won't buy anything. Simply put, the states of the sales process must be defined. If a customer has already been called by someone at the telemarketing company that customer should not be called again the same day, and preferably not for a number of days. As illustrated, the states of the process are often connected to business rules. It is a business rule that no two employees of the same company should call the same customer on the same day.

Applicability

The Process Instance State pattern is used to model process and activity states in order to understand them before building support systems, such as information systems. Typical problem situations where this pattern can be applied are supervising applications, project management tools, and simulators.

Structure

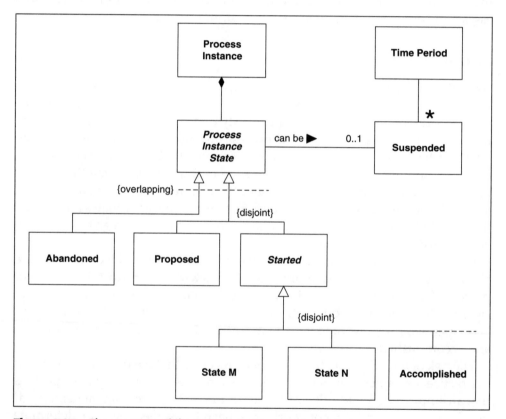

Figure 9.23   The structure of the Process Instance State pattern.

Participants

Process Instance represents the actual execution of a process and its activities.

Process Instance State represents the state of a Process Instance, for example, how the process instance is related to other process instances and how it reacts

when an event occurs. The Process Instance State is an abstract class, meaning that only the subclasses (Abandoned, Proposed, and Started) can be instantiated.

Suspended means that a Process Instance is temporarily stopped. A Process Instance can be Suspended for a Time Period.

Time Period represents the period of time that a Process Instance is Suspended.

Abandoned means that a Process Instance has been terminated.

Proposed is a state that represents a submitted Process Instance.

Started indicates that a Process Instance has begun.

State M is a subclass to the abstract superclass Started. State M is the first start state.

State N is a subclass to the abstract superclass Started. State N is the second start state. More concrete states such as O, P, and Q, and so on can be added.

Accomplished is a subclass to the abstract superclass Started. It is the last concrete state, meaning that a Process Instance has completed execution.

Note that a Process Instance State is always Started (including the specialization M, N, Accomplished) or Proposed. It can also be Abandoned and Suspended.

Consequences

The possible states for process or activity instances can be expressed using this pattern to develop systems that support those processes and activities. The pattern also helps to define business rules. If a process is interrupted, abandoned, or suspended, it may affect the definition of the business rules that govern the execution of the process or activity. One good example is if a food production process is suspended too long. The food may go bad and directly affect the business rules for producing food.

Example

The consulting company A&A develops products for the chemical industry. Based on a marketing analysis, it is preparing to contact customers to try and sell some new chemical substances or custom-made machine equipment. Many of these contacts result in negotiations, which may lead to the go-ahead for A&A to develop its ideas and deliver them. A&A's product development process consists of a number of phases, each of which can be suspended for a certain time. For example, the development of a machine to package Pharmatica's new drug Sniftron was suspended because Pharmatica considered the machine too expensive. Later, however, Pharmatica returned to A&A with a partner that was willing to pay for some of the development cost. This enabled A&A to restart the machine's development.

Figure 9.24 shows two diagrams of product development at A&A. The process diagram shows the product development process with its four sub-processes. The class diagram shows a state machine for the process modeled in the process diagram. The product development state can be Preparation, Negotiation, Accomplish, or Acceptance; at the same time, it can be Abandoned, Sus-

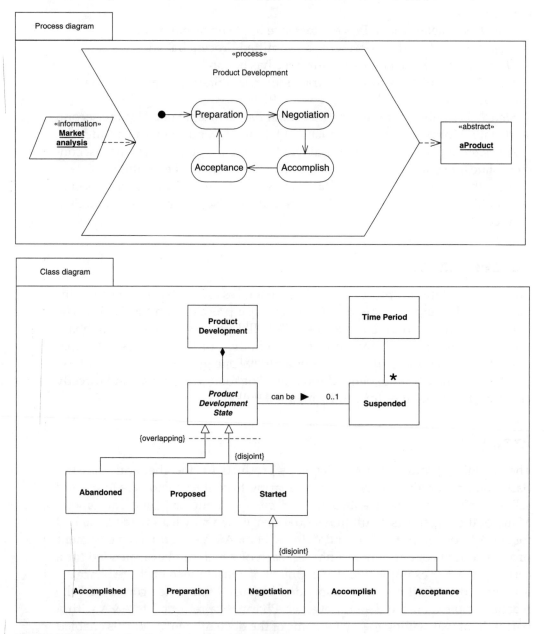

Figure 9.24 Using the Process Instance State pattern.

pended, Proposed, or Started. The product development state thus has two parallel states.

Related Patterns

The Process Instance State pattern uses the Process Instance pattern to define the concept of process and process instance.

Source/Credit

This pattern is well known, but goes by many names and in various forms. The book, *Design Patterns*, by Erich Gamma, Richard Helm, Ralph Johnson, John Vlissides, Grady Booch, (Addison-Wesley, 1994) refers to it as the State pattern.

Summary

The process patterns are *packaged knowledge* about frequently used and high-quality structures in process modeling. There are several kinds of process patterns: Process Model patterns are concerned with how to model processes to achieve high quality in both the model and in the execution of the model—that is, the actual work carried out in accordance to the process descriptions. Instance patterns refer to the difference between the process descriptions and the actual executions of the descriptions. Process Support patterns describe common problems and solutions in the context of "running" or executing processes.

Process patterns can be summarized as insights into the context of business process modeling. They are solutions to common problems encountered while structuring, improving, and describing the nature of the activities performed in a business.

CHAPTER

10

From Business Architecture to Software Architecture

A business model can act as the basis for modeling and designing the supporting software systems in a business. It is advantageous to use the same modeling language and the same concepts to model the business and the software, but rarely is this possible today (although exceptions exists, as some modern development processes now have a business modeling activity). Typically, business modeling and software modeling use different languages, techniques, and concepts, making integration of the two models difficult. This is a primary reason that this book shows how to use UML for business modeling. UML is a well-known technique for modeling software systems; consequently, many companies that today use UML for software modeling can use UML for their business modeling as well.

The business model and the software model are often developed as part of two different projects with two different teams. The models do not have a one-to-one relationship; many elements in the business model will not be part of the software model since not all of the business processes will be developed or represented in software. Many processes contain activities that are performed manually outside the software system, and so don't become part of the software model. Business concepts, such as the goal model, are also normally left out of the software system. Likewise, many elements in the software model comprise detailed technical software solutions and constructs that are not part of the business model.

353

This chapter reviews the software development process and discusses how a business model is used to define a software architecture. We assume here that you are familiar with software development and the characteristics of software architectures, and therefore only touch briefly on these topics in this chapter. For a detailed discussion of a software project's life cycle and the phases and activities of software development, refer to Murray Cantor's *Object-Oriented Project Management with UML* (Wiley, 1998). And for a detailed description of software architecture, refer to *Software Architecture in Practice*, by Len Bass, Paul Clements, and Rick Kazman (Addison-Wesley, 1998). A practical example that demonstrates the connection between a business model and software development follows in Chapter 11, "A Business Model Example."

Software Development Process

Software development processes specify the activities to perform in software development, instructions for how to perform the activities, the results of each activity, and the order and synchronization of the various activities. A process makes use of a notation such as UML. More advanced development processes also include checklists, guidelines, metrics, documentation standards, and recommended tools. These advanced processes are often configurable, meaning that the process can be adapted or configured to different types of organizations or projects.

There are many processes for software development, each with different recommended activities. For the purposes of our discussion, we divide software development into nine common activities:

Requirements analysis. Captures the correct requirements on the system. These requirements come from the business architecture and the business processes and must be transferred into functional requirements on the information systems. Use-case modeling is a well-known method for capturing the requirements on the information system.

Analysis. Creates an object-oriented model of an ideal solution, which disregards any technical solutions or details. This activity often also involves a sketch of the graphical user interface that can be tested and evaluated by end users so that the developers can incorporate early feedback to the design process.

Architectural design. Defines a basic structure and a set of guidelines, on which detailed designs are based.

Design. Creates an object-oriented model that expands on the analysis and architectural design activities by including technical solutions such as an implementation of a graphical user interface, database mapping, and communication protocols.

Implementation. Programs the object-oriented design model using an object-oriented programming language. In this activity, final design issues are modeled in the programming language. Often the activity also involves a review of the code produced.

Unit test. Tests the individual classes or groups of classes, to identify programming errors. This activity is a test of the implementation and is often performed by the individual developers who test the classes they have programmed.

Integration test. Integrates and tests subsystems or parts of systems that were developed by different teams or programmers. This test validates the architectural design and is often performed by an integration team with a good understanding of the overall architecture.

System test. Tests the entire system from the viewpoint of an external actor. This is a final test of the requirements analysis and analysis processes, and validates and verifies that a correct and working system has been produced.

Deployment. Deploys the system to the customer and establishes all activities that prepare the software for use by the end users: packaging, installation, documentation, training, and customer support.

Each activity is defined with the input, a more detailed list of subactivities, and the expected results. Figure 10.1 shows the anatomy of a traditional software development process. The V-like structure shows the activities of software development, their sequence, and their relationship to each other. Business modeling takes place prior to the software development process and is verified through the actual business results (the results are tested against the business goals, as defined in the business model).

A traditional software development process performs the activities in sequence; each activity is performed only once. That said, as software systems become more complex, it may become necessary for the development process to iterate through these activities multiple times. Modern software development process uses an iterative, incremental approach, as shown in Figure 10.2.

An iterative, incremental process suggests that the system is developed in increments, where each increment produced runs through the activities previously mentioned. Each increment adds functionality to the system; thereafter, the result is evaluated in terms of technical goals, time and economy goals, and process goals (e.g., an evaluation of the development process itself, how is it working, and what could be improved). Some factors need to be clear before the first increment begins, such as the base requirements of the system. The

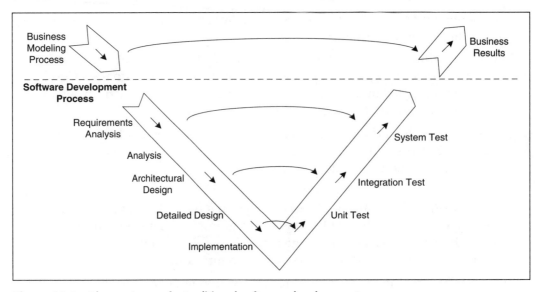

Figure 10.1   The anatomy of a traditional software development process.

requirements activity in each iteration should detail only those base requirements needed in that iteration and, if necessary, take into account experiences from previous iterations or, in some cases, suggestions from users who have tested earlier iterations. Business modeling should be done separately from

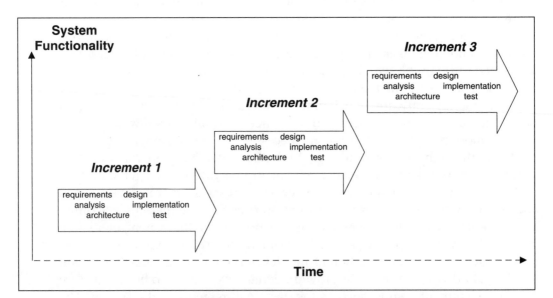

Figure 10.2   An iterative and incremental approach to software development.

the development iterations, so that a stable business model exists before these iterations begin. (The business model in itself can also be produced in iterations, but not in conjunction with the development iterations.)

Running through the main activities only once reduces the possibility of detection of serious defects or misunderstandings in the requirements and early analysis and design. Errors identified late in the cycle lead to higher costs, delays in the development, and sometimes to a poor end-product. If the process is iterative instead—running through all the activities in each iteration that result in the completion of an incremental step or version of the final system—problems can be detected continuously. In this way, the project can be better controlled, errors can be detected earlier, and thus can be better handled. Iterative development also allows developers to prioritize the incremental steps (each subversion of the system), so that more important or more risky steps can be developed and delivered early. By creating a base architecture in an early step, then adding functionality in the steps that follow, the more difficult parts of the system can be completed early.

In all kinds of development, insights and discoveries may also be discovered during design that might affect the initial requirements or business models. When this happens, it is necessary to go back and change, detail, or evolve the business models. Furthermore, new questions arise as the business model is examined from the system architects' viewpoint, and these questions must be answered and modeled in order to be able to design the software system. This is a natural part of the process, and development should plan for and include such correcting steps.

Many software development processes are available that can be used with the business modeling techniques presented in this book. Philippe Kruchten describes the Rational Unified Process [Kruchten 1998], a commercially available development process, and discusses best practices in software development, such as incremental development and its advantages, in more detail. Ivar Jacobson, Grady Booch, and James Rumbaugh illustrate a theoretical framework for a development process using the UML language in their book *Unified Software Development Process* [Jacobson 1998]. Describing a software development process is beyond the scope of this book; instead, we discuss how a business model can be used when designing the software models and architecture that support the business.

As mentioned, a key concept needed for iterative development is a well-defined software architecture. Functionality can then be added incrementally to a base architecture to thus achieve better control over the development. Another advantage is that changes and extensions not initially planned for the system can be added to better support a business in flux. As in a building or bridge, a well-defined base architecture for software is essential; it is what "holds up" the system and ensures that the system doesn't deteriorate into a jumble of unstructured code that is impossible to maintain.

What Is Software Architecture?

In Chapter 3, the concept of business architecture was defined as "an organized set of elements with clear relationships to one another, which together form a whole defined by its functionality." A software architecture can be defined in similar terms, except that the system being constructed and defined is a software system. And like a business architecture, a software architecture can be defined in different views and modeled using a visual modeling language such as UML (describing a software architecture was in fact the initial purpose of UML).

The term software architecture is a familiar one, but remarkably, no distinct definition exists for it. For our purposes here, software architecture can be defined as:

> [T]he structure or structures of the [computing] system, which comprise software components, the externally visible properties of those components, and the relationships among them [Bass, Clements, Kazman 1998].

It is important to note that:

> Software architecture is concerned not only with structure and behavior but also with usage, functionality, performance, resilience, reuse, comprehensibility, economic and technology constraints and trade-offs, and aesthetic issues [Kruchten 1998].

The primary building blocks of software architecture are subsystems or components, modules that are at a higher level than the class concept used in object-oriented programming. These modules are typically groups of classes rather than individual classes (although often one or a few classes in the group make up the interface to the subsystem).

An architecture has functional, nonfunctional, and development characteristics that can be used to evaluate it. Being able to provide the correct function on time is often considered the most important goal, but a good architect can't neglect other goals. The different characteristics are:

Functional. The capability of the system to perform the functions required by its users. Naturally, this is often the characteristic most in focus. Besides just defining the essential functions, it also involves finding ways that simplify the usability of the system. Much of the basis for finding the functional requirements on the system can be derived from the business model.

Nonfunctional. Nonfunctional goals, such as performance, security, and availability, are not directly connected to a specific function; rather, they affect the system as a whole. The support for these characteristics must be designed into the overall architecture. Nonfunctional requirements of the system also can be taken from the business model, although the functional requirements typically dominate. Nonfunctional characteristics can be distinguished into constraints (such as data arrival rates and hardware platforms) and quality attributes (such as integrity or security).

Development. These are characteristics that concern the development of the system and the qualities of the system produced, in terms of modifiability, reusability, cost, and integrity. These are vital considerations for making architectural decisions. Usually, little material for defining the development characteristics can be derived from the business model, since this has more to do with the software and its characteristics than the overall business.

The functional characteristics are inherently connected to a specific system, while the nonfunctional characteristics can exist both at the enterprise level and the individual system level. For example, a nonfunctional characteristic such as a security requirement may concern all systems in the business. This also means that architecture often transcends systems and that many architectural decisions concern the entire enterprise. It is important to realize that even though architecture is often discussed in terms of a specific system, architecture often spans several systems or even all systems in the business.

Architecture will not affect only the functional and technical context; it will affect the organization of the development team as well as project management. The architecture is also the basis for long-range issues such as reuse, product line development, and handling of legacy systems. All of these issues involve more than a single software system, and only by developing and having similar architectures in the various systems can they be resolved (e.g., making a part of one system reusable in another, or making systems easy to integrate with the legacy systems). When all systems have a similar and flexible architecture, it is possible to handle changes in the business and in the business models in the supporting systems.

All of these characteristics must be weighed against one another because it's impossible to maximize all of them. A balance must be established that makes the architecture a success. There are interactions and dependencies between all architectural characteristics; some go hand in hand, such as modifiability and modularity, while others stand in conflict with each other, such as performance and security. The architect must weigh the characteristics and make trade-offs or compromises to achieve the best possible result. In addition, the architect must ensure that all the characteristics have been addressed in the architectural design.

All systems have an architecture. Unfortunately, in many systems this architecture will have been built in an unplanned manner, where the software development process was driven by writing code. Really good programmers sometimes can build a vision of an architecture in their head when the development team is small, but as soon as the development team increases in size or includes programmers with different skill levels, the system degenerates. The result is often disastrous: the system consists of hundreds of classes that are not structured and are impossible to administrate and have many complex dependencies to each other. In these situations, very few of the promises made by object-oriented programming can be fulfilled (i.e., creating flexible, extensible, changeable systems with high productivity). The solution is to define the architecture in a planned, deliberate way and to base the functionality on the requirements of the business, that is, on the business model. This has to be balanced against the need for rapid results at the project level, and that is one advantage with using an iterative, incremental life cycle in which the architecture is continuously evaluated and detailed in each iteration.

A current trend in software architecture is the development of architectural styles or patterns, that is, the definition of well-proven architectural constructions that have worked well in the past. Architectural patterns typically show a specific set of subsystems, relationships between the subsystems, and the interaction or communication between the subsystems. Experienced architects have several patterns that they reuse in their architectural designs. A well-known example of a pattern is the Layers pattern in which a certain functionality is handled through a layered set of subsystems, each handling the functionality at a more detailed level. A system is rarely designed with just a single pattern, rather with a combination of patterns, and a subsystem that is part of one pattern can be designed internally with another software architectural pattern. For more on software architectural patterns, consult Frank Buschmann, Regine Meuer, Hans Rohnert, and Peter Sommerlad's *Pattern-Oriented Software Architecture: A System of Patterns* [1996]. Note that software architectural patterns are different from the business patterns presented in Chapters 7 to 9. Software architectural patterns address the structure and organization of software systems, whereas the business patterns in Chapters 7 to 9 describe common structures in the modeling of businesses.

Myths about Software Architectures

There are many common misconceptions, which need to be dispelled, about software architectures:

Architecture is part of program design. The word design often is associated with program code or syntax. Architectural design is not, however, affected by the programming language used. It focuses on the modularization, the interaction mechanisms, and the communication at the highest level of the software system.

Architecture is contained in middleware or infrastructure products. Many of the most common middleware product suppliers (such as suppliers of databases, frameworks, and component systems) use the word architecture in association with their products, leading buyers to believe that purchasing those products eliminates the need to design a software architecture, since it "comes with the product." There is no such product on the market. Not even object/component architectures such as CORBA, Enterprise JavaBeans, or COM+ provide the user with a complete architecture, though they can provide a very important part of the technical infrastructure in a software system architecture. There is always a part of the architecture that is completely dependent on the current application, and there are also technical issues that the component architectures can handle today. Components will be discussed in further detail later in this chapter.

Architecture means choosing between a two-tier, three-tier, or *n*-tier architecture. Two-tier (a user-interface part of the system accessing the database part of the system) or three-tier (with a business object part, containing business logic in between the two other parts) reference architectures can be used as the basis for defining an architecture (for all nontrivial systems, the three-tier architecture should be used). But the complete architecture specification must also deal with all the other issues in a system, such as usability, security, portability, and modifiability. Each of the tiers in any of these architectures can be viewed as a system in itself with its own architecture; the dependencies and communication mechanisms between its different parts must be designed.

High-quality architecture is created by geniuses, much in the same way as good art. A lot of literature is available on designing a good architecture. The area is being extensively researched and developed, and more and more experience is being gained. Architecture design is a very vital part of the creation of software systems, and should be neither trivialized into a few simple decisions nor be considered as a mythical area that only a selected few are capable of understanding.

Designing a Good Architecture

The question remains: How is a good architecture achieved? What is the process or technique to use to create great software architectures? Is there a fully scientific definition of how to do this? The answer to the last question seems to be no, though at the same time some people do seem able to create good architectures over and over again. But their success is based on experience, and the use of common patterns or styles, along with the willingness to make meaningful compromises or trade-offs when they weigh different characteristics of the architecture against each other. Good architects have the ability to look backward (asking: in this situation, what has worked previously?) and to look forward (asking: this is a new situation, what could possibly work here?). The architect has to be able to create a vision of a working software architecture for the system.

Defining a good software architecture is not that much different from defining a good business architecture, which was discussed in Chapter 3, "Modeling the Business Architecture." The same goals for finding a correct, flexible, and understandable description of the system (or systems) abide, and the same concepts of multiple views, the right level of abstraction, and visual models are also present. A vital difference is that the software architecture will be expanded into a very detailed artifact, namely the detailed programming code. When the business architecture is defined, the development is often stopped at an appropriate level of abstraction, and further details are not elaborated upon (the appropriate level is dependent on the actual purpose of the model, as discussed in Chapters 1, 3, and 4). The software architecture will have to be expanded and detailed in order to produce a working system.

This vision is based on a combination of knowledge about factors such as: the domain at hand, old and new technology and its possibilities, available products and frameworks, information strategies, and architecture patterns and styles. Because finding this combined knowledge in just one person is rare, the role of architect often has to be played by different individuals in the project. That said, the architecture should be developed by a team of *not more than five* persons and headed by a lead architect. The work of the architect and his or her team is not only to define the system architecture, but to communicate and lead other developers in understanding and using the architecture correctly.

As with a business architecture, a number of principles signify a good software architecture:

Well-defined subsystems with clear interfaces. The system is based on a set of well-defined subsystems that are encapsulated and separated from each other. A subsystem is a group of classes that handles a specific area of functionality (technical or application-oriented) with a well-defined interface. Each area of functionality, be it technical or application-oriented, should be placed into a distinct subsystem. Abstraction is used to hide the underlying implementation or representation; the representation of data and the implementation of each unit should be encapsulated into subsystems or classes.

Simple and few one-way dependencies between subsystems. The subsystems have as few simple dependencies to each other as possible. Ideally, there are no two-way dependencies (where two subsystems both need to know of each other).

Independently developed subsystems. The subsystems should be defined thoroughly enough so that it is possible for them to be developed independently.

Simple and clear communication mechanisms and interaction patterns. The subsystems need to communicate and transfer data between one another. Here, too, the communication mechanisms should be as simple and as few as possible.

Isolated technical choices. Whenever specific products, such as databases, communication solutions, components, and other types of middleware, have been chosen as part of the architecture, they should be isolated through clear interfaces so that it is possible to switch to other products in the future. Replaceability is a key principle in component-based development, and services unique to a product should be avoided or at least their use limited to a few places in the system. This prevents the system from becoming too dependent on a specific product.

Clear and synchronized parallel execution. Parallel execution can enhance the performance and functionality of a system tremendously, but it also can create very tough debugging problems. The solution is to try to isolate the use of separate processes or threads inside a subsystem and clearly identify which resources are to be shared between the processes or threads, then synchronize them. A system in which processes and threads have been introduced without planning will become almost impossible to debug completely.

Easily visualized and communicated. The architecture should be expressed visually so that it can be used as a map that indicates where the component currently being developed fits into the overall picture. The architecture defines a playing field for the detailed design on which each developer performs. If the architecture is expressed only in text, each developer will inevitably create his or her own mental picture of the architecture, resulting in different visions for each developer. This increases the risk of mistakes. A modeling language, such as UML, plays an important role in visually presenting the architecture.

The common threads running through these key principles are simplicity and clarity. This does not mean that the system as a whole has to be simple, rather that all large, complex systems should be based on a set of few, simple principles or constructs that can be combined or expanded. The same principles can be applied at the subsystem level, as well as within a subsystem if it is viewed as a system in itself, where each part of that subsystem is another subsystem.

Modeling the Software Architecture

In both business and software, a well-defined architecture is the most important tool for managing the complexity of a large and difficult system, and it is also the basis for creating a system that can be extended and changed as the needs to do so arises. Good architecture helps in structuring both the system being built and the actual work performed to build the system. When the architecture is applied at the enterprise level, affecting all or many systems in the business, it also transcends systems so that they can be integrated more easily. Just as a business architecture describes the elements in a business along with their relationships and collaborations, a software system architecture describes the elements that make up a software system (or systems) along with their relationships and collaborations. The business architecture can be difficult to see, however, since it's even more of an abstraction than the software architecture. The software architecture is more apparent because it affects both the structure of the code and the actual work done by software designers, programmers, and testers.

Architecture, then, also involves defining a common infrastructure among the systems, and the use or definition of interface standards that enable the different systems in the enterprise to exchange data and commands. The architecture encompasses the entire system and, in the same way that the architectural drawings for a building are the base for all detail decisions, work planning, and evaluation of the finished result, the software architecture is the foundation for constructing the software system. A business architecture differs, as discussed earlier in Chapter 3, in that it "looks outward" toward customers, and contains business goals and involves people and other nontechnical resources, whereas the software architecture looks inward at the software system and is much more technical and clear-cut in its nature.

Using UML to model the software architecture is a well-established and commonly used technique. Many different development processes, although varying in their activities, agree on using UML as the modeling language to describe the software and its architecture. The techniques described earlier in this book, which use UML to model the businesses, will be used here to supply some of the information for that software model.

By modeling the business first, you gain a good understanding of the business requirements on its support systems; in addition, the software model is provided with a lot of vital information that increases the quality of the software system. A third advantage is that the same modeling language can be used in both models, increasing the traceability between the models. This means that a specific function in the information system can be traced back to a specific requirement in the business. Subsequently, a change in the business model can more easily be propagated to the software model.

Software Architectural Views

Similar to the business architecture, a software architecture is described in a number of views, each of which depicts a specific aspect of the system. A view

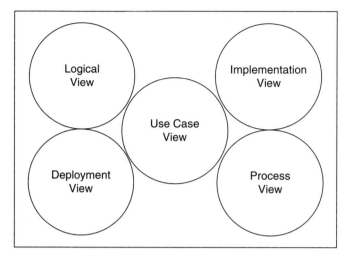

Figure 10.3   The five views used to capture the architecture of a software system.

is an abstraction from a given viewpoint that addresses a certain family of issues or concerns, and is expressed in a number of diagrams. Whenever a new diagram is drawn, it is allocated to the most suitable view, organizing all the diagrams in a model. The software architecture views (there are five) of a system, shown in Figure 10.3, have been implemented and used in many software development projects, and hence are more established than the business views.

The five software architecture views are:

Use case. Illustrates the key functionality of the system as perceived by external actors (people or other systems) through the communication that takes place between the actors and the system (use-case diagrams). This view drives the development of other views since the ultimate goal of the system is to achieve the use cases, which are used to validate other views. The use cases must be connected with the requirements from the business. They are the link between the business processes and the implementation of information support in a software system.

Logical. Shows the realization of the functional requirements through the grouping of classes into packages (class diagrams with packages), the significant classes in the architecture and their relationships (class diagrams), their state and behavior (statechart diagrams), and collaboration (sequence diagrams, collaboration diagrams, or activity diagrams).

Deployment. Describes the system in terms of the physical nodes (i.e., computers and devices) and allocates components and processes to these nodes (deployment diagrams). The components implement the classes defined in the logical view. The deployment view shows the system topology.

Implementation. Structures the development of the system in terms of code modules, both in source code and in binary modules, such as libraries and executables (component diagrams). Note that UML uses the term component in a more general sense, whereby a component is considered an executable unit of code based on a component technology such as JavaBeans or COM+. For example, a source code file is also considered a component in UML. The implementation view also handles configuration and version management and the release strategy of a system.

Process. Structures the system into processes and threads (e.g., active objects that execute concurrently) and the interaction and synchronization mechanisms between these active objects (class diagrams, sequence diagrams, collaboration diagrams, and activity diagrams). The process view also describes specific issues such as the startup and shutdown of the system, along with special nonfunctional requirements such as fault tolerance and distribution issues.

Though not officially part of the UML specification, these five views (originally described in Philippe Kruchten's article *The 4+1 View Model of Architecture* (IEEE Software 1995)) are referred to in most books, processes, and tools as the basis for organizing UML diagrams. As with the business views discussed in Chapter 4, "Business Views," it is not mandatory to use all five views to model the software architecture.

Figures 10.4 and 10.5 are examples of the some of the most familiar diagrams used to capture a software architecture. But note that they do not capture the entire architecture; they illustrate how aspects of the same architecture can be studied from different views.

Figure 10.4 shows the top-level diagram for the logical view with a number of packages and their dependencies to each other. In contrast, Figure 10.5 shows the deployment view of the system, with the nodes (computers and devices) in the system and their connections to each other. It is also possible to show the executable components allocated to each of the nodes by drawing components inside the nodes, but that hasn't been done in this example. The figure shows the same diagram twice: in the top figure, the diagram uses standard UML symbols; in the bottom figure, the diagram uses special icons attached to the different stereotypes, such as PC, Printer, and Server. None of these stereotypes is standard in UML, but all can be used to get special icons for the different node types, thus making the deployment diagram more like a "normal" system diagram that has been hand-drawn with a drawing tool. The second picture uses the correct set of stereotypes and thus adheres to the UML specification.

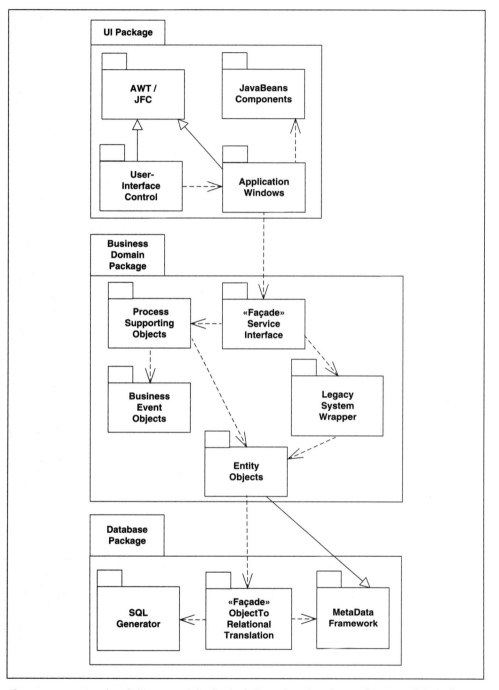

Figure 10.4 Top-level diagram of the logical view, showing the packages and their dependencies in the system. This is a class diagram, which shows only packages (UML does not have a specific diagram for packages).

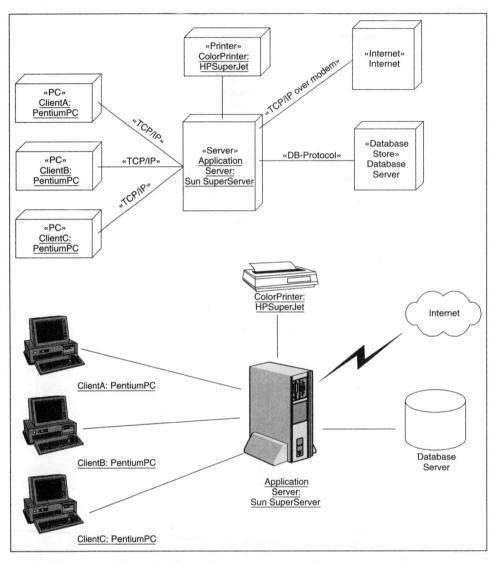

Figure 10.5 A deployment diagram showing the physical structure of the hardware nodes and their connections. The top uses standard UML symbols; the others have special icons for the different node stereotypes. A tool should be able to switch between both of these representations.

Using the Business Architecture to Define the Software Architecture

Transferring the information in the business model to the software model is not a simple or automatic process. Unfortunately, there isn't a one-to-one mapping for this process, and there is no simple algorithm to translate the business model into a software model. They are two different models, with different purposes. The business model describes a business or a specific part of a business, and not all parts of the business transfer into the software systems (for example, the people, manual activities, and many business goals). Nor can the classes and objects in the business model be directly converted into corresponding software classes and objects; doing so often leads to a very confusing software architecture where things that can't or shouldn't go into the software system becomes classes and objects in the system.

When a business model is created with the explicit and exclusive purpose of finding requirements and working as the basis for a software model, it is important not to over-model, by which we mean describe things that are of no relevance to the software model. Numerous interactions and discussions about all aspects of the business are important, but they need to be described in a way that directly addresses the software requirements. It is more fruitful to concentrate on the business concepts that do carry through smoothly to software. Naturally, if the purpose of the business model is broader (e.g., to document the business or to identify innovations in the business), more work has to be put into the business model.

With all that in mind, the software developer has to critically view and evaluate the information in the business model in order to decide which parts of the model are relevant to the software system being developed and to determine how that information is best represented in software classes. Connections between the two architectures can be made and conclusions can be drawn when defining a software architecture based on the business architecture. Figure 10.6 is a process diagram of the business and software development processes, as well as the connections and the resources used or produced in the processes. Although this figure presents an overview rather than a detailed description, it serves to illustrate the complexity and the many activities and resources involved in these two processes.

The ultimate goal is of course to create the software system(s) that best support and fit the business; therefore, the business model is a very important foundation both for specifying the requirements and for designing the software. The business model is used in software modeling to:

Identify the information systems that best support the operation of the business. The systems can be new, standard, or legacy.

Find functional requirements. The business model is used as a basis for identifying the correct set of functions or use cases that the system should supply to the business processes.

Find nonfunctional requirements. These requirements, such as robustness, security, availability, and performance, typically span and involve the entire system.

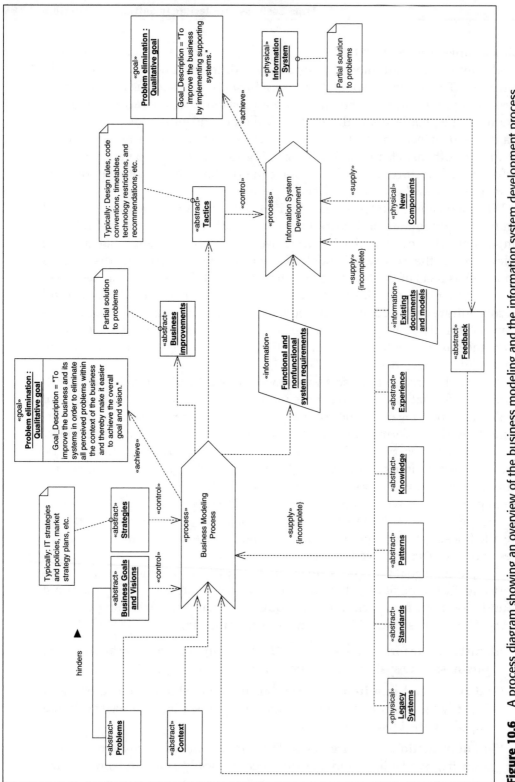

Figure 10.6 A process diagram showing an overview of the business modeling and the information system development process.

Act as a basis for analysis and design of the system. For example, information about resources in the business model can be used to identify classes in the system. However, it is not possible to directly transfer the classes in the business model to the software model.

Identify suitable components. Modern software development makes use of components, which are autonomous packages of functionality that are not specific to a certain system but can be used in several systems. Most component technology has concentrated on technical components, but increasingly, there is interest in defining business components that encapsulate a specific and reusable area of business functionality. Business models are a good way to identify these areas of functionality and to define the appropriate set of services.

The next sections explore these uses in more detail.

Identify the Information Systems

A very basic use of the business model is to identify the most suitable information systems for the business, that is, which systems are necessary and suitable to enable and run the processes? Often, such decisions regarding which information systems are needed are made ad hoc or are based on the type of systems that are traditionally required in this type of business. Critically reviewing the needs of the business and the current system topology will often pinpoint ways to improve the support for the business. Not all systems in the business will need to be newly developed. In fact, an important goal is usually to minimize the amount of new development because of the high cost involved.

There are three systems in a business:

New. Systems specifically developed to support this business. They are developed from scratch and are optimized to support the processes.

Standard. Systems sold by third-party suppliers. Typical offerings in this category are accounting, workflow, and personnel administration systems. Though standard systems are often cheaper to buy than to develop, keep in mind the services in these systems are generic and not always optimized to the specific business.

Legacy. Existing systems that are in use in the business. These represent a previous investment and should be incorporated in the new solution if possible. In many cases, the legacy systems can be adapted or extended to include new services that better support the business.

Rarely, when deciding which systems are needed, can the "ideal" solution—one in which totally new and highly adapted and optimized systems have been created—be used. More likely, some of the legacy system must be used or enhanced, even if a new system has clear advantages in terms of functionality. In some cases, a standard system may be cheaper than developing a new system in-house or through subcontractors. Economical considerations are always an important factor in choosing the new system topology. Replacing systems requires a *replacement and phase-out plan*. This plan describes how the new system will replace the old systems and how the information in the old system will be transferred to the new system. Typically, this plan requires a phase during which both systems run in parallel, so that if the new system fails, the old system can be reverted to.

The process and the assembly line diagrams in the business model are used to develop the correct system topology. These diagrams help the architect to identify activities that require services from an information system. Though it's not important to see the services defined in detail at this point, it is important to identify the information systems that are required by or that are of use to the processes.

Activities in the business processes that indicate the use of services from information systems are typically:

Information storage, retrieval, organization, and administration. Information is used as an asset to the business processes. Much of the information stored will be about other objects in the business process, such as process state, instructions, or facts about resources and business events.

Processing, conversion, and presentation. Stored information must be processed (e.g., summarized), converted into different formats, or presented in various pedagogical ways.

Knowledge and decision making. When so-called intelligent software can draw conclusions or make decisions from the information. It implies that the software system refines and enhances the information.

Communication. Whenever information, events, or instructions need to be sent from one location to another.

Control of hardware. Whenever hardware resources, such as machines, need to be controlled and monitored.

Today, many businesses would be impossible to run without the support of information technology. Systems that contain online business-to-business commerce, just-in-time delivery, workflow support, high distribution, shopping on the Internet, or finance information cannot be visualized without high-level software systems. Unfortunately, identifying exactly which systems are needed and what functionality should go into each system is not easy to define or describe in a simple process. The architect must balance the functionality in legacy systems, the functionality that can be bought in standard systems, and the functionality that is unique or specific enough to the business in question that makes the development of a new system worthwhile or nec-

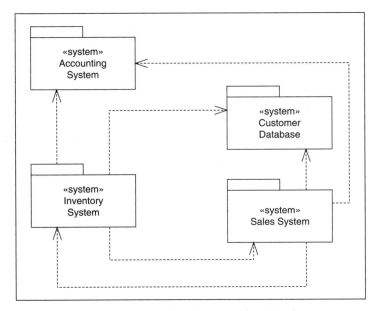

Figure 10.7 A system topology diagram showing the support systems for a business.

essary. Technical constraints, such as the environments in which the legacy systems operate, may also be a factor in deciding between what can be bought or developed.

Using the assembly line diagram as described earlier would result in a list of the services needed by the processes, but it then would have to be compared to the current system configuration and weighed against the cost constraint. Instead, to identify a suitable strategy for the systems, a system topology diagram, illustrated in Figure 10.7, is used. A system topology diagram is a class diagram with packages and dependencies between the packages. Each package, stereotyped to «system» (using standard UML), denotes a system in this business. The systems can be either legacy, standard, or planned. Characteristics for each system are documented as properties for each system package. By iterating and trying out different possibilities in such a system topology diagram, the final system topology is slowly discovered. There are many things to consider, such as estimating the cost for each new system or defining the order in which existing systems will be replaced. (These considerations are beyond the scope of this book.)

Find Functional Requirements

Perhaps the most important use of the business model in the context of software engineering is as the basis for identifying the functional requirements of a system, that is, the functions or use cases that the system should provide.

Functional requirements of the system are described in use cases, textual descriptions of the sequence of interactions between an information system and an external actor (the actor can be either the role of a person or of another system). A use case discusses each step of the communication between the system and its surroundings. Actually, this text description specifies the functional requirements, not the UML use-case diagram, which is only an overview of the actors and the use cases present in the system. A use-case description concentrates on functional requirements, but sometimes also contains nonfunctional requirements specific to the use case in question (e.g., such as performance issues). Actors in the use-case model are typically resources in the process, such as people or machines.

A use case is not equivalent to a process. A use case provides a service that is required as part of a process outside the system. A use case is fully implemented in software, whereas a process is normally only partly implemented in software (the term use case is an abstraction to define communication between actors and a system). Use cases can be considered as the specification of the services the software system provides to the business process.

The use cases are identified through a use-case analysis as part of the requirements analysis activity of the software development process. The use-case analysis uses parts of the business model to find the required services that the information system should provide (and that the business needs). Resources (people, machines, or other systems) in the business become actors to the analyzed system, and the interaction of these resources in the activities are captured in terms of use cases. A resource is considered an actor only in terms of a specific system and from the system architect's viewpoint, so there is no change to the business model.

The assembly line diagram is a powerful tool for identifying the required use cases for the system. It depicts the necessary references from activities in a process to packages of objects in an information system. A package of objects (represented by a package stereotyped to «assembly line») could represent an entire information system, a subsystem or component in an information system, or even a specific class of objects. The first iteration of analysis usually begins with references to systems (each assembly line is a system) and is then repeated with a special assembly line diagram for each system, where the packages represent logical subsystems in that system. Naturally, if the purpose of the business model is to find the requirements for a specific system, you begin directly with the assembly line diagram for that system. The subsystems packages are identified by looking at the resource and information models in the business model to find suitable and logical divisions of functionality that should be part of the system in question.

When an assembly line diagram has been completed on the subsystem level for a specific system, it may be necessary to revisit, refine, and detail the assembly line diagrams in the business model. When analyzing the process from the viewpoint of a specific system, these questions may arise: What needs to be clarified in order to specify the system in detail? What requests are met by the process to the information system that enable and support the process? The references from the processes or activities to the assembly line packages are communication requests between resources (actors) in the process to the information system. A sequence of such references becomes a use case in the system.

The integration point between the business process and the use case is the assembly line diagram. The use case should not be defined by collecting references from the process to an assembly line and labeling them a use case. The use case must be a complete functionality, from its initiation by an actor to the return of a result from the system. When using the business model to define the use cases, you must look from both the view of the business process (asking what is needed from the information system?) and from the view of the system (asking what will make up a complete and well-defined use case?). Otherwise, you might end up with rather poor, ill-formed, and partial use cases.

The business model can also be used to identify the suitable incremental steps in an iterative development cycle; it can aid in defining which use cases are most important for the processes (while technological considerations define which use cases carry the most risk or cover the architecture of the system, two other means of defining the suitable incremental steps).

Figure 10.8 shows an assembly diagram and its references to different information systems. References can be linked to define a use case according to the guidelines for a use case. For each of the information systems, a use-case model can be created (see Figure 10.9) that defines the use cases in more detail.

In Figures 10.8 and 10.9, communication between the systems has not been defined. One could imagine that, for example, the accountant only works with the accounting system. The accounting system then retrieves the order information from the sales system as part of registering a transaction. In that case, the reference in Figure 10.8 from the registering transaction process should go to the accounting system. The accounting system then becomes an actor to the sales system in Figure 10.9.

A part of the software design that is indirectly affected by the functional requirements is the graphical user interface, the GUI. The GUI can be designed at an early stage of development, after the actors and the use cases in the system have been defined, and often leads to the development of a prototype. The prototype can then be put in the hands of real-life users early, for their feedback. The user-interface design uses the actor definition as well as both the functional and nonfunctional requirements as its basis. The user interface is implemented by boundary objects that handle the presentation, navigation, and communication of information between the actors (a boundary object is, for example, what a window object in the user interface represents). These

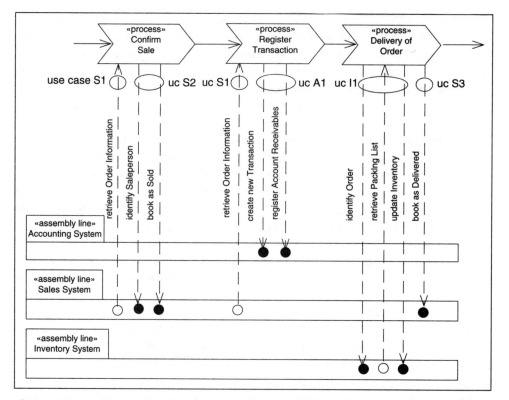

Figure 10.8 A business process uses services from different information systems. (Note: the use-case ellipses are not part of the diagram—they are only an illustration in this figure.)

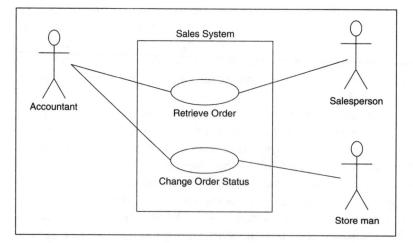

Figure 10.9 A use-case diagram as seen from the order system.

boundary objects will have relationships to other objects that represent the communicated information. The detailed collaboration between the boundary objects and the other objects are later designed in detail and documented in interaction diagrams, such as sequence or collaboration diagrams in UML.

Find Nonfunctional Requirements

Nonfunctional requirements, such as performance, availability, and security, are not normally connected to a specific use case or functionality; instead, they are usually generic properties that affect and must be maintained and handled in many use-cases. Often the nonfunctional requirements aren't even specific to a certain system but are applicable to the enterprise level, that is, all the systems in a business. These requirements normally are not designed or implemented in a specific component or subsystem, but affect many or all components and subsystems. The process diagrams and descriptions in the business model are studied to identify nonfunctional requirements. Nonfunctional requirements are identified by looking at the following needs in the business processes:

- Lead times (the time between an order and a delivered product)
- Response time
- Business process performance tracking
- Quality measurements
- Availability
- Resource consumption
- Security

Values for these nonfunctional requirements may not be specified in the process diagram, in which case they are specified in the requirements activity of the software development process. Specifications that typically indicate the affect of nonfunctional requirements on the entire software system also reside in the goal models, another part of the business model that affects the nonfunctional requirements.

It is a good idea to illustrate the functional requirements (like use cases) and the nonfunctional requirements together at an early stage in a matrix, as shown in Figure 10.10. The matrix can list those nonfunctional requirements that affect a specific function (an X indicates a connection) or can contain specific values for the nonfunctional requirement. The measurement of each value depends on the properties of each nonfunctional requirement; for example, performance is typically a time value, whereas security might be a level value. This relatively simple tool illustrates that nonfunctional requirements typi-

	Performance	Availibity	Security	Usability
use case 1	10 ms	98 %	high	n/a
use case 2	2 s	99 %	none	n/a
use case 3	n/a	90 %	n/a	high

Figure 10.10   A matrix cross-referencing functional and nonfunctional requirements.

cally span more than one function, and often more than system; that is, nonfunctional requirements are often at the enterprise level.

The matrix clearly visualizes that the nonfunctional requirements normally are not connected to a specific use case, but span several functions. It is important to describe both the functional and nonfunctional requirements at the system and the subsystem levels. The requirements are documented in a requirements specification that includes the use-case specification. The requirement specification is the contract between the customer or user and the development organization that is responsible for developing the correct system.

Act as Basis for Analysis and Design

Even though there is no one-to-one correlation between the business model and the software model, a lot in the business model can be used in the analysis and design of the software. Tasks such as identifying classes, their attributes and operations, their structures and relationships, and collaborations between objects of classes can be carried over to the software model. Since the software system handles and supports the business, many of the classes in the business model will be reflected and implemented in software. That said, it's still important to look at the business model from the viewpoint of each system and to identify which classes are actually required in each system.

Process and assembly line diagrams can indicate software classes. Resources that are used in the diagrams are sometimes represented in software; and a process can also be represented in software as a *process supporting object*, an object that runs or tracks the execution of the process. A process supporting object holds the order of activities and the state of the process and coordinates the resources involved in the process. To clarify: The process supporting object is not the process, it is a software object that supports and coordinates the support of the process. Some of the resources involved in the process are not implemented in software but are communicated with, through the interface of the system. For example, people outside of the system would not be depicted in the software system; but, from the systems point of view, they would be seen as actors that use use cases in the system. The objects in the system that handle communication with actors are referred to as *boundary objects*.

The process and assembly line diagrams also define collaborations between objects; answering, how do the objects collaborate to perform a specific service (use case)? These collaborations are also part of the software design, since they describe software objects that perform operations on each other or communicate with actors outside the system. The objects involved in a collaboration can be categorized as *active, reactive,* or *passive*. An active object runs independently of other objects and initiates collaborations itself, for example at specific points in time. A reactive object reacts to specific events (implemented as *business event objects*) or needs to be triggered in order to start a collaboration. A passive object never initiates a collaboration; it only delivers information and executes when called upon by other objects. Process supporting objects are either active or reactive. Passive objects are often referred to as *entity objects* (objects holding information that are typically stored in a database). Process supporting objects cannot be passive, since they execute and represent the process.

Many of the concepts and relationships defined in the conceptual model that was defined in the business vision will be entity objects. The resource diagrams (including information and organization diagrams) that are part of the business structural view are also a good basis for identifying entity objects since information and state of resources are stored in an information system.

The meta-model in Figure 10.11 is an overview of the mapping of the business model concepts and their information system concepts. The implementation classes, shown in the upper right of the diagram, are process supporting objects, entity objects, boundary objects, and business event objects. All these classes refer to actual software classes that are implemented in the software system. The process supporting classes implement support for the business processes in the business model and obtain information from the process diagrams and descriptions (the processes are not shown in the meta-model).

The entity classes implement and map to the information objects in the business model. An information object will contain information about other concepts in the business model: An information object can contain information about a person or a physical product in the business or about an abstract resource such as an order, or about another information object, or hold information about a process (holding the state of the process). It is the information about these concepts that is implemented to the information system; the actual resources cannot usually be implemented in software. Separating the object itself from the information about it in the business model is not always done; this is, in our experience one of the reasons that translating business models

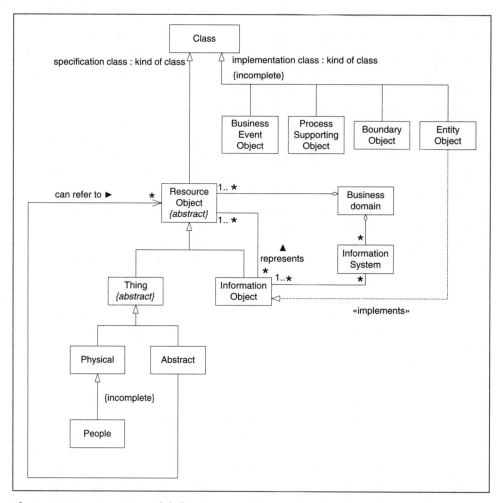

Figure 10.11 A meta-model showing categories of specification classes in the business model and categories of implementation classes in the software model.

into information systems has proven to be so difficult. The event classes implement the business events from the business model, and represent events that typically trigger the start of a process or decide the next state of a process. The process supporting classes, the entity classes, and the event classes are all seen as *business object classes*, since they all represent business concepts.

The boundary classes implement the interface to the system, that is, the system's interaction with other resources in the overall process. The boundary object classes are more technically oriented, and implement interfaces such as user interfaces, interfaces to other systems, or interfaces to hardware devices (e.g., that control or instruct a machine). Boundary classes are part of the technical design of the information system and thus are not considered business objects. There are also other technical classes in the information system archi-tecture, such as classes for handling a specific database product, a class library abstracting a specific operating system, or classes for connecting different information systems together.

One important area comprises business rules, which are scattered through-out the business models and affect all types of implementation classes. Guide-lines for implementing the different types of rules mentioned in Chapter 5, "Business Rules," are:

Invariants. Implemented in the class to which the invariant refers.

Pre- and postconditions. Implemented in the operation of the class to which the conditions refer (precondition tested before and postcondition after).

Derivational and computational constraints. Implemented in the class that makes the derivation, computation, or conclusion.

Relationship constraints. Implemented in the class that creates or adminis-trates the structure (or possibly in both classes if a relationship is admin-istered in more than one class).

Guards. Implemented in a process supporting class, where the guard con-dition is used to decide which and when the next activity of the process should be performed.

Identify Suitable Components

Component-based development has almost replaced object-oriented develop-ment as the programming paradigm of today. A number of competing compo-nent models have emerged: Microsoft's COM+, Sun's Enterprise JavaBeans, and CORBA. Component-based development is, however, a continuation of object-oriented development, and the two go very well together.

Component-based development has arisen from the realization that reusing object-oriented systems at the source code level is very difficult, and that the reuse of software requires a common infrastructure so that different compo-nents can be exposed to one another and cooperate. Software solutions must adapt as the business adapts, and to do that, software must be as technically neutral as possible. A key to achieving that neutrality is to reuse business com-ponents based on one of the common component models. The most successful business components are those that can be "rewired" in many configurations in effective response to business change.

A component can be defined as:

[A]n executable unit of code that provides physical black-box encapsulation of related services. Its services can only be accessed through a consistent, published interface that includes an interaction standard [Allen 1998].

A component exposes properties, methods, and events through an interface standard (such as COM+, CORBA, or JavaBeans) that makes the component configurable and that enables the component to cooperate with other components about which it previously had no knowledge. A component also exposes its interface through meta-data, data that at runtime describes the properties and behavior of the component.

As component-based development becomes more popular, and the components become more business-oriented rather than technically oriented, the business model will be capable of being used to identify the components in a software system. The goal for identifying and defining components is to find the correct set of services for each component, so that the component becomes autonomous and can be reused in more than one system (i.e., it can be configured or adapted to a certain degree for each system). A component is configurable through its exposed properties so that, for example, a process supporting object in a system can configure a component to suit its specific needs. To date, techniques for identifying suitable business components have been desperately lacking, and this activity is still an area under research.

In software architecture, a component is defined in its own package, which supplies a number of services. A component package has a connection to both the logical view of the software architecture, in that it implements a specific part of the functionality in the logical view, and to the component view, in terms of a physical component that is deployed on one or more computers. The idea is that the functionality of the component package is reusable and that the component package can be allocated and deployed in several nodes in the hardware architecture (which in turn deploys the process and deployment views in the software architecture). Here, the hardware architecture can refer to either a system or, more so, the architecture on an enterprise level (all of the systems in the business).

The assembly line diagram from the business model can be used to identify components, similar to the process of identifying systems or subsystems. The assembly line packages then represent a specific component. Finding the appropriate level of functionality for a component (i.e., assembly line package) is an iterative task for which the designer will have to experiment with different levels of abstraction. When the services of an assembly line package defined at the component level can be used by more than one process, the appropriate component level has been identified. The services are identified as references from the process to the assembly line package. This process is similar to trying to identify subsystems through assembly line diagrams, but with the added requirement that the services be generic and reusable by more than one application and more than one business process. The difference between trying to identify components with the assembly line diagram and studying use-cases in several systems is that the former is done by identifying commonality among business process and the latter is done by finding similarities in the information systems. The techniques are not necessarily exclusive; they can be used together.

The component package contains classes that implement the services of the components, but it presents a single component interface to its users (users in this context are other classes or components in a system). Depending on the component model, there may also be technical requirements for defining the component package. Most of the component models allow the definition of events, so that a component can generate events to other components that notify them about important situations. In the case of a business component, such an event is a business event. Often, component technology is used to encapsulate legacy applications, in which case, the component designer has to look at the services available from the legacy system as well as the services desired by the business processes. The component then must handle conversions or additional functionality that can adapt the services of the legacy system to better work with the current business processes.

Another special case is when a component is designed without the requirements for a specific system. Instead, a business domain model is defined that models a generic domain. This model is used to define generic components for this domain. Examples of domains are financial price, accounting, or network administration services. Designing domain-based components has proven difficult, because software development often requires the real-life test of a specific system to determine whether the component really works (both technically and in terms of the functionality offered). Some early initiatives in this area are IBM's San Francisco project and Microsoft's BizTalk framework.

The relationship between a business process, use case, and component can be summarized in this way: A business process will use one or more use cases that a system supplies, and the use cases can be internally implemented through generic components that supply all or part of the use cases. Figure 10.12 illustrates this relationship.

Summary

A software architecture describes the key mechanisms of a system (or systems), along with their relationships and collaborations. Architectural design is not concerned with code design, nor is it dependent on features of a programming language. It is the base design of the overall system or of a suite of systems in the enterprise. Even though interface standards, such as CORBA or COM+, exist and can serve as a base technology for the architecture of a system, they don't replace the need to define an architecture for the system or for the business as a whole.

A number of characteristics or properties of an architecture must be prioritized and weighed against each other. Functional characteristics include the

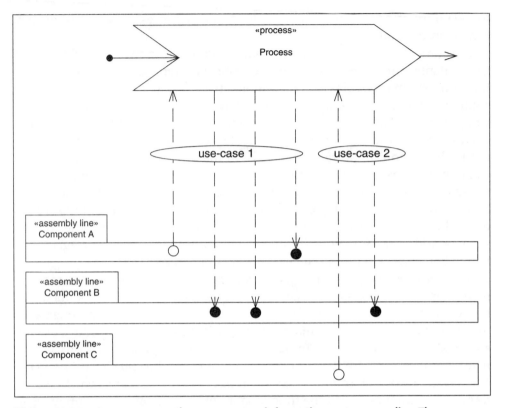

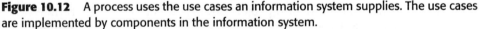

Figure 10.12 A process uses the use cases an information system supplies. The use cases are implemented by components in the information system.

functionality of the system; nonfunctional characteristics are properties such as performance, security, usability, and availability. The development characteristics, such as modifiability, portability, reusability, and the amount of reuse, integrateability, and testability, are not visible at runtime but are increasingly important to consider. The economic characteristics, such as time to produce the system, cost, and lifetime of the system, are also aspects for the architect to consider before making architectural decisions. It is impossible to achieve maximum benefit from all of these characteristics because they are in conflict with each other; therefore, tradeoffs have to be made.

The software architecture is organized in five views, as defined by Philippe Kruchten [Kruchten 1995]: a use-case view to capture the functional requirements; a logical view to capture the high-level subsystem and conceptual design; a deployment view to define the physical structure of hardware nodes; an implementation view to specify the structure of the code; and the process view to capture parallel execution and its synchronization.

The knowledge and information in a business architecture is used to define the software architecture. This isn't a one-to-one mapping, and there is no simple algorithm to convert the business model into a software model. They are two different models that serve different purposes. The business model describes a business or a specific part of a business; not all of the business goes into the software systems. To define a software architecture, the business architecture is used to:

- Identify suitable support systems.
- Identify functional requirements.
- Identify nonfunctional requirements.
- Act as basis for analysis and design.
- Identify suitable components.

Creating a business model before the software models, then using the information in that business model for the creation of software models, will increase the quality of the software systems. Systems that better support the business of which they are a part will be the result.

The next chapter gives a practical example of a business model that is created and then used as the basis for a software model.

A Business Model Example

Chapters 3 and 4 presented the steps for business modeling. Recall that business modeling begins with expressing the visions and goals of the business, and defining the business terminology. After the visions, goals, and terminology are clearly defined and understood, the business processes, organization, resources, and rules can be modeled. During the business modeling process, supporting systems may be created, removed, or changed. The last step is to evaluate and adjust the project results.

This chapter applies these steps and the patterns described in Chapters 6 through 9 to model an example mail order firm that has to migrate into the new world of e-business and network economy. This example is based on our experience in modeling these types of projects. The company is fictitious, but the business structure is based on existing businesses.

Bob's Mail Order

Bob's Mail Order, established in 1983, sells office equipment, such as copy and fax machines, switchboards, mobile phones, computers, software, and other office supplies to larger companies. Under its trademark, Top, the company sells products purchased from subcontractors or products it manufactures itself. Conducting business in this way allows Bob's Mail Order to be independent of anyone else's trademark, branding, and marketing. Bob's management also realized that by advertising and attempting to sell a new product before manufacturing it, they could reduce the capital investment.

In recent years, the means of doing business has changed, and Internet-based mail order firms have become a serious threat to Bob's Mail Order, whose internal systems are old and inefficient, and can't meet the demands of the changing business environment. In addition, the new Internet-based firms have lower sell expenses because of smart Internet solutions, enabling them to offer lower prices and to invest more money in marketing, thereby increasing their marketing shares. This business model example uses the concepts previously discussed in Chapters 1 through 10 to demonstrate how Bob's Mail Order can overcome these strategic business problems and update its support systems accordingly. The four views introduced in Chapter 4, "Business Views," are the basis for the analysis:

- Business Vision
- Business Structure
- Business Behavior
- Business Process

Because the views are different aspects of the business and not separate diagrams, one view at one time may be considered, while several views are considered simultaneously at another.

The intent of this business model example is to demonstrate business modeling and specify requirements of software systems, rather than actually build software systems. The result of the business model in this case study is a requirement specification that will serve as the input for building supporting software systems. From that point, numerous methods can be used to build the software systems, such as Rational Unified Process, OMT, Fusion, Catalyst, or Select Perspective.

Visions and Goals

The Business Vision view of a business contains the business idea and its goals expressed in a vision statement and a goal model. Because it is difficult to formulate a vision statement and goals without defining the key concepts, a conceptual model can be created in parallel to complement this view, to help clarify the key concepts of the business.

The vision statement for Bob's Mail Order is:

We should be the leading supplier of office equipment and supplies. We should offer customers attractive solutions and good value for their money. By not going through a retailer, we cut the sales expenses. Integrating our sales processes with our customers' purchase processes results in highly efficient communication and delivery. To be able to integrate these processes, we must provide several interfaces, such as Internet, e-mail, FTP, telephone, and fax. We can integrate further by offering additional services such as inventory tracking and automatic purchasing.

Goal Model

The goal of Bob's Mail Order is to increase its market share from 15 percent to 55 percent in a 24-month period. This is achievable by satisfying its customers, having a highly motivated staff, conducting 5,000 transactions per day, and earning a high profit from those transactions. However, increasing the current number of transactions, 1,000, to 5,000 will not be easy. To do this, Bob's Mail Order has to increase both the number of regular telephone customers as well as Internet customers. To realize the increase in Internet customers, Bob's Mail Order home page must be easy to find, and its visitors must be encouraged to register. Therefore, registration must be made clearly beneficial to these visitors, or they won't register. Bob's Mail Order must offer something in return for registering, such as a discount off the first order. But increasing the number of visitors and making it beneficial to register is an expensive undertaking for Bob's, and can impact the profit in negative terms. On the other hand, making these investments in the home page is necessary to achieve an increase in the number of market shares and ensure a high profit in the future. These goals are marked as contradictory.

The goal of high profit is hindered by that fact that Bob's Mail Order has too much restricted equity. The amount of restricted equity is caused by inefficient production and purchasing, as well as inaccurate predictions about the incoming orders. In addition, the product lines do not always meet the customers' needs; clearly, market analysis and product development have a high potential for improvement. Some of the problems in production, product development, and market analysis stem from confusion about terminology. For example, the marketing department refers to new product sets as "new products," whereas to the production department, the term "new products" means variations on items. Other problems stem from system issues. For example, the legacy sales systems cannot be connected directly to the Internet; many manual steps are required for each sale or transaction on the home page.

The goals for Bob's Mail Order are diagrammed in the goal model shown in Figure 11.1. It carries out the vision by directly relating concrete goals to the business and its processes. The objective of the goal model is to serve as a starting point for setting up a project that implements the vision; in this case, turning Bob's Mail Order firm into the leading supplier of office equipment and supplies.

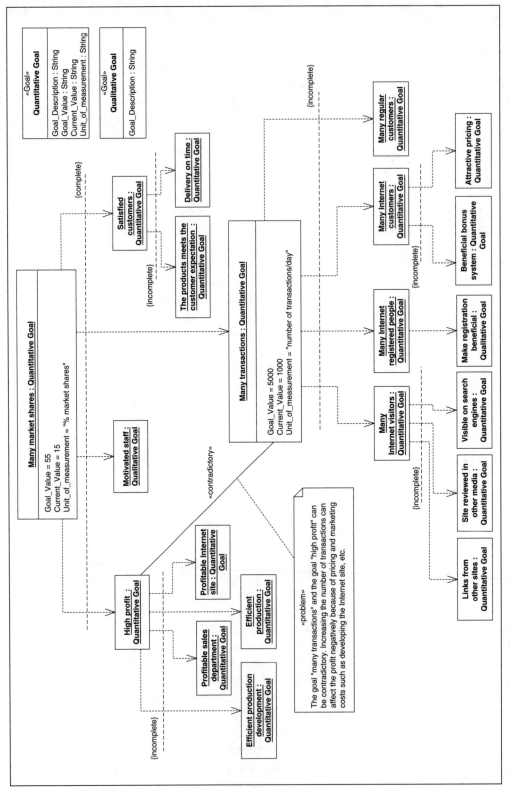

Figure 11.1 Goal model for Bob's Mail Order firm.

Conceptual Model

The conceptual model that complements the goal model for Bob's Mail Order firm is shown in Figure 11.2. This model defines the key concepts that are important for modeling this business.

The *business plan* is one of the key concepts in Bob's Mail Order firm. It consists of the marketing plan, product strategy, Internet strategy, and the busi-

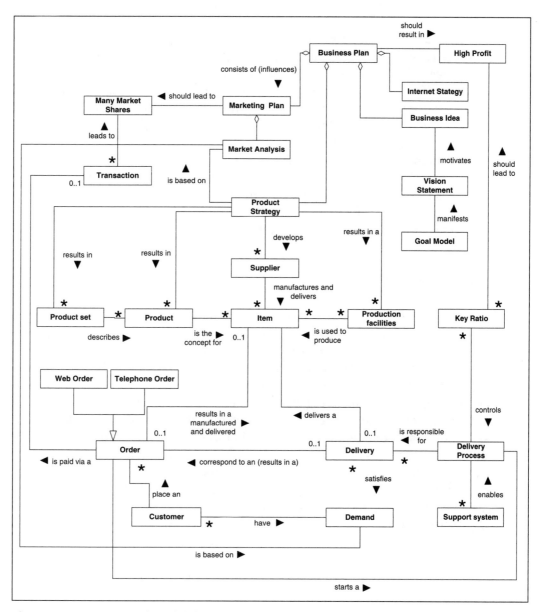

Figure 11.2 Conceptual model describing the key concepts of Bob's Mail Order firm.

ness ideas. It should result in high profit. The conceptual model also indicates that the marketing plan that is a part of the business plan also influences the business plan. The vision statement that is manifested in the goal model motivates the business idea.

The *product strategy* is another key concept in Bob's Mail Order firm. It develops the supplier that manufactures and delivers items. The product strategy also results in production facilities, products, and product sets. The product strategy is based on the market analysis and is also a part of the business plan.

The *product sets* describe the products. Examples of product sets include printers, copying machines, and handbooks. The *products* are concepts for the actual *items*. For example, the product printer HP/5000 (which belongs to the product set printers) is the concept or term that encompasses all actual HP/5000 printers. Typical product attributes are description, design reference, and version number. The items are the actual printers, and they have attributes such as a serial number and age.

Implementing the *market plan* leads to an increased number of market shares. Customers place orders and pay via transactions, which leads to more market shares. An order results in a manufactured and delivered item. The delivered items satisfy a customer's demand. The delivery process is controlled via key ratios, such as optimum delivery times or quality requirements.

Business Processes

The Business Process view focuses on how to carry out the vision and goals outlined in the vision statement, goal model, and conceptual model. The process diagram, shown in Figure 11.3, is used to model the business processes for Bob's Mail Order 24 months from now. Each process is allocated the specific goal that it must achieve. In addition, the processes can also indicate the steps necessary for improving a business or the supporting systems.

The market development process of Bob's Mail Order takes a market analysis as input and delivers a marketing plan as output. The goal of the market development process is to increase the number of market shares. The marketing plan, which is also a part of the whole business plan, controls the process of business development. The goal of the business development process is to achieve an increase in transactions and high profit, which would aid in achieving the overall goal of an increase to 55 percent of market share. The business development process is responsible for developing the business and its strategies, to meet the demands of the market. It delivers a business plan, which is, according to the conceptual model, composed of a market plan, a product strategy, an Internet strategy, and a business idea. In addition to the business plan, the business development process follows the plan itself. For example,

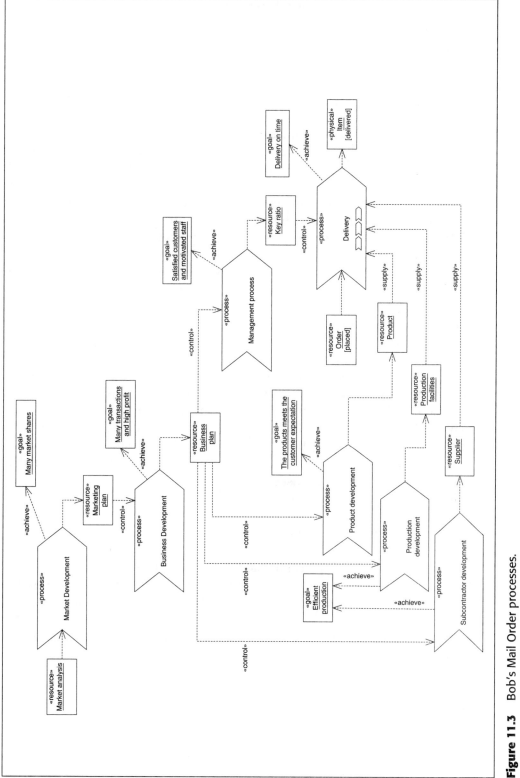

Figure 11.3 Bob's Mail Order processes.

the business development process is responsible for developing Bob's Mail Order home page, a critical aspect because it is one of the resources that will be used to increase the number of transactions.

The business plan controls the management process, product development process, production development process, and subcontractor development process. The management process aims to achieve the goal of satisfying customers and motivating staff. It also defines key ratios that control the delivery process. The product development process supplies the delivery process with products that meet the customers' expectations. The production development process aims to increase the efficiency of production; it also supplies the delivery process with production facilities. The subcontractor development process is responsible for the subcontractors' delivery processes. This process ensures that the subcontractors deliver the specified items on time.

The delivery process takes a customer's order as input and delivers an item to that customer. The goal of the delivery process is timely delivery. The process is controlled by the key ratio defined in the management process. When an order is placed, it should be filled as soon as possible. The customer should make payment before delivery. It is also important to reduce inventory, because maintaining too many items in stock is expensive. This means that Bob's staff must be able to accurately predict the number of incoming orders and plan production and purchase based on that prediction. Later on in this case study this process is further decomposed and detailed.

The business processes for Bob's Mail Order were modeled with the Process Control Layer pattern and the Process Supply Layer pattern, discussed in Chapter 9, "Process Patterns." These powerful patterns are often used together to facilitate the structuring of most businesses.

Resources and Organization

Resources and organizations are modeled in the Business Structure view. Organization models show the structure of the human resources, and the resource models show both structure and behavior of other resources, such as products, documents, and machines. The resources in the resource model are mainly those used in the process model. The conceptual model describing the overall concepts for Bob's Mail Order will help us to explore the resource model and, later, the organization.

Resource Modeling

Order and item are two of the key concepts in the conceptual model for Bob's Mail Order (Figure 11.2) that are used in the process model in Figure 11.3. The behavior of the order resource is modeled in Figure 11.4. An order has three

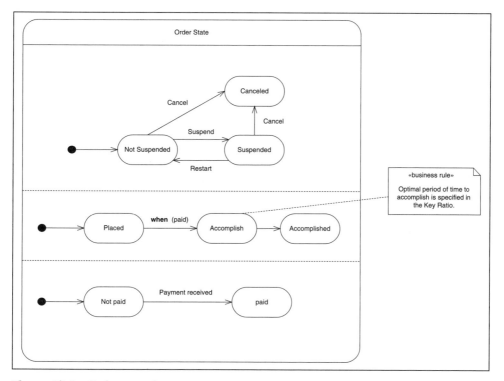

Figure 11.4   Order statechart.

states: placed, not paid, and not suspended. An order can be paid and filled, but during that time it can also be suspended for a period or it can be canceled. There are several situations in which orders might be canceled, for instance, when an order is placed but the customer does not pay, or when it is impossible to deliver for some reason (trade embargo, bankruptcies, etc.). Production stoppages and credit risks are two other factors that might cause an order to be canceled. A cancelation is normally temporary and resolved when the cause is handled.

Figure 11.5 models the behavior of an item resource. An item can be proposed, then enter the Started state, where it moves from the manufacturing state to manufactured. The manufactured item can then be delivered. At any point, the item also can be suspended for a period of time, or canceled if the movement from proposed item to delivered item is stopped.

Figure 11.6 shows the item and order resources and their organization in relation to additional resources, such as product, production facilities, supplier, key ratio, and product set. The item resource is described with a serial number and a placement. The Placement, Site, and Geographical Location classes are structured according to the Geographical Location pattern, discussed in Chapter 7, "Resource and Rule Patterns." Production facilities are

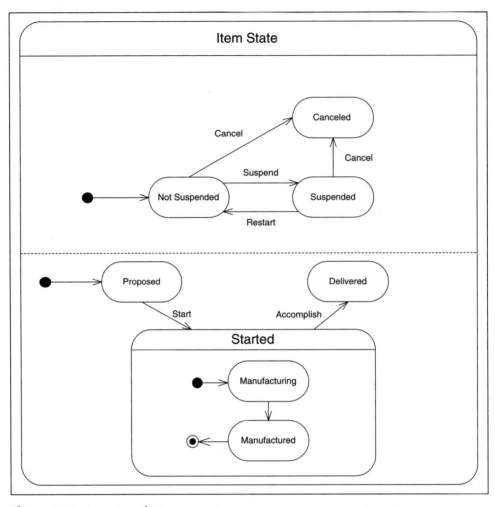

Figure 11.5 Item statechart.

those necessary to produce the items. The Supplier delivers items; it can be a subcontractor or an internal production department. Key Ratio controls restrict equity, delivery time, the optimum time for introduction of new products, and error rate in production. Product is the concept for Item; it can be an object, such as the Nokia mobile phone 6150, while the items are the actual phones, with a serial number.

The product sets are used to organize and group the products. For example, writing tables, desk lamps, chairs, bookshelves, file cabinets, and wastebaskets can be organized by grouping them as office furniture. Office furniture can be subject to certain sales campaigns and package solutions; and the office furniture department is staffed with skilled people.

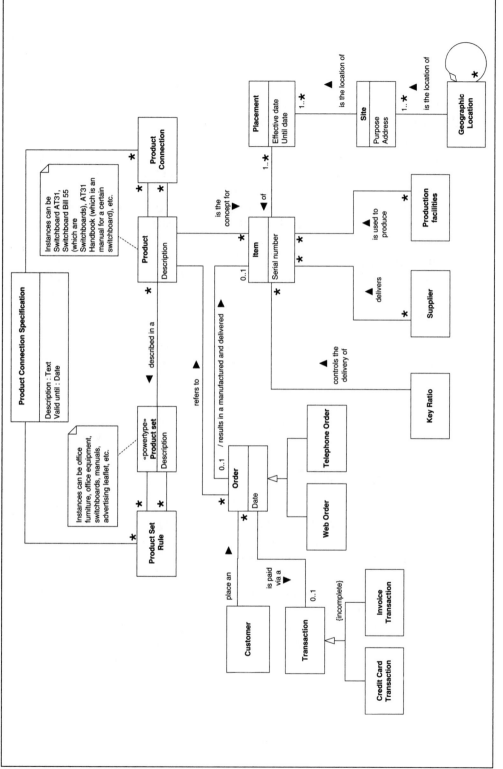

Figure 11.6 Resource model for Bob's Mail Order.

397

The Product Data Management pattern discussed in Chapter 7, "Resource and Rule Patterns," was used to structure the products and the product sets shown in Figure 11.6. The description attribute, in the Product Connection Specification class, can have values such as parts, refill, or refinement. For example, Bob's Mail Order product set Switchboard Solution can either be the product Office 2000 or the product Small Switchboard Solution. Both products contain other products, including the actual switchboard, computers, fax machines, software, and headsets. The relationship between these two products and their parts is captured by the class Product Connections, and is specified by the class Product Connection Specification. The class Product Set Rule is used to specify that product sets can be connected to each other; for example, the product set Switchboard Solution can consist of Computers, which is also a product set in itself.

Resource models are complemented with business rules. One such rule might be a restriction on a customer's credit rating, or the relationship between incoming orders and production rate. Some of these rules, credit rating for example, are candidates for Fuzzy Business Rules. Other rules, especially constraints, are candidates for OCL. The following OCL rule is a business rule that specifies (constrains) that the number of placed orders should be equal to the number of manufactured items.

```
context order:
self->select( state = #placed )->size =
product.item->select( state = #manufactured )->size
```

Organizational Modeling

The Business Structure view also includes the organizational aspects of Bob's Mail Order firm. The structure of an organization is important to understand not only for restructuring purposes, but also for clarifying the responsibilities of each organizational unit. The object diagram in Figure 11.7 aims to clarify the structure of the organizational units in Bob's Mail Order firm. This diagram is based on the Organization and Party pattern, discussed in Chapter 7, "Resource and Rule Patterns."

Bob's Mail Order has a Board composed of the president and other shareholders. There are seven departments at Bob's Mail order firm and one of them, the Sales Department, consists of two additional departments—Telesales and Web sales. Bob's Mail Order includes the following organizational units:

- The Financial Department is responsible for the firm's finances, including credit references, credit card checks, and accounts receivable.

- The Production Department produces items, either by assembling items that they manufacture or by relabeling items purchased from subcontractors.

- The Purchase Department works with purchasing outside products and developing subcontractor relationships.

- The System Department is responsible for the technical infrastructure and information technology of the business. It comprises system analysts, programmers, system architects, operators, and support staff.

- The Sales Department, which is divided into Telesales and Web Sales, is responsible for selling products.

- The Product Department develops new products and product sets.

- The Marketing Department is responsible for marketing and implementing the marketing plan.

The next subsection shows how the organizational units interact with each other and how responsibility for each of them can be established.

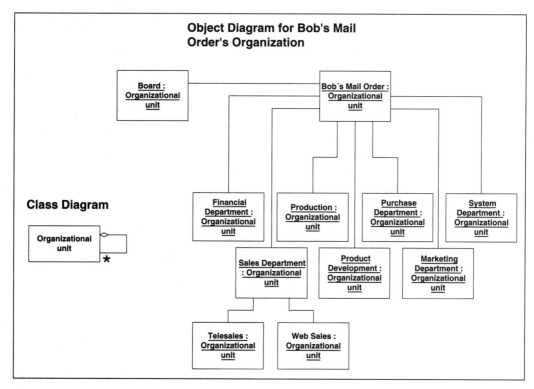

Figure 11.7 Bob's Mail Order organization.

Interaction Analysis

The Business Behavior view uses interaction analysis to allocate responsibility to organizational units and the business processes that intersect with them. Interaction analysis is performed simultaneously with organizational modeling and business process modeling. Sequence diagrams are used to show the interactions between organizational units as well as the processes that take place within or cross each organizational unit.

An interaction is a sequence or a scenario that begins with a business event, such as a question or an order, and ends with a result. For example, Bob's Mail Order accepts credit card orders from customers. Assume that prior marketing and telemarketing have resulted in an inquiry from a customer to the Sales Department. The customer wants to know if a particular item is available and the cost of the item. The customer might also try to negotiate for a better price. If the customer is satisfied with the offer for the item, he or she places an order, pays for it, and receives the ordered item. The Financial Department is responsible for processing the payment, in this case a credit card transaction. The Production Department is responsible for taking the order and delivering the item. The sequence of events for this interaction is shown in Figure 11.8. The organizational units in the figure are picked up from the object diagram in Figure 11.7. Figure 11.8 is based on the Action Workflow pattern discussed in Chapter 9, "Process Patterns," which is a useful pattern for modeling interactions.

Figure 11.9 is the sequence diagram for an interaction analysis for purchasing. The Purchase Department is responsible for purchasing items. It must confer with other organizational units in order to determine what to purchase, when to make the purchase, and the quantity to purchase. The first step is to ask the Sales and Marketing Departments for prognosis to determine whether there is a demand for the product, and, if so, how much of a demand. The Purchase Department then asks the Production Department about the stock figures, that is, how much of the product in question is in stock. The Financial Department supplies information regarding the liquidity. Once this information is received, the Purchase Department begins negotiations with the Supplier, which should result in the purchase of items. The model shown in Figure 11.9 is also based on the Action Workflow pattern described in Chapter 9, "Process Patterns."

The credit card order scenario in Figure 11.8 is an instance of the order process, which is a subprocess to the delivery process (illustrated in Figure 11.3). The order process is responsible for the result: delivering the ordered and paid item. The Sales Department is responsible for conducting the actual sale of the item; the Production Department is responsible for providing the correct stock figures and for delivering on time; and the Financial Department is responsible for checking the credit card transactions.

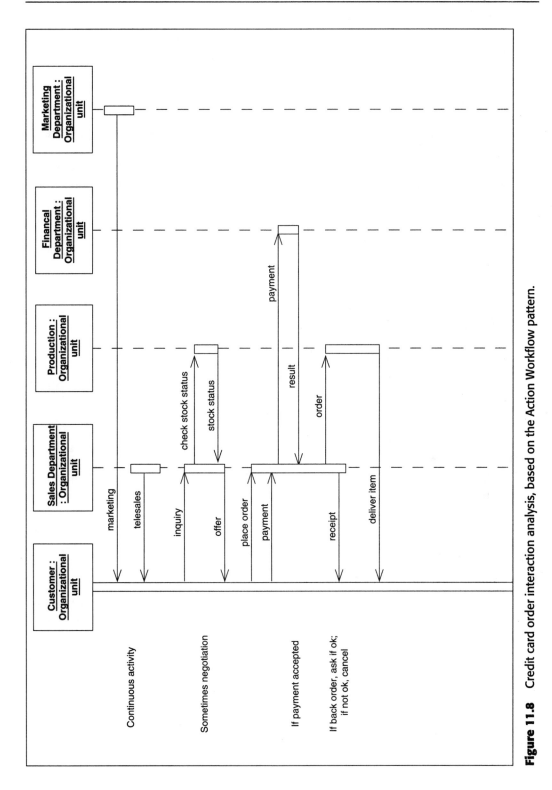

Figure 11.8 Credit card order interaction analysis, based on the Action Workflow pattern.

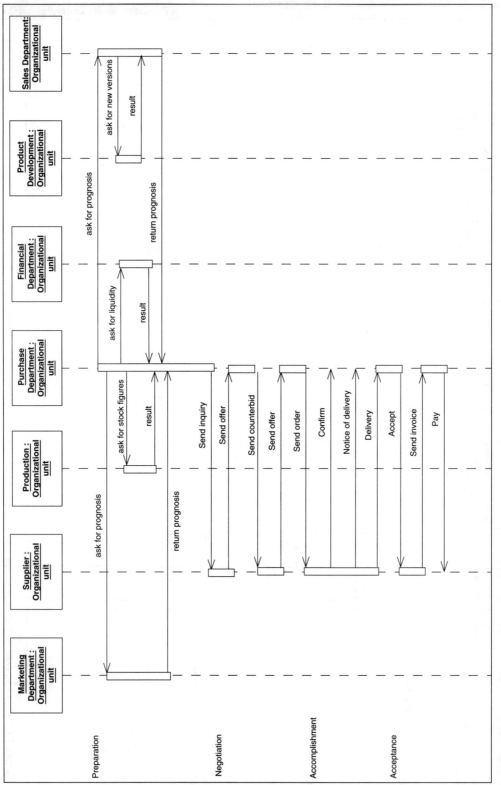

Figure 11.9 Purchase interaction analysis based on the Action Workflow pattern.

Process Decomposition

Complex processes can be decomposed to enable better understanding. For example, the delivery process in Bob's Mail Order is a complex process that can be decomposed using the overall process diagram in Figure 11.3, the sequence diagrams in Figures 11.8 and 11.9, and Time-to-Customer Process pattern discussed in Chapter 9, "Process Patterns." The result is three subprocesses:

- Order
- Procurement
- Customer interaction

Figure 11.10 shows the decomposed delivery process.

The order process is responsible for on-time delivery, invoice and credit card payments, and customer satisfaction. The process is triggered by a placed order and ends with a delivered item and a satisfied buyer. The order process is controlled by key ratios (discussed previously in the "Resource Modeling" section), items, and products. The order process is primarily executed in the Sales and Financial Departments, but it also may involve the procurement process—if, for example, the supply of items is affected.

The procurement process is responsible for delivering items on time to the order process and for satisfying customers. This process is triggered by market and sales prognosis. It then purchases, refines, and sometimes manufactures items, and finally delivers them to the order process. The key ratios that control the efficiency of this process are defined in terms of quality and stock figures. The procurement process involves all organizational units, including the subcontractors and suppliers. The customers are not involved in the procurement process.

The customer interaction process is responsible for taking many orders. It is supplied with customer information, item information, and product information. This interaction takes place via Bob's Mail Order home page, telephone, e-mail, or fax.

The assembly line diagram shown in Figure 11.11 is used to further clarify the delivery process. This diagram visually depicts the synchronization, interaction, and resources of the three subprocesses. For example, the procurement process delivers manufactured items that supply the order process, which delivers the items to customers. Notice how orders delivered from the customer interaction process are used in both the procurement and the order process.

Support Systems

Bob's Mail Order firm has several support systems that supply the business processes. Some of them are old and must be replaced while others require

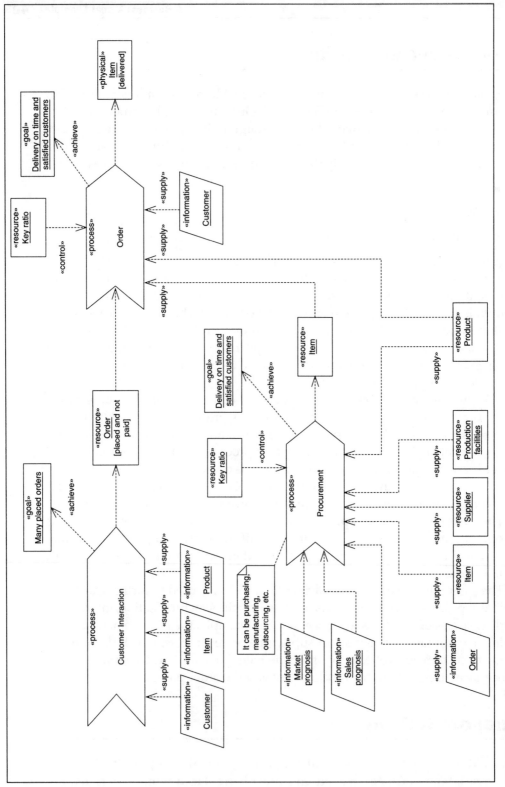

Figure 11.10 The decomposed delivery process.

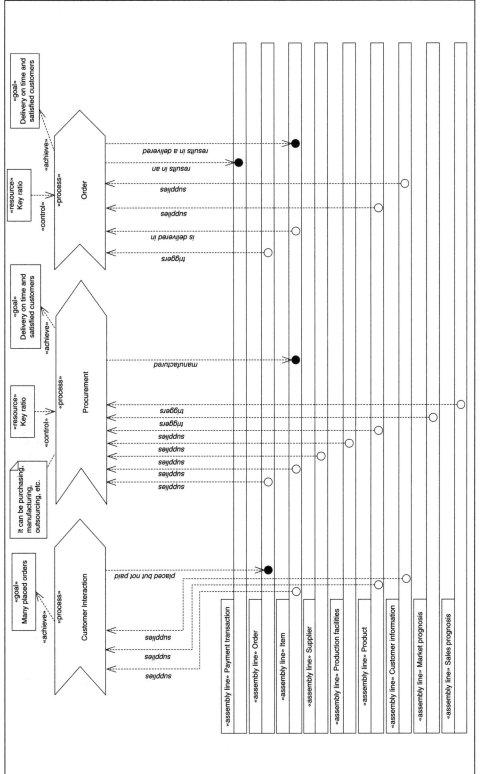

Figure 11.11 Assembly line diagram describing the interaction, synchronization, and the supply of the delivery process subprocesses.

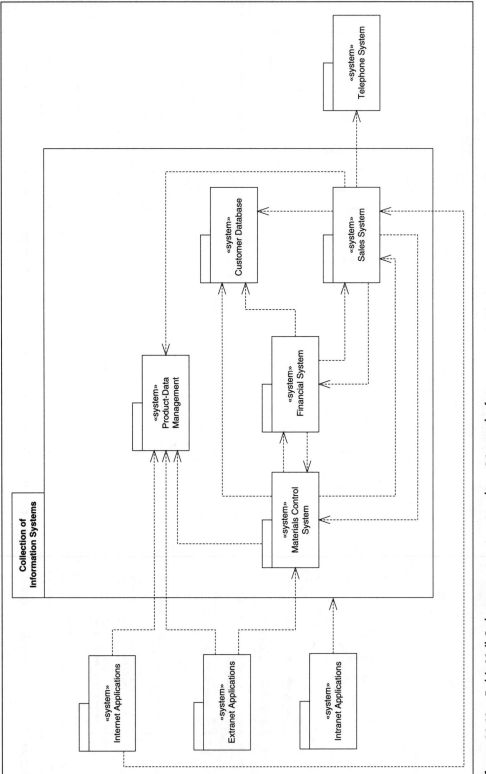

Figure 11.12 Bob's Mail Order support system topology, 24 months from now.

minor changes in order to achieve the goals of the business. Information about products and documents spans multiple systems and is poorly integrated.

Figure 11.12 shows the system topology that should be implemented simultaneously with the business processes and the organization within the next 24 months if Bob's is to meet the goals defined for the firm. Two systems that do not currently exist are: the Product Data Management system and the Materials Control system.

The Product Data Management system (PDM) is one of the more important systems that must be built, and as soon as possible. A PDM system is an information system that organizes and supplies the business with adequate information about the product set, the individual products, and the documents (external documents, such as advertising material, product sheets, data sheets, and manuals, as well as internal documents such as requirement specifications and blueprints). The PDM system is used by all organizational units, including subcontractors, who will obtain information from an extranet, and customers, who will download some of the documents from the Internet.

The PDM system requirements come from the assembly line diagrams, which indicate the business processes supplied by the system; the diagrams also show which resources, such as information, should be used, and how they should be organized to facilitate the execution of the processes. In context of the PDM system, this means the information the system delivers and how the system delivers it.

In addition to the PDM system, a Materials Control system is required. This system, which should be built and integrated with the other systems, supports the production process with production and manufacturing planning, materials purchase, and others. Its requirements are found in the assembly line diagram for the production process.

As mentioned, in addition to these two new systems, existing systems require evaluation. Some require changes; others even need to be replaced entirely.

- Internally, Bob's Mail Order firm is migrating from outdated terminals to modern PCs with Web browsers that are connected to an intranet. This means that the whole infrastructure must be built upon Web technology and include an Internet sever with Bob's external home page, an internal intranet server, and an extranet server for subcontracts.

- The Customer Database, another of the existing support systems, is a database application that contains customer information. The processes use it to store, find, and change customer information. This system will not be changed. It provides a well-defined interface to the other systems and can be integrated easily.

- The Sales system is an existing system that supports the sales staff. The system requires a new interface in order for it to be integrated with the rest of the supporting systems in Bob's Mail Order firm.

■ The Telephone system must be replaced as soon as possible. The new Telephone system should be integrated with the Sales system, which already contains functionality that can be integrated with a modern switchboard.

■ The Financial system, used for accounting, invoicing, and credit card transactions, currently works satisfactorily; the business processes that use it do not have additional requirements. This system will remain unchanged.

In the new software architecture shown in Figure 11.12, the systems are stereotyped packages shown with the standard stereotype: «system». Dependencies are shown with dependency arrows. The Sales system is dependent upon the Financial system, the Telephone system, the Customer Database, the Materials Control system, and the PDM system. The Financial system is dependent upon the Sales system, the Customer Database system, and the Materials Control system. The Materials Control system is dependent upon the Sales system, the Financial system, the Customer Database, and the PDM system. The Internet Application system is dependent upon the Sales system, and the PDM system. The Extranet Application system is dependent upon the PDM system, and the Materials Control system. The Intranet Application system is dependent upon all other information systems (the one bundled in the package Collection of Information Systems). However, access from the Internet and extranet applications is restricted.

The system topology can be complemented with an interaction analysis. As is the case with organizational interaction analysis, the system interactions are analyzed using the sequence diagrams, and aim to allocate responsibility to the units (in this case, the systems).

Systems must be prioritized for development planning. Giving priority to systems or subsystems in case of project problems, such as delays, should be based on the goal model; in Bob's case, the goal model in Figure 11.1. For example, it is better to prioritize the building of the Internet applications and add interfaces to the Sales system before building the Material Control system, since the number of goals concerned with Internet and Sales is greater in number than the number of goals concerned with production and production development. Note, however, though counting goals is a straightforward method of prioritizing, it is not always the most appropriate. Another technique for prioritizing goals is to weigh the goals against each other.

System Requirements

A system requirement specification itemizes what to develop, change, or remove in terms of support systems. The PDM system is a candidate for a requirement specification because it must be developed and integrated with existing systems. Old data spread out over many of the other systems has to be handled in conjunction with the development of the system itself. Let's take a look at how to write a requirement specification for the PDM system.

All business processes are supplied by the PDM system, which stores all documents. If all processes use the PDM system the same way, it will be easy to define the system functionality. However, if the processes use the PDM system in different ways, all the processes will have to be considered to ensure the proper system functionality and to avoid partial and ill-formed use cases. If a system is used by many processes in many different ways, the system functionality will have to be described in general and common use cases that capture the essential functionality desired by the identified actors, then extended or specialized as necessary.

The actors interested in the PDM system in Bob's Mail Order firm are other existing systems: Internet Applications, Extranet Applications, Intranet Applications, Sales, and Materials Control. All of these systems interact with people outside the systems. All organizational units except the System Department are involved in using the PDM system, and so might be suitable target groups for prototype evaluation. Interaction analysis, as in Figures 11.8 and 11.9, and assembly line diagrams like the one shown in Figure 11.11 are useful for determining which organizational units use which system.

Functional Requirements and Information Analysis

The PDM system for Bob's Mail Order firm is used by all actors in the same way. The system's expected functionality can be found in the assembly line diagrams for the processes. The assembly line diagram in Figure 11.11 showed that products and documents, such as the market prognosis, supply the processes. If this diagram were even more detailed, supply would be interpreted as finding and getting information about products and documents. Of course, before information can be found, it must be created first. The product development process creates the information and defines new products and documents. The business development process defines new product sets, which are added to the PDM system. Other processes generate and store documents in the PDM system in this manner as well.

It is common to model required information and its structure in requirement specifications, especially for complex information structures such as the PDM systems. The PDM pattern discussed in Chapter 7, "Resource and Rule Patterns," was used to model the products in the resource diagram. It also can be used to handle both the documents and the products in information modeling. The information model, based on the earlier resource model and the PDM pattern, is shown in Figure 11.13. If the PDM system should be able to handle different document versions and several document copies, the Docu-

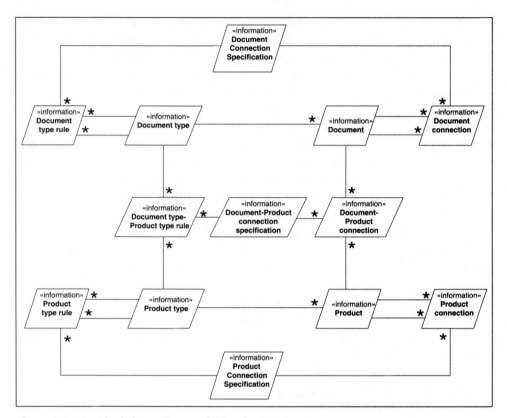

Figure 11.13   The information model for the PDM system.

ment pattern discussed in Chapter 7 could be used to extend the model in Figure 11.13.

Several actors and processes interact with the PDM system, but there are only two ways of using the system (two use cases): to update products and documents and to find products and documents. The update products and documents use case also requires creating, deleting, and registering new types of documents and new product sets. The finds products and documents use case delivers the functionality of finding and getting documents or information about products. Figure 11.14 illustrates the two use cases.

Different levels of access rights must be considered when several different actors are using the system, as in the case of the PDM system. The Internet Application, which is used by regular customers, should have access only to public documents, such as product sheets or advertising material. The Intranet Application has unlimited access to the PDM system, while the Extranet Application has limited access. Subcontractors use the extranet to download blueprints and data sheets.

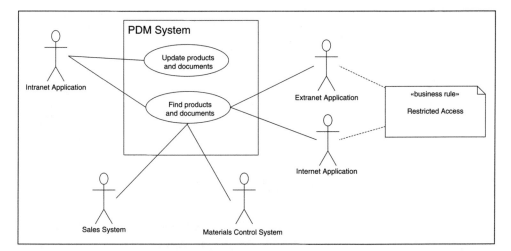

Figure 11.14.   A use-case model describing the PDM system functionality.

Use cases are described textually. The find products and documents use case is described as follows:

Goal. To supply the business processes with adequate information about products and documents

Participate in the business processes. Market development, business development, management process, delivery, product development, productions development, subcontractor development.

Actors. Internet Application, the Intranet Application, the Extranet Application, the Sales system, and the Materials Control system. Each has a different level of access right.

Precondition. Information about products and documents must be registered.

Main flow. The actor identifies or formulates a question about products, product sets, documents, or document types. The actor gets an answer, and in some cases a document file as a result.

Postconditions. The question is answered, and, if requested, a document file is downloaded.

Exceptions. If the question cannot be answered, ask again, and suggest a proper action.

Both uses cases are exemplified in the sequence diagrams in Figures 11.15 and 11.16, which connect the information model with the actors and the business processes. Note that an interaction within a system is a part of an interac-

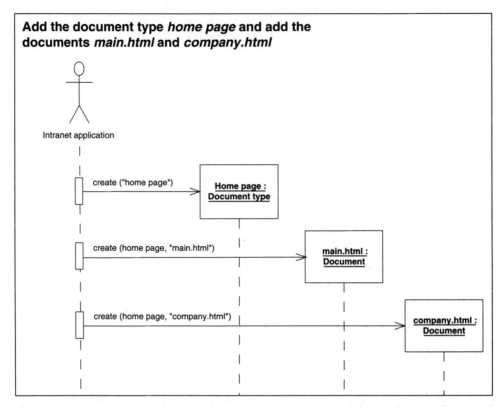

Figure 11.15   Sequence diagram describing one instance of the update products and documents use case.

tion that takes place inside a business process or between business processes. Also note that the assembly line diagrams, which show the information and resources used by the processes, how they are used, and who uses them (the process actors), are the common links between the business and its systems.

Figure 11.15 shows how to create the document type home page and then how to add the home page documents main.html and company.html.

Figure 11.16 shows how to retrieve all stored home pages by asking the class document type for all home pages. The document type identifies its home page object and asks it for all corresponding documents (the stored home pages). When all home pages have been identified and returned, the Intranet Application actor downloads the main.html file from the PDM system.

Nonfunctional Requirements

Security issues, such as the level of access rights and illegal use of computer information, are considered nonfunctional requirements. Other such issues that should be considered include availability, reliability, performance, integ-

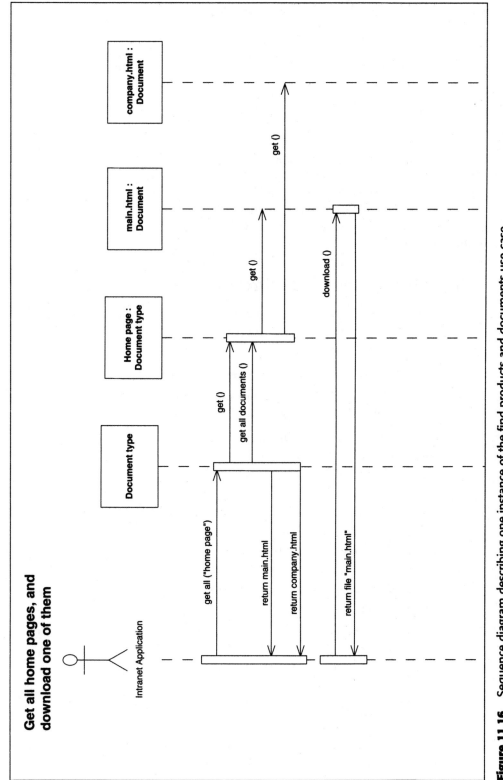

Figure 11.16 Sequence diagram describing one instance of the find products and documents use case.

413

rity, usability and reusability, adaptability, maintainability, and information accuracy.

GUI and Users

There are no graphical user interfaces (GUIs) directly connected to the PDM system. Instead, the systems using the PDM system have GUIs. The Internet, Intranet, and Extranet Applications are all Web-based and provide the GUIs for other applications. It is important to define style guidelines for the GUIs at an early stage to avoid confusing the different interfaces at the end of the project. It is also a good idea to sketch the GUIs or to prototype them using some of the end users.

System Requirement Specification

System requirements specifications detail how the system is developed. The content of a requirements specification for an information system such as the PDM system might include:

1. *Summary.* Summarize the requirement specification.
2. *Problem and background.* Gives a brief introduction to the perceived problem, and includes some background information.
3. *Procurement regulations.* Public tenders are regulated by procurement regulations, and there might also be other situations where procurement regulations are involved. The procurement regulations should be stated here.
4. *The business vision and goals.* A short description of the business goals and vision.
5. *The structure of the business, the business processes, and the business rules.* A short description of the business processes and rules.
6. *Description of legacy systems.* A description of legacy systems affected by the system being specified.
7. *Use cases.* Specifies functional and nonfunctional system requirements.
8. *Prioritization.* Specifies and motivates prioritization of requirements (if there are any).
9. *Requirements of commercial software and commercial hardware.* Specifies demands or requirements of commercial software and hardware used in the solution, if there are any.
10. *IT strategies.* Identifies and describes anything in the IT strategies that affects the development of the systems being specified.

11. *GUI sketch.* Illustrates the graphical user interfaces, if there are any.

12. *Information structure.* Sometimes includes the information structure in the requirement specification, especially in PDM systems where the information structure is rather complex.

13. *System collaboration, integration, and interfaces.* Describes the systems dependent on the system being specified. Explains how to integrate the system being specified and how to formalize the interface descriptions and the interface realizations. This section also discusses database schemas; many times only one database is used and the database schemas are integrated.

14. *Migration of old data.* Itemizes old data that has to be moved into the system being specified, as in the case with the PDM system in Bob's Mail Order. Database schemas and old data should be documented to ease the migration.

15. *Financial prerequisites.* Defines assumptions and conditions such as budgets, etc.

16. *Organizational prerequisites.* Considers important organizational aspects.

17. *Delivery conditions.* States the conditions for the delivery of the systems being specified.

  17.1 *Time of delivery.* Specifies when to deliver.

  17.2 *Requirements on part deliveries.* Specifies requirements on part deliveries. For instance, a part delivery that is a computer program that cannot be executed without getting the next part delivery should not be allowed.

  17.3 *Requirements on staff training.* Requirements of training programs. Typically containing requirements on course material, online learning concepts, etc.

  17.4 *Guarantee.* Covers delivery promises.

18. *Terminology (based on the conceptual model).* A glossary explaining the business concepts used in the requirement specification.

Note that the content in the preceding sample specification comprises only suggestions; often, it is desirable to separate the technical issues (management, financial, contractual) from the nontechnical issues (e.g., guarantee, delivery). It is may also be preferable to separate factors that are, at some point, becoming stable and immutable (e.g., use cases, nonfunctional requirements) from those that remain volatile, such as financial assumptions, GUI prototypes, or training.

From this point, development processes such as the Rational Unified Process (RUP) and the Select Perspective can be used to analyze, design, build, and test the systems specified. In fact, much of the content shown in the suggested system requirement specification is included in the Inception phase of RUP and the Feasibility stage of Perspective.

Also, remember that it is important to verify and evaluate the supporting systems built using the business model. In Bob's case, it is important to verify and evaluate the new and improved systems to determine whether the goals were reached and the vision was carried out with the new and improved systems, business processes, and organization.

Summary

Bob's Mail Order firm needed to update to compete with other mail order firms that had migrated to the Web and implemented e-commerce systems. Bob's systems were outdated, necessitating the remodeling and improving of the entire business and the support systems. The goal was established to increase market share from 15 percent to 55 percent in a 24-month period. To accomplish this, Bob realized it would be necessary not only to rebuild or switch the old systems, but also to change the business processes.

Many years ago, Bob recognized that a lucrative way to conduct business was to market products before they existed, producing them only if the demand was there. The problem was that the sales channels had moved partly to the Internet, and that the products had become increasingly complex. The solution was to integrate not just the customer purchasing process with the Internet, but also the suppliers' delivery process, via an extranet solution. This would cut the lead-times and increase the quality; then, together with marketing and motivating the sales force, Bob's would be able to achieve its goal.

As shown in this example, a business can be described with a vision statement, a goal model, a conceptual model, an organization model, and a process model. When the processes are detailed, as was Bob's delivery process, and connected to the support systems structured in the system topology, the resource model, the assembly line diagrams, and interaction analyses become useful tools. All businesses need support systems, such as Bob's Product Data Management system, Materials Control system, and Telephone system; those are what the resource model and the assembly line diagram captures.

The interaction analysis facilitates the structuring and allocating of responsibility to the processes and resources, and clarifies the connection between them, as expressed in the assembly line diagram. The support systems are specified by functional and nonfunctional requirements. The functional requirements are identified via assembly line diagrams; nonfunctional requirements are identified via process properties (lead-times, cost, process owners, process actors, etc.). Use cases are a way of describing functional requirements of support systems. The actors using the use cases are also process actors following the processes described. The use-case actors can be specified by investigating process actors described with processes. The use cases are connected to the resources in the assembly line diagrams (resources can be information, things, etc.), and should specify how the processes (and their actors) use the assembly line diagrams (via object-to and object-from assembly lines).

Appendix A

Eriksson-Penker
Business Extensions

The Eriksson-Penker Business Extensions are a powerful set of concepts aimed to help you rapidly conduct high-quality business modeling. The extensions comprise views, diagrams, models, constraints, tagged values, and stereotypes.

Views

The Eriksson-Penker Business Extensions recommend four views for modeling businesses. These views are not diagrams or models; they are four practical and useful perspectives that facilitate the modeling process. A given problem should be iterated until it is fully understood and described. The four views are:

Business Vision. Focuses the overall vision, the key concepts, and the goal structures, and points to problems that need to be eliminated.

Business Process. Focuses the business processes that represent the activities and value created in the business, and illustrates the process interaction and use of resources in order to achieve the goals and the overall vision.

Business Structure. Focuses the resource structures, such as organizational units, products, documents, information, knowledge, and so on.

Business Behavior. Focuses the individual behaviors and interactions. Both resources and processes have individual behaviors as well as interactions. Interaction analysis is an important tool when allocating responsibility to resources and processes (theoretically, processes are resources).

Diagrams and Models

Recall that a model is the idea and that the diagrams are the blueprints. The Eriksson-Penker Business Extensions suggest a set of models and diagrams suitable for business modeling. Most models are expressed with the nine UML standard diagrams, but some of the suggested models are expressed in one kind of diagram, while other models are expressed in a specialized version of one of the diagrams. For example, the Conceptual model, the Resource model, the Information model, and the Organization model are all expressed with class diagrams. The Process diagram and the Assembly Line diagram are both specializations of the Activity diagram; they are not just models expressed in the standard diagrams, they are also specialized diagrams (all according to the UML specification). In contrast, the Vision Statement and the System Topology diagram are two new diagrams that are neither standard nor specialized diagrams. According to the UML standard, new kinds of diagrams can be added, but we have tried not to add more new diagrams than necessary; instead, we have used standard diagrams and specializations of standard diagrams. The diagrams and models included in Eriksson-Penker Business are:

Vision Statement diagram. States the overall vision. This diagram is expressed in plan text.

Conceptual model. Aims at defining the business key concepts. It is expressed as a class diagram.

Goal model. States the business goals, and is used for validation. It is expressed in an object diagram

Process diagram. Shows the business processes and their collaboration. It is a specialization of the Activity diagram.

Assembly Line diagram. Focuses on the connection between the business processes and the objects involved. This diagram is also the point of connection between the world of business modeling and the world of software engineering. The Assembly Line diagram is a specialization of the Activity diagram.

Use-Case diagram. A standard UML diagram that can be used to capture the functional aspects of supporting systems. Note that functionality can also be described in plain text.

Resource model. Captures the resources of a business, which can be information or things; the things can be either abstract or concrete. Concrete things include people, machines, and items; abstract things typically are organizational units, departments, and the like. The Resource model is expressed in a class diagram.

Organization model. Shows the organizational structures of a business. The Organization model is a special case (specialization) of the Resource model. The Organization model is expressed in class diagrams or, in some cases, object diagrams.

Information model. Shows the information in a structured manner to facilitate decisions regarding what information should be organized in which system. The Information model is a special case (specialization) to the Resource model. The Information model is normally expressed in a class diagram, but it can also be expressed in an object diagram.

Statechart diagram. This standard UML diagram is used to express the behavior of resources.

Interaction diagrams. Used to conduct interaction analysis. They are Sequence and Collaboration diagrams.

System Topology diagram. A new diagram used to specify supporting systems and their dependencies.

Stereotypes and Constraints

The Eriksson-Penker Business Extensions provide a set of business model elements called stereotypes that allow you to model and capture the essence of a business. The stereotypes are divided into four categories: process, resource and rules, goals, and miscellaneous. The goal category also contains a small set of constraints, necessary to model the goal hierarchies. Table A.1 itemizes the process extensions, A.2 lists the resources and rules extensions, A.3.1, A3.2, and A3.3 contain the goal extensions, and A.4 has the miscellaneous extensions.

Table A.1 Process Extensions

NAME	STEREOTYPED TO	SYMBOL	DEFINITION/DESCRIPTION
Process	Activity	«process» Name «process» «process»	A process is a description of a set of related activities that, when correctly performed, will satisfy an explicit goal.
Activity (atomic process)	Activity	Name	A process might be divided into further processes. If these processes are atomic, they are called activities.
Process start	Start	●→	Starts a process.
Process end	End	◉↑	Ends a process.
Object-to-Assembly Line	Object	●	A delivered object from a process to the Assembly Line.
Object-from-Assembly Line	Object	○	An object that goes from the Assembly Line to a process.
Process flow	Control Flow	[condition] →	A process control flow with a condition.
Resource flow	Object flow	Name ⇢	Object flow shows that an object is produced by one process and consumed by another process.

Table A.1 Process Extensions (*Continued*)

NAME	STEREOTYPED TO	SYMBOL	DEFINITION/DESCRIPTION
Noncausal resource flow	Object flow	------«non-causal»----▷	Noncausal object flow shows that an object might be produced by one process and consumed by another process.
Process control	Object flow	------«control»----▷	Shows that a process is controlled by an object.
Goal connection	Dependency	------«achieve»----▷	Allocates a goal to a process.
Process supply	Object flow	------«supply»----▷	Shows that a process is supplied by an object.
Process decision	Decision	◇	Decision point between two or more processes.
Fork and Join of processes	Fork and Join	▬	Forks and joins processes.
Receive business event	Signal Receipt	Name	Shows a receive business event.
Send business event	Signal Send	Name	Shows a send business event.
Assembly Line	Package	«assembly line»	The Assembly Lines synchronize and supply processes in terms of objects.

Table A.2 Resources and Rules Extensions

NAME	STEREOTYPE TO	SYMBOL	DEFINITION/DESCRIPTION
Information	Class	«information» **Name**	Information is a kind of resource. It is the knowledge increment brought about by a receiving action in a message transfer; that is, it is the difference between the conceptions interpreted from a received message and the knowledge before the receiving action. [Falkenberg 1996]
Resource	Class	«resource» **Name**	Resources can be produced, consumed, used, or refined in processes. Resources are either information or things. Things can be abstract or physical.
Abstract resource	Class	«abstract» **Name**	An abstract resource is an intangible asset, for example, mathematics, concepts, and so on.
People	Class	«people» **Name**	A physical resource; specifically, human beings.
Physical resource	Class	«physical» **Name**	A physical resource, excluding people. For example, machines, documents, and so on.
Business event	Signal	«business event» **Name**	A significant occurrence in time or space. A business event is one that impacts the business.
Business rule	Note	«business rule» Rule statement	Rules restrict, derive, and establish conditions of existence. Business rules are used to specify state of affairs, including allowed business object states.

Table A.3.1 Goal Extensions

NAME	STEREOTYPE TO	SYMBOL	DEFINITION/DESCRIPTION
Goal	Class	«goal» **Name**	Denote desired states, meaning that goals motivate actions leading to state changes in a desired direction.
Problem	Note	«problem» Problem name	Something that prevents us from meeting goals. Cause, measure, and prerequisite are other stereotype notes that are useful when modeling problems. A cause leads to problems; a problem can be solved if the cause is removed. The cause can be removed if a certain measure is taken and certain prerequisites are valid.
Goal dependency	Dependency	⟶	Goals are organized in dependency hierarchies, in which one or several goals are dependent on subgoals.
Contradictory goal	Association	«contradictory»	Goals can be contradictory, but must be fulfilled.

Table A.3.2 Goal Extensions

NAME	CONSTRAINT TO	SYMBOL	DEFINITION/DESCRIPTION
Incomplete goal decomposition	Dependency	{incomplete} – – –	Goals are organized in dependency hierarchies that are sometimes incomplete.
Complete goal decomposition	Dependency	{complete} – – –	Goals are organized in dependency hierarchies that are sometimes complete.

Table A.3.3 Goal Extensions

NAME	INSTANCE OF	SYMBOL	DEFINITION/DESCRIPTION
Quantitative goal	Goal	«goal» **Quantitative Goal** — Goal_Description : String, Goal_Value : String, Current_Value : String, Unit_of_measurement : String	A goal that can be described with a target value in a specific unit of a measurement (a quantity).
Qualitative goal	Goal	«goal» **Qualitative Goal** — Goal_Description : String	A goal normally described in a natural language. A qualitative goal involves human judgment, in the process of determining whether it has been fulfilled.
Instance of a qualitative goal	Qualitative goal	**Many Customers : Quantitative Goal** — Goal_Value = 500000, Current_Value = 0, Unit_of_measurement = "registrered customers"	Both qualitative and quantitative goals can be instantiated.

Table A.4 Miscellaneous Extensions

NAME	STEREOTYPE TO	SYMBOL	DEFINITION/DESCRIPTION
Reference note	Note	«reference» Name	A stereotyped note that contains a reference to another diagram or another document.
Business package	Package	«business package» Name	Used to package business models or parts of business models.

Tagged Values

UML defines and includes many useful tagged values, but the Eriksson-Penker Business Extensions offer a set of new tagged values for describing business processes. They are:

Goal. A textual value that describes the goal of the process if a goal object is not explicitly attached to it. The goal, which is a part of the goal model, is used to control, measure, and decide the created value of the process.

Purpose. A textual value that informally describes the purpose of the process; for example, anticipated effect. The purpose is typically communicated to the process actors and to customers.

Documentation. A textual value that informally describes the work of the process; for example, the activities completed and the resources involved.

Process owner. A textual value that defines the person in the organization who has the overall responsibility for the process in question and who manages the changes and plans for changes.

Process actors. A textual value that defines the actors needed to run the process. Typically, their skill levels are described.

Priority. A textual value that describes the priority of this process; for example, whether it's a core process, a support process, an administrative process, and so on.

Risks. A textual value that describes the risk of the process; for example, what can go wrong either when executing the process in question or when implementing it to the business.

Possibilities. A textual value that describes the potential of a given process; for example, the opportunities for improving or using the process in the future.

Time. A numerical value that approximates the execution duration of the process.

Cost. A numerical value that approximates the cost of executing the process.

Business Patterns Summary

Resource and Rules Patterns

PATTERN NAME	INTENT	RELATED PATTERNS	PAGE
Actor-Role	Provides guidelines for using actor and role concepts, including how they should be separated and how they can be combined.	▪ Organization and ▪ Party Employment	191
Business Definitions	Captures and organizes business term definitions, then creates systems for managing them.	▪ None	199
Business Event-Result History	Used to track significant business events and then to connect these events to their results. Capturing the different business events, along with their results—such as decisions, contracts, statements, or products, will help you to make better business decisions. The goal of this pattern is to enable you to keep a record of all important business events, which are typically described with attributes such as description, purpose, and result.	▪ Contract pattern ▪ Product Data Management pattern ▪ Document pattern	207

(continues)

Resource and Rules Patterns (*Continued*)

PATTERN NAME	INTENT	RELATED PATTERNS	PAGE
Contract	Provides guidelines for modeling the important and very common concept of contracts.	■ Business Event-Result History pattern ■ Product Data Management pattern ■ Core-Representation pattern	215
Core-Representation	Structures the essentials in a problem domain with the purpose of building well-structured and easily changeable models. The core objects of a business, such as debt, agreement, customer, product, delivery, and order, are objects that rarely change fundamentally; conversely, the representations of these objects often change or are extended. A modeler should take this into consideration and separate the core objects from their representations. This process is aided by this pattern.	■ Contract pattern	219
Document	Documents are used in all businesses, and they can cause a lot of confusion for modelers. One common problem is when a copy is made of a document. This raises the question: Is the copy another document, the same document, or a "copy document" linked to the original document? Also, a document might exist in several different versions; the basic content and purpose of the document may be the same but the details are different. When information systems are used to handle documents, other problems can raise additional questions, such as: If I copy my Word file, does it become two documents? If so, which is considered the original? What happens if I switch the names on them; which then is the original and why? This pattern provides a practical way to approach the issues inherent in the modeling of documents, including different versions and copies of documents.	■ Product Data Management pattern ■ Geographical Location pattern	223

Resource and Rules Patterns (*Continued*)

PATTERN NAME	INTENT	RELATED PATTERNS	PAGE
Employment	Employment is a contract between a person (employee) and an organization that indicates factors such as assigned responsibilities, contract of employment, and start and end dates. This pattern breaks down then organizes these underlying concepts with the purpose of describing and representing that information to handle both present and future forms of employment.	■ Organization and Party pattern	229
Geographic Location	Prevents the modeling of addresses or locations using formats that may become obsolete in a short period of time.	■ All patterns that require addresses locations to be modeled.	235
Organization and Party	Used to create flexible and qualitative organizational charts in object-oriented models.	■ Product Data Management pattern ■ Employment pattern	241
Product Data Management (PDM)	All businesses have many products and/or documents that must be organized and structured. Capturing the structure of the relationship between documents and products is a difficult but common problem in all businesses. This pattern is used for that purpose.	■ Title Item pattern ■ Contract pattern ■ Business Event-Result pattern	247
Thing-Information	Eliminates the focus-shifting that occurs during the modeling process by referring to two frequently used foci (thing focus and information focus) in business modeling and how they are related to each other.	■ All patterns that are used to structure information or resources.	257
Title-Item	Helps modelers to simplify the design process for systems that involve objects that exist in multiple copies or instances. It separates the information about the title from the information about individual instances of that title.	■ PDM pattern	261
Type-Object-Value	Models the relationships between a type, its object, and value.	■ All resource and rule patterns	267

Goal Patterns

PATTERN NAME	INTENT	RELATED PATTERNS	PAGE
Business Goal Allocation	Used to assign goals to specific business processes, resources, and rules in order to facilitate the description and validation of those business processes, resources, and rules during business modeling.	■ Business Goal Decomposition pattern	277
Business Goal Decomposition	Used to streamline the goal-modeling process by breaking down the business goals into hierarchies. In this way, high-level business goals can be divided into more concrete subgoals that are then allocated to specific business processes.	■ Business Goal Allocation pattern ■ Business Goal-Problem pattern	283
Business Goal-Problem	Used to identify the connection between business goals and their related problems in order to correct the problems and achieve the goals.	■ Business Goal Decomposition pattern	289

Process Patterns

PATTERN NAME	INTENT	RELATED PATTERNS	PAGE
Action Workflow	A tool for analyzing communication between parties, with the purpose of understanding and optimizing this communication.	■ None.	329
Basic Process Structure	A Process Modeling pattern; it shows how to form the business process concept in terms of supplying business resources, goals for the process, and the transformation or refinement of input and output resource objects. It provides the basic structure for describing a business process.	■ All patterns	295
Process Feedback	A Process Modeling pattern that evaluates the business process results, and, based on those results, adjusts the process accordingly to achieve the business process goal.	■ All Process Modeling patterns	305
Process Instance State	Also known as the State Design pattern; shows how a well-known design pattern can be used to improve the quality of business modeling—not to reinvent the pattern wheel, so to speak.	■ Process Instance pattern	347

Process Patterns (*Continued*)

PATTERN NAME	INTENT	RELATED PATTERNS	PAGE
Process Interaction	A Process Modeling pattern; it shows how to model and organize the numerous interactions that occur between different business processes.	■ All Process Modeling patterns.	299
Process Layer Control	A Process Modeling pattern that helps to structure complex businesses for the purpose of reengineering or understanding them. The fundamental principle is that all businesses can be layered into processes, where each layer controls the layer underneath.	■ Process Layer Supply pattern	323
Process Layer Supply	A Process Modeling pattern that organizes the structure of complex organizations into primary and supporting business processes. Breaking the organization down into primary and supporting processes allows for a better understanding of the entire organization and provides a stable foundation for future reengineering efforts.	■ Process Layer Control pattern	315
Process-Process Instance	A Process Instance pattern that clarifies the distinction between a process and a process instance, and the impact that clarification has on process models and process thinking.	■ Resource Use pattern ■ Process Instance State patterns	339
Resource Use	A Process Support pattern that structures the resources used in process instances in order to model and implement their use in a supporting information system.	■ Process-Process Instance pattern ■ All other business process patterns	341
Time-To-Customer	A Process Modeling pattern that demonstrates how to describe a business with two main processes: enable and available, in order to shorten the lead time from customer demand to customer satisfaction.	■ Process Layer Supply pattern	309

Glossary

Abstract class   A class that cannot be directly instantiated.

Abstraction   The principle of ignoring those aspects of a subject that are not relevant to the current purpose in order to concentrate more fully on those that are. When focusing on something for the purpose of modeling it, the objective is to separate the aspects that interest us from those that do not.

Activity diagram   A diagram used to describe activities and actions taking place in a system or a process. (Can also be used to express the operations in a class.)

Actor   An external object that interacts with the system. As described in use cases, an actor is the role played by a human or other system.

Agent   An active system that has a certain task. A human being and an information system are examples of agents.

Aggregate   A class that represents the whole in a whole-part relationship.

Analysis   The examination of a problem for the purpose of producing a hypothesis or a solution. In object-oriented analysis, a model is created that reflects a set of or, in some cases, all real-world entities, including their relationship and collaboration, without taking into consideration a technical solution.

Architecture   The organizational structure of a system. Architectures may be decomposed into parts or organized in hierarchies. The purpose of an architecture is to organize thoughts and resources, to create efficient systems with minimum effort.

Assembly line   Stereotyped packages that contain objects (read and write objects). The business processes in the Assembly diagram pick up objects (read) from the assembly lines and put down objects (write) to the assembly lines in a certain sequence. The business processes refine the objects in the assembly lines. The read and write objects are stereotyped object flows.

Assembly line diagram   A diagram that connects business processes to assembly lines, for example, to illustrate the services a business process uses from an information system.

Association   The semantic relationship between two or more classifiers that specify connections among their instances.

Association class   A class connected to an association.

Association end   The endpoint of an association, which connects the association to a classifier.

Attribute   A feature within a classifier that describes a range of values that instances of the classifier may hold.

Behavior   The actions a business object is capable of performing to fulfill its purpose. This includes recognizing events in its environment, changing its attributes, and interacting with other business objects.

Boolean   An enumeration whose value can be either true or false.

Boundary object   A class whose objects are used to communicate with actors.

Business   A context capturing relationships between customers and suppliers.

Business Behavior view   Depicts the behavior of each important resource and process in the business, so they can be modeled individually.

Business event   A significant occurrence in time/space that impacts the business.

Business object   A representation of something within a business. The representation might be expressed in natural languages, modeling languages, programming languages, and others. For example, an invoice is a business object that can be a textual representation of an invoice, a binary component representing invoices, or even a model representing invoices. Business objects are expressed in some language, defined with objectives, rules, and needs of collaborations with others. Business objects are also assumed to have a clear and well-defined interface.

Business process   A description of a set of related activities that, when correctly performed, will satisfy an explicit business goal.

Business Process view   Describes the business processes that represent the activities and value created in the business; the processes interact with resources to achieve the goal of each process and to show the interaction between different processes.

Business rules   Statements that constrain, derive, and give conditions of existence. Business rules are used to specify allowed state of affairs, including allowed business object states.

Business Structure view   The structures of the resources in the business, such as the organization of the business or the structure of the products created.

Business view A way of looking at or studying a business. There are numerous business views, each with its own purpose, advantages, and disadvantages. Examples of business views are organizations, human capital, business ideas, business goal models, business processes, and workflow models.

Business Vision view The overall vision of the business; describes a goal structure for the company, and illustrates problems that must be eliminated to reach those goals.

Class A model element used to model objects, both intellectual and physical. A class can be instantiated to objects that are individual entities (objects). A class is described with members, which are attributes, operations, and relationships to other classes. A class can be generalized and specialized; extension mechanisms may also be attached to the class.

Class diagram Used to describe structures. The structures are built up from classes and relationships. The classes can represent and structure objects such as information, products, documents, and organizations.

Collaboration Describes how a set of objects interact to perform some specific function. A collaboration describes both a context and an interaction. The context shows the set of objects involved in the collaboration, along with their links to each other. The interaction shows the communication that the objects perform in the collaboration.

Collaboration diagram A UML diagram that describes a complete collaboration among a set of objects.

Component A physical implementation of logical model elements as defined in class diagrams or interaction diagrams. A component can be viewed at different stages of development, such as compile time, link time, or runtime.

Component diagram A UML diagram used to describe components and their dependencies within a software system.

Composition An aggregation where the whole owns its parts (strong ownership). The parts live inside the whole and will be destroyed together with its whole.

Conceptual modeling Definitions of the important concepts used in the business, along with their relationships to each other.

Constraint A semantic condition or restriction.

Control object Objects whose purpose is to control in some sense. *See* Process supporting object.

Control process A process that is controlling some other process, typically strategic and tactic processes.

CORBA Acronym for Common Object Request Broker Architecture. The architecture in which the nodes in a distributed system all have an Object Request Broker (ORB) enabling objects on that system to register and expose their services or establish contact with objects on other nodes in the system. The ORB handles the differences in programming language, operating system, hardware architecture, and so on. The ORB is supplemented with a set of services (CORBAservices) that handles things such as naming of objects, event handling, transactions, and more, and a set of facilities (CORBAfacilities) that handles things such as compound documents. Not all the services or facilities defined in the CORBA standard are present in all available ORB implementations (in fact, there is currently no ORB that contains all the services or facilities).

CORBA domains Standard models for finance, health care, manufacturing, telecommunications, transportation, electronic commerce, and so on. The definition of these CORBA domains are defined using IDL and CDL.

Data Any set of representations of knowledge, expressed in any language [FRISCO 1996]. Data might carry information. *See* Information.

Denotation A precise and unambiguous representation of a model.

Dependency A relationship between two model elements, in which a change to one model element (the independent model element) will affect the other model element (the dependent model element).

Deployment diagram A special case of Class diagram used to describe hardware within a software system.

Derivations Rules that define how knowledge in one form may be transformed into other knowledge (how some information is derived from other information). A derivation can either be a computation rule, such as a formula for calculating a value, or an inference rule, such as the determination that if some fact is true, then another inference fact must also be true.

Enterprise A business system that consists of collaborating objects that are in functional symbiosis.

Eriksson-Penker Business Extensions Extensions to UML that make it possible to model both a business and its supporting systems.

Event A significant occurrence in time or space.

Existence Rules that define when something may exist and when it should come into existence, that is, when an object is created or destroyed.

Extends A relationship between one use case to another, specifying how the behavior defined for the first use case can be inserted into the behavior defined for the second use case.

Extension The population corresponding to the intensional model, whereby the population must obey all rules determined in that intensional model. *See* Intension.

Façade A stereotyped package that refers only to elements from other packages (imports, via friend dependency, etc.). The façade does not own any elements. A façade typically presents an interface to the services provided by a package.

Fuzzy business rule Rules that are modeled with fuzzy logic. Fuzzy logic is a way of handling uncertainties, where conditions do not result in Boolean (either true or false) values.

Generalizable element   A model element that can participate in a generalization relationship.

Generalization   A relationship between a general element and a more specific element. The more specific element is fully consistent with the more general element, and contains additional information or behavior. An instance of the more specific element may be used wherever the more general element can be used.

Goal   Desired asset states. Goals motivate actions leading to state changes in a desired direction.

Goal patterns   Patterns that provide guidelines for modeling business goals. Goal modeling is a critical issue in business modeling. The goals are what the business models and what the corresponding business strive for; therefore, goals are the basis for designing the processes correctly, finding the right resources, and tuning the business rules.

Goal–problem modeling   Definition of the goals of the company, including the breakdown of goals into subgoals and the problems that hinder the achievement of goals.

Guard-condition   A Boolean expression of a state transition. If the guard-condition is combined with an event-signature, both the event must occur and the guard-condition must be true for the state to change. However, only a guard-condition can be attached to a state transition; that is, the state will change when the condition becomes true.

Hierarchical systems   A system comprising several layers hierarchically organized, where the higher layer controls the lower layer.

Import   The stereotyped dependency between packages that indicates that a package imports and can access elements within another package that has the public visibility.

Incomplete   A generalization that indicates new subclasses may be added in the future. Incomplete generalization is the opposite of complete generalization, and it is the default.

Information   The knowledge increment brought about by a receiving action in a message transfer; that is, the difference between the conceptions interpreted after a received message and the knowledge before the receiving action [FRISCO 1996].

Information system   A system that organizes and handles information. Information systems should be seen as a part of a surrounding business. They are built up from business objects that represent things in the business outside the information systems. Control objects are used to organize and handle the information that the business objects carry. While they support the business processes, these control objects are called process supporting objects. Boundary objects are used to manipulate or present information carried by the business objects. The actors use the boundary objects to obtain access to the business objects, and the process supporting objects are used to control and hold the information in the business objects for the actors.

Instance   An individual member described by a classifier.

Intension   Part of a model comprising the possibilities and necessities of a domain only, that is, the types and rules [FRISCO 1996]. *See* extension.

Interaction   Actions that occur between things.

Interaction diagram   A type of diagram that emphasizes object interactions. This type of diagram includes collaboration diagrams and sequence diagrams.

Interface   A declaration of a collection of operations that may be used for defining a service offered by an instance.

Intra-action   Actions that occur inside things.

Invariant   A type. Specifies a property (i.e., condition) that must be preserved over the lifetime of an instance of the type.

Kind of system   The classification of a system. There is no single universal and true classification theory; instead, there are numerous theories for classifying systems, some of which are useful. Systems can be classified based on internal structure, such as hierarchical systems versus layered systems. Another way to classify a system is to base it on the system's nature, such as artificial versus organic.

Knowledge   The relatively stable and sufficiently consistent set of conceptions possessed by single human actors [FRISCO 1996].

Link   A semantic connection between instances. An instantiation of an association; the actual connection between two (or more) objects.

Link role   An instance of an association role.

Message   A communication between objects that conveys information, with the expectation that activity will ensue. The receipt of a message is normally considered an event.

Meta-class   A class that can be instantiated to other classes (a class for classes).

Meta-language   A natural or formal language used to describe another language (the object language). A formal semantics theory provides an axiomatic or otherwise systematic theory of meaning for the object language. The meta-language specifies the object language's symbols and formation rules, which determine its grammatical structure or well-formed formulas, and assigns meanings or interpretations to these sentences or formulas [Cambridge 1995].

Meta-model   A model that describes other models, expressed in a meta-language. Meta-models are used to describe UML and many other languages. Languages like UML are both a modeling language and a meta-language because they are expressed using themselves.

Meta-type   A type whose instances are types.

Method   A procedure for attending something. Method comes from the Latin *methodus,* meaning pursuit, especially of knowledge.

Model   An abstract description of a system. A model is expressed with diagrams (graphs) and the diagrams are expressed in a modeling language. A model is an expression of something (a business, etc.) and always has objectives. It is possible to model the same thing with different objectives and to model different things with the same objectives.

Model coordination   Integration and relation of different models of the same thing to each other. Models should be coordinated on each level of abstraction (e.g., structure and behavior) and among the different levels of abstraction (e.g., system versus subsystem and analysis versus design).

Model element   The concepts within a modeling language, for example, class, object, node, and state. Most model elements have a corresponding view element that shows their graphical appearance; they may therefore be projected within diagrams.

Model integration   Combination of a set of models that have the same purpose and represent the same thing without inconsistencies.

Modeling language   A language used to express models. The expressions are called diagrams or graphs. A modeling language is defined with syntax and semantics. Some modeling languages also have pragmatic rules.

Multilayer system   A system that consists of several layers, where the layers are each a different abstraction of the system. Each layer consists of several subsystems interacting with each other.

Node   Physical objects (devices) that have some kind of computational resource, including computers with processors and devices such as printers, card readers, communication devices, and the like.

Note   A comment attached to an element or a collection of elements. A note has no semantics.

Object   A (unique) instance of a class.

Object diagram   A diagram that expresses possible object combinations of a certain Class diagram. An object diagram is used to exemplify a class diagram.

Object flow state   A state in an activity graph that represents the passing of an object from the output of actions in one state to the input of actions in another state.

Object lifeline   A line in a sequence diagram that represents the existence of an object over a period of time.

Operation   A member of a class. The operation is defined as a function with a signature and an implementation.

Overlapping   One object exists in more than one class in a subclass.

Package   A mechanism that groups common elements. A package is used for creating groups of diagrams, classes, nodes, and so on.

Parameter   The specification of a variable that can be changed, passed, or returned. A parameter can include a name, type, and direction. Parameters are used for operations, messages, and events.

Pattern   A generalized solution that can be implemented and applied in a problem situation (a context), and thereby eliminate one or more of the inherent problems in order to satisfy one or more objectives.

Pragmatics   Intentions. Modeling languages can have intentions, called pragmatic rules.

Problem   A hindrance to achieving goals.

Process   A description of a set of related activities that, when correctly performed, will satisfy an explicit goal. Process comes from the Latin *processus*, meaning advance or progress.

Process patterns   High-quality, well-proven, and easy-to-use patterns that are used to model business processes. These patterns provide solutions to typical problems in the context of process modeling.

Process supporting object   A specialization of control objects; also called process business objects. The process supporting object's purpose is to support the processes and the actors following the processes.

Process user   The users of a process. In the context of software engineering, the process users are normally developers.

Relationship   A semantic connection among model elements. A relationship is specialized to generalization, dependency, association, transition, and link.

Resource and rule patterns   Patterns that describe typical problem situations that can arise when modeling the structures and relationships (including rules) between resources. They provide guidelines and common solutions to these problems in pattern form.

Resources   The objects within the business, such as people, material, information, and products, that are used or produced in the business. The resources are arranged in structures and have relationships with each other. Resources are manipulated (used, consumed, refined, or produced) through processes. Resources can be categorized as physical, abstract, and informational.

Role   A technique used to specify the context for a class and its objects. An association (or aggregate) can have roles connected to each class involved. Role-names are part of the association, not part of the classes.

Rule   *See* Business rules.

Semantics   The link between the concept and the symbol for that concept. The semantics of a concept must be known when communicating about the concept, otherwise misunderstandings will result.

Send (a message)   To pass a message instance from a sender object to a receiver object.

Sequence diagram   A diagram that shows one or several sequences of messages among a set of objects.

State   The condition of an object. An object state is determined by its attribute values and the links to other objects. A state is a result of previous activities in the object.

Statechart diagram   A diagram that expresses possible states of a class (or a system).

Stereotype   A modeling element that extends the semantics of the UML. Stereotypes must be based on elements that already are defined in the UML. Stereotypes can extend the semantics but not the structure of preexisting elements. Certain stereotypes are predefined in UML; others may be user-defined.

Strategy definition   Position of the company with regard to the current and future world and the strategic goals or necessary changes in the business.

Subactivity state   A state in an activity graph that represents the execution of a nonatomic sequence of steps that have some duration.

Subprocess   The result of dividing a process into further processes.

Substate   A state within another state.

Subsystem   The result of dividing a system into further systems. A subsystem is represented as a package in UML.

Subtype   A specialization of another type.

Superclass   A generalization of another class.

Superstate   A state that contains other states or substates.

Supertype   A generalization of another type.

Supporting process   A process whose purpose is to support other processes.

Swimlanes   A grouping mechanism used to organize concepts. Swimlanes do not have any particular semantics.

Syntax   The rules that restrict how concepts (elements) can be combined with each other.

System   A special model, used to reduce complexity. A system is defined with a system border and system components. The system border delimits the system components from its environment. System goals are always outside the systems, meaning that a system cannot exist without an environment (this is true even for closed systems; a closed system is defined without references to the environment but is motivated by the environment). A system is conceived of as having assigned to it, as a whole, a specific characterization (the systemic properties) that cannot be attributed to any of its system components. This means that if you put some system components together, the system as a whole might come up with brand new properties. Chemical systems such as sal ammoniac have totally different properties from the components they are built from. The components, hydrochloric acid and ammonia, which as separate components are dangerous to humans, when composed are safe (and commonly used in candy).

Tagged value   The explicit definition of a property as a name-value pair. In a tagged value, the name is referred to as the tag. Certain tags are predefined in the UML. In UML, property is used in a general sense to mean any value connected to an element, including attributes in classes, associations, and tagged values.

Transition   A relationship between two states that indicates that an object in the first state will perform certain specified actions and enter the second state when a specified event occurs and/or specified conditions are satisfied.

UML   Unified Modeling Language; an OMG standard for visual object-oriented modeling.

Use case   A description of how a system can be used (from an external actor's point of view). Use cases show the functionality of a system, and are described in terms of external actors, use cases, and the system being modeled. A use case should yield an observable result of value to a particular actor.

Use-case diagram   A use-case model. A use-case diagram contains elements for the system, the actors, and the use cases, and shows the different relationships between these elements.

Use-case model   A model that describes a system's functional requirements in terms of use cases.

Uses   A relationship from a use-case to another use-case in which the behavior defined for the former use-case employs the behavior defined for the latter.

View   An abstraction, consisting of a number of diagrams, that show different aspects of the modeled system.

View element   A projection of one or more model elements; also called notation.

Visibility   An enumeration where the set of allowed values are public, protected, private, and implementation. The visibility specifies the allowed access to elements within types and packages.

References

[Alexander 79] Alexander, Christopher. *Timeless Way of Building*. New York: Oxford University Press, 1979.

[Alexander 87] Alexander, Christopher. *A Pattern Language*. New York: Oxford University Press, 1987.

[Allen 98] Allen, Paul and Stuart Frost. *Component-Based Development for Enterprise Systems: Applying the Select Perspective*. New York: Cambridge University Press, 1998.

[Ambler 98] Ambler, Scott W. *Process Patterns: Delivering Large-Scale Systems Using Object Technology*. New York: Cambridge University Press, 1998.

[Astrakan 97]Astrakan: *The Astrakan Method*. Stockholm: Astrakan, 1997.

[Bass 98] Bass, Len, Paul Clements, and Rick Kazman. *Software Architecture in Practice*. Reading, MA: Addison-Wesley, 1998.

[Beedle 97] Beedle, Michael A. *cOOherentBPR:– A Pattern language to Build Agile Organizations*. PLoP-97 conference, 1997.

[Booch 94] Booch, Grady. *Object-Oriented Analysis and Design with Applications*. 2nd edition. Reading, MA: Addison-Wesley, 1994.

[Booch 98] Booch, Grady, Ivar Jacobson, and James Rumbaugh. *The Unified Modeling Language Users Guide*. Reading, MA: Addison-Wesley, 1998.

[Buschmann 96] Buschmann, Frank, Regine Meuer, Hans Rohnert, and Peter Sommerlad. *Pattern-Oriented Software Architecture: A System of Patterns*. New York: John Wiley & Sons, Inc., 1996.

[Cambridge 95] *Cambridge Dictionary of Philosophy*. Cambridge University Press, USA, 1995.

[Cantor 98] Cantor, Murray R. *Object-Oriented Project Management with UML*. New York: John Wiley & Sons, Inc., 1998.

[Checkland 81] Checkland P. B. *Systems Thinking, Systems Practice*. New York: John Wiley & Sons, Inc., 1981.

[Coplien 95] Coplien, James and Doug Schmidt (eds.). *Pattern Languages of Program Design.* Reading, MA: Addison-Wesley, 1995.

[Darnton 97] Darnton, Geoffrey and Moksha Darnton. *Business Process Analysis.* Cambridge, U.K.: Thomson Business Press, 1997.

[Davenport 92] Davenport, Thomas. *Process Innovation: Reengineering Work through Information Technology.* Cambridge, MA: Harvard Business School Books, 1992.

[Eriksson 96] Eriksson, Hans-Erik and Magnus Penker. *Objektorientering: Handbok och lexikon.* Lund, Sweden: Studentlitteratur, 1996.

[Eriksson 98] Eriksson, Hans-Erik and Magnus Penker. *UML Toolkit.* John Wiley & Sons, Inc., 1996.

[F3 91] *From Fuzzy to Forma.* ESPRIT III Project 6612, Technical Annex II, 1991.

[F3 94] *The F3 Requirement Engineering Handbook.* Kista, Sweden: SISU, 1994.

[Flores 88] Flores F., M. Gaves, B. Hartfield, and T. Winograd. "Computer Systems and Design of Organizational Interaction," *ACM Transactions on Office Information Systems*, vol. 6. no .2, 1988.

[Fowler 97] Fowler, Martin. *Analysis Patterns: Reusable Object Models.* Reading, MA: Addison-Wesley, 1997.

[FRISCO 96] Falkenberg, D., J.L. Han Oei, W. Hesse, P. Lindgreen, B. Nilsson, C. Rolland, R. Stamper, F. van Assche, A. Verrijn-Stuart, and K. Voss. *A Framework of Information System Concepts.* The IFIP WG 8.1 Task Group FRISCO, 1996.

[Gale 96] Gale, Thornton and James Eldred. *Getting Results with the Object-Oriented Enterprise Model.* New York: SIGS Books, 1996.

[Gamma 95] Gamma, Erich, Richard Helm, Ralph Johnson, and John Vlissides. *Design Patterns.* Reading, MA: Addison-Wesley, 1995.

[Gordon 69] Gordon, M. J., and G. Shillinglaw. *Accounting: A Management Approach,* 4th ed. Richard D. Irving, 1969.

[Graham 94] Graham, Ian. *Object-Oriented Methods.* Reading, MA: Addison-Wesley, 1994.

[GUIDE 95] Hay, D., Allan Kolber, and Keri Anderson Healy. "Guide Business Rule Project: Final Report," 1995.

[Hammer 94] Hammer, Mike and James Champy. *Reengineering the Corporation: A Manifesto for Business Revolution.* New York: Harper Business Books, 1994.

[Harrington 1991] Harrington, James. *Business Process Improvement.* New York: McGraw-Hill, 1991.

[Haugen 97] Haugen, Robert. *Dependent Demand: A Business Pattern for Balancing Supply and Demand.* Paper PloP'97, 1997.

[Hay 96] Hay, David C. *Data Model Patterns: Conventions of Thought.* New York: Dorset House, 1996.

[IDEF0 93] *Announcing the Standard for INTEGRATION DEFINITION FOR FUNCTION MODELING (IDEF0),* Federal Information Processing Standards Publication 183, 1993.

[Jacobson 98] Jacobson, Ivar, Grady Booch, and James Rumbaugh. *The Unified Software Development Process.* Reading, MA: Addison-Wesley, 1998.

[Jacobson 92] Jacobson, I., M. Christerson, P. Jonsson, and G. Övergaard. *Object-Oriented Software Engineering.* Reading, MA: Addison-Wesley, 1992.

[Kendell 98] Kendell, Elizabeth A., Uma Palanivelan, and Satya Kalikivayi. *Capturing and Structuring Goals: Analysis Patterns.* EuroPloP'98 paper, 1998.

[Kosko 93] Kosko, Bart. *Fuzzy Thinking.* New York: Hyperion, 1993.

[Kruchten 95] Kruchten, Philippe. *The 4+1 View Model of Architecture.* Piscataway, NJ: IEEE Software, November 1995.

[Kruchten 98] Kruchten, Philippe. *The Rational Unified Process.* Reading, MA: Addison-Wesley, 1998.

[Leavitt 72] Leavitt H. *The Volatile Organization: Everything Triggers Everything Else, Managerial Psychology.* Chicago: The University of Chicago Press, 1972.

[Martin 98] Martin, Robert C., Dirk Riehle, Frank Buschmann, and John Vlissides (eds.). *Pattern Languages of Program Design 3.* Reading, MA: Addison-Wesley, 1998.

[McNeill 93] McNeill, Daniel and Paul Freiberger. *Fuzzy Logic: The Revolutionary Computer Technology That Is Changing Our World.* Touchstone, 1993.

[Morgan 86] Morgan, G. *Images of Organization.* Thousand Oaks, CA: Sage Publications 1986.

[Mylopoulos 99] Mylopoulos, John, Lawrence Chung, and Eric Yu. "From Object-Oriented to Goal-Oriented: Requirements Analysis." *Communication of the ACM,* vol. 42, no. 1, January 1999, pp. 3–37.

[Nilsson 79] Nilsson, Björn. *On Models and Mappings in a Data Base Environment:–A Holistic Approach to Data Modeling.* Ph.D dissertation, University of Stockholm, 1979.

[Nilsson 91] Nilsson, Björn. "Vision 95." CaiSE91 Conference on Advanced Information Systems Engineering, 1991.

[Nilsson 94] Nilsson, Björn. "Perspective on Modeling the Business and Its IT-Support." ER94 conference presentation, 1994.

[Nilsson 95] Nilsson, Björn. "Towards a Framework of Information System Concepts." ISCO3 conference presentation, 1995.

[Nilsson 99] Nilsson A.G., C. Tollis, and C. Nellborn. *Perspective on Business Modeling.* New York: Springer-Verlag, 1999.

[Odell 98] Odell, James. *Advanced Object-Oriented Analysis and Design Using UML.* New York: SIGS Books, 1998.

[OMG 92] OMG, *Analysis and Design Reference Model.* Framingham, MA: OMG, 1992.

[OMG 98] OMG, *Business Object Architecture Proposal*. Framingham, MA: OMG, 1998.

[OMG 99] OMG, *Object Constraint Language Specification*, version 1.3. Framingham, MA: OMG, 1999.

[OMG 99] OMG, *UML Semantics*, version 1.3. Framingham, MA: OMG, 1999.

[Porter 90] Porter, Michael E. *The Competitive Advantage of Nations.* New York: Free Press, 1990.

[Rising 98] Rising, Linda (ed). *The Patterns Handbook: Techniques, Strategies and Applications.* New York: Cambridge University Press, 1998.

[Rüping 99] Rüping, Andreas. *Project Documentation Management.* EuroPLoP '99 paper, 1999.

[Steneskog 91] Steneskog, Gösta. *Process Management.* Stockholm, Sweden: Liber, 1991.

[Stoll 63] Stoll, Robert R. *Set Theory and Logic.* New York: Freeman, 1963.

[Taylor 91] Taylor, David. *Object-Oriented Technology: A Managers Guide.* Reading, MA: Addison-Wesley, 1991.

[Tilli 93] Tilli, F. *Fuzzy-Logik Grundlagen, Anwendungen, Hard- und Software.* Poing,Germany: Franzis-Verlag, 1993.

[Vernadat 96] Vernadat, Francois. *Enterprise Modeling and Integration.* London, England: Chapman & Hall 1996.

[Vlissides 96] Vlissides, John, James Coplien, and James and Norman Kerth (eds.). *Pattern Languages of Program Design 2.* Reading, MA: Addison-Wesley, 1996.

[Warmer 99] Warmer, Jos B. and Anneke G. Kleppe. *The Object Constraint Language: Precise Modeling with UML.* Reading, MA: Addison-Wesley, 1999.

[Weirich 82] Weirich, H. *The TOWS Matrix: A Tool for Situational Analysis.* Long Range Planning, 1982.

[Willars 91] Willars, Hans. *Amplification of Business Cognition through Modeling Techniques.* IEA Congress, 1991.

Index

Page references followed by italic *t* indicate material in tables. Information about specific patterns can be located in several ways. The three broad headings "goal patterns", "process patterns", and "resource and rule patterns"; have subheadings listing the primary discussion point of all patterns of that type. Additional information, such as using one pattern with another pattern, can be found at the location of each pattern as a main heading. Finally, all the business pattern template elements, which are listed on pages 175–182, are present in the index. For example to look up information on the applicability of various patterns, look under the index heading "Applicability section."